# Deliberative Democracy

# Deliberative Democracy

Essays on Reason and Politics

*edited by James Bohman and William Rehg*

The MIT Press
Cambridge, Massachusetts
London, England

©1997 Massachusetts Institute of Technology

This book was set in Baskerville using Ventura Publisher under Windows 95 by Wellington Graphics and was printed and bound in the United States of America

Library of Congress Cataloging-in-Publication Data

Deliberative democracy : essays on reason and politics / edited by
  James Bohman and William Rehg.
      p.    cm.
  Includes bibliographical references and index.
  ISBN 0-262-02434-9 (hc : alk. paper). — ISBN 0-262-52241-1 (pbk. : alk. paper)
  1. Democracy. 2. Representative government and representation.
I. Bohman, James.   II. Rehg, William.
JC423.D389   1997
321.—dc21                                                           97–8350
                                                                       CIP

10 9 8 7 6 5 4

# Contents

# Acknowledgments

The editors gratefully acknowledge the following permissions to reprint essays in this volume.

Joshua Cohen, "Deliberation and Democratic Legitimacy," from A. Hamlin and P. Pettit, eds., *The Good Polity* (Oxford: Blackwell, 1989), 17–34. Reprinted with the permission of the author and Blackwell Publishers.

Joshua Cohen, "Procedure and Substance in Deliberative Democracy," from S. Benhabib, ed., *Democracy and Difference* (Princeton: Princeton University Press, 1996), 95–119. Reprinted with the permission of the author and Princeton University Press.

Jon Elster, "The Market and the Forum," from J. Elster and A. Aanund, eds., *The Foundations of Social Choice Theory* (Cambridge: Cambridge University Press, 1986), 103–132. Reprinted with the permission of the author and Cambridge University Press.

Jürgen Habermas, "Popular Sovereignty as Procedure," from *Between Facts and Norms: Contributions to a Discourse Theory of Law and Democracy* (Cambridge, MA: MIT Press, 1996), 463–490. Reprinted with the permission of the author and The MIT Press.

John Rawls, "Introduction" and "The Public Use of Reason" from *Political Liberalism* (New York: Columbia University Press, 1993, 1996), xxxvii–xxxviii, xliii–xlvii, 212–254. Reprinted with the permission of the author and Columbia University Press.

# Introduction

The idea that legitimate government should embody the "will of the people" has a long history and appears in many variants. As the beneficiary of this rich heritage, the concept of deliberative democracy that has emerged in the last two decades represents an exciting development in political theory. Broadly defined, *deliberative democracy* refers to the idea that legitimate lawmaking issues from the public deliberation of citizens. As a normative account of legitimacy, deliberative democracy evokes ideals of rational legislation, participatory politics, and civic self-governance. In short, it presents an ideal of political autonomy based on the practical reasoning of citizens. But is this ideal feasible or even desirable? What exactly is public deliberation? Given the complex issues that confront contemporary societies, is an intelligent, broad-based participation possible? In societies as culturally diverse as our own, is it reasonable to expect deliberating citizens to converge on rational solutions to political problems? Does deliberation actually overcome or only exacerbate the more undesirable features of majority rule?

The essays in this volume address questions such as these, whose importance for contemporary constitutional democracies can hardly be overestimated. The volume is divided into two parts. In part 1, we provide a selection of some of the more influential essays in the revival of deliberative models. The essays in part 2, the majority of which were presented at the Second Henle Conference held at Saint Louis University in April 1996, represent the latest round of attempts by some leading political theorists to elaborate the idea of deliberative democracy. Before indicating the range of positions the reader will find in these essays, though, we shall establish the context by reviewing some earlier trends in democratic theory that set the stage for the revival of the deliberative model.

Conceptions of legitimate government have been a site of intense conflict—both in theory and in practice—since the onset of modernity. To understand what is at stake in deliberative politics, we must give one issue particular attention. On one side are theorists who emphasize the plurality of citizens' interests and the potential for civil strife; on the other are those who see possibilities for civil harmony based on a commonality of interests, values, or traditions. On the standard reading of the classical moderns, liberal theorists such as Thomas Hobbes and John Locke are pitted in this debate against civic republicans such as James Harrington and Jean-Jacques Rousseau. Although the idea of deliberative democracy does not necessarily lead to republicanism and does not preclude a keen awareness of social conflict, it arises on the terrain staked out by the debates between these two traditions. For a democracy based on public deliberation presupposes that citizens or their representatives can take counsel together about what laws and policies they ought to pursue as a commonwealth. And this in turn means that the plurality of competing interests is not the last word, or sole perspective, in deciding matters of public importance. The problem, to use Kant's terms, is to bring about "the public use of reason."

Perhaps the critical question along this axis of debate is whether citizens with a variety of individual interests can also come to affirm a common good in some sense. This question has become especially clear in the twentieth century. The theories of democracy dominant in the middle part of this century were generally suspicious of public deliberation. Several theoretical developments ratified this antipopulist sentiment. The first was the *elitist theory* of democracy propounded by Joseph Schumpeter and his disciples. Driven by the empirical findings of political sociology, which suggested that citizens in modern democracies were politically uninformed, apathetic, and manipulable, and also by the history of the rise of National

Introduction

Socialism, which suggested that participation could be downright dangerous, this theory tended to emphasize stability at the expense of popular participation. In the tradition of Max Weber's pessimistic realism about politics (as the place where "gods and demons fight it out"), Schumpeter concluded that "there is, first, no such thing as a uniquely determined common good that all people could agree on." In this vision, governance was best left in the hands of leadership elites, and democracy was reduced to a negative control over leaders through the possibility of turning them out of office at the next election.[1] To be sure, Talcott Parsons and his followers opposed self-interested and Hobbesian approaches and offered a less pessimistic view of democratic stability: indeed, Parsons's account of value consensus and the expansion of citizenship pointed toward central motifs of participatory politics. However, Parsonian functionalism employed a theoretical strategy that could not go very far in the direction of a deliberative model.[2]

In a second influential development, democratic theorists retreated enough from sociological realism to model the competitive political process on rational-choice assumptions. Anthony Downs attempted to apply economic categories to politics, suggesting that parties function as entrepreneurs who compete to sell their policies in a market of political consumers.[3] The *economic theory of democracy* was spawned by this union between empirical assumptions about actors' motivations and the formal techniques of the theories of games and social choice.[4] Although this approach introduced a more rationalistic view of the citizen and was more optimistic about the responsiveness of government to the citizens' prepolitical interests, it followed Schumpeter's approach on at least two key points: it viewed citizens primarily as passive consumers who exerted democratic control primarily through voting, and it conceived the political process as a struggle for power among competing interests rather than as a search for the common good.[5] Like sociological realism, the economic view precluded active public deliberation by citizens about a common good. One could perhaps speak of voting as a mechanism for aggregating individual preferences, but, as social choice theorists pointed out, aggregation mechanisms do not yield a public opinion about a common good. Indeed, given sufficient diversity of preferences, the theory suggests that there is no such good that is acceptable to all citizens. According to some, the results of social choice theory led to a critique of populism.[6]

These two developments, one sociological and the other economic, were the two main sources for liberal democratic theory up to 1970. The central motifs of these lines of research also had an impact on constitutional theory. In this context, the *pluralist model of democracy* proposed by Robert Dahl and others provided an influential framework for interpreting Madisonian democracy. Dahl was interested in the social conditions under which egalitarian democratic ideals could be approximately realized in complex industrialized societies. In line with James Madison's *Federalist Paper* no. 10, he identified competition among group interests as a crucial condition for democracy. Although Dahl's decentralized, "polyarchal" version of pluralism shed much of Schumpeter's elitism, it retained the emphasis on competition, interests, and voting.[7]

This climate was a rather inhospitable one for conceptions of public deliberation about a common good. Although other theorists, such as John Dewey and Hannah Arendt, were prominent in postwar political theory, the competitive-pluralist trend only began to reverse itself in the late 1960s. This reversal can be traced, at least in part, to broad dissatisfaction with the debacles and anonymity of liberal government (e.g., the war in Vietnam and the increasing perception that decision making in government was bureaucratic and beyond the control of citizens). More specifically, leftist political activism, with its emphasis on participatory democracy, sparked renewed interest in the possibilities for consensual forms of self-government.[8]

The theoretical critique of liberal democracy and revival of participatory politics gradually developed through the 1970s.[9] It was only in the 1980s, however, that a concept of deliberative democracy began to take definite shape. The term "deliberative democracy" seems to have been first coined by Joseph Bessette, who argued against elitist (or "aristocratic") interpretations of the Constitution.[10] Bessette's challenge joined the chorus of voices calling for a participatory view of democratic politics. These theorists questioned the key assumptions underlying the earlier economic and pluralist models: that politics should be understood mainly in terms of a conflict of competing interests—and thus in terms more of bargaining than of public reason; that rational-choice frameworks provide the sole model for rational decision making; that legitimate government is minimalist, dedicated to the preservation of the negative liberty of atomic individuals; that democratic participation reduces to voting; and so on. In a more positive vein, they took their cue from a variety of deliberative contexts and motifs: direct democracy, town-hall meetings and small organizations, workplace democracy, mediated forms of public reason among citizens with diverse moral doctrines, voluntary associations, and deliberative constitutional and judicial practices regulating society as a whole, to name just a few.[11]

## The Idea of Deliberative Democracy: Major Statements

The papers in part 1 should give the reader a sense of the key theoretical issues that were initially raised with the concept of deliberative democracy. Deliberative theorists are in general agreement on at least this: the political process involves more than self-interested competition governed by bargaining and aggregative mechanisms. But rejection of the rational-choice model leaves the further question unanswered: what, positively speaking, differentiates political behavior from market behavior? The first essay in part 1, Jon Elster's "The Market and the Forum," provides a helpful initial orientation by distinguishing two different answers to this question. Both views agree that politics involves a public activity that cannot be reduced to the private choices of consumers in the "market." Both agree that political engagement requires citizens to adopt a civic standpoint, an orientation toward the common good, when they consider political issues in the "forum." On the view represented by such thinkers as John Stuart Mill and Hannah Arendt, however, this transformative power of politics makes democratic engagement an end in itself; deliberative democracy should be advocated precisely because of the beneficial educative effects it has on citizens. Elster argues that this view is incoherent. Although we may applaud democratic politics because of its educative "by-products," we should advocate it only if it has inherent advantages as a method of deciding political questions. In contrast, Elster sees politics as involving both market and forum institutions, since it is "public in nature and instrumental in purpose."

Elster's essay brings out two key elements in the deliberative conception of democracy: that political deliberation requires citizens to go beyond private self-interest of the "market" and orient themselves to public interests of the "forum"; and that deliberation from this civic standpoint is defensible only if it improves political decision making, especially with regard to achieving common ends. Both points invite further questions. Exactly how, for example, should one conceive the civic standpoint and public good? The classical civic-republican view stemming from Plato and Aristotle conceived the common good substantively, in terms of shared traditions, values, conceptions of virtue, and so forth. The quality of deliberation requires insight into, and the retrieval of, these traditions and values. However, the republican answer is plausible today only if one defines the relevant traditions more pluralistically and procedurally; here the American constitutional tradition has provided sympathetic theorists such as Frank Michelman and Cass Sunstein with a fruitful starting point.[12]

In developing his conception of politics as "public in nature," Elster alludes to a somewhat different approach to the common good: Jürgen Habermas's idealized model of rational, consensus-oriented discourse. According to Elster's reading of this model, engagement in political debate has an inherent tendency to produce in participants an openness to considerations of the public interest. But this leads to further questions regarding the nature, likelihood, and desirability of consensus in pluralistic and time-constrained political settings.[13] To answer the questions that Elster raises, one must say more about the normative standards for rational consensus, the relation between deliberation and decision, and proper institutional design.

In his "Popular Sovereignty as Procedure," Jürgen Habermas attempts to provide a normative response to such questions that is both historically and sociologically plausible. Habermas asks whether the radical democratic ideals associated with the French Revolution can still speak to us today. His answer seeks to combine the best features of the two dominant conceptions of democracy: civic republicanism and liberalism. As in civic republicanism, Habermas wants to develop the participatory features of democracy; as in liberalism, he wants to emphasize the role of institutions and of law. Because he takes the disillusioning sociological literature—in particular, systems theory—so seriously, the central question for Habermas is this: how can the normative force of reasons generated by the public deliberation of citizens have an effect on government administrations that respond only to power? The key to his solution lies in the internal relation between the exercise of political power and the rule of law: in constitutional regimes, government officials are at least constrained by the arguments and reasons that have held up in the public sphere. Insofar as a broadly dispersed, "subjectless communication" among citizens is allowed to develop in autonomous public spheres and enter into receptive representative bodies with formal decision-making power, the notion of popular sovereignty—a democratically self-organizing society—is not beyond the pale of feasibility.

Models such as Habermas's differ from updated republicanism and rights-based liberalism by elaborating an idealized deliberative procedure as its point of departure. In the next two essays, Joshua Cohen and John Rawls try to work out the philosophical details of a conception of political justification based on deliberation and public reason. The third essay in part 1, Joshua Cohen's "Deliberation and Democratic Legitimacy," provides a good example of how such an ideal proceduralism could be elaborated. Like Habermas, Cohen defines political legitimacy in relation to an ideal consensus: "outcomes are democratically legitimate if and only if they could be the object of a free and reasoned agreement among equals."[14] Similar to Elster in his discussion of the constraints of the forum, Cohen maintains that the orientation toward reasoned agreement should constrain citizens to focus their proposals on the common good. But Cohen takes a step beyond Elster by specifying procedural standards, such as freedom and lack of coercion and the formal and substantive equality of participants, designed to preserve autonomy and guard against objectionable deliberative outcomes. Cohen then goes on to argue that his ideal procedure provides a suitable model for democratic institutions, one that should be broadly acceptable, stable, just, and institutionally feasible, given the proper mediating structures (such as voting and party competition).

As Cohen has argued elsewhere, an ideal procedural model provides the basis for an "epistemic" interpretation of democratic outcomes.[15] This interpretation presupposes that deliberation involves a cognitive process of assessing arguments and forming judgments about the common good, and that there is some standard, independent of the actual process, according to which the outcome of deliberation is either correct or incorrect. Because the relevant standard is an ideal procedure, correctness does not imply a realist or metaphysical conception of political truth or the common good. Rather, the ideal procedure specifies the counterfactual conditions for public debate and practical reasoning that would allow for the best possible discussion of a political issue on the merits; consequently, an agreement reached under such conditions defines the best solution possible for the available information and arguments. One can then construe real democratic procedures as imperfect approximations of this ideal. Hence, an epistemic interpretation suggests how one might address the second key tenet of the deliberative model, the claim that deliberation should improve decision making. As Cohen puts it, a real decision-making procedure could at least provide "evidence" for the correct political judgment insofar as the real procedure is properly designed to reflect the requirements of the ideal.[16]

Whether Cohen's proposal holds up or not, it opens up the large area of research having to do with the relationship between deliberation and democratic decision making—whether and how deliberation improves decisions, how these two are best linked, and so forth. Such questions can be studied from a number of perspectives. Some theorists, for example, have called for more collaboration between deliberative democratic theory and rational choice theory.[17] Others have attempted to resurrect Condorcet's Jury Theorem, whose epistemic analysis of voting suggests obvious points of contact with an epistemic model of deliberation.[18] However, the epistemic interpretation is in tension with other features of democratic decision making, as discussion in part 2 will show.

The last essay in part 1, John Rawls's "Idea of Public Reason," takes a closer look at the connection between deliberation and the common good. Rawls thus brings us back to the first tenet of deliberative democracy, that deliberation constrains citizens to cast their proposals in relation to the common good. Only now the main challenge to deliberation lies not in the competition of private interests but in the plurality of normative conceptions of the good and worldviews.

Not content with vague assumptions, Rawls seeks to elaborate exactly what such an orientation substantively requires at the level of public reason-giving in pluralistic settings. For Rawls, this means "forswearing the whole truth" and basing one's proposals on widely accepted "plain truths." At least for constitutional essentials and issues of justice, the "duty of civility" normally precludes appeals to comprehensive doctrines: political association should rest on shared political values, which provide public reasons that "all might reasonably be expected to endorse."[19] Although this commitment presupposes a background consensus on political values and constitutional essentials, it does not define correct outcomes against an ideal consensus—here Rawls's model of deliberation differs from Habermas's and Cohen's. Rawls is concerned to specify the limits of the public use of reason.

Rawls concludes his essay by considering difficulties raised by particular cases, such as the use of religious appeals in the antislavery and civil rights movements. Here he allows for some use of comprehensive doctrines, to the extent that they "support" the public use of reason. In the postscript, which is taken from the new introduction to the paperback edition of *Political Liberalism,* Rawls further expands his conception into a "wide view of public reason," which allows even greater scope for appeals to comprehensive doctrines and for more radical forms of criticism of the sort that Habermas finds missing in his account. The postscript also highlights the "criterion of reciprocity" that governs public reason. Rawls's recent work articulates a conception of justification that is committed to both pluralism and publicity, specifying a kind of politics that is consistent with his claim in *Theory of Justice* (sec. 6.4) that the ultimate form of practical rationality is deliberative. Norms of reasonableness and reciprocity govern and limit the public use of reason by citizens in a pluralistic society.

**Reason, Politics, and Justification: The Process, Conditions, and Goal of Deliberation**

The essays in part 2 continue the work of specifying the details of the ideal of deliberative democracy. They primarily address controversies that have emerged after the initial statements of Elster,

Habermas, Cohen, and Rawls. Perhaps the main focus of these disputes is the relation between reason and politics in a democracy based on the ideal of achieving "reasoned agreement among free and equal citizens under ideal conditions." Even if existing procedures and practices are broadly fair and democratic, they might not yet be deliberative; they might not promote such agreement, offer sufficient opportunities for public input, or the requisite access of citizens to relevant public arenas. A fully developed and practical version of the deliberative ideal adequate to this constructive task would require at least four aspects. First, it would have to specify a *goal* for deliberative decision making: should this goal be consensus, or something weaker such as cooperation or compromise? Second, it would have to say more about the *process* of deliberation, involving public discussion, formal institutions and various methods of decision making. How does such a process improve the quality of decision making, particularly its epistemic value? Third, it would have to specify certain *conditions* necessary for deliberation to be democratic, and these are usually discussed broadly as freedom and equality of citizens. But in what sense are citizens to be free and equal in deliberation? How are freedom and equality related to each other? Finally, the conditions of deliberation also must be *shown to apply,* even if only approximately, to current social conditions, including increasing cultural pluralism and social complexity. Should deliberative democracy take into account group identity as pluralists urge, or should it adopt a normative individualism as liberals insist? What role should experts play? Different ways of specifying the goal, process and conditions of deliberation lead to quite different conceptions of a practical relation of reason to politics, ranging from David Estlund's epistemic proceduralism, to Joshua Cohen's emphasis on consensus, to Gerald Gaus's and Thomas Christiano's doubts regarding the importance of deliberation as a method for discovering political truths.

Before turning to such issues, some background might be needed to put the current discussion in the context of the debate among deliberative theorists. David Estlund's previous work provides a good starting point for this purpose. In various papers, Estlund has pointed out a fundamental ambiguity in the conception of political justification implied by the ideal proceduralist conceptions of Habermas, Michelman, and Cohen, among others.[20] He has rejected claims that a purely proceduralist conception of justification can provide the basis for deliberative democracy, and for that reason rejects any conception of legitimacy according to which the agreement of citizens is *constitutive* of the correctness of a particular decision. Claims about the constitutive character of procedures for justification are quite common among defenders of deliberative democracy, who see procedural justification as an alternative to appeals to metaphysical truths or moral expertise.[21] Indeed, deliberative democracy accepts the liberal insistence that such appeals cannot provide convincing public reasons in democratic debate. However, if one identifies rightness with what citizens agree upon in an institution that approximates an ideal procedure, then it is difficult to underwrite some of the central claims of the deliberative ideal: that public deliberation somehow improves the quality of decisions; that deliberation makes it more likely for outcomes to be rational, well-justified, true, or just. For such epistemic claims to be defensible, Estlund argues, it seems that deliberative theorists must appeal to a procedure-independent standard of correctness or truth (whatever it may be). Estlund's argument is therefore conceptual: the very idea of a cognitive judgment involves appeals to "objective standards." This contrasts with the view that Estlund calls "fair proceduralism," which claims only that decisions are legitimate or fair to the extent that they are based on the equal power of citizens over outcomes.

In his essay in this volume, Estlund sets forth one of the basic themes of the second part of the volume: how are deliberative procedures related to political justification and legitimation? As he refines his argument for "epistemic proceduralism," the basic lines of dispute among deliberative theorists about political justification and thus about the goal of deliberation become clear. Representing one view are theorists such as Estlund, who defend deliberative procedures in terms of their epistemic value. A second position is staked out by Cohen and followers of Habermas, who defend the weaker epistemic claim that democratic procedures and their goal of consensus embody norms of reasonableness or communicative rationality. Finally, there are defenders of fair proceduralism, such

as Christiano and Gaus, who acknowledge the intrinsic or instrumental significance of deliberation but sever it from the question of
justification.

Frank Michelman's contribution shows the political stakes involved in what may seem a rather abstract philosophical debate
about justification, independent standards, and epistemic values in
deliberation. Employing a new color scheme to designate the advocates of deliberation, Michelman describes deliberative democracy
as an overall political program: the program of the "blue" party.
Michelman then asks whether deliberative democracy is a practical
ideal in a specific sense: not in terms of its feasibility, but rather in
terms of whether its goals conceptually cohere on the practical level.
Michelman argues that the practical goal of "blue" thought is tied to
popular sovereignty: to "the ongoing project of authorship of a
country's laws by the country's people in some nonfictively attributable sense." According to Michelman, however, the special recursive-
ness or circularity built into his ideal confronts its advocates with a
practical dilemma. On the one hand, the people make the laws; on
the other hand, basic or fundamental laws must already be in place
for the process of deliberation to begin. Specifically, there is a
conflict between the blue commitment to "deep democracy" and to
liberal deontological principles such as rights that are the basis for
decisions among free and equal citizens. All of these deontological
ideals are "process-bound" and thus open to political debate; at the
same time, this very process of debate presupposes deontological-liberal principles as conditions of its possibility. Michelman's solution
to this "regress problem" is pragmatic: if the ongoing practices of
making laws are sufficiently self-critical, then we can accept both
sides of the dilemma in practice. That is, if the people not only make
the laws but also revise their practices of self-determination when
these violate their ideal of political rightness, then it is possible to
combine respect for persons with the commitment to a norm of
political truth internal to the deliberative process.[22]

Much like Michelman, Estlund has the goal of cutting through
some of the dilemmas and antinomies that are built into the deliberative ideal. In his essay, Estlund wants to show how a proceduralist
account of legitimacy is compatible with epistemic criteria of right-

ness, that is, standards of justice and the common good that are independent of *actual* procedures (though not necessarily of all conceivable procedures or ideal procedures). Reinforcing his earlier arguments on the link between deliberation and truth, Estlund argues against attempts to eliminate or moderate the epistemic value of deliberation. "Fair deliberative proceduralism," for example, drops epistemic claims and highlights instead the fairness of deliberation or equality of voice; but why settle for this when we can have procedures that are both fair and improve reasons? Habermasian attempts to construct a moderate position—which identify the epistemic standard with a conception of reason embodied in the fair procedure—must either collapse into fair proceduralism or invoke independent standards of good reasons.[23] At the same time, one must also avoid the overly epistemic view associated with correctness theories, which identify legitimacy with correctness of outcome. Such views—which Estlund attributes not only to Plato, Rousseau, and Condorcet but also to Cohen—threaten the democratic character of deliberation and make it difficult to account for how minority views are to be respected.

The "epistemic proceduralism" that emerges from this dialectic links legitimacy with deliberative procedures that have an imperfect tendency to produce epistemically correct outcomes. On this view, a procedure such as majority rule is legitimate because it is both fair and epistemically superior to alternative procedures. Armed with this set of distinctions, proponents of deliberation might begin to solve some of the conceptual difficulties raised by Michelman's antinomy. Epistemic proceduralism corrects for the excesses of deep democracy, including deference to the general will as an independent standard of correctness. In light of the weaker standard of democratic legitimacy, for example, we need not appeal to the cognitive capacities of individuals (which, as Gaus insists, the empirical evidence shows to be often rather suspect), but to more general and more easily attainable social/structural and institutional considerations.

By directly challenging the sort of epistemic claims advanced by Cohen or Estlund, Gaus and Christiano develop nonepistemic versions of the deliberative ideal, both of which do not depend on the goal of consensus or correctness. Both think that the facts of deep disagreement challenge the core assumptions of proceduralism: that each citizen must be given reasons that he or she could accept, or at least not reasonably reject. But for Gaus and Christiano the social fact of deep disagreement means that we must reject the idea that any procedure, even a deliberative one, could be the source of political justification. For Christiano, procedures themselves can be evaluated by an independent standard, but that standard is the norm of equality that ensures the fairness of the result of discussion and voting by giving each citizen equal influence in the decision-making process. The standard here is thus moral rather than epistemic: it is the equal respect due to persons that is intrinsic to justice. Thus, the significance of deliberation is not that it produces better justifications or more informed decisions, but rather that it approximates the intrinsic standard of political equality. Besides such intrinsic worth of a properly constituted deliberative process, deliberation can also have instrumental value, such as increasing understanding in a community. According to Christiano, the dilemmas facing deliberative democracy around issues of intractable disagreement can be avoided by uncoupling deliberation from epistemic values and the goal of maximizing agreement. Gaus, too, rejects consensus as the goal of deliberation on conceptual and empirical grounds. While emphasizing the problem of disagreement, unlike Christiano he still insists on the use of reason and public justification in politics. But he rejects any appeal to the norm of reasonableness, which requires what Joseph Raz has called the internally incoherent stance of "epistemic abstinence." The problem with reasonableness for Gaus is that it gives us a hopelessly thin principle of public justification that is unsuitable to deliberative democracy: it provides no basis for judging any substantive proposals about basic political issues. He thus proposes a form of "adjudicative democracy," which accepts the fact of fundamental and intractable disagreements between persons and groups. Like Christiano's goal of fairness through equality, Gaus sees democracy itself as an umpiring mechanism by which all parties seek public, rational, and most importantly impartial adjudication of their differences. Whatever one's view of the results of these debates about justification, one thing is clear: the facts of pluralism and persistent disagreement must now be made central to any case for epistemic improvement as a goal of deliberation.[24]

### Deliberative Democracy as a Substantive Ideal: Equality, Pluralism, and Liberty

The remaining essays by Knight and Johnson, Bohman, Richardson, Young, and Cohen concern more substantive issues about the process and conditions necessary for deliberative democracy: political equality, cultural difference, the formation of joint intentions, and the role of the substantive liberal and egalitarian values that inform deliberative procedures. Taken together, they show not only the variety of positions within deliberative theory, but also the robustness of the deliberative ideal in dealing with the problems facing contemporary democracy.

Rather than focusing on the outcome of deliberation, Bohman and Knight and Johnson take up the most fundamental condition of deliberation for either epistemic or nonepistemic versions: political equality. Both essays develop substantive conceptions that attempt to go beyond merely building equality into procedures, ideal or otherwise. Certainly, procedural equality, understood as the equality of opportunity to participate in political decision making, is crucial for democratic legitimacy. But deliberative democracy also requires elaborating the substantive aspects of political equality appropriate to its particular ideal. Whereas for Knight and Johnson this is "equal opportunity of access to political influence," for Bohman it is "equally effective social freedom." In order to develop procedural aspects of equality, Knight and Johnson turn to analogies to the axioms of social choice theory; Bohman, by contrast, develops this aspect of political equality in terms of Habermas's ideal speech situation where all have equal opportunity to speak. But the main innovation in both essays is to develop the more substantive account in which the work of Amartya Sen on "capability equality" is the primary inspiration.[25] Knight and Johnson argue that this approach has considerable advantages over the Rawlsian approach and answer objections put forward by Cohen that the resource-based account is more practically useful. However, they see problems with Sen's account, even as it is modified by Bohman to accommodate the uncertainties of social freedom and the inequalities that undermine effective democratic participation in political deliberation.

The difficulties motivating the turn to Sen's conception of capability equality are not only the weaknesses of procedural equality of opportunity and equality of resources, but also the possible elitism of deliberative theories. Deliberative conceptions of democracy must have demanding requirements of political equality, if they are not to favor the more virtuous, the better educated, or simply the better off. Even if the design of deliberative institutions must ensure that all citizens have the equal opportunity to influence political decisions, the capacity to make effective use of such opportunities may vary widely whenever there are considerable differences in wealth and power among the citizenry. Bohman argues that a capabilities-based account begins by establishing a minimum threshold for equality in political decision making: that citizens must be capable of adequate political functioning, such that they are able to avoid being consistently included or excluded from the decision-making process. This threshold of adequate public functioning marks the "floor" of "political poverty," below which citizens cannot reasonably expect to be able to influence the outcomes of deliberation. It establishes a "ceiling" as well, when citizens have so much social power as to be able to causally influence outcomes without enlisting the cooperation of others. The problem of intermediate cases raised by Knight and Johnson can be solved in a preliminary way by considering the effects that differences in the extent of both effective agency and social freedom among differently situated deliberators may have on outcomes.

Richardson and Young focus on a different practical issue for deliberative democracy: who are the subjects of deliberation? To whom or to what do the norms of freedom and equality apply? Richardson proposes that the dispute between epistemic and fair proceduralism can best be resolved by shifting the focus of the debate. Instead of seeing agreements about truth or fairness as the outcome of deliberation, deliberation is the process by which "partially joint intentions" are formed and acted upon. Richardson opens up the conceptual space between the different forms of pro-

ceduralism that Estlund is at pains to deny. Using Raimo Tuomela's
individualist model of collective intentions, Richardson explicates
his conception of joint intentions through a process by which various
goods are recognized and given a place. He then provides a detailed,
step-by-step model of how majority rule might be interpreted as
forming joint intentions, where reaching informal agreements about
the nature of the issues at stake is the indispensable step. Most of all,
Richardson thinks that the formation of partially joint intentions
best accounts for why democracy respects each individual as a "self-
originator of claims." Thus, while his model does not reduce joint
intentions to merely individual ones, it is committed to a normative
individualism. By contrast, Young thinks that without the recognition
of group-based identities in the decision-making process, deliberative democracy will be blind to sources of inequality and asymmetries
of power. Adding to her previous work on "group differentiated
citizenship," Young argues here that making groups (rather than
individuals) the subjects of deliberation has distinct epistemic advantages. These advantages follow from her nonessentialist understanding of social groups as occupying different, relational positions,
each with its own particular social perspective. Critical public discussion ought to be about the expression and exchange of different
social perspectives, so that each can be transformed into a more
reflective and objective social judgment. Deliberation is thus the
mutual openness and accountability of different groups to each
other's perspectives, each of which is committed to thinking from
the standpoint of everyone else. Young makes communication across
differences essential to the creation of a wider and potentially shared
perspective that is infused with the comprehensive social knowledge
derived from the situated knowledge of every particular social
group. Difference is thus "a resource" (and not just a burden) for
democratic communication among and across various groups, the
outcome of which is the more comprehensive and effective form of
social knowledge.

Given the intense scrutiny to which Joshua Cohen's work has been
submitted in this volume, it is only fitting that it end with an essay
by him. Here Cohen gives a revised general statement of the deliberative conception, showing how "the fact of reasonable pluralism"

provides a way to give concrete shape to the conception of citizens as free and equal. Deliberative democracy, he argues, is not merely based on a procedural conception of justification. Rather, it establishes a substantive conception of politics, containing a very specific interpretation of egalitarian and liberal values of rights and liberties. Under reasonable pluralism, citizens are free to the extent that they do not have to share some particular religious or moral doctrine; they are equal to the extent that "each is recognized as having the capacities required for participating in discussion aimed at authorizing the exercise of power." Using Rawls's terminology, the idealized procedure is still a model characterization of free reasoning among equals, the features of which can be built into institutions. The added norm of reasonableness is the crucial addition to the model that he develops in "Deliberation and Democratic Legitimacy." This assumption is strongly challenged by Knight and Johnson, Gaus, Young, and Christiano as an inadequate normative basis for settling problems of difference. Its main use for Cohen is to define what is an acceptable public reason without presupposing substantive agreement in moral doctrines. As a norm, reasonableness sets the parameters of debate about such morally contentious issues as abortion or censorship in pluralistic settings and even suggests political solutions that are publicly acceptable.

Once we see how deliberation works under conditions of reasonable pluralism, it is clear why deliberative democracy must ensure "a wide guarantee" of religious, moral, and expressive liberties. Their purpose is to ensure full membership to all citizens in the sovereign body that exercises power. Thus, deliberative inclusion can be justified as a requirement of liberty of conscience, itself guaranteed by the deeper political values of freedom and equality. The substantive values of freedom and equality thus extend such guarantees beyond the political-deliberative process itself. Indeed, the very disagreements that are an ineliminable feature of a democratic community of free and equal citizens demand "wide" liberties of conscience, religion, and expression by denying the community or the majority the legitimate power to enforce its contingent consensus on moral matters. The fact and origins of disagreement do indeed demand limits on public reason, as Rawls has argued; but these limits also imply substantive solutions to pressing matters of moral conflict and political legitimacy. Reasonableness is thus a central norm to be built into deliberative procedures.

## Conclusion

These essays show the continued fruitfulness of thinking about democracy in terms of the deliberative ideal. They also show that there remain certain internal tensions in the ideal: tensions between procedural justification and the need for independent standards of judgment and reason; tensions between freedom and equality; tensions between pluralism and publicity; and the tensions between its ideal and the actual conditions of pluralism and complexity in contemporary societies. Resolving such tensions within it will go a long way toward showing how this demanding ideal can inform our judgment about many pressing issues of pluralist democracy. More than that, the deliberative ideal provides the basis for the reform of democratic institutions and practices, starting with how campaigns are financed and conducted and how representative bodies do their business.[26] The ultimate test of the fully developed conception of deliberative democracy will be practical: whether its proposed reforms can enrich and improve democratic practice and overcome the many obstacles to the public use of reason in contemporary political life.

## Notes

1. Joseph A. Schumpeter, *Capitalism, Socialism and Democracy* (New York: Harper, 1942; 1976), p. 251; more generally, see chaps. 20–22. For a criticism of Schumpeter's legacy, see also Carole Pateman, *Participation and Democratic Theory* (Cambridge: Cambridge University Press, 1970), chap. 1.

2. Specifically, the abstract functionalist framework and orientation toward noncognitivist cultural explanations of political behavior prevented Parsonians from fully grasping the nature and scope of reasonable public deliberation; for a critical discussion of key works by Parsons and others, see Brian Barry, *Sociologists, Economists and Democracy* (London: Collier-Macmillan, 1970), chaps. 3–4, 7–8. See also Jürgen Habermas, *Theory of Communicative Action*, vol. 2, trans. T. McCarthy (Boston: Beacon, 1987), chap. 7, esp. pp. 256–282. Parsons's own writings in this area are conveniently available in his *Politics and Social Structure* (New York: Free Press, 1969). Note that Habermas has critically appropriated elements of Parsonian functionalism (such as the

Introduction

conception of the "societal community") for a deliberative model; see Habermas, *Between Facts and Norms: Contributions to a Discourse Theory of Law and Democracy*, trans. W. Rehg (Cambridge, MA: MIT Press, 1996), pp. 66, 73–81, 139ff, 363ff.

3. Anthony Downs, *An Economic Theory of Democracy* (New York: Harper, 1957); also Barry, *Sociologists, Economists and Democracy*, chaps. 2 and 5.

4. Prominent developments are represented by Kenneth Arrow, *Social Choice and Individual Values*, 2nd ed. (New Haven: Yale University Press, 1963); Duncan Black, *The Theory of Committees and Elections* (Cambridge: Cambridge University Press, 1958); for an introduction, see William H. Riker, *Liberalism against Populism: A Confrontation between the Theory of Democracy and the Theory of Social Choice* (Prospect Heights, Ill.: Waveland, 1982).

5. The similarities uniting these two approaches led C. B. Macpherson to group them under a single, broader model; see his *Life and Times of Liberal Democracy* (Oxford: Oxford University Press, 1977), chap. 4; compare also Benjamin Barber, *Strong Democracy: Participatory Politics for a New Age* (Berkeley: University of California Press, 1984), part 1.

6. See Riker, *Liberalism against Populism*, chap. 10.

7. Robert A. Dahl, *A Preface to Democratic Theory* (Chicago: University of Chicago Press, 1956); for Dahl's later critical assessment of pluralist theory, see his *Democracy and Its Critics* (New Haven: Yale University Press, 1989), pp. 289–298. The influence of the pluralist model in constitutional scholarship is noted by Cass R. Sunstein, "Interest Groups in American Public Law," *Stanford Law Review* 38 (1985): 30–35.

8. For a brief review of developments, see Jane Mansbridge, *Beyond Adversary Democracy* (Chicago: University of Chicago Press, 1983), chap. 2.

9. One of the earlier book-length contributions to the revival was Pateman's *Participation and Democratic Theory*. Neo-Marxist theorists were also prominent in this trend; for example, Jürgen Habermas, *Legitimation Crisis*, trans. Thomas McCarthy (Boston: Beacon, 1975); Macpherson, *Life and Times of Liberal Democracy*, chap. 5. A nonaggregative conception of the common good also re-emerged with John Rawls's *Theory of Justice* (Cambridge: Harvard University Press, 1971).

10. Joseph M. Bessette, "Deliberative Democracy: The Majority Principle in Republican Government," in *How Democratic Is the Constitution?*, eds. Robert A. Goldwin and William A. Schambra (Washington: American Enterprise Institute, 1980), pp. 102–116; Bessette has subsequently worked out his position in greater detail in *The Mild Voice of Reason: Deliberative Democracy and American National Government* (Chicago: University of Chicago Press, 1994).

11. For representative works that highlight these motifs, see, respectively, Barber, *Strong Democracy;* Mansbridge, *Beyond Adversarial Democracy;* Pateman, *Participation and Democratic Theory;* Rawls, *Theory of Justice;* Joshua Cohen and Joel Rogers, *On Democracy: Toward a Transformation of American Society* (New York: Penguin, 1983); Bessette, "Deliberative Democracy"; and Sunstein, "Interest Groups."

12. For a historical overview of the republican tradition and adaptation of it to the United States, see especially Frank Michelman, "The Supreme Court 1985 Term—Foreword: Traces of Self-Government," *Harvard Law Review* 100 (1985): 4–77; for

further links with American law, see Cass Sunstein, "Beyond the Republican Revival," *Yale Law Journal* 97 (1988): 1539–1578, as well as his "Interest Groups."

13. The desirability of consensualist models of legitimacy has also been notably questioned by Bernard Manin, "On Legitimacy and Political Deliberation," trans. E. Stein and J. Mansbridge, *Political Theory* 15 (1987): 338–368.

14. Compare Habermas, *Between Facts and Norms,* p. 110: "Only those statutes may claim legitimacy that can meet with the assent of all citizens in a discursive process of legislation that in turn has been legally constituted."

15. Joshua Cohen, "An Epistemic Conception of Democracy," *Ethics* 97 (1986): 26–38. Note that Thomas Christiano's contribution to this volume argues that Cohen's current account of deliberation is inconsistent with this particular epistemic formulation of proceduralism.

16. Cohen, "Epistemic Conception," p. 32.

17. See, for example, Jack Knight and James Johnson, "Aggregation and Deliberation: On the Possibility of Democratic Legitimacy," *Political Theory* 22 (1994): 277–296; compare Bernard Grofman, "Public Choice, Civic Republicanism, and American Politics: Perspectives of a 'Reasonable Choice' Modeler," *Texas Law Review* 71 (1993): 1541–1587.

18. According to Condorcet's Jury Theorem, the probability that a majority is correct approaches certainty as the size of the group increases, assuming each voter is a "competent judge" (or is better than chance in being correct); see Black, *Theory of Committees,* pp. 159–180. See Bernard Grofman and Scott Feld, "Rousseau's General Will: A Condorcetian Perspective," *American Political Science Review* 82 (1988): 567–576.

19. The idea that political argumentation should avoid controversial conceptions of the good life has also been championed by Bruce Ackerman, *Social Justice in the Liberal State* (New Haven: Yale University Press, 1980).

20. David Estlund, "Who's Afraid of Deliberative Democracy? On the Strategic/Deliberative Dichotomy in Recent Constitutional Jurisprudence," *Texas Law Review* 71 (1993): 1437–1477; and "Making Truth Safe for Democracy" in *The Idea of Democracy,* ed. D. Copp et al. (Cambridge: Cambridge University Press, 1992), pp. 72–100.

21. See, for example, Barber, *Strong Democracy,* pp. 64–65 and 166–168. Estlund cites Frank Michelman and Lani Guinier as possible examples of deliberative theorists who make constitutive claims about public justification. In earlier work, Habermas has also used a constitutivist idiom, asserting that public consensus has a "constitutive significance [for truth] beyond its pragmatic value." See Habermas, *The Structural Transformation of the Public Sphere,* trans. Thomas Burger and Frederick Lawrence (Cambridge: MIT Press, 1989), pp. 105–106.

22. Compare Frank Michelman, "Law's Republic," *The Yale Law Journal* 97 (1988): 1518, arguing that it is best to hold both the epistemic and the deep democratic moments in "a generative tension."

23. Estlund attributes this view to Seyla Benhabib in his contribution to this volume, while Rawls finds it in Habermas. In his "Reply to Habermas," *Journal of Philosophy* 92

(1995): 132–180, Rawls interprets Habermas as taking this moderate approach. Both Rawls and Estlund reject the moderate position, but for very different reasons.

24. For two quite different treatments of this problem see Amy Gutmann and Dennis Thompson, *Democracy and Disagreement* (Cambridge: Harvard University Press, 1996) and Fred D'Agostino, *Free Public Reason* (Oxford: Oxford University Press, 1996). The latter uses the contestability of public reason as a reason for skepticism about deliberative democracy; the former uses it to argue for "deliberative universalism." For an argument against skepticism about the scope of public reason motivated by deep conflicts and disagreements on basic principles, see James Bohman, *Public Deliberation* (Cambridge: MIT Press, 1996), chapter 2. On the notion of epistemic abstinence, see Joseph Raz, "Facing Diversity: The Case for Epistemic Abstinence," *Philosophy and Public Affairs* 19 (1990): 3–46.

25. See Amartya Sen, *Inequality Reexamined* (Cambridge: Harvard University Press, 1992).

26. See, for example, James Fishkin's "deliberative opinion poll," in *Democracy and Deliberation* (New Haven: Yale University Press, 1991), pp. 81–104. Fishkin has applied this idea in several televised experiments in the United States and the United Kingdom. For an analysis of the decline of deliberation in the United States Congress as a deliberative body, see Bessette, *Mild Voice of Reason*, pp. 152ff.

# I

## The Idea of Deliberative Democracy: Major Statements

# 1

## The Market and the Forum: Three Varieties of Political Theory

*Jon Elster*

I want to compare three views of politics generally, and of the democratic system more specifically. I shall first look at social choice theory, as an instance of a wider class of theories with certain common features. In particular, they share the conception that the political process is instrumental rather than an end in itself, and the view that the decisive political act is a private rather than a public action, viz. the individual and secret vote. With these usually goes the idea that the goal of politics is the optimal compromise between given, and irreducibly opposed, private interests. The other two views arise when one denies, first, the private character of political behavior and then, secondly, goes on also to deny the instrumental nature of politics. According to the theory of Jürgen Habermas, the goal of politics should be rational agreement rather than compromise, and the decisive political act is that of engaging in public debate with a view to the emergence of a consensus. According to the theorists of participatory democracy, from John Stuart Mill to Carole Pateman, the goal of politics is the transformation and education of the participants. Politics, on this view, is an end in itself—indeed many have argued that it represents the good life for man. I shall discuss these views in the order indicated. I shall present them in a somewhat stylized form, but my critical comments will not, I hope, be directed to straw men.

Jon Elster

# I

Politics, it is usually agreed, is concerned with the common good, and notably with the cases in which it cannot be realized as the aggregate outcome of individuals pursuing their private interests. In particular, uncoordinated private choices may lead to outcomes that are worse for all than some other outcome that could have been attained by coordination. Political institutions are set up to remedy such *market failures,* a phrase that can be taken either in the static sense of an inability to provide public goods or in the more dynamic sense of a breakdown of the self-regulating properties usually ascribed to the market mechanism.[1] In addition there is the redistributive task of politics—moving along the Pareto-optimal frontier once it has been reached.[2] According to the first view of politics, this task is inherently one of interest struggle and compromise. The obstacle to agreement is not only that most individuals want redistribution to be in their favor, or at least not in their disfavor.[3] More basically consensus is blocked because there is no reason to expect that individuals will converge in their views on what constitutes a just redistribution.

I shall consider social choice theory as representative of the private-instrumental view of politics, because it brings out supremely well the logic as well as the limits of that approach. Other varieties, such as the Schumpeterian or neo-Schumpeterian theories, are closer to the actual political process, but for that reason also less suited to my purpose. For instance, Schumpeter's insistence that voter preferences are shaped and manipulated by politicians[4] tends to blur the distinction, central to my analysis, between politics as the aggregation of given preferences and politics as the transformation of preferences through rational discussion. And although the neo-Schumpeterians are right in emphasizing the role of the political parties in the preference-aggregation process,[5] I am not here concerned with such mediating mechanisms. In any case, political problems also arise within the political parties, and so my discussion may be taken to apply to such lower-level political processes. In fact, much of what I shall say makes better sense for politics on a rather small scale—within the firm, the organization or the local community—than for nationwide political systems.

In very broad outline, the structure of social choice theory is as follows.[6] (1) We begin with a *given* set of agents, so that the issue of a normative justification of political boundaries does not arise. (2) We assume that the agents confront a *given* set of alternatives, so that for instance the issue of agenda manipulation does not arise. (3) The agents are supposed to be endowed with preferences that are similarly *given* and not subject to change in the course of the political process. They are, moreover, assumed to be causally independent of the set of alternatives. (4) In the standard version, which is so far the only operational version of the theory, preferences are assumed to be purely ordinal, so that it is not possible for an individual to express the intensity of his preferences, nor for an outside observer to compare preference intensities across individuals. (5) The individual preferences are assumed to be defined over all pairs of individuals, i.e. to be complete, and to have the formal property of transitivity, so that preference for $A$ over $B$ and for $B$ over $C$ implies preference for $A$ over $C$.

Given this setting, the task of social choice theory is to arrive at a social preference ordering of the alternatives. This might appear to require more than is needed: why not define the goal as one of arriving at the choice of one alternative? There is, however, usually some uncertainty as to which alternatives are really feasible, and so it is useful to have an ordering if the top-ranked alternative proves unavailable. The ordering should satisfy the following criteria. (6) Like the individual preferences, it should be complete and transitive. (7) It should be Pareto-optimal, in the sense of never having one option socially preferred to another which is individually preferred by everybody. (8) The social choice between two given options should depend only on how the individuals rank these two options, and thus not be sensitive to changes in their preferences concerning other options. (9) The social preference ordering should respect and reflect individual preferences, over and above the condition of Pareto-optimality. This idea covers a variety of notions, the most important of which are *anonymity* (all individuals should count equally), *nondictatorship* (a fortiori no single individual should dictate the social choice), *liberalism* (all individuals should have some private domain within which their preferences are decisive), and *strategy-proofness* (it should not pay to express false preferences).

Jon Elster

   The substance of social choice theory is given in a series of impossibility and uniqueness theorems, stating either that a given subset of these conditions is incapable of simultaneous satisfaction or that they uniquely describe a specific method for aggregating preferences. Much attention has been given to the impossibility theorems, yet from the present point of view these are not of decisive importance. They stem largely from the paucity of allowable information about the preferences, i.e. the exclusive focus on ordinal preferences.[7] True, at present we do not quite know how to go beyond ordinality. Log-rolling and vote-trading may capture some of the cardinal aspects of the preferences, but at some cost.[8] Yet even should the conceptual and technical obstacles to intra- and interindividual comparison of preference intensity be overcome,[9] many objections to the social choice approach would remain. I shall discuss two sets of objections, both related to the assumption of given preferences. I shall argue, first, that the preferences people choose to express may not be a good guide to what they really prefer; and secondly that what they really prefer may in any case be a fragile foundation for social choice.
   In fact, preferences are never "given," in the sense of being directly observable. If they are to serve as inputs to the social choice process, they must somehow be *expressed* by the individuals. The expression of preferences is an action, which presumably is guided by these very same preferences.[10] It is then far from obvious that the individually rational action is to express these preferences as they are. Some methods for aggregating preferences are such that it may pay the individual to express false preferences, i.e. the outcome may in some cases be better according to his real preferences if he chooses not to express them truthfully. The condition for strategy-proofness for social choice mechanisms was designed expressly to exclude this possibility. It turns out, however, that the systems in which honesty always pays are rather unattractive in other respects.[11] We then have to face the possibility that even if we require that the social preferences be Pareto-optimal with respect to the expressed preferences, they might not be so with respect to the real ones. Strategy-proofness and collective rationality, therefore, stand and fall together. Since it appears that the first must fall, so must the second.

It then becomes very difficult indeed to defend the idea that the outcome of the social choice mechanism represents the common good, since there is a chance that everybody might prefer some other outcome.

Amos Tversky has pointed to another reason why choices—or expressed preferences—cannot be assumed to represent the real preferences in all cases.[12] According to his "concealed preference hypothesis," choices often conceal rather than reveal underlying preferences. This is especially so in two sorts of cases. First, there are the cases of anticipated regret associated with a risky decision. Consider the following example (from Tversky):

On her twelfth birthday, Judy was offered a choice between spending the weekend with her aunt in the city ($C$), or having a party for all her friends. The party could take place either in the garden ($GP$) or inside the house ($HP$). A garden party would be much more enjoyable, but there is always the possibility of rain, in which case an inside party would be more sensible. In evaluating the consequences of the three options, Judy notes that the weather condition does not have a significant effect on $C$. If she chooses the party, however, the situation is different. A garden party will be a lot of fun if the weather is good, but quite disastrous if it rains, in which case an inside party will be acceptable. The trouble is that Judy expects to have a lot of regret if the party is to be held inside and the weather is very nice.

Now, let us suppose that for some reason it is no longer possible to have an outside party. In this situation, there is no longer any regret associated with holding an inside party in good weather because (in this case) Judy has no other place for holding the party. Hence, the elimination of an available course of action (holding the party outside) removes the regret associated with an inside party, and increases its overall utility. It stands to reason, in this case, that if Judy was indifferent between $C$ and $HP$, in the presence of $GP$, she will prefer $HP$ to $C$ when $GP$ is eliminated.

What we observe here is the violation of condition (8) above, the so-called "independence of irrelevant alternatives." The expressed preferences depend causally on the set of alternatives. We may assume that the real preferences, defined over the set of possible outcomes, remain constant, contrary to the case to be discussed below. Yet the preferences over the *pairs* (choice, outcome) depend on the set of available choices, because the "costs of responsibility" differentially associated with various such pairs depend on what else one "could have done." Although Judy could not have escaped her predicament by deliberately making it physically impossible to have an outside party,[13] she might well have welcomed an event outside her control with the same consequence.

The second class of cases in which Tversky would want to distinguish the expressed preferences from the real preferences concerns decisions that are unpleasant rather than risky. For instance, "society may prefer to save the life of one person rather than another, and yet be unable to make this choice." In fact, losing both lives through inaction may be preferred to losing only one life by deliberate action. Such examples are closely related to the problems involved in act utilitarianism versus outcome utilitarianism.[14] One may well judge that it would be a good thing if state A came about, and yet not want to be the person by whose agency it comes about. The reasons for not wanting to be that person may be quite respectable, or they may not. The latter would be the case if one were afraid of being blamed by the relatives of the person who was deliberately allowed to die, or if one simply confused the causal and the moral notions of responsibility. In such cases the expressed preferences might lead to a choice that in a clear sense goes against the real preferences of the people concerned.

A second, perhaps more basic, difficulty is that the real preferences themselves might well depend causally on the feasible set. One instance is graphically provided by the fable of the fox and the sour grapes.[15] For the "ordinal utilitarian," as Arrow for instance calls himself,[16] there would be no welfare loss if the fox were excluded from consumption of the grapes, since he thought them sour anyway. But of course the cause of his holding them to be sour was his conviction that he would in any case be excluded from consuming them, and then it is difficult to justify the allocation by invoking his preferences. Conversely, the phenomenon of "counter-adaptive preferences"—the grass is always greener on the other side of the fence, and the forbidden fruit always sweeter—is also baffling for the social choice theorist, since it implies that such preferences, if respected, would not be satisfied—and yet the whole point of respecting them would be to give them a chance of satisfaction.

Adaptive and counter-adaptive preferences are only special cases of a more general class of desires, those which fail to satisfy some substantive criterion for acceptable preferences, as opposed to the purely formal criterion of transitivity. I shall discuss these under two headings: autonomy and morality.

Autonomy characterizes the way in which preferences are shaped rather than their actual content. Unfortunately I find myself unable to give a positive characterization of autonomous preferences, so I shall have to rely on two indirect approaches. First, autonomy is for desires what judgment is for belief. The notion of judgment is also difficult to define formally, but at least we know that there are persons who have this quality to a higher degree than others: people who are able to take account of vast and diffuse evidence that more or less clearly bears on the problem at hand, in such a way that no element is given undue importance. In such people the process of belief formation is not disturbed by defective cognitive processing, nor distorted by wishful thinking and the like. Similarly, autonomous preferences are those that have not been shaped by irrelevant causal processes—a singularly unhelpful explanation. To improve somewhat on it, consider, secondly, a short list of such irrelevant causal processes. They include adaptive and counter-adaptive preferences, conformity and anti-conformity, the obsession with novelty and the equally unreasonable resistance to novelty. In other words, preferences may be shaped by adaptation to what is possible, to what other people do or to what one has been doing in the past—or they may be shaped by the desire to differ as much as possible from these. In all of these cases the source of preference change is not in the person, but outside him—detracting from his autonomy.

Morality, it goes without saying, is if anything even more controversial. (Within the Kantian tradition it would also be questioned whether it can be distinguished at all from autonomy.) Preferences are moral or immoral by virtue of their content, not by virtue of the way in which they have been shaped. Fairly uncontroversial examples of unethical preferences are spiteful and sadistic desires, and arguably also the desire for positional goods, i.e. goods such that it is logically impossible for more than a few to possess them.[17] The desire for an income twice the average can lead to less welfare for everybody, so that such preferences fail to pass the Kantian generalization test.[18] Also they are closely linked to spite, since one way of getting more than others is to take care that they get less—indeed this may often be a more efficient method than trying to excel.[19]

To see how the lack of autonomy may be distinguished from the lack of moral worth, let me use *conformity* as a technical term for a desire caused by a drive to be like other people, and *conformism* for a desire to be like other people, with anti-conformity and anti-conformism similarly defined. Conformity implies that other people's desires enter into the causation of my own, conformism that they enter irreducibly into the description of the object of my desires. Conformity may bring about conformism, but it may also lead to anti-conformism, as in Theodore Zeldin's comment that among the French peasantry "prestige is to a great extent obtained from conformity with traditions (so that the son of a nonconformist might be expected to be one too)."[20] Clearly, conformity may bring about desires that are morally laudable, yet lacking in autonomy. Conversely, I do not see how one could rule out on a priori grounds the possibility of autonomous spite, although I would welcome a proof that autonomy is incompatible not only with anti-conformity, but also with anti-conformism.

We can now state the objection to the political view underlying social choice theory. It is, basically, that it embodies a confusion between the kind of behavior that is appropriate in the market place and that which is appropriate in the forum. The notion of consumer sovereignty is acceptable because, and to the extent that, the consumer chooses between courses of action that differ only in the way they affect him. In political choice situations, however, the citizen is asked to express his preference over states that also differ in the way in which they affect other people. This means that there is no similar justification for the corresponding notion of the citizen's sovereignty, since other people may legitimately object to social choice governed by preferences that are defective in some of the ways I have mentioned. A social choice mechanism is capable of resolving the market failures that would result from unbridled consumer sovereignty, but as a way of redistributing welfare it is hopelessly inadequate. If people affected each other only by tripping over each other's feet, or by dumping their garbage into one another's backyards, a social choice mechanism might cope. But the task of politics is not only to eliminate inefficiency, but also to create justice—a goal to which the aggregation of prepolitical preferences is a quite incongruous means.

This suggests that the principles of the forum must differ from those of the market. A long-standing tradition from the Greek *polis* onwards suggests that politics must be an open and public activity, as distinct from the isolated and private expression of preferences that occurs in buying and selling. In the following sections I look at two different conceptions of public politics, increasingly removed from the market theory of politics. Before I go on to this, however, I should briefly consider an objection that the social choice theorist might well make to what has just been said. He could argue that the only alternative to the aggregation of given preferences is some kind of censorship or paternalism. He might agree that spiteful and adaptive preferences are undesirable, but he would add that any institutional mechanism for eliminating them would be misused and harnessed to the private purposes of power-seeking individuals. Any remedy, in fact, would be worse than the disease. This objection assumes (i) that the only alternative to aggregation of given preferences is censorship, and (ii) that censorship is always objectionable. I shall now discuss a challenge to the first assumption, viz. the idea of a *transformation* of preferences through public and rational discussion.

## II

Today this view is especially associated with the writings of Jürgen Habermas on "the ethics of discourse" and "the ideal speech situation." As mentioned above, I shall present a somewhat stylized version of his views, although I hope they bear some resemblance to the original.[21] The core of the theory, then, is that rather than aggregating or filtering preferences, the political system should be set up with a view to changing them by public debate and confrontation. The input to the social choice mechanism would then not be the raw, quite possibly selfish or irrational, preferences that operate in the market, but informed and other-regarding preferences. Or rather, there would not be any need for an aggregating mechanism, since a rational discussion would tend to produce unanimous preferences. When the private and idiosyncratic wants have been shaped and purged in public discussion about the public good, uniquely determined rational desires would emerge. Not optimal compromise, but unanimous agreement is the goal of politics on this view.

There appear to be two main premises underlying this theory. The first is that there are certain arguments that simply cannot be stated publicly. In a political debate it is pragmatically impossible to argue that a given solution should be chosen just because it is good for oneself. By the very act of engaging in a public debate—by arguing rather than bargaining—one has ruled out the possibility of invoking such reasons.[22] To engage in discussion can in fact be seen as one kind of self-censorship, a pre-commitment to the idea of rational decision. Now, it might well be thought that this conclusion is too strong. The first argument only shows that in public debate one has to pay some lip service to the common good. An additional premise states that over time one will in fact come to be swayed by considerations about the common good. One cannot indefinitely praise the common good "du bout des lèvres," for—as argued by Pascal in the context of the wager—one will end up having the preferences that initially one was faking.[23] This is a psychological, not a conceptual premise. To explain why going through the motions of rational discussion should tend to bring about the real thing, one might argue that people tend to bring what they mean into line with what they say in order to reduce dissonance, but this is a dangerous argument to employ in the present context. Dissonance reduction does not tend to generate autonomous preferences. Rather one would have to invoke the power of reason to break down prejudice and selfishness. By speaking with the voice of reason, one is also exposing oneself to reason.

To sum up, the conceptual impossibility of expressing selfish arguments in a debate about the public good, and the psychological difficulty of expressing other-regarding preferences without ultimately coming to acquire them, jointly bring it about that public discussion tends to promote the common good. The *volonté générale*, then, will not simply be the Pareto-optimal realization of given (or expressed) preferences,[24] but the outcome of preferences that are themselves shaped by a concern for the common good. For instance, by mere aggregation of given preferences one would be able to take account of some negative externalities, but not of those affecting future generations. A social choice mechanism might prevent persons now living from dumping their garbage into one another's backyards, but not from dumping it on the future. Moreover, considerations of distributive justice within the Pareto constraint would now have a more solid foundation, especially as one would also be able to avoid the problem of strategy-proofness. By one stroke one would achieve more rational preferences, as well as the guarantee that they will in fact be expressed.

I now want to set out a series of objections—seven altogether—to the view stated above. I should explain that the goal of this criticism is not to demolish the theory, but to locate some points that need to be fortified. I am, in fact, largely in sympathy with the fundamental tenets of the view, yet fear that it might be dismissed as Utopian, both in the sense of ignoring the problem of getting from here to there, and in the sense of neglecting some elementary facts of human psychology.

The *first objection* involves a reconsideration of the issues of paternalism. Would it not, in fact, be unwarranted interference to impose on the citizens the obligation to participate in political discussion? One might answer that there is a link between the right to vote and the obligation to participate in discussion, just as rights and duties are correlative in other cases. To acquire the right to vote, one has to perform certain civic duties that go beyond pushing the voting button on the television set. There would appear to be two different ideas underlying this answer. First, only those should have the right to vote who are sufficiently *concerned* about politics to be willing to devote some of their resources—time in particular—to it. Secondly, one should try to favor *informed* preferences as inputs to the voting process. The first argument favors participation and discussion as a sign of interest, but does not give it an instrumental value in itself. It would do just as well, for the purpose of this argument, to demand that people should pay for the right to vote. The second argument favors discussion as a means to improvement—it will not only select the right people, but actually make them more qualified to participate.

These arguments might have some validity in a near-ideal world, in which the concern for politics was evenly distributed across all relevant dimensions, but in the context of contemporary politics they miss the point. The people who survive a high threshold for participation are disproportionately found in a privileged part of the population. At best this could lead to paternalism, at worst the high ideals of rational discussion could create a self-elected elite whose members spend time on politics because they want power, not out of concern for the issues. As in other cases, to be discussed later, the best can be the enemy of the good. I am not saying that it is impossible to modify the ideal in a way that allows both for rational discussion and for low-profile participation, only that any institutional design must respect the trade-off between the two.

My *second objection* is that even assuming unlimited time for discussion, unanimous and rational agreement might not necessarily ensue. Could there not be legitimate and unresolvable differences of opinions over the nature of the common good? Could there not even be a plurality of ultimate values?

I am not going to discuss this objection, since it is in any case preempted by the *third objection.* Since there are in fact always time constraints on discussions—often the stronger the more important the issues—unanimity will rarely emerge. For any constellation of preferences short of unanimity, however, one would need a social choice mechanism to aggregate them. One can discuss only for so long, and then one has to make a decision, even if strong differences of opinion should remain. This objection, then, goes to show that the transformation of preferences can never do more than supplement the aggregation of preferences, never replace it altogether.

This much would no doubt be granted by most proponents of the theory. True, they would say, but even if the ideal speech situation can never be fully realized, it will nevertheless improve the outcome of the political process if one goes some way towards it. The *fourth objection* questions the validity of this reply. In some cases a little discussion can be a dangerous thing, worse in fact than no discussion at all, viz. if it makes some but not all persons align themselves on the common good. The following story provides an illustration:

Once upon a time two boys found a cake. One of them said, "Splendid! I will eat the cake." The other one said, "No, that is not fair! We found the cake together, and we should share and share alike, half for you and half for me." The first boy said, "No, I should have the whole cake!" Along came an adult who said, "Gentlemen, you shouldn't fight about this: you should *compromise*. Give him three quarters of the cake."[25]

What creates the difficulty here is that the first boy's preferences are allowed to count twice in the social choice mechanism suggested by the adult: once in his expression of them and then again in the other boy's internalized ethic of sharing. And one can argue that the outcome is socially inferior to that which would have emerged had they both stuck to their selfish preferences. When Adam Smith wrote that he had never known much good done by those who affected to trade for the public good, he may only have had in mind the harm that can be done by *unilateral* attempts to act morally. The categorical imperative itself may be badly served by people acting unilaterally on it.[26] Also, an inferior outcome may result if discussion brings about partial adherence to morality in all participants rather than full adherence in some and none in others, as in the story of the two boys. Thus Serge Kolm argues that economies with moderately altruistic agents tend to work less well than economies where either everybody is selfish or everybody is altruistic.[27]

A *fifth objection* is to question the implicit assumption that the body politic as a whole is better or wiser than the sum of its parts. Could it not rather be the case that people are made more, not less, selfish and irrational by interacting politically? The cognitive analogy suggests that the rationality of beliefs may be positively as well as negatively affected by interaction. On the one hand there is what Irving Janis has called "group-think," i.e. mutually reinforcing bias.[28] On the other hand there certainly are many ways in which people can, and do, pool their opinions and supplement each other to arrive at a better estimate.[29] Similarly autonomy and morality could be enhanced as well as undermined by interaction. Against the pessimistic view of Reinhold Niebuhr that individuals in a group show more unrestrained egoism than in their personal relationships,[30] we may set Hannah Arendt's optimistic view:

American faith was not all based on a semireligious faith in human nature, but on the contrary, on the possibility of checking human nature in its singularity, by virtue of human bonds and mutual promises. The hope for man in his singularity lay in the fact that not man but men inhabit the earth and form a world between them. It is human worldliness that will save men from the pitfalls of human nature.[31]

Niebuhr's argument suggests an aristocratic disdain of the *mass*, which transforms individually decent people—to use a characteristically condescending phrase—into an unthinking horde. While rejecting this as a general view, one should equally avoid the other extreme, suggested by Arendt. Neither the Greek nor the American assemblies were the paradigms of discursive reason that she makes them out to be. The Greeks were well aware that they might be tempted by demagogues, and in fact took extensive precautions against this tendency.[32] The American town surely has not always been the incarnation of collective freedom, since on occasion it could also serve as the springboard for witch hunts. The mere decision to engage in rational discussion does not ensure that the transactions will in fact be conducted rationally, since much depends on the structure and the framework of the proceedings. The random errors of selfish and private preferences may to some extent cancel each other out and thus be less to be feared than the massive and coordinated errors that may arise through group-think. On the other hand, it would be excessively stupid to rely on mutually compensating vices to bring about public benefits as a general rule. I am not arguing against the need for public discussion, only for the need to take the question of institutional and constitutional design very seriously.

A *sixth objection* is that unanimity, were it to be realized, might easily be due to conformity rather than to rational agreement. I would in fact tend to have more confidence in the outcome of a democratic decision if there was a minority that voted against it, than if it was unanimous. I am not here referring to people expressing the majority preferences against their real ones, since I am assuming that something like the secret ballot would prevent this. I have in mind that people may come to change their real preferences, as a result of seeing which way the majority goes. Social psychology has amply shown the strength of this bandwagon effect,[33] which in political theory is also known as the "chameleon" problem.[34] It will not do to argue that the majority to which the conformist adapts his view is likely to pass the test of rationality even if his adherence to it does not, since the majority could well be made up of conformists each of whom would have broken out had there been a minority he could have espoused. To bring the point home, consider a parallel case of nonautonomous preference formation. We are tempted to say that a man is free if he can get or do whatever it is that he wants to get or do. But then we are immediately faced with the objection that perhaps he only wants what he can get, as the result of some such mechanism as "sour grapes."[35] We may then add that, other things being equal, the person is freer the more things he wants to do which he is not free to do, since these show that his wants are not in general shaped by adaptation to his possibilities. Clearly, there is an air of paradox over the statement that a man's freedom is greater the more of his desires he is not free to realize, but on reflection the paradox embodies a valid argument. Similarly, it is possible to dissolve the air of paradox attached to the view that a collective decision is more trustworthy if it is less than unanimous.

My *seventh objection* amounts to a denial of the view that the need to couch one's argument in terms of the common good will purge the desires of all selfish arguments. There are in general many ways of realizing the common good, if by that phrase we now only mean some arrangement that is Pareto-superior to uncoordinated individual decisions. Each such arrangement will, in addition to promoting the general interest, bring an extra premium to some specific group, which will then have a strong interest in that particular arrangement.[36] The group may then come to prefer the arrangement because of that premium, although it will argue for it in terms of the common good. Typically the arrangement will be justified by a causal theory—an account, say, of how the economy works—that shows it to be not only *a* way, but the only way of promoting the common good. The economic theories underlying the early Reagan administration provide an example. I am not imputing insincerity to the proponents of these views, but there may well be an element of wishful thinking. Since social scientists disagree so strongly among themselves as to how societies work, what could be more human than to pick on a theory that uniquely justifies the arrangement from which one stands to profit? The opposition between general interest and special interests is too simplistic, since the private benefits may causally determine the way in which one conceives of the common good.

These objections have been concerned to bring out two main ideas. First, one cannot assume that one will in fact approach the good society by acting as if one had already arrived there. The fallacy inherent in this "approximation assumption"[37] was exposed a long time ago in the economic "theory of the second best":

It is *not* true that a situation in which more, but not all, of the optimum conditions are fulfilled is necessarily, or is even likely to be, superior to a situation in which fewer are fulfilled. It follows, therefore, that in a situation in which there exist many constraints which prevent the fulfillment of the Paretian optimum conditions, the removal of any one constraint may affect welfare or efficiency either by raising it, by lowering it or by leaving it unchanged.[38]

The ethical analogue is not the familiar idea that some moral obligations may be suspended when other people act nonmorally.[39] Rather it is that the nature of the moral obligation is changed in a nonmoral environment. When others act nonmorally, there may be an obligation to deviate not only from what they do, but also from the behavior that would have been optimal if adopted by everybody.[40] In particular, a little discussion, like a little rationality or a little socialism, may be a dangerous thing.[41] If, as suggested by Habermas, free and rational discussion will only be possible in a society that has abolished political and economic domination, it is by no means obvious that abolition can be brought about by rational argumentation. I do not want to suggest that it could occur by force—since the use of force to end the use of force is open to obvious objections. Yet something like irony, eloquence or propaganda might be needed, involving less respect for the interlocutor than what would prevail in the ideal speech situation.

As will be clear from these remarks, there is a strong tension between two ways of looking at the relation between political ends and means. On the one hand, the means should partake of the nature of the ends, since otherwise the use of unsuitable means might tend to corrupt the end. On the other hand, there are dangers involved in choosing means immediately derived from the goal to be realized, since in a nonideal situation these might take us away from the end rather than towards it. A delicate balance will have to be struck between these two opposing considerations. It is in fact an open question whether there exists a ridge along which we can move to the good society, and if so whether it is like a knife-edge or more like a plateau.

The second general idea that emerges from the discussion is that even in the good society, should we hit upon it, the process of rational discussion could be fragile, and vulnerable to adaptive preferences, conformity, wishful thinking and the like. To ensure stability and robustness there is a need for structures—political institutions or constitutions—that could easily reintroduce an element of domination. We would in fact be confronted, at the political level, with a perennial dilemma of individual behavior. How is it possible to ensure at the same time that one is bound by rules that protect one from irrational or unethical behavior—and that these rules do not turn into prisons from which it is not possible to break out even when it would be rational to do so?[42]

## III

It is clear from Habermas's theory, I believe, that rational political discussion has an *object* in terms of which it makes sense.[43] Politics is concerned with substantive decision-making, and is to that extent instrumental. True, the idea of instrumental politics might also be taken in a more narrow sense, as implying that the political process is one in which individuals pursue their selfish interests, but more broadly understood it implies only that political action is primarily a means to a nonpolitical end, only secondarily, if at all, an end in itself. In this section I shall consider theories that suggest a reversal of this priority and that find the main point of politics in the educative or otherwise beneficial effects on the participants. And I shall try to show that this view tends to be internally incoherent, or self-defeating. The benefits of participation are by-products of political activity. Moreover, they are *essentially* by-products, in the sense that any attempt to turn them into the main purpose of such activity would make them evaporate.[44] It can indeed be highly satisfactory to engage in political work, but only on the condition that the work is defined by a serious purpose which goes beyond that of achieving this satisfaction. If that condition is not fulfilled, we get a narcissistic view of politics—corresponding to various consciousness-raising activities familiar from the last decade or so.

My concern, however, is with political theory rather than with political activism. I shall argue that certain types of arguments for political institutions and constitutions are self-defeating, since they justify the arrangement in question by effects that are essentially by-products. Here an initial and important distinction must be drawn between the task of justifying a constitution ex ante and that of evaluating it ex post and at a distance. I argue below that Tocqueville, when assessing the American democracy, praised it for consequences that are indeed by-products. In his case, this made perfectly good sense as an analytical attitude adopted after the fact and at some distance from the system he was examining. The incoherence arises when one invokes the same arguments before the fact, in public discussion. Although the constitution-makers may secretly have such side effects in mind, they cannot coherently invoke them in public.

Kant proposed a *transcendental formula of public right:* "All actions affecting the rights of other human beings are wrong if their maxim is not compatible with their being made public."[45] Since Kant's illustrations of the principle are obscure, let me turn instead to John Rawls, who imposes a similar condition of publicity as a constraint on what the parties can choose in the original position.[46] He argues, moreover, that this condition tends to favor his own conception of justice, as compared to that of the utilitarians.[47] If utilitarian principles of justice were openly adopted, they would entail some loss of self-esteem, since people would feel that they were not fully being treated as ends in themselves. Other things being equal, this would also lead to a loss in average utility. It is then conceivable that public adoption of Rawls's two principles of justice would bring about a higher average utility than public adoption of utilitarianism, although a lower average than under a secret utilitarian constitution introduced from above. The latter possibility, however, is ruled out by the publicity constraint. A utilitarian could not then advocate Rawls's two principles on utilitarian grounds, although he might well applaud them on such grounds. The fact that the two principles maximize utility would essentially be a by-product, and if chosen on the grounds that they are utility-maximizing they would no longer be so. Utilitarianism, therefore, is self-defeating in Kant's sense: "it essentially lacks openness."[48]

Derek Parfit has raised a similar objection to act consequentialism (AC) and suggested how it could be met:

This gives to all one common aim: the best possible outcome. If we try to achieve this, we may often fail. Even when we succeed, the fact that we are disposed to try might make the outcome worse. AC might thus be indirectly self-defeating. What does this show? A consequentialist might say: "It shows that AC should be only one part of our moral theory. It should be the part that covers successful acts. When we are certain to succeed, we should aim for the best possible outcome. Our wider theory should be this: we should have the aim and dispositions having which would make the outcome best. This wider theory would not be self-defeating. So the objection has been met."[49]

Yet there is an ambiguity in the word "should" in the penultimate sentence, since it is not clear whether we are told that it is good to have certain aims and dispositions, or that we should aim at having them. The latter answer immediately raises the problem that having certain aims and dispositions—i.e., being a certain kind of person— is essentially a by-product. When instrumental rationality is self-defeating, we cannot decide on instrumentalist grounds to take leave of it—no more than we can fall asleep by deciding not to try to fall asleep. Although spontaneity may be highly valuable on utilitarian grounds, "you cannot both genuinely possess this kind of quality and also reassure yourself that while it is free and creative and uncalculative, it is also acting for the best."[50]

Tocqueville, in a seeming paradox, suggested that democracies are less suited than aristocracies to deal with long-term planning, and yet are superior in the long-run to the latter. The paradox dissolves once it is seen that the first statement involves time at the level of the actors, the second at the level of the observer. On the one hand, "a democracy finds it difficult to coordinate the details of a great undertaking and to fix on some plan and carry it through with determination in spite of obstacles. It has little capacity for combining measures in secret and waiting patiently for the result."[51] On the other hand, "in the long run government by democracy should increase the real forces of a society, but it cannot immediately assemble at one point and at a given time, forces as great as those at the disposal of an aristocratic government."[52] The latter view is further elaborated in a passage from the chapter on "The Real Advantages Derived by American Society from Democratic Government":

That constantly renewed agitation introduced by democratic government into political life passes, then, into civil society. Perhaps, taking everything into consideration, that is the greatest advantage of democratic government, and I praise it much more on account of what it causes to be done than for what it does. It is incontestable that the people often manage public affairs very badly, but their concern therewith is bound to extend their mental horizon and to shake them out of the rut of ordinary routine. . . . Democracy does not provide a people with the most skillful of governments, but it does that which the most skillful government often cannot do: it spreads throughout the body social a restless activity, superabundant force, and energy never found elsewhere, which, however little favored by circumstances, can do wonders. Those are its true advantages.[53]

The advantages of democracies, in other words, are mainly and essentially by-products. The avowed aim of democracy is to be a good system of government, but Tocqueville argues that it is inferior in this respect to aristocracy, viewed purely as a decision-making apparatus. Yet the very activity of governing democratically has as a by-product a certain energy and restlessness that benefits industry and generates prosperity. Assuming the soundness of this observation, could it ever serve as a public justification for introducing democracy in a nation that had not yet acquired it? The question is somewhat more complex than one might be led to think from what I have said so far, since the quality of the decisions is not the only consideration that is relevant for the choice of a political system. The argument from *justice* could also be decisive. Yet the following conclusion seems inescapable: if the system has no inherent advantage in terms of justice or efficiency, one cannot coherently and publicly advocate its introduction because of the side effects that would follow in its wake. There must be a *point* in democracy as such. If people are motivated by such inherent advantages to throw themselves into the system, other benefits may ensue—but the latter cannot by themselves be the motivating force. If the democratic method is introduced in a society solely because of the side effects on economic prosperity, and no one believes in it on any other ground, it will not produce them.

Tocqueville, however, did not argue that political activity is an end in itself. The justification for democracy is found in its effects, although not in the intended ones, as the strictly instrumental view would have it. More to the point is Tocqueville's argument for the jury system: "I do not know whether a jury is useful to the litigants, but I am sure that it is very good for those who have to decide the case. I regard it as one of the most effective means of popular education at society's disposal."[54] This is still an instrumental view, but the gap between the means and the end is smaller. Tocqueville never argued that the effect of democracy was to make politicians prosperous, only that it was conducive to general prosperity. By contrast, the justification of the jury system is found in the effect on the jurors themselves. And, as above, that effect would be spoilt if they believed that the impact on their own civic spirit was the main point of the proceedings.

John Stuart Mill not only applauded but advocated democracy on the ground of such educative effects on the participants. In current discussion he stands out both as an opponent of the purely instrumental view of politics, that of his father James Mill,[55] and as a forerunner of the theory of participatory democracy.[56] In his theory the gap between means and ends in politics is even narrower, since he saw political activity not only as a means to self-improvement, but also as a source of satisfaction and thus a good in itself. As noted by Albert Hirschman, this implies that "the benefit of collective action for an individual is not the difference between the hoped-for result and the effort furnished by him or her, but the *sum* of these two magnitudes."[57] Yet this very way of paraphrasing Mill's view also points to a difficulty. Could it really be the case that participation would yield a benefit even when the hoped-for results are nil, as suggested by Hirschman's formula? Is it not rather true that the effort is itself a function of the hoped-for result, so that in the end the latter is the only independent variable? When Mill refers, critically, to the limitations of Bentham, whose philosophy "can teach the means of organizing and regulating the merely *business* part of the social arrangement,"[58] he seems to be putting the cart before the horse. The nonbusiness part of politics may be the more valuable, but the value is contingent on the importance of the business part.

For a fully developed version of the noninstrumental theory of politics, we may go to the work of Hannah Arendt. Writing about the distinction between the private and the public realm in ancient Greece, she argues that:

Without mastering the necessities of life in the household, neither life nor the "good life" is possible, but politics is never for the sake of life. As far as the members of the *polis* are concerned, household life exists for the sake of the "good life" in the *polis*.[59]

The public realm . . . was reserved for individuality; it was the only place where men could show who they really and inexchangeably were. It was for the sake of this chance, and out of love for a body politic that it made it possible to them all, that each was more or less willing to share in the burden of jurisdiction, defence and administration of public affairs.[60]

Against this we may set the view of Greek politics found in the work of M. I. Finley. Asking why the Athenian people claimed the right of every citizen to speak and make proposals in the Assembly, yet left its exercise to a few, he finds that "one part of the answer is that the *demos* recognized the instrumental role of political rights and were more concerned in the end with the substantive decisions, were content with their power to select, dismiss and punish their political leaders."[61] Elsewhere he writes, even more explicitly: "Then, as now, politics was instrumental for most people, not an interest or an end in itself."[62] Contrary to what Arendt suggests, the possession or the possibility of exercising a political right may be more important than the actual exercise. Moreover, even the exercise derives its value from the decisions to be taken. Writing about the American town assemblies, Arendt argues that the citizens participated "neither exclusively because of duty nor, and even less, to serve their own interests but most of all because they enjoyed the discussions. the deliberations, and the making of decisions."[63] This, while not putting the cart before the horse, at least places them alongside each other. Although discussion and deliberation in other contexts may be independent sources of enjoyment, the satisfaction one derives from *political* discussion is parasitic on decision making. Political debate is about what to *do*—not about what ought to be the case. It is defined by this practical purpose, not by its subject matter.

Politics in this respect is on a par with other activities such as art, science, athletics or chess. To engage in them may be deeply satisfactory, if you have an independently defined goal such as "getting it right" or "beating the opposition." A chess player who asserted that he played not to win, but for the sheer elegance of the game, would be in narcissistic bad faith—since there is no such thing as an elegant way of losing, only elegant and inelegant ways of winning. When the artist comes to believe that the process and not the end result is his real purpose and that defects and irregularities are valuable as reminders of the struggle of creation, he similarly forfeits any claim to our interest. The same holds for E. P. Thompson, who, when asked whether he really believed that a certain rally in Trafalgar Square would have any impact at all, answered: "That's not really the point, is it? The point is, it shows that democracy's alive. . . . A rally like that gives us self-respect. Chartism was terribly good for the Chartists, although they never got the Charter."[64] Surely, the Chartists, if asked whether they thought they would ever get the Charter, would not have answered: "That's not really the point, is it?" It was because they believed they might get the Charter that they engaged in the struggle for it with the seriousness of purpose that also brought them self-respect as a side effect.[65]

## IV

I have been discussing three views concerning the relation between economics and politics, between the market and the forum. One extreme is "the economic theory of democracy," most outrageously stated by Schumpeter, but in essence also underlying social choice theory. It is a market theory of politics, in the sense that the act of voting is a private act similar to that of buying and selling. I cannot accept, therefore, Alan Ryan's argument that "On any possible view of the distinction between private and public life, voting is an element in one's public life."[66] The very distinction between the secret and the open ballot shows that there is room for a private-public distinction within politics. The economic theory of democracy, therefore, rests on the idea that the forum should be like the market, in its purpose as well as in its mode of functioning. The purpose is defined in economic terms, and the mode of functioning is that of aggregating individual decisions.

At the other extreme there is the view that the forum should be completely divorced from the market, in purpose as well as in institutional arrangement. The forum should be more than the distributive totality of individuals queuing up for the election booth. Citizenship is a quality that can only be realized in public, i.e., in a collective joined for a common purpose. This purpose, moreover, is not to facilitate life in the material sense. The political process is an end in itself, a good or even the supreme good for those who participate in it. It may be applauded because of the educative effects on the participants, but the benefits do not cease once the education has been completed. On the contrary, the education of the citizen leads to a preference for public life as an end in itself. Politics on this view is not *about* anything. It is the agonistic display of excellence,[67] or the collective display of solidarity, divorced from decision making and the exercise of influence on events.

In between these extremes is the view I find most attractive. One can argue that the forum should differ from the market in its mode of functioning, yet be concerned with decisions that ultimately deal with economic matters. Even higher-order political decisions concern lower-level rules that are directly related to economic matters. Hence constitutional arguments about how laws can be made and changed, constantly invoke the impact of legal stability and change on economic affairs. It is the concern with substantive decisions that lends the urgency to political debates. The ever-present constraint of *time* creates a need for focus and concentration that cannot be assimilated to the leisurely style of philosophical argument in which it may be better to travel hopefully than to arrive. Yet within these constraints arguments form the core of the political process. If thus defined as public in nature and instrumental in purpose, politics assumes what I believe to be its proper place in society.

## Notes

1. Elster (1978, Ch. 5) refers to these two varieties of market failure as *suboptimality* and *counterfinality* respectively, linking them both to collective action.

2. This is a simplification. First, as argued in Samuelson (1950), there may be political constraints that prevent one from attaining the Pareto-efficient frontier. Secondly, the very existence of several points that are Pareto-superior to the status quo, yet involve differential benefits to the participants, may block the realization of any of them.

3. Hammond (1976) offers a useful analysis of the consequences of selfish preferences over income distributions, showing that "without interpersonal comparisons of some kind, any social preference ordering over the space of possible income distributions must be dictatorial."

4. Schumpeter (1961, p. 263): "the will of the people is the product and not the motive power of the political process." One should not, however, conclude (as does Lively 1975, p. 38) that Schumpeter thereby abandons the market analogy, since on his view (Schumpeter 1939, p. 73) consumer preferences are no less manipulable (with some qualifications stated in Elster 1983a, Ch. 5).

5. See in particular Downs (1957).

6. For fuller statements, see Arrow (1963), Sen (1970), Kelly (1978), and Hylland (1986).

7. Cf. d'Aspremont and Gevers (1977).

8. Riker and Ordeshook (1973, pp. 112–113).

9. Cf. Davidson (1986) and Gibbard (1986).

10. Presumably, but not obviously, since the agent might have several preference orderings and rely on higher-order preferences to determine which of the first-order preferences to express, as suggested for instance by Sen (1976).

11. Pattanaik (1978) offers a survey of the known results. The only strategy-proof mechanisms for social choice turn out to be the dictatorial one (the dictator has no incentive to misrepresent his preferences) and the randomizing one of getting the probability that a given option will be chosen equal to the proportion of voters that have it as their first choice.

12. Tversky (1981).

13. Cf. Elster (1979, Ch. II) or Schelling (1980) for the idea of deliberately restricting one's feasible set to make certain undesirable behavior impossible at a later time. The reason this does not work here is that the regret would not be eliminated.

14. Cf. for instance Williams (1973) or Sen (1979).

15. Cf. Elster (1983b, Ch. III) for a discussion of this notion.

16. Arrow (1973).

17. Hirsch (1976).

18. Haavelmo (1970) offers a model in which everybody may suffer a loss of welfare by trying to keep up with the neighbors.

19. One may take the achievements of others as a parameter and one's own as the control variable, or conversely try to manipulate the achievements of others so that they fall short of one's own. The first of these ways of realizing positional goods is clearly less objectionable than the second, but still less pure than the noncomparative desire for a certain standard of excellence.

20. Zeldin (1973, p. 134).

21. I rely mainly on Habermas (1982). I also thank Helge Høibraaten, Rune Slagstad, and Gunnar Skirbekk for having patiently explained to me various aspects of Habermas's work.

22. Midgaard (1980).

23. For Pascal's argument, cf. Elster (1979, Ch. II.3).

24. As suggested by Runciman and Sen (1965).

25. Smullyan (1980, p. 56).

26. Sobel (1967).

27. Kolm (1981a, b).

28. Janis (1972).

29. Cf. Hogarth (1977) and Lehrer (1978).

30. Niebuhr (1932, p. 11).

31. Arendt (1973, p. 174).

32. Finley (1973); see also Elster (1979, Ch. II.8).

33. Asch (1956) is a classic study.

34. See Goldman (1972) for discussion and further references.

35. Berlin (1969, p. xxxviii); cf. also Elster (1983b, Ch. III.3).

36. Schotter (1981, pp. 26 ff., pp. 43 ff.) has a good discussion of this predicament.

37. Margalit (1983).

38. Lipsey and Lancaster (1956–57, p. 12).

39. This is the point emphasized in Lyons (1965).

40. Cf. Hansson (1970) as well as Føllesdal and Hilpinen (1971) for discussions of "conditional obligations" within the framework of deontic logic. It does not appear,

however, that the framework can easily accommodate the kind of dilemma I am concerned with here.

41. Cf. for instance Kolm (1977) concerning the dangers of a piecemeal introduction of socialism—also mentioned by Margalit (1983) as an objection to Popper's strategy for piecemeal social engineering.

42. Cf. Ainslie (1982) and Elster (1979, Ch. II.9).

43. Indeed, Habermas (1982) is largely concerned with maxims for *action,* not with the evaluation of states of affairs.

44. Cf. Elster (1983b, Ch. III) for a discussion of the notion that some psychological or social states are essentially by-products of actions undertaken for some other purpose.

45. Kant (1795, p. 126).

46. Rawls (1971, p. 133).

47. Rawls (1971, pp. 177 ff., esp. p. 181).

48. Williams (1973, p. 123).

49. Parfit (1981, p. 554).

50. Williams (1973, p. 131); also Elster (1983b, Ch. II.3).

51. Tocqueville (1969, p. 229).

52. Tocqueville (1969, p. 224).

53. Tocqueville (1969, pp. 243–244).

54. Tocqueville (1969, p. 275).

55. Cf. Ryan (1972). His contrast between "two concepts of democracy" corresponds in part to the distinction between the first and the second of the theories discussed here, in part to the distinction between the first and the third, as he does not clearly separate the public conception of politics from the noninstrumental one.

56. Pateman (1970, p. 29).

57. Hirschman (1982, p. 82).

58. Mill (1859. p. 105).

59. Arendt (1958, p. 37).

60. Arendt (1958, p. 41).

61. Finley (1976, p. 83).

62. Finley (1981, p. 31).

63. Arendt (1973, p. 119).

64. *Sunday Times,* 2 November 1980.

65. Cf. also Barry (1978, p. 47).

66. Ryan (1972, p. 105).

67. Veyne (1976) makes a brilliant statement of this noninstrumental attitude among the elite of the Ancient World.

## References

Ainslie, G. (1982) "A behavioral economic approach to the defense mechanisms." *Social Science Information* 21, 735–780.

Arendt, H. (1958) *The Human Condition.* Chicago: University of Chicago Press.

Arendt, H. (1973) *On Revolution.* Harmondsworth: Pelican Books.

Arrow, K (1963) *Social Choice and Individual Values.* New York: Wiley.

Arrow, K. (1973) "Some ordinal-utilitarian notes on Rawls's theory of justice." *Journal of Philosophy* 70, 245–263.

Asch, S. (1956). "Studies of independence and conformity: I. A minority of one against a unanimous majority." *Psychology Monographs* 70, No. 9, 1–70.

Barry, B. (11978) "Comment," in S. Benn et al. (eds.), *Political Participation.* Canberra: Australian National University Press, pp. 37–48.

Berlin, I. (1969) *Two Concepts of Liberty.* Oxford: Oxford University Press.

d'Aspremont, C. and Gevers, L. (1977) "Equity and the informational basis of collective choice." *Review of Economic Studies* 44, 199–210.

Davidson, D. (1986) "Judging interpersonal interests," in J. Elster and A. Hylland (eds.), *Foundations of Social Choice Theory.* Cambridge: Cambridge University Press, pp. 195–211.

Downs, A. (1957) *An Economic Theory of Democracy.* New York: Harper.

Elster, J. (1978) *Logic and Society.* Chichester: Wiley.

Elster, J. (1979) *Ulysses and the Sirens.* Cambridge: Cambridge University Press.

Elster, J. (1983a) *Explaining Technical Change.* Cambridge: Cambridge University Press; Oslo: Universitetsforlaget.

Elster, J. (1983b) *Sour Grapes.* Cambridge: Cambridge University Press.

Finley, M. I. (1973) *Democracy: Ancient and Modern.* London: Chatto and Windus.

Finley, M. I. (1976) "The freedom of the citizen in the Greek world," reprinted as Ch. 5 in M. I. Finley, *Economy and Society in Ancient Greece*. London: Chatto and Windus 1981.

Finley, M. I. (1981) "Politics," in M. I. Finley (ed.), *The Legacy of Greece*. Oxford: Oxford University Press, pp. 22–36.

Føllesdal, D. and Hilpinen, R. (1971) "Deontic logic: an introduction," in R. Hilpinen (ed.), *Deontic Logic: Introductory and Systematic Readings*. Dordrecht: Reidel, pp. 1–35.

Gibbard, A. (1986) "Interpersonal comparisons: Preference, good, and the intrinsic reward of a life," in J. Elster and A. Hylland (eds.), *Foundations of Social Choice Theory*. Cambridge: Cambridge University Press, pp. 165–193.

Goldman, A. (1972) "Toward a theory of social power." *Philosophical Studies* 23, 221–268.

Haavelmo, T. (1970) "Some observations on welfare and economic growth," in W. A. Eltis, M. Scott and N. Wolfe (eds.), *Induction, Growth, and Trade: Essays in Honour of Sir Roy Harrod*. Oxford: Oxford University Press, pp. 65–75.

Habermas, J. (1982) Diskursethik—notizen zu einem Begründingsprogram. Mimeographed. (English: "Discourse ethics: Notes on a program of philosophical justification," in J. Habermas, *Moral Consciousness and Communicative Action*, tr. C. Lenhardt and S. W. Nicholsen. Cambridge, Mass.: MIT Press, 1990, pp. 43–115.)

Hammond, P. (1976) "Why ethical measures need interpersonal comparisons." *Theory and Decision* 7, 263–274.

Hansson, B. (1970) "An analysis of some deontic logics." *Nous* 3, 373–398.

Hirsch, F. (1976) *Social Limits to Growth*. Cambridge, Mass.: Harvard University Press.

Hirschman, A. (1982) *Shifting Involvements*. Princeton: Princeton University Press.

Hogarth, R. M. (1977) "Methods for aggregating opinions," in H. Jungermann and G. de Zeeuw (eds.), *Decision Making and Change in Human Affairs*. Dordrecht: Reidel, pp. 231–256.

Hylland, A. (1986) "The purpose and significance of social choice theory," in J. Elster and A. Hylland (eds.), *Foundations of Social Choice Theory*. Cambridge: Cambridge University Press, pp. 45–73.

Janis, I. (1972) *Victims of Group-Think*. Boston: Houghton Mifflin.

Kant, I. (1795) *Perpetual Peace*, in H. Reiss (ed.), *Kant's Political Writings*. Cambridge: Cambridge University Press.

Kelly, J. (1978) *Arrow Impossibility Theorems*. New York: Academic Press.

Kolm, S.-C. (1977) *La transition socialiste*. Paris: Editions du Cerf.

Kolm, S.-C. (1981a) "Altruismes et efficacités." *Social Science Information* 20, 293–354.

Kolm, S.-C. (1981b) "Efficacité et altruisme." *Revue Economique* 32, 5–31.

Lehrer, K. (1978) "Consensus and comparison: A theory of social rationality." in C. A. Hooker, J. J. Leach, and E. F. McClennen (eds.), *Foundations and Applications of Decision Theory.* Vol. 1: *Theoretical Foundations.* Dordrecht: Reidel, pp. 283–310.

Lipsey, R. G. and Lancaster, K. (1956–57) "The general theory of the second-best." *Review of Economic Studies* 24, 11–32.

Lively, J. (1975) *Democracy.* Oxford: Blackwell.

Lyons, D. (1965) *Forms and Limits of Utilitarianism.* Oxford: Oxford University Press.

Margalit, A. (1983) "Ideals and second bests," in S. Fox (ed.), *Philosophy for Education.* Jerusalem: Van Leer Foundation, pp. 77–90.

Midgaard, K. (1980) "On the significance of language and a richer concept of rationality," in L. Lewin and E. Vedung (eds.), *Politics as Rational Action.* Dordrecht: Reidel, pp. 83–97.

Mill, J. S. (1859) "Bentham," in J. S. Mill, *Utilitarianism.* London: Fontana Books (1962), pp. 78–125.

Niebuhr, R. (1932) *Moral Man and Immoral Society.* New York: Scribner's.

Parfit, D. (1981) "Prudence, morality, and the prisoner's dilemma," *Proceedings of the British Academy.* Oxford: Oxford University Press.

Pateman, C. (1970) *Participation and Democratic Theory.* Cambridge: Cambridge University Press.

Pattanaik, P. (1978) *Strategy and Group Choice.* Amsterdam: North-Holland.

Rawls, J. (1971) *A Theory of Justice.* Cambridge, Mass.: Harvard University Press.

Riker, W. and Ordeshook, P. C. (1973) *An Introduction to Positive Political Theory.* Englewood Cliffs, N.J.: Prentice-Hall.

Runciman, W. G. and Sen, A. (1965) "Games, justice, and the general will." *Mind* 74, 554–562.

Ryan, A. (1972) "Two concepts of politics and democracy: James and John Stuart Mill," in M. Fleisher (ed.), *Machiavelli and the Nature of Political Thought.* London: Croom Helm, pp. 76–113.

Samuelson, P. (1950) "The evaluation of real national income." *Oxford Economic Papers* 2, 1–29.

Schelling, T. C. (1980) "The intimate contest for self-command." *The Public Interest* 60, 94–118.

Schotter, A. (1981) *The Economic Theory of Social Institutions.* Cambridge: Cambridge University Press.

Schumpeter, J. (1939) *Business Cycles*. New York: McGraw-Hill.

Schumpeter, J. (1961) *Capitalism, Socialism, and Democracy*. London: Allen and Unwin.

Sen, A. K. (1970) *Collective Choice and Social Welfare*. San Francisco: Holden-Day.

Sen, A. K. (1976) "Liberty, unanimity, and rights." *Economica* 43, 217–245.

Sen, A. K. (1979) "Utilitarianism and welfarism." *Journal of Philosophy* 76, 463–488.

Sobel, J. H. (1967) "'Everyone,' consequences, and generalization arguments." *Inquiry* 10, 373–404.

Smullyan, R. (1980) *This Book Needs No Title*. Englewood Cliffs, N.J.: Prentice-Hall.

Tocqueville, A. de (1969) *Democracy in America*. New York: Anchor Books.

Tversky, A. (1981) "Choice, preference and welfare: some psychological observations," paper presented at a colloquium on "Foundations of social choice theory." Ustaoset (Norway).

Williams, B. A. O. (1973) "A critique of utilitarianism," in J. J. C. Smart and B. A. O. Williams (eds.), *Utilitarianism: For and Against*. Cambridge: Cambridge University Press, pp. 77–150.

Veyne, P. (1976) *Le pain et le cirque*. Paris: Seuil.

Zeldin, T. (1973) *France 1848–1945*, Vol. 1. Oxford: Oxford University Press.

# 2

# Popular Sovereignty as Procedure

*Jürgen Habermas*

In view of its impressive historical influence, the French Revolution can "scarcely be compared with any other historical event."[1] This one undisputed statement explains why almost any other statement is subject to debate. In our day a new controversy has arisen: whether the Great Revolution has ceased to be relevant.

Under the banner of postmodern farewells, we are now also supposed to distance ourselves from that exemplary event whose effects have been felt for the last two hundred years. The eminent Leipzig historian of the Revolution, Walter Markov, still claimed in 1967 that "The French Revolution has been experienced by no subsequent generation as a self-contained episode or museum piece."[2] At that time François Furet and Denis Richet had just published an impressive analysis of the Revolution in terms of the *histoire des mentalités*.[3] A decade later, when the self-criticism of the Left in Paris developed into the more extreme poststructuralist critique of reason, Furet could laconically conclude that "the French Revolution has ended."[4] Furet wanted to escape the hold of a "testamentary historiography" that conceived the French Revolution as the action-orienting origin of the present. He declared the French Revolution finished, so that the "contamination of the past" by narcissistic reference to the present would stop.

This impulse toward a more dispassionate, scholarly approach must not be confused with the most recent attempt to faith heal an allegedly contaminated present by normalizing and leveling out another, *negatively* charged past. The clocks of collective memory keep different time in France and Germany. In France, liberal and socialist interpretations of the Revolution have determined the nation's self-understanding. In contrast, since the initial enthusiasm of the Revolution's contemporaries died down, we Germans have constantly been suspicious of the terrorist consequences of the "ideas of 1789." This was not only true of the earlier Prussian self-understanding of the German nation. Traces of a conservative, even aggressively hostile, historiography were still to be found on this side of the Rhine up to 1945.[5] International differences in reception history do not, by themselves, say anything about the truth of a thesis, but the same thesis takes on a different significance in different contexts. Furet was responding to the tradition in which the French Revolution stands as a model alongside the Bolshevik revolution. This dialectical relation supports his thesis of the end of the French Revolution—and simultaneously relativizes it.[6]

A nonhistorian cannot contribute much to that controversy. Instead, I want to take the perspective of political theory and address the question of whether the orienting power of the French Revolution is exhausted. I am concerned with the normative issue of whether the shift in mentality that occurred during the French Revolution still represents, in some respects, an unclaimed heritage. Can we read the "revolution in ideas" of 1789 in a way that might still inform our own needs for orientation?

**1**

*1.1*

We can discuss the question concerning the still promising aspects of the French Revolution from various points of view.

(a) In France, the Revolution in part made possible, in part only accelerated, the development of a mobile bourgeois society and a capitalist economic system. It furthered processes that had occurred in other countries without a revolutionary reorganization of political authority and the legal system. Since then, this economic and social modernization has become not only permanently crisis-ridden but overtly secular as well. Today, with its dysfunctional side effects, we are more aware of the dangers; we now experience the inexorable development of productive forces and the global expansion of Western civilization more as threats. One can no longer coax an unredeemed promise from the production-centered capitalist project. The workers' social utopia is exhausted.

(b) Something similar holds for the rise of the modern state apparatus. As Alexis de Tocqueville already saw, the French Revolution by no means signified an innovation in the development of state bureaucracies. At most, it accelerated trends that were already under way. Today, the integrative capabilities of the state continue to diminish under the pressure of regional movements, on the one hand, and worldwide corporations and transnational organizations, on the other. Where the ethos of instrumental rationality still survives, it hardly finds any support in the unpredictable organizational accomplishments of self-programming government administrations.

(c) We find a genuine product of the French Revolution, however, in the nation-state that could require universal conscription of its patriotic citizens. With national consciousness, a new form of social integration developed for enfranchised citizens who were released from the bonds of estates and corporations. This French model also guided the last generation of states emerging from decolonization. But, with their multiethnic societies, the superpowers of the United States and the Soviet Union have never fit into the nation-as-state scheme. And the contemporary heirs of the European system of states, having taken nationalism beyond its limits, find themselves on the path to a postnational society.

(d) There seems to be only one remaining candidate for an affirmative answer to the question concerning the relevance of the French Revolution: the ideas that inspired constitutional democracy. Democracy and human rights form the universalist core of the constitutional state that emerged from the American and French Revolutions in different variants. This universalism still has its explosive power and vitality, not only in Third World countries and the Soviet bloc, but also in European nations, where constitutional patriotism acquires new significance in the course of an identity transformation. This, at least, is the opinion recently expressed by Rudolf von Thadden at the German-French meeting in Belfort: "With immigration at seven to eight percent, nations run the risk of changing their identity; soon they will no longer be able to understand themselves as monocultural societies, if they do not provide any points of integration beyond pure ethnic descent. In these circumstances it becomes urgent that we return to the idea of the citizen as the *citoyen,* which is at once more open and less rigid than the traditional idea of ethnic belonging."[7]

Of course, if the institutionalization of equal liberties were the only still promising idea, it would suffice, as many believe, to draw upon the heritage of the American Revolution: we could emerge from the shadows of the *terreur.*

Von Thadden does not draw this conclusion. Moreover, it is unlikely that the occasion of his speech (the opening of the celebration of the two-hundredth anniversary of the Great Revolution) is enough to explain why he reaches back to specifically French ideas. In the spirit of Jean-Jacques Rousseau, he contrasts the *citoyen* with the *bourgeoisie;* in line with the republican tradition, he links civil rights and participation with fraternity or solidarity. One can still hear the echoes of the old revolutionary slogans in what he says: "The Europe of citizens that we must build needs the forces of fraternity, of mutual aid and solidarity, so that the weak, the needy, and the unemployed are also able to accept the European Community as an advance over existing conditions. This appeal for the promotion of fraternity, connected with the idea of citizenship, must be the central message of the celebration of the two-hundredth anniversary of the French Revolution."[8]

Unlike the American Revolution, which was, so to speak, the *outcome* of events, the French Revolution was *carried forward* by its protagonists in the consciousness of a revolution. Furet also sees in the consciousness of revolutionary practice a new modality of historical action. One could even say that the bourgeois revolutions—the Dutch, English, and American—became aware of themselves *as* revolutions only in the French Revolution. Neither capitalistic economic trade (a, above), nor the bureaucratic form of legal authority (b), nor even national consciousness (c) and the modern constitutional state (d) had to emerge from a radical change experienced *as* revolution. "France, however, is the country that invents democratic culture through the Revolution and reveals to the world one of the foundational postures of conscious historical action."[9] Our current posture has two features: we still appeal to the readiness to act and to the political-moral orientation to the future, on the part of those who want to rebuild the existing order; at the same time, however, we have lost our confidence that conditions can be changed by revolution.

### 1.2

The revolutionary consciousness gave birth to a new mentality, which was shaped by a new time consciousness, a new concept of political practice, and a new notion of legitimation. The historical consciousness that broke with the traditionalism of nature-like continuities; the understanding of political practice in terms of self-determination and self-realization; and the trust in rational discourse, through which all political authority was supposed to legitimate itself—each of these is specifically modern. Under these three aspects, a radically this-worldly, postmetaphysical concept of the political penetrated the consciousness of a mobilized population.

Of course, looking back over the last two hundred years can arouse the suspicion that this understanding of politics has become so far removed from its intellectual and cultural origins that the revolutionary consciousness has ceased to be relevant at all. Is it not precisely the revolutionary signature, specifically inscribed on the years between 1789 and 1794, that has faded?

(a) The revolutionary consciousness was expressed in the conviction that a new beginning could be made. This reflected a change in historical consciousness.[10] Drawn together into a single process, world history became the abstract system of reference for a future-oriented action considered capable of uncoupling the present from the past. In the background lay the experience of a break with tradition: the threshold to dealing reflexively with cultural transmissions and social institutions was crossed. The process of modernization was experienced as the acceleration of events that were open, as it were, to single-minded collective intervention. The current generation saw itself burdened with responsibility for the fate of future generations, while the example of past generations lost its binding character. Within the enlarged horizon of future possibilities, the topicality of the present moment acquired excessive prominence in contrast to the normativity of an existing reality that merely protruded into the present. Hannah Arendt associated this emphatic confidence with our "natality," the moving affection that is always aroused on seeing a newborn infant and that brings the expectation of a better future.

This vitality, however, lost its revolutionary form long ago. For the reflexive liquefaction of traditions has by now become permanent; the hypothetical attitude toward existing institutions and given forms of life has become the norm. The Revolution has itself slipped into tradition: 1815, 1830, 1848, 1871, and 1917 represent the caesurae of a history of revolutionary struggles, but also a history of disappointments. The Revolution dismisses its dissidents, who no longer rebel against anything except the Revolution itself. This self-destructive dynamic is also rooted in a concept of progress, already discredited by Walter Benjamin, that dedicates itself to the future without remembering the victims of past generations. On the other hand, the effects of student revolts and new social movements in Western-style societies lead one to suspect that the cultural dynamic unleashed by the French Revolution is having an effect in the less-conspicuous value transformations of broad strata of the population, whereas the esoteric consciousness of contemporary relevance, penetrating continuity, and violated normativity has retreated into areas of post-avant-gardist art.

(b) Revolutionary consciousness was further expressed in the conviction that emancipated individuals are jointly called to be authors of their destiny. In their hands lies the power to decide about the rules and manner of their living together. As citizens, they give *themselves* the laws they want to obey, thereby producing their own life context. This context is conceived as the product of a cooperative practice centered in conscious political will-formation. A radically this-worldly politics understands itself as the expression and confirmation of the freedom that springs simultaneously from the subjectivity of the individual and the sovereignty of the people. At the level of political theory, individualist and collectivist approaches, which respectively give priority to the individual and the nation, have no doubt competed with one another from the beginning. But political freedom has always been conceived as the freedom of a subject that determines and realizes itself. Autonomy and self-realization are the key concepts for a practice with an immanent purpose, namely, the production and reproduction of a life worthy of human beings.[11]

This holistic concept of political practice has also lost its luster and motivating power. As the equal participation of all citizens in political will-formation was laboriously institutionalized according to the rule of law, the contradictions built into the concept of popular sovereignty itself became manifest. The people from whom all governmental authority is supposed to derive does not comprise a subject with will and consciousness. It only appears in the plural, and *as* a people it is capable of neither decision nor action as a whole. In complex societies, even the most earnest endeavors at political self-organization are defeated by resistant elements originating in the stubborn systemic logics of the market and administrative power. At one time, democracy was something to be asserted against the despotism palpably embodied in the king, members of the aristocracy, and higher-ranking clerics. Since then, political authority has been depersonalized. Democratization now works to overcome not genuinely political forms of resistance but rather the systemic imperatives of differentiated economic and administrative systems.

(c) Revolutionary consciousness was expressed, finally, in the conviction that the exercise of political domination could be legitimated neither religiously (by appeal to divine authority) nor metaphysically (by appeal to an ontologically grounded natural law). From now on, a politics radically situated in this world should be justifiable on the basis of reason, using the tools of postmetaphysical theorizing. Doctrines of rational natural law, that is, social-contract theories, were proposed with this purpose in mind. Such theories translated the Aristotelian concept of political authority—the self-rule of free and equal persons—into the basic concepts of the philosophy of the subject. In doing so, they finally satisfied the demands of individual freedom as well as those of universal justice. Revolutionary practice could thus be understood as a theoretically informed realization of human rights; the Revolution itself seemed to be derived from principles of practical reason. This self-understanding also explains the influence of the "sociétés de penser" and the active role of the "ideologues."

This intellectualism did not just awaken the suspicion of conservative opponents. The assumption that political will-formation is immediately receptive to theory, that it can be guided by a prior consensus on moral principles, had consequences that were unfortunate for democratic theory and disastrous for political practice. Theory must cope with the tension between sovereign will-formation and the apodictic insight of reason; practice must deal with the false apotheosis of reason, such as that manifested in the cult of the supreme being and the emblems of the French Revolution.[12] In the name of an authoritarian reason prior to every actual process of mutual understanding, a dialectic of spokespersons unfolded that blurred the difference between morality and tactics and ended by justifying "virtuous terror." Hence, thinkers from Carl Schmitt to Hermann Lübbe, from Cochin to Furet, have denounced the discourse that converts power into word; that is, they have portrayed it as a mechanism that inevitably gives rise to the consensually veiled domination of intellectual spokespersons—in other words, avant-gardism.[13]

## 1.3

Our review seems to suggest that the mentality created by the French Revolution became both permanent and trivial: no longer surviving today as revolutionary consciousness, it has forfeited its explosive utopian power and much of its rhetorical power as well. But has this transformation of form also depleted its energies? The *cultural* dynamic released by the French Revolution has obviously *not* come to a standstill. Today, for the first time, this dynamic has created the conditions for a cultural activism stripped of all high-cultural privileges and stubbornly eluding administrative manipulation. To be sure, the highly diversified pluralism of these activities, which are not confined by socioeconomic class, is opposed to the revolutionary self-understanding of a more or less homogeneous nation. Nevertheless, the cultural mobilization of the masses goes back to this source. In urban centers one can discern the emerging contours of a social intercourse characterized by both socially de-differentiated forms of expression and individualized lifestyles. The ambiguous physiognomy is not easy to decipher. One is not quite sure whether this "culture society" reflects only the commercially and strategically "exploited power of the beautiful"—a semantically desiccated, privatistic mass culture—or whether it might provide receptive ground for a revitalized public sphere where the ideas of 1789 could finally take root.

In what follows, I must leave this question open and restrict myself to normative arguments. My aim is simply to determine how a radically democratic republic might even be *conceived* today, assuming we can reckon on a resonant political culture that meets it halfway. A republic of this sort is not a possession we simply accept as our fortunate inheritance from the past. Rather it is a project we must carry forward in the consciousness of a revolution both permanent and quotidian. I am not speaking of a trivial continuation of the revolution by other means. One can already learn from Büchner's *Danton* how soon the revolutionary consciousness became enmeshed in the aporias of revolutionary instrumentalism. Melancholy is inscribed in the revolutionary consciousness—a mourning over the failure of a project that *nonetheless cannot be relinquished*. One can explain both the failure and this unrelinquishable character by the fact that the revolutionary project overshoots the revolution itself; it eludes the revolution's own concepts. Hence I will endeavor to translate the normative content of this unique revolution into our own concepts. In view of the double anniversary of the years 1789 and 1949—and stung by *other* "anniversaries"—a leftist in the Federal Republic must consider this undertaking an imperative: the principles of the Constitution will not take root in our souls until reason has assured itself of its orienting, future-directed contents. It is only as a historical project that constitutional democracy points beyond its legal character to a normative meaning—a force at once explosive and formative.

From the viewpoint of political theory, history is a laboratory for arguments. The French Revolution comprised in any case a chain of events fortified with arguments: the Revolution robed itself in the discourses of modern natural law. And it left behind prolix traces in the political ideologies of the nineteenth and twentieth centuries. From the distance available to later generations, the ideological struggles between democrats and liberals, between socialists and anarchists, between conservatives and progressives—to summarize loosely—display basic patterns of argumentation that are still instructive today.

## 2

### 2.1

The *dialectic between liberalism and radical democracy* that was intensely debated during the French Revolution has exploded worldwide. The dispute has to do with how one can reconcile equality with liberty, unity with diversity, or the right of the majority with the right of the minority. Liberals begin with the legal institutionalization of equal liberties, conceiving these as rights held by individual subjects. In their view, human rights enjoy normative priority over democracy, and the constitutional separation of powers has priority over the will of the democratic legislature. Advocates of egalitarianism, on the other hand, conceive the collective practice of free and equal persons as sovereign will-formation. They understand human rights as an expression of the sovereign will of the people, and the constitutional separation of powers *emerges* from the enlightened will of the democratic legislature.

Thus the starting constellation is already characterized by Rousseau's answer to John Locke. Rousseau, the forerunner of the French Revolution, understands liberty as the autonomy of the people, as the equal participation of each person in the practice of *self-legislation*. Immanuel Kant, as a philosophical contemporary of the French Revolution who admitted that Rousseau first "set him straight," formulates this point as follows:

The legislative authority can be attributed only to the united will of the people. Because all right and justice is supposed to proceed from this authority, it can do absolutely no injustice to anyone. Now, when someone prescribes for another, it is always possible that he thereby does the other an injustice, but this is never possible with respect to what he decides for himself (for *volenti non fit injuria*—"he who consents cannot receive an injury"). Hence, only the united and consenting will of all—that is, a general and united will of the people by which each decides the same for all and all decide the same for each—can legislate.[14]

The point of this reflection is the unification of practical reason and sovereign will, of human rights and democracy. A rational structure is inscribed in the autonomy of the legislative practice itself, so that the reason that legitimates political authority no longer has to rush ahead of the sovereign will of the people and anchor human rights in an imaginary state of nature, as it did in Locke. Because it can express itself only in general and abstract laws, the united will of the citizens must perforce exclude all nongeneralizable interests and admit only those regulations that guarantee equal liberties to all. The exercise of popular sovereignty simultaneously secures human rights.

Through Rousseau's Jacobin disciples, this idea kindled practical enthusiasm and provoked liberal opposition. The critics insisted that the fiction of the unified popular will could be realized only at the cost of masking or suppressing the heterogeneity of individual wills. In fact, Rousseau had already imagined the constitution of the popular sovereign as something like an existential act of sociation through which isolated individuals were transformed into citizens oriented toward the common good. These citizens comprise the members of a collective *body;* they are the subject of a legislative practice that has been freed from the individual interests of private persons who are merely passively subjected to legal statutes. All the radical varieties of Rousseauianism labor under this moral overburdening of the virtuous citizen. The assumption of republican virtues is realistic only for a polity with a normative consensus that has been secured in advance through tradition and ethos: "Now the less the individual wills relate to the general will, that is to say customary conduct to the laws, the more repressive force has to be increased."[15] Liberal objections to Rousseauianism can thus draw on Rousseau himself: modern societies are not homogeneous.

## 2.2

The opponents emphasize the diversity of interests that must be brought into balance and the pluralism of opinions that must be brought into a majority consensus. In fact, the critique leveled against the "tyranny of the majority" appears in two different variants. The classical liberalism of Tocqueville understands popular sovereignty as a principle of equality that needs to be limited. It is the fear the *bourgeoisie* have of being overpowered by the *citoyen:* if the constitutional regime with its separation of powers does not *set boundaries* on the democracy of the people, then the prepolitical liberties of the individual are in danger. With this, of course, liberal theory falls back into its earlier difficulties: the practical reason incorporated in the constitution once again comes into conflict with the sovereign will of the political masses. The problem Rousseau sought to solve with the concept of self-legislation reappears. A democratically enlightened liberalism must therefore hold on to Rousseau's intention.

At this end of the political spectrum, the critique led not to a limitation but to a redefinition of the principle of popular sovereignty: such sovereignty should express itself only under the discursive conditions of an internally differentiated process of opinion- and will-formation. In 1848—hence before John Stuart Mill, in his "On Liberty" (1859), united equality and liberty in the idea of the discursive public sphere—the German democrat Julius Fröbel issued a flyer in which he conceived the idea of a total will a*long completely nonutilitarian lines.* This will should emerge from the free will of all citizens through discussion and voting: "We seek the social republic, that is, the state in which the happiness, freedom, and dignity of each individual are recognized as the common goal of all, and the perfection of the law and power of society springs from the *mutual understanding* and agreement *of all its members.*"[16]

A year earlier Fröbel had published *System der socialen Politik* (System of Social Politics),[17] in which he connects the principle of free discussion with majority rule in an interesting way. He assigns to public discourse the role that Rousseau ascribed to the supposedly universalizing force of the mere *form* of the legal statute. The normative meaning of the validity of laws that deserve general assent cannot be explained by the semantic properties of abstract and general laws. Instead, Fröbel has recourse to the communicative conditions under which opinion-formation oriented to truth can be combined with majoritarian will-formation. At the same time, he holds on to Rousseau's concept of autonomy: "A law exists only for the one who has made it himself or agreed to it; for everyone else it is a command or an order" (p. 97). Hence laws require the justified assent of all. The democratic legislature, however, decides by majority. Consensus and majority rule are compatible only if the latter has an internal relation to the search for truth: public discourse must mediate between reason and will, between the opinion-formation of all and the majoritarian will-formation of the representatives.

A majority decision may come about only in such a way that its content is regarded as the rationally motivated but *fallible* result of an attempt to determine what is right through a discussion that has been brought to a *provisional* close under the pressure to decide: "The discussion allows convictions as they have developed in the minds of different human beings to have an effect on one another, it clarifies them and enlarges the circle in which they find recognition. The . . . practical specification of law results from the development and recognition of the theoretical legal consciousness already present in the society, but it can . . . succeed in one way only, namely that of voting and deciding according to the majority" (p. 96). Fröbel interprets the majority decision as a *conditional* consensus, as the consent of the minority to a practice that conforms to the will of the majority: "Certainly one does not require that the minority, by resigning their will, declare their opinion to be incorrect; indeed, one does not even require that they abandon their aims, but rather . . . that they forego the practical application of their convictions, until they succeed in better establishing their reasons and procuring the necessary number of affirmative votes" (pp. 108f.).

## 2.3

Fröbel's position shows that the normative tension between equality and liberty can be resolved as soon as one renounces an *overly concrete reading of the principle of popular sovereignty.* Unlike Rousseau, who focused on the mere form of general law, Fröbel does not imbue the sovereign will of a collectivity with practical reason but anchors the latter in a procedure of opinion- and will-formation that determines when a political will not identical with reason has the presumption of reason on its side. This preserves Fröbel from a normative devaluation of pluralism. Public discourse mediates between reason and will: "For the progress of knowledge, a unity of convictions would be a misfortune; in the affairs of society, a unity of aims is a necessity" (p. 108). The majoritarian production of a unified will is compatible with the "principle of the equal validity of the personal will of each" only in connection with the principle "of reducing error on the way to conviction" (p. 105). And the latter principle can be asserted against tyrannical majorities only in public discourses.

Fröbel therefore proposes popular education, a high level of education for all, as well as the freedom to express "theoretical" opinions and to campaign (*Propaganda*). He is also the first to recognize the constitutional significance of parties and of their political struggles for the majority of votes conducted with the instruments of "theoretical propaganda." Only open structures of communication can prevent the ascendancy of avant-garde parties. Only "parties" and not "sects" should exist: "The party wants to validate its separate aims in the state, the sect wants to use its separate aims to overcome the state. The party seeks to come to power in the state, the sect seeks to impose its own form of existence on the state. By coming to power in the state, the party seeks to dissolve into it, whereas the sect, by dissolving the state into itself, seeks to come to power" (p. 277). Fröbel stylizes the loose parties of his day as free associations that specialize in bringing influence to bear, primarily through arguments, on the process of public opinion- and will-formation. They represent the organizational core of an enfranchised public citizenry that, engaged in a multivocal discussion and deciding by majority, occupies the seat of the sovereign.

Whereas with Rousseau the sovereign *embodied* power and the legal monopoly on power, Fröbel's public is no longer a body. Rather, it is only the medium for a multivocal process of opinion-formation that substitutes mutual understanding for power and rationally motivates majoritarian decisions. Party competition in the political public sphere thus serves to establish the Rousseauian act of the social contract for the long run, in the form of a "legal and permanent revolution," as Fröbel puts it. Fröbel's constitutional principles strip the constitutional order of everything substantial. Strictly postmetaphysical, they delineate not "natural rights" but simply the procedure of opinion- and will-formation that secures equal liberties via general rights of communication and participation:

> With the constitutional compact the parties make an agreement to have their opinions affect one another through free discussion alone and to forego the implementation of any theory until it has the majority of citizens on its side. With the constitutional compact the parties agree to the following: to determine the unity of aims according to the majority of those supporting the theory; but to leave publicity for the theory to the freedom of each individual; and to give further shape to their constitution and legislation according to the outcome of all the individual efforts as shown by the votes. (p. 113)

Whereas the first three articles of the constitution establish the conditions and procedures of a rational democratic will-formation, the fourth article rules out the unchangeability of the constitution as well as every *external* limitation on proceduralized popular sovereignty. Human rights do not *compete* with popular sovereignty; they are identical with the constitutive conditions of a self-limiting practice of publicly discursive will-formation. The separation of powers is then explained by the logic of application and supervised implementation of laws that have been enacted through such a process.

# 3

## *3.1*

The discourse over liberty and equality is carried on at another level in the *dispute between socialism and liberalism.* This dialectic, too, was already built into the French Revolution: it appeared when Jean-Paul Marat opposed the formalism of legal statutes and spoke of "legal tyranny," when Jacques Roux complained that the equality of legal statutes was aimed against the poor, and when François Babeuf, appealing to an equal satisfaction of the needs of each, criticized the institutionalization of equal liberties.[18] This discussion first acquired clear contours in early socialism.

In the eighteenth century, the critique of social inequality was directed against the social effects of political inequality. Legal arguments, that is, arguments based on modern natural law, provided a sufficient basis to plead for the equal liberties of constitutional democracy and bourgeois private law in opposition to the ancien régime. However, as constitutional monarchy and the Code Napoléon were implemented, social inequalities of *another* kind came to light. The inequalities connected with political privilege were replaced by ones that first appeared in the process of institutionalizing equal liberties according to private law. The social effects of the unequal distribution of a nonpolitical economic power were now at issue. When Karl Marx and Friedrich Engels denounced the bourgeois legal order as the juridical expression of unjust relations of production, they were borrowing arguments from political economy, thereby enlarging the concept of the political itself. No longer was just the organization of the state open to our control but the arrangement of society as a whole.[19]

With this change in perspective, a functional relationship between class structure and the legal system came into view. This connection made it possible to criticize legal formalism, and thus to criticize the substantive inequality of rights that were formally equal (i.e., equal according to their literal meaning). However, this same shift in perspective simultaneously made it difficult to see the problem that arises for political will-formation once the social is politicized. Marx and Engels, satisfied with allusions to the Paris Commune, more or less put aside questions of democratization. The philosophical background of these authors could also partly explain their blanket rejection of legal formalism (in fact a rejection of the legal sphere as a whole). Specifically, one could argue that they read Rousseau and Hegel too much through the eyes of Aristotle; that they failed to appreciate the normative substance of Kantian universalism and the Enlightenment; and that their idea of a liberated society was too concrete. They conceived socialism as a historically privileged form of concrete ethical life (*Sittlichkeit*) and not as the set of necessary conditions for emancipated forms of life about which participants *themselves* would have to reach an understanding.

The expanded concept of the political was not matched by a deeper understanding of the functional modes, forms of communication, and institutional conditions of egalitarian will-formation. The holistic notion of a politicized society of workers remained central. The early socialists were still confident that the convivial forms of life of freely associated workers would emerge spontaneously from properly organized production processes. Faced with the complexity of developed, functionally differentiated societies, this idea of workers' self-governance had to fail—and fail even if the workers' social utopia was imagined, with Marx, as a realm of freedom to be established on the basis of an ongoing, systemically regulated realm of necessity. Even Lenin's strategy, the seizure of power by professional revolutionaries, could not make up for the lack of political theory. The practical effects of this deficit are evident in those aporias that to this day still grip bureaucratic socialism, with its political avant-garde frozen into *nomenklatura*.

### 3.2

On the other hand, achieving the social-welfare compromise has been a disappointing experience for the reformist unions and parties that operate within the framework of constitutional democracy. That is, they had to be content with an adjusted version of bourgeois liberalism and forego the redemption of radical democratic promises. The intellectual kinship between reformism and left liberalism (between Eduard Bernstein and Friedrich Naumann, still the godsons of the social-liberal coalition) rests on the shared goal of universalizing basic rights from a social-welfare perspective.[20] Normalizing the status of dependent wage labor through participatory political and social rights is supposed to provide the mass of the population with the opportunity to live in security, social justice, and growing prosperity. On the basis of a capitalist growth that is both domesticated and nurtured, the parties in power are supposed to operate the levers of administrative power so as to implement these goals via interventions. According to orthodox Marxism, social emancipation was to be achieved through a political revolution that took possession of the state apparatus only to smash it to pieces. Reformism can bring about social pacification solely by way of social-welfare interventions, but in doing so parties are absorbed into an expanding state apparatus. As parties become arms of the state, political will-formation shifts into a political system that is largely self-programming. To the extent that it succeeds in *extracting* mass loyalty from the public sphere, the political system becomes independent of the democratic sources of its legitimation. Thus the flip side of a halfway successful welfare state is a mass democracy in which the process of legitimation is *managed* by the administration. At the programmatic level, this is associated with resignation: both the acceptance of the scandalous "natural fate" imposed by the labor market and the renunciation of radical democracy.

This explains the relevance of the *discourse between anarchism and socialism* that has been carried on since the nineteenth century. What was already practiced in the petit bourgeois revolution of the sansculottes finally received rational justification and partial theoretical elaboration in anarchist social criticism and the idea of council democracy. Here the techniques of self-organization (such as permanent consultation, imperative mandates, rotation of offices, and interlocking powers) were probably less important than the organizational form itself: the model of the voluntary association.[21] Such associations displayed only a minimal degree of institutionalization. The horizontal contacts at the level of face-to-face interactions were supposed to coalesce into an intersubjective practice of deliberation and decision making strong enough to maintain all the *other* institutions in the fluid condition of the founding phase, more or less preserving them from coagulation. This anti-institutionalism coincided with the classical liberal idea that associations could support a public sphere in which the communicative practices of opinion- and will-formation would occur, guided of course by argumentation. When Donoso Cortes complained that liberalism erroneously made discussion into the principle of political decision, and when Carl Schmitt likewise denounced the liberal bourgeoisie as the discussing class, both had the anarchistic, hence *power-dissolving,* consequences of public discussion in view. The same motive still drives the numerous disciples of Schmitt in their shadowboxing with the intellectual instigators of a "European civil war."

In contrast to the individualistic, natural-*law* construct of the state of nature, the organizational form of voluntary association is a *sociological* concept that allows one to think of spontaneously emergent, domination-free relationships in noncontractualist terms. Then one no longer needs to conceive of domination-free society as an instrumental and hence prepolitical order established on the basis of contracts, that is, through the self-interested agreements of private persons oriented toward success. A society integrated through associations instead of through markets would be a political, yet nevertheless domination-free, order. The anarchists trace spontaneous sociation back to a different impulse than does modern natural law, that is, not to the interest in the useful exchange of goods but rather to the willingness to solve problems and coordinate action through mutual understanding. Associations differ from formal organizations in that the purpose of the union has not yet become functionally autonomous vis-à-vis the associated members' value orientations and goals.

### 3.3

This anarchist projection of a society made up entirely of horizontal networks of associations was always utopian; today it is still less workable, given the regulatory and organizational needs of modern societies. Media-steered interactions in the economic and administrative systems are defined precisely by the uncoupling of organizational functions from members' orientations. From the actor's perspective, this uncoupling manifests itself as an inversion of ends and means; processes of utilization and administration appear to acquire a fetishistic life of their own. But the anarchist's suspicion can be given a methodological turn; indeed it can be turned critically against both sides: against the system-blindness of a normative theory of democracy that disregards the bureaucratic expropriation of the grassroots level, and against the fetishizing gaze of a systems theory that dismisses all normative considerations. By methodological flat, systems theory excludes the possibility of communication in which a society could examine itself as a whole.[22]

The classical theories of democracy start with the assumption that society has an effect or influence on itself through the sovereign legislature. The people program the laws, and these in turn program the implementation and application of law, so that through the collectively binding decisions of administration and judiciary the members of society receive the benefits and regulations that they themselves have programmed in their role of citizens. This *idea of an action-upon-self programmed by laws* appears plausible only on the supposition that society as a whole can be represented as an association writ large, which governs itself through the media of law and political power. Today we know better, now that sociological analyses have enlightened us about the actual circulation of power. We also know that as an organizational form, an association lacks the complexity necessary to structure the social fabric as a whole. But this is not my concern here. I am interested, rather, in the conceptual analysis of the reciprocal constitution of law and political power. Such an analysis already shows that, in the medium proper to action-upon-self programmed by laws, there exists *an opposing, self-programming circulation* of power.

Before law and political power can take on *their own* functions, namely, stabilization of behavioral expectations and collectively binding decisions, they must fulfill functions for each other. Thus law, which borrows its coercive character from power, first bestows on power the legal form that provides power with its binding character. Each of these two codes requires its own perspective: law requires a normative perspective, and power an instrumental one. From the perspective of law, policies as well as laws and decrees have need of normative justification, whereas from the perspective of power they function as means for and constraints upon the reproduction of power. The perspective of legislation and adjudication yields a normative approach to law; the perspective of preserving power yields a corresponding instrumental approach. From the perspective of power, the circulation of normative action-upon-self programmed through laws acquires the opposite character of a self-programming circulation of power: the administration programs itself by steering the behavior of the voting public, preprogramming the executive branch (*Regierung*) and legislature, and functionalizing the judiciary.

As the welfare state develops, the opposing element that is already *conceptually* present in the medium of legal-administrative action-upon-self also begins to have an empirical effect that gradually increases in strength. By now it is clear that the administrative instruments for implementing social-welfare programs are by no means a passive medium without properties of its own, as it were. To an increasing degree, the interventionist state has contracted into a subsystem steered by power and centered in itself; to an increasing degree, it has displaced legitimation processes into its environment. In fact, this process has progressed to the point where we would do well to consider modifications in the normative idea of a self-organizing society. I thus propose that we make a distinction in the concept of the political itself, consonant with the duality of normative and instrumental perspectives.[23]

We can distinguish between *communicatively generated* power and *administratively employed* power. In the political public sphere, then, two contrary processes encounter and cut across each other: the communicative generation of legitimate power, for which Arendt sketched a normative model, and the political-systemic acquisition of legitimacy, a process by which administrative power becomes reflexive. How these two processes—the spontaneous forming of opinion in autonomous public spheres and the organized extraction of mass loyalty—interpenetrate, and which overpowers which, are empirical questions. What primarily interests me is this: insofar as this distinction comes to have any empirical relevance, the normative understanding of a democratic self-organization of the legal community must also change.

**4**

*4.1*

The first question concerns the mode of action-upon-self. Because the administrative system must translate all normative inputs into its own language, one must explain how this system can be programmed at all through the policies and laws emerging from processes of public opinion- and will-formation. The administration obeys its own rationality criteria as it operates according to law; from the perspective of employing administrative power, what counts is not the practical reason involved in applying norms but the effectiveness of implementing a given program. Thus the administrative system primarily deals with the law instrumentally. Normative reasons, which justify adopted policies and enacted norms in the language of law, are regarded in the language of administrative power as rationalizations appended to decisions that were previously induced. Naturally, because of its juridical character, political power still depends on normative reasons. Normative reasons thus constitute the means by which communicative power makes itself felt. The indirect measures by which the administration manages the economy illustrate how influence can be brought to bear on self-regulating mechanisms (e.g., "help to self-help"). Perhaps we can apply this model to the relation between the democratic public sphere and the administration. Communicatively generated legitimate power can have an effect on the political system insofar as it assumes responsibility for the pool of reasons from which administrative decisions must draw their rationalizations. If the normative arguments appended by the system have been discursively invalidated by counterarguments from prior political communication, then it is simply not the case that "anything goes," that is, anything feasible for the political system.

The next question concerns the possibility of democratizing opinion- and will-formation themselves. Normative reasons can achieve an indirect steering effect only to the extent that the political system does not, for its part, steer the very production of these reasons. Now, democratic procedures are meant to institutionalize the forms of communication necessary for a rational will-formation. From this standpoint, at least, the institutional framework in which the legitimation process occurs today can be submitted to critical evaluation. With some institutional imagination, moreover, one can think of how existing parliamentary bodies might be supplemented by institutions that would allow affected clients and the legal public sphere to exert a stronger pressure for legitimation on the executive and judicial branches. The more difficult problem, however, is how to ensure the autonomy of the opinion- and will-formation that have already been institutionalized. After all, these generate communicative power only to the extent that majority decisions satisfy the conditions stated by Fröbel, that is, only insofar as they come about discursively.

The assumed internal relation between political will-formation and opinion-formation can secure the expected rationality of decision making only if parliamentary deliberations do not proceed according to ideologically *pregiven* assumptions. Elitist interpretations of the principle of representation respond to this requirement by shielding organized politics from a forever-gullible popular opinion. In normative terms, however, this way of defending rationality against popular sovereignty is contradictory: if the voters' opinion is irrational, then the election of representatives is no less so. This dilemma turns our attention toward a relation Fröbel did not discuss, that between formally structured political will-formation and the surrounding environment of unstructured processes of opinion-formation. The former issues in decisions (and is also the level at which general elections are located), whereas the latter remains informal, because it is not under any pressure to decide. Fröbel's own assumptions compel one to conclude that the democratic procedure can lead to a rational will-formation only insofar as organized opinion-formation, which leads to accountable decisions within government bodies, remains permeable to the free-floating values, issues, contributions, and arguments of a surrounding political communication that, as such, cannot be *organized* as a whole.

Thus the normative expectation of rational outcomes is grounded ultimately in the interplay between institutionally structured political will-formation and spontaneous, unsubverted circuits of communication in a public sphere that is not programmed to reach decisions and thus is not organized. In this context, the public sphere functions as a normative concept. Voluntary associations represent the nodal points in a communication network that emerges from the intermeshing of autonomous public spheres. Such associations specialize in the generation and dissemination of practical convictions.

They specialize, that is, in discovering issues relevant for all of society, contributing possible solutions to problems, interpreting values, producing good reasons, and invalidating others. They can become effective only indirectly, namely, by altering the parameters of institutionalized will-formation by broadly transforming attitudes and values. The manner in which general voting behavior is increasingly affected by opaque mood swings in the political culture indicates that the foregoing reflections are not entirely out of touch with social reality. But here we must restrict ourselves to the normative implications of this descriptive analysis.

### 4.2

Following Arendt's lead, Albrecht Wellmer has underscored the self-referential structure of the public practice issuing from communicative power.[24] This communicative practice bears the burden of stabilizing itself; with each important contribution, public discourse must keep alive both the meaning of an undistorted political public sphere as such and the very goal of democratic will-formation. The public sphere thereby continually thematizes itself as it operates, for the existential presuppositions of a nonorganizable practice can be secured only by this practice itself. The institutions of public freedom stand on the shifting ground of the political communication of those who, by using them, at the same time interpret and defend them. The public sphere thus reproduces itself *self-referentially,* and in doing so reveals the place to which the expectation of a sovereign self-organization of society has withdrawn. The idea of popular sovereignty is thereby desubstantialized. Even the notion that a network of associations could replace the dismissed "body" of the people— that it could occupy the vacant seat of the sovereign, so to speak—is too concrete.

This fully dispersed sovereignty is not even embodied in the heads of the associated members. Rather, if one can still speak of "embodiment" at all, then sovereignty is found in those subjectless forms of communication that regulate the flow of discursive opinion- and will-formation in such a way that their fallible outcomes have the presumption of practical reason on their side. Subjectless and anonymous, an intersubjectively dissolved popular sovereignty withdraws into democratic procedures and the demanding communicative presuppositions of their implementation. It is sublimated into the elusive interactions between culturally mobilized public spheres and a will-formation institutionalized according to the rule of law. Set communicatively aflow, sovereignty makes itself felt in the power of public discourses. Although such power originates in autonomous public spheres, it must take shape in the decisions of democratic institutions of opinion- and will-formation, inasmuch as the responsibility for momentous decisions demands clear institutional accountability. Communicative power is exercised in the manner of a siege. It influences the premises of judgment and decision making in the political system without intending to conquer the system itself. It thus aims to assert its imperatives in the only language the besieged fortress understands: it takes responsibility for the pool of reasons that administrative power can handle instrumentally but cannot ignore, given its juridical structure.

Naturally, even a proceduralized "popular sovereignty" of this sort cannot operate without the support of an accommodating political culture, without the basic attitudes, mediated by tradition and socialization, of a population *accustomed* to political freedom: rational political will-formation cannot occur unless a rationalized lifeworld meets it halfway. This thesis could appear to be just one more guise for a civic-republican ethos and its expectations of virtue that have morally overburdened citizens since time immemorial. If we are to dispel this suspicion, then we must finally argue for what neo-Aristotelian political theory slips in with its concept of ethos: we must explain how it is possible in principle for civic virtue and self-interest to intermesh. If it is to be *reasonable to expect* the political behavior that is normatively required, then the moral substance of self-legislation—which for Rousseau was concentrated in a single act—must be parceled out over many stages: the process of proceduralized opinion- and will-formation must break down into numerous smaller particles. It must be shown that political morality is exacted only in small increments.[25] Here I can illustrate this point only briefly.

Why should representatives base their decisions on correct and, as we are here assuming, more or less discursively formed judgments

Jürgen Habermas

and not merely advance legitimating reasons as a pretext? It is because the institutions are designed in such a way that representatives normally do not want to expose themselves to the criticism of their voters. After all, voters can sanction their representatives at the next opportunity, but representatives do not have any comparable way of sanctioning voters. But why should voters base their ballot choices on, as we here assume, a more or less discursively formed public opinion, instead of ignoring the legitimating reasons? It is because normally they can choose only between the highly generalized policies and vague profiles of popular parties, and they can perceive their own interests only in the light of pregeneralized interest positions. But are not these two assumptions themselves unrealistic? Not entirely, so long as we are only normatively assessing the alternatives that are possible in principle. As we have seen, democratic procedures should produce rational outcomes insofar as opinion-formation inside parliamentary bodies remains sensitive to the results of a surrounding informal opinion-formation in autonomous public spheres. No doubt this second assumption of an unsubverted political public sphere is unrealistic; properly understood, however, it is not utopian in a bad sense. It would be realized to the extent that opinion-forming associations developed, catalyzed the growth of autonomous public spheres, and, in virtue of the natural visibility such associations enjoy, changed the spectrum of values, issues, and reasons. This would both innovatively unleash and critically filter the elements of discourse that have been channeled by the mass media, unions, associations, and parties, according to the dictates of power. In the final analysis, of course, the emergence, reproduction, and influence of such a network of associations remains dependent on a liberal-egalitarian political culture sensitive to problems affecting society as a whole—a culture that is even jumpy or in a constant state of vibration, and thus responsive.

## 4.3

Let us assume that complex societies would be open to such fundamental democratization. In that case, we are immediately confronted with *objections that conservatives* since Edmund Burke have repeatedly marshaled against the French Revolution and its effects.[26] In this final round of reflection, we must take up the arguments that such thinkers as Joseph de Maistre and Louis de Bonald have used to remind overly naive believers in progress of the limits of what can be done. The overextended project of a self-organizing society, so the argument goes, carelessly disregards the weight of traditions, organically developing reserves and resources that cannot be created at will. As a matter of fact, the instrumentalism underlying a practice that directly attempts to realize theory has had disastrous effects. Robespierre already set up an opposition between revolution and constitution: the Revolution exists for war and civil war, the Constitution for the victorious peace. From Marx to Lenin, the theoretically informed intervention of revolutionaries was merely supposed to complete the teleology of history driven by the forces of production. Proceduralized popular sovereignty, however, no longer has any place for such trust in a philosophy of history. Once the subject is removed from practical reason, the progressive institutionalization of procedures of rational collective will-formation can no longer be conceived as purposive action, as a kind of sublime process of production. Rather, today the controversial *realization* of universalist constitutional principles has become a permanent process that is already under way in ordinary legislation. The debates that precede decisions take place under conditions of a social and politicocultural transformation whose direction, though certainly not open to control by direct political intervention, can be indirectly accelerated or inhibited. The constitution has thus lost its static character. Even if the wording of norms has not changed, their interpretations are in flux.

Constitutional democracy is becoming a project, at once the outcome and the accelerating catalyst of a rationalization of the lifeworld reaching far beyond the political. The sole substantial aim of the project is the gradual improvement of institutionalized procedures of rational collective will-formation, procedures that cannot prejudge the participants' concrete goals. Each step along this path has repercussions on the political culture and forms of life.

Conversely, without the support of the sociopolitical culture, which cannot be produced upon demand, the forms of communication adequate to practical reason cannot emerge.

Such a culturalistic understanding of constitutional *dynamics* seems to suggest that the sovereignty of the people should be relocated to the cultural dynamics of opinion-forming avant-gardes. This conjecture will fuel suspicions against intellectuals all the more: powerful in word, they grab for themselves the very power they profess to dissolve in the medium of the word. But at least one obstacle stands in the way of domination by intellectuals: communicative power can become effective only indirectly, insofar as it limits the implementation of administrative, hence actually exercised, power. And unstructured public opinion can in turn function as a siege of this sort only by way of accountable decision making organized according to democratic procedures. What is more important, the influence of intellectuals could coalesce into communicative power at all only under conditions that exclude a concentration of power. Autonomous public spheres could crystallize around free associations only to the extent that current trends toward an uncoupling of culture from class structures continue.[27] Public discourses find a good response only in proportion to their diffusion, and thus only under conditions of a broad and active participation that simultaneously has a *dispersing effect*. This in turn requires a background political culture that is egalitarian, divested of all educational privileges, and thoroughly intellectual.

There is certainly no necessity that this increasingly reflexive transmission of cultural traditions be associated with subject-centered reason and future-oriented historical consciousness. To the extent that we become aware of the intersubjective constitution of freedom, the possessive-individualist illusion of autonomy as self-ownership disintegrates. The self-assertive subject that wants to have everything at its disposal lacks an adequate relation to any tradition. Benjamin's youthful conservative sensibility detected another time consciousness in the culture revolution itself, a consciousness that turned our attention away from the horizon of our own "future presents" and back to the claims that past generations make on us. But one reservation still remains. The sobriety of a secular, unreservedly egalitar-

ian mass culture does not just defeat the pathos of the holy seriousness that seeks to ensure social status to the prophetic alone. The
fact that everyday affairs are necessarily banalized in political communication also poses a danger for the semantic potentials from
which this communication must still draw its nourishment. A culture
without thorns would be absorbed by mere needs for compensation;
as M. Grefrath puts it, it settles over the risk society like a foam
carpet. No civil religion, however cleverly adjusted, could forestall
this entropy of meaning.[28] Even the moment of unconditionality
insistently voiced in the context-transcending validity claims of everyday life does not suffice. *Another* kind of transcendence is preserved
in the unfulfilled promise disclosed by the critical appropriation of
identity-forming religious traditions, and *still another* in the negativity
of modern art. The trivial and everyday must be open to the shock
of what is absolutely strange, cryptic, or uncanny. Though these no
longer provide a cover for privileges, they refuse to be assimilated by
pregiven categories.[29]

*Translated by William Rehg*

## Notes

This was presented as a lecture in December, 1988, and was first published in Forum
für Philosophie Bad Homburg, ed., *Die Ideen von 1789* (Frankfurt am Main, 1989),
pp. 7–36.

1. E. Schulin, *Die Französische Revolution* (Munich, 1988), p. 11.

2. W. Markov, *Die Jakobinerfrage heute* (Berlin, 1967), p. 3.

3. F. Furet and D. Richet, *La Révolution* (Paris, 1965); citations are from the German
translation, *Die Französische Revolution* (Frankfurt am Main, 1968); here see p. 84. An
English translation is available under the title *French Revolution*, trans. S. Hardman
(New York, 1970).

4. F. Furet, *Penser la Révolution française* (Paris, 1978); citations are taken from the
German translation, 1789—*Vom Ereignis zum Gegenstand der Geschichtswissenschaft*
(Frankfurt am Main, 1980).

5. Schulin, *Die Französische Revolution*, pp. 9ff.

6. Furet himself has since adopted this relativizing view. See F. Furet, *La Révolution
1780–1880* (Paris, 1988); and his "La France Unie," in *La République du Centre* (Paris,

1988); cf. A. I. Hartig, "Das Bicentennaire—eine Auferstehung?" *Merkur* 43 (1989): 258ff.

7. R. v. Thadden, "Die Botschaft der Brüderlichkeit," *Süddeutsche Zeitung*, Nov. 26/27, 1988.

8. Ibid.

9. Furet, 1789—*Vom Ereignis*, p. 34.

10. R. Koselleck, *Futures Past*, trans. K. Tribe (Cambridge, Mass., 1985); J. Habermas, *The Philosophical Discourse of Modernity*, trans. F. Lawrence (Cambridge, Mass., 1987), chap. 1.

11. C. Taylor, "Legitimation Crisis?" in Taylor, *Philosophy and the Human Sciences* (Cambridge, 1985), pp. 248–88.

12. J. Starobinski, *1789: The Emblems of Reason*, trans. B. Bray (Charlottesville, Va., 1982).

13. For an astounding agreement with Carl Schmitt, see Furet, *1789—Vom Ereignis*, pp. 197ff.

14. I. Kant, *Metaphysical Elements of Justice*, trans. J. Ladd (New York, 1965), p. 78 [translation altered. Trans.].

15. J.-J. Rousseau, *On the Social Contract*, trans. C. M. Sherover (New York, 1984), bk. 3, chap. 1, sec. 159 (p. 55).

16. J. Fröbel, *Monarchie oder Republik* (Mannheim, 1848), p. 6.

17. J. Fröbel, *System der socialen Politik* (Mannheim, 1847; reprint, Scientia Verlag, Aalen, 1975; intralinear page numbers refer to the latter edition).

18. H. Dippel, "Die politischen Ideen der französischen Revolution," in *Pipers Handbuch der Politischen Ideen*, vol. 4 (Munich, 1986), pp. 21ff.

19. O. Negt and E. T. Mohl, "Marx und Engels—der unaufgehobene Widerspruch von Theorie und Praxis," in *Pipers Handbuch der Politischen Ideen*, vol. 4, pp. 449ff.

20. O. Kallscheuer, "Revisionismus und Reformismus," in *Pipers Handbuch der Politischen Ideen*, vol. 4, pp. 545ff.

21. P. Lösche, "Anarchismus," in *Pipers Handbuch der Politischen Ideen*, vol. 4, pp. 415ff.

22. N. Luhmann, *Political Theory in the Welfare State*, trans. J. Bednarz, Jr. (New York, 1990).

23. J. Habermas, *Die Neue Unübersichtlichkeit* (Frankfurt am Main, 1985).

24. A. Wellmer, "Hannah Arendt on Judgment: The Unwritten Doctrine of Reason," in L. May and J. Kohn, eds., *Hannah Arendt: Twenty Years Later* (Cambridge, Mass., 1996); see H. Arendt, *On Violence* (New York, 1970); J. Habermas, "Hannah Arendt:

On the Concept of Power," in Habermas, *Philosophical-Political Profiles,* trans.
F. Lawrence (Cambridge, Mass., 1985), pp. 173–89.

25. U. Preuß, "Was heißt radikale Demokratie heute?" in Forum für Philosophie Bad
Homburg, ed., *Die Ideen von 1789* (Frankfurt am Main, 1989), pp. 37–67.

26. H. J. Puhle, "Die Anfänge des politischen Konservatismus in Deutschland," in
*Pipers Handbuch der Politischen Ideen,* vol. 4, pp. 255ff.

27. H. Brunkhorst, "Die Ästhetisierung der Intellektuellen," *Frankfurter Rundschau,*
November 28, 1988.

28. H. Kleger and R. Müller, eds., *Religion des Bürgers* (Munich, 1986); H. Dubiel,
"Zivilreligion in der Massendemokratie," ms. 1989.

29. C. Menke-Eggers, *Die Souveränität der Kunst* (Frankfurt am Main, 1988); English
translation forthcoming (Cambridge, Mass., 1996).

# 3

## Deliberation and Democratic Legitimacy

*Joshua Cohen*

In this essay I explore the ideal of a "deliberative democracy."[1] By a deliberative democracy I shall mean, roughly, an association whose affairs are governed by the public deliberation of its members. I propose an account of the value of such an association that treats democracy itself as a fundamental political ideal and not simply as a derivative ideal that can be explained in terms of the values of fairness or equality of respect.

The essay is in three sections. In section I, I focus on Rawls's discussion of democracy and use that discussion both to introduce certain features of a deliberative democracy, and to raise some doubts about whether their importance is naturally explained in terms of the notion of a fair system of social cooperation. In section II, I develop an account of deliberative democracy in terms of the notion of an *ideal deliberative procedure*. The characterization of that procedure provides an abstract model of deliberation which links the intuitive ideal of democratic association to a more substantive view of deliberative democracy. Three features of the ideal deliberative procedure figure prominently in the essay. First, it helps to account for some familiar judgments about collective decision making, in particular about the ways that collective decision making ought to be different from bargaining, contracting, and other market-type interactions, both in its explicit attention to considerations of the common advantage and in the ways that that attention helps to form the aims of the participants. Second, it accounts for the

Joshua Cohen

common view that the notion of democratic association is tied to notions of autonomy and the common good. Third, the ideal deliberative procedure provides a distinctive structure for addressing institutional questions. And in section III of the paper I rely on that distinctive structure in responding to four objections to the account of deliberative democracy.

# I

The ideal of deliberative democracy is a familiar ideal. Aspects of it have been highlighted in recent discussion of the role of republican conceptions of self-government in shaping the American constitutional tradition and contemporary public law.[2] It is represented as well in radical democratic and socialist criticisms of the politics of advanced industrial societies.[3] And some of its central features are highlighted in Rawls's account of democratic politics in a just society, particularly in those parts of his account that seek to incorporate the "liberty of the ancients" and to respond to radical democrats and socialists who argue that "the basic liberties may prove to be merely formal." In the discussion that follows I shall first say something about Rawls's remarks on three such features, and then consider his explanation of them.[4]

First, in a well-ordered democracy, political debate is organized around alternative conceptions of the public good. So an ideal pluralist scheme, in which democratic politics consists of fair bargaining among groups each of which pursues its particular or sectional interest, is unsuited to a just society (Rawls 1971, pp. 360–361).[5] Citizens and parties operating in the political arena ought not to "take a narrow or group-interested standpoint" (p. 360). And parties should only be responsive to demands that are "argued for openly by reference to a conception of the public good" (pp. 226, 472). Public explanations and justifications of laws and policies are to be cast in terms of conceptions of the common good (conceptions that, on Rawls's view, must be consistent with the two principles of justice), and public deliberation should aim to work out the details of such conceptions and to apply them to particular issues of public policy (p. 362).

Second, the ideal of democratic order has egalitarian implications that must be satisfied in ways that are manifest to citizens. The reason is that in a just society political opportunities and powers must be independent of economic or social position—the political liberties must have a fair value[6]—and the fact that they are independent must be more or less evident to citizens. Ensuring this manifestly fair value might, for example, require public funding of political parties and restrictions on private political spending, as well as progressive tax measures that serve to limit inequalities of wealth and to ensure that the political agenda is not controlled by the interests of economically and socially dominant groups (Rawls 1971, pp. 225–226, 277–278; 1982, pp. 42–43). In principle, these distributional requirements might be more stringently egalitarian than those fixed by the difference principle (Rawls 1982, p. 43).[7] This is so in part because the main point of these measures is not simply to ensure that democratic politics proceeds under fair conditions, nor only to encourage just legislation, but also to ensure that the equality of citizens is manifest and to declare a commitment to that equality "as the public intention" (1971, p. 233).

Third, democratic politics should be ordered in ways that provide a basis for self-respect, that encourage the development of a sense of political competence, and that contribute to the formation of a sense of justice;[8] it should fix "the foundations for civic friendship and [shape] the ethos of political culture" (Rawls 1971, p. 234). Thus the importance of democratic order is not confined to its role in obstructing the class legislation that can be expected from systems in which groups are effectively excluded from the channels of political representation and bargaining. In addition, democratic politics should also shape the ways in which the members of the society understand themselves and their own legitimate interests.

When properly conducted, then, democratic politics involves *public deliberation focused on the common good*, requires some form of *manifest equality* among citizens, and *shapes the identity and interests* of citizens in ways that contribute to the formation of a public conception of common good. How does the ideal of a fair system of social cooperation provide a way to account for the attractiveness and importance of these three features of the deliberative democratic

Joshua Cohen

ideal? Rawls suggests a formal and an informal line of argument. The formal argument is that parties in the original position would choose the principle of participation[9] with the proviso that the political liberties have their fair value. The three conditions are important because they must be satisfied if constitutional arrangements are to ensure participation rights, guarantee a fair value to those rights, and plausibly produce legislation that encourages a fair distribution according to the difference principle.

Rawls also suggests an informal argument for the ordering of political institutions, and I shall focus on this informal argument here:

Justice as fairness begins with the idea that where common principles are necessary and to everyone's advantage, they are to be worked out from the viewpoint of a suitably defined initial situation of equality in which each person is fairly represented. The principle of participation transfers this notion from the original position to the constitution . . . [thus] preserv[ing] the equal representation of the original position to the degree that this is feasible. (Rawls 1971, pp. 221–222)[10]

Or, as he puts it elsewhere: "The idea [of the fair value of political liberty] is to incorporate into the basic structure of society an effective political procedure which *mirrors* in that structure the fair representation of persons achieved by the original position" (1982, p. 45; emphasis added). The suggestion is that, since we accept the intuitive ideal of a fair system of cooperation, we should want our political institutions themselves to conform, insofar as it is feasible, to the requirement that terms of association be worked out under fair conditions. And so we arrive directly at the requirement of equal liberties with fair value, rather than arriving at it indirectly, through a hypothetical choice of that requirement under fair conditions. In this informal argument, the original position serves as an *abstract model* of what fair conditions are, and of what we should strive to mirror in our political institutions, rather than as an initial-choice situation in which regulative principles for those institutions are selected.

I think that Rawls is right in wanting to accommodate the three conditions. What I find less plausible is that the three conditions are natural consequences of the ideal of fairness. Taking the notion of fairness as fundamental, and aiming (as in the informal argument) to model political arrangements on the original position, it is not clear why, for example, political debate ought to be focused on the common good, or why the manifest equality of citizens is an important feature of a democratic association. The pluralist conception of democratic politics as a system of bargaining with fair representation for all groups seems an equally good mirror of the ideal of fairness.

The response to this objection is clear enough: the connection between the ideal of fairness and the three features of democratic politics depends on psychological and sociological assumptions. Those features do not follow directly from the ideal of a fair system of cooperation, or from that ideal as it is modeled in the original position. Rather, we arrive at them when we consider what is required to preserve fair arrangements and to achieve fair outcomes. For example, public political debate should be conducted in terms of considerations of the common good because we cannot expect outcomes that advance the common good unless people are looking for them. Even an ideal pluralist scheme, with equal bargaining power and no barriers to entry, cannot reasonably be expected to advance the common good as defined by the difference principle (1971, p. 360).

But this is, I think, too indirect and instrumental an argument for the three conditions. Like utilitarian defenses of liberty, it rests on a series of highly speculative sociological and psychological judgments. I want to suggest that the reason why the three are attractive is not that an order with, for example, no explicit deliberation about the common good and no manifest equality would be unfair (though of course it might be). Instead it is that they comprise elements of an independent and expressly political ideal that is focused in the first instance[11] on the appropriate conduct of public affairs—on, that is, the appropriate ways of arriving at collective decisions. And to understand that ideal we ought not to proceed by seeking to "mirror" ideal fairness in the fairness of political arrangements, but instead to proceed by seeking to mirror a system of ideal deliberation in social and political institutions. I want now to turn to this alternative.

Joshua Cohen

**II**[12]

The notion of a deliberative democracy is rooted in the intuitive ideal of a democratic association in which the justification of the terms and conditions of association proceeds through public argument and reasoning among equal citizens. Citizens in such an order share a commitment to the resolution of problems of collective choice through public reasoning, and regard their basic institutions as legitimate insofar as they establish the framework for free public deliberation. To elaborate this ideal, I begin with a more explicit account of the ideal itself, presenting what I shall call the "formal conception" of deliberative democracy. Proceeding from this formal conception, I pursue a more substantive account of deliberative democracy by presenting an account of an *ideal deliberative procedure* that captures the notion of justification through public argument and reasoning among equal citizens, and serves in turn as a model for deliberative institutions.

The formal conception of a deliberative democracy has five main features:

D1  A deliberative democracy is an ongoing and independent association, whose members expect it to continue into the indefinite future.

D2  The members of the association share (and it is common knowledge that they share) the view that the appropriate terms of association provide a framework for or are the results of their deliberation. They share, that is, a commitment to coordinating their activities within institutions that make deliberation possible and according to norms that they arrive at through their deliberation. For them, free deliberation among equals is the basis of legitimacy.

D3  A deliberative democracy is a pluralistic association. The members have diverse preferences, convictions, and ideals concerning the conduct of their own lives. While sharing a commitment to the deliberative resolution of problems of collective choice (D2), they also have divergent aims, and do not think that some particular set of preferences, convictions, or ideals is mandatory.

D4 Because the members of a democratic association regard deliberative procedures as the source of *legitimacy,* it is important to them that the terms of their association not merely *be* the results of their deliberation, but also be *manifest* to them as such.[13] They prefer institutions in which the connections between deliberation and outcomes are evident to ones in which the connections are less clear.

D5 The members recognize one another as having deliberative capacities, i.e., the capacities required for entering into a public exchange of reasons and for acting on the result of such public reasoning.

A theory of deliberative democracy aims to give substance to this formal ideal by characterizing the conditions that should obtain if the social order is to be manifestly regulated by deliberative forms of collective choice. I propose to sketch a view of this sort by considering an ideal scheme of deliberation, which I shall call the "ideal deliberative procedure." The aim in sketching this procedure is to give an explicit statement of the conditions for deliberative decision making that are suited to the formal conception, and thereby to highlight the properties that democratic institutions should embody, so far as possible. I should emphasize that the ideal deliberative procedure is meant to provide a model for institutions to mirror—in the first instance for the institutions in which collective choices are made and social outcomes publicly justified—and not to characterize an initial situation in which the terms of association themselves are chosen.[14]

Turning then to the ideal procedure, there are three general aspects of deliberation. There is a need to decide on an agenda, to propose alternative solutions to the problems on the agenda, supporting those solutions with reasons, and to conclude by settling on an alternative. A democratic conception can be represented in terms of the requirements that it sets on such a procedure. In particular, outcomes are democratically legitimate if and only if they could be the object of a free and reasoned agreement among equals. The ideal deliberative procedure is a procedure that captures this principle.[15]

Joshua Cohen

I1    Ideal deliberation is *free* in that it satisfies two conditions. First, the participants regard themselves as bound only by the results of their deliberation and by the preconditions for that deliberation. Their consideration of proposals is not constrained by the authority of prior norms or requirements. Second, the participants suppose that they can act from the results, taking the fact that a certain decision is arrived at through their deliberation as a sufficient reason for complying with it.

I2    Deliberation is *reasoned* in that the parties to it are required to state their reasons for advancing proposals, supporting them, or criticizing them. They give reasons with the expectation that those reasons (and not, for example, their power) will settle the fate of their proposal. In ideal deliberation, as Habermas puts it, "no force except that of the better argument is exercised" (1975, p. 108). Reasons are offered with the aim of bringing others to accept the proposal, given their disparate ends (D3) and their commitment (D2) to settling the conditions of their association through free deliberation among equals. Proposals may be rejected because they are not defended with acceptable reasons, even if they could be so defended. The deliberative conception emphasizes that collective choices should be *made in a deliberative way,* and not only that those choices should have a desirable fit with the preferences of citizens.

I3    In ideal deliberation, parties are both formally and substantively *equal.* They are formally equal in that the rules regulating the procedure do not single out individuals. Everyone with the deliberative capacities has equal standing at each stage of the deliberative process. Each can put issues on the agenda, propose solutions, and offer reasons in support of or in criticism of proposals. And each has an equal voice in the decision. The participants are substantively equal in that the existing distribution of power and resources does not shape their chances to contribute to deliberation, nor does that distribution play an authoritative role in their deliberation. The participants in the deliberative procedure do not regard themselves as bound by the existing system of rights, except insofar as that system establishes the framework of free deliberation among equals. Instead they regard that system as a potential object of their deliberative judgment.

I4    Finally, ideal deliberation aims to arrive at a rationally motivated *consensus*—to find reasons that are persuasive to all who are committed to acting on the results of a free and reasoned assessment of alternatives by equals. Even under ideal conditions there is no promise that consensual reasons will be forthcoming. If they are not, then deliberation concludes with voting, subject to some form of majority rule.[16] The fact that it may so conclude does not, however, eliminate the distinction between deliberative forms of collective choice and forms that aggregate nondeliberative preferences. The institutional consequences are likely to be different in the two cases, and the results of voting among those who are committed to finding reasons that are persuasive to all are likely to differ from the results of an aggregation that proceeds in the absence of this commitment.

Drawing on this characterization of ideal deliberation, can we say anything more substantive about a deliberative democracy? What are the implications of a commitment to deliberative decisions for the terms of social association? In the remarks that follow I shall indicate the ways that this commitment carries with it a commitment to advance the common good and to respect individual autonomy.

### Common Good and Autonomy

Consider first the notion of the common good. Since the aim of ideal deliberation is to secure agreement among all who are committed to free deliberation among equals, and the condition of pluralism obtains (D3), the focus of deliberation is on ways of advancing the aims of each party to it. While no one is indifferent to his/her own good, everyone also seeks to arrive at decisions that are acceptable to all who share the commitment to deliberation (D2). (As we shall see just below, taking that commitment seriously is likely to require a willingness to revise one's understanding of one's own preferences and convictions.) Thus the characterization of an ideal deliberative procedure links the formal notion of deliberative democracy with the more substantive ideal of a democratic association in which public debate is focused on the common good of the members.

Of course, talk about the common good is one thing; sincere efforts to advance it are another. While public deliberation may be organized around appeals to the common good, is there any reason to think that even ideal deliberation would not consist in efforts to disguise personal or class advantage as the common advantage? There are two responses to this question. The first is that in my account of the formal idea of a deliberative democracy, I stipulated (D2) that the members of the association are committed to resolving their differences through deliberation, and thus to providing reasons that they sincerely expect to be persuasive to others who share that commitment. In short, this stipulation rules out the problem. Presumably, however, the objection is best understood as directed against the plausibility of realizing a deliberative procedure that conforms to the ideal, and thus is not answerable through stipulation.

The second response, then, rests on a claim about the effects of deliberation on the motivations of deliberators.[17] A consequence of the reasonableness of the deliberative procedure (I2) together with the condition of pluralism (D3) is that the mere fact of having a preference, conviction, or ideal does not by itself provide a reason in support of a proposal. While I may take my preferences as a sufficient reason for advancing a proposal, deliberation under conditions of pluralism requires that I find reasons that make the proposal acceptable to others who cannot be expected to regard my preferences as sufficient reasons for agreeing. The motivational thesis is that the need to advance reasons that persuade others will help to shape the motivations that people bring to the deliberative procedure in two ways. First, the practice of presenting reasons will contribute to the formation of a commitment to the deliberative resolution of political questions (D2). Given that commitment, the likelihood of a sincere representation of preferences and convictions should increase, while the likelihood of their strategic misrepresentation declines. Second, it will shape the content of preferences and

convictions as well. Assuming a commitment to deliberative justification, the discovery that I can offer no persuasive reasons on behalf
of a proposal of mine may transform the preferences that motivate
the proposal. Aims that I recognize to be inconsistent with the
requirements of deliberative agreement may tend to lose their force,
at least when I expect others to be proceeding in reasonable ways
and expect the outcome of deliberation to regulate subsequent
action.

Consider, for example, the desire to be wealthier come what may.
I cannot appeal to this desire itself in defending policies. The motivational claim is the need to find an independent justification that
does not appeal to this desire and will tend to shape it into, for
example, a desire to have a level of wealth that is consistent with a
level that others (i.e., equal citizens) find acceptable. I am of course
assuming that the deliberation is known to be regulative, and that
the wealth cannot be protected through wholly nondeliberative
means.

Deliberation, then, focuses debate on the common good. And the
relevant conceptions of the common good are not comprised simply
of interests and preferences that are antecedent to deliberation.
Instead, the interests, aims, and ideals that comprise the common
good are those that survive deliberation, interests that, on public
reflection, we think it legitimate to appeal to in making claims on
social resources. Thus the first and third of the features of deliberative democracy that I mentioned in my discussion of Rawls comprise
central elements in the deliberative conception.

The ideal deliberative scheme also indicates the importance of
autonomy in a deliberative democracy. In particular, it is responsive
to two main threats to autonomy. As a general matter, actions fail to
be autonomous if the preferences on which an agent acts are,
roughly, given by the circumstances, and not determined by the
agent. There are two paradigm cases of "external" determination.
The first is what Elster (1982) has called "adaptive preferences."[18]
These are preferences that shift with changes in the circumstances
of the agent without any deliberate contribution by the agent to that
shift. This is true, for example, of the political preferences of in-
stinctive centrists who move to the median position in the political

Joshua Cohen

distribution, wherever it happens to be. The second I shall call "accommodationist preferences." While they are deliberately formed, accommodationist preferences represent psychological adjustments to conditions of subordination in which individuals are not recognized as having the capacity for self-government. Consider Stoic slaves, who deliberately shape their desires to match their powers, with a view to minimizing frustration. Since the existing relations of power make slavery the only possibility, they cultivate desires to be slaves, and then act on those desires. While their motives are deliberately formed, and they act on their desires, the Stoic slaves do not act autonomously when they seek to be good slaves. The absence of alternatives and consequent denial of scope for the deliberative capacities that defines the condition of slaves supports the conclusion that their desires result from their circumstances, even though those circumstances shape the desires of the Stoic slaves through their deliberation.

There are then at least two dimensions of autonomy. The phenomenon of adaptive preferences underlines the importance of conditions that permit and encourage the deliberative formation of preferences; the phenomenon of accommodationist preferences indicates the need for favorable conditions for the exercise of the deliberative capacities. Both concerns are met when institutions for collective decision making are modeled on the ideal deliberative procedure. Relations of power and subordination are neutralized (I1, I3, I4), and each is recognized as having the deliberative capacities (D5), thus addressing the problem of accommodationist preferences. Further, the requirement of reasonableness discourages adaptive preferences (I2). While preferences are "formed" by the deliberative procedure, this type of preference formation is consistent with autonomy, since preferences that are shaped by public deliberation are not simply given by external circumstances. Instead they are the result of "the power of reason as applied through public discussion."[19]

Beginning, then, from the formal ideal of a deliberative democracy, we arrive at the more substantive ideal of an association that is regulated by deliberation aimed at the common good and that respects the autonomy of the members. And so, in seeking to embody the ideal deliberative procedure in institutions, we seek, inter alia, to design institutions that focus political debate on the common good, that shape the identity and interests of citizens in ways that contribute to an attachment to the common good, and that provide the favorable conditions for the exercise of deliberative powers that are required for autonomy.

## III

I want now to shift the focus. While I shall continue to pursue the relationship between the ideal deliberative procedure and more substantive issues about deliberative democratic association, I want to do so by considering four natural objections to the conception I have been discussing, objections to that conception for being sectarian, incoherent, unjust, and irrelevant. My aim is not to provide a detailed response to the objections, but to clarify the conception of deliberative democracy by sketching the lines along which a response should proceed. Before turning to the objections, I enter two remarks about what follows.

First, as I indicated earlier, a central aim in the deliberative conception is to specify the institutional preconditions for deliberative decision making. The role of the ideal deliberative procedure is to provide an abstract characterization of the important properties of deliberative institutions. The role of the ideal deliberative procedure is thus different from the role of an ideal social contract. The ideal deliberative procedure provides a model for institutions, a model that they should mirror, so far as possible. It is not a choice situation in which institutional principles are selected. The key point about the institutional reflection is that it should *make deliberation possible.* Institutions in a deliberative democracy do not serve simply to implement the results of deliberation, as though free deliberation could proceed in the absence of appropriate institutions. Neither the commitment to nor the capacity for arriving at deliberative decisions is something that we can simply assume to obtain independent from the proper ordering of institutions. The institutions themselves must provide the framework for the formation of the will; they determine whether there is equality, whether deliberation is free and reasoned, whether there is autonomy, and so on.

Second, I shall be focusing here on some requirements on "public" institutions that reflect the ideal of deliberative resolution. But there is of course no reason to expect as a general matter that the preconditions for deliberation will respect familiar institutional boundaries between "private" and "public" and will all pertain to the public arena. For example, inequalities of wealth, or the absence of institutional measures designed to redress the consequences of those inequalities, can serve to undermine the equality required in deliberative arenas themselves. And so a more complete treatment would need to address a wider range of institutional issues (see Cohen and Rogers 1983, chs. 3, 6; Cohen 1988).

### Sectarianism

The first objection is that the ideal of deliberative democracy is objectionably sectarian because it depends on a particular view of the good life—an ideal of active citizenship. What makes it sectarian is not the specific ideal on which it depends, but the (alleged) fact that it depends on some specific conception at all. I do not think that the conception of deliberative democracy suffers from the alleged difficulty. In explaining why not, I shall put to the side current controversy about the thesis that sectarianism is avoidable and objectionable, and assume that it is both.[20]

Views of the good figure in political conceptions in at least two ways. First, the *justification* of some conceptions appeals to a notion of the human good. Aristotelian views, for example, endorse the claim that the exercise of the deliberative capacities is a fundamental component of a good human life, and conclude that a political association ought to be organized to encourage the realization of those capacities by its members. A second way in which conceptions of the good enter is that the *stability* of a society may require widespread allegiance to a specific conception of the good, even though its institutions can be justified without appeal to that conception. For example, a social order that can be justified without reference to ideals of national allegiance may none the less require widespread endorsement of the ideal of patriotic devotion for its stability.

A political conception is objectionably sectarian only if its *justification* depends on a particular view of the human good, and not simply because its stability is contingent on widespread agreement on the value of certain activities and aspirations. For this reason the democratic conception is not sectarian. It is organized around a view of political justification—that justification proceeds through free deliberation among equal citizens—and not a conception of the proper conduct of life. So, while it is plausible that the stability of a deliberative democracy depends on encouraging the ideal of active citizenship, this dependence does not suffice to show that it is objectionably sectarian.

### Incoherence

Consider next the putative incoherence of the ideal. We find this charge in an important tradition of argument, including Schumpeter's *Capitalism, Socialism, and Democracy* and, more recently, William Riker's work on social choice and democracy. I want here to say a word about the latter, focusing on just one reason that Riker gives for thinking that the ideal of popular self-government is incoherent.[21]

Institutionalizing a deliberative procedure requires a decision rule short of consensus—for example, majority rule. But majority rule is globally unstable: as a general matter, there exists a majority-rule path leading from any element in the set of alternatives to any other element in the set. The majority, standing in for the people, wills everything and therefore wills nothing. Of course, while anything can be the result of majority decision, it is not true that everything will be the result. But, because majority rule is so unstable, the actual decision of the majority will not be determined by preferences themselves, since they do not constrain the outcome. Instead decisions will reflect the particular institutional constraints under which they are made. But these constraints are "exogenous to the world of tastes and values" (Riker 1982, p. 190). So the ideal of popular self-government is incoherent because we are, so to speak, governed by the institutions, and not by ourselves.

Joshua Cohen

I want to suggest one difficulty with this argument that highlights the structure of the deliberative conception. According to the argument I just sketched, outcomes in majority-rule institutions reflect "exogenous" institutional constraints, and not underlying preferences. This suggests that we can identify the preferences and convictions that are relevant to collective choices apart from the institutions through which they are formed and expressed. But that is just what the deliberative conception denies. On this conception, the relevant preferences and convictions are those that could be expressed in free deliberation, and not those that are prior to it. For this reason, popular self-government *premises* the existence of institutions that provide a framework for deliberation; these arrangements are not "exogenous constraints" on the aggregation of preferences, but instead help to shape their content and the way that citizens choose to advance them. And, once the deliberative institutions are in place, and preferences, convictions, and political actions are shaped by them, it is not clear that instability problems remain so severe as to support the conclusion that self-government is an empty and incoherent ideal.

## Injustice

The third problem concerns injustice. I have been treating the ideal of democracy as the basic ideal for a political conception. But it might be argued that the ideal of democracy is not suited to the role of fundamental political ideal because its treatment of basic liberties is manifestly unacceptable. It makes those liberties dependent on judgments of majorities and thus endorses the democratic legitimacy of decisions that restrict the basic liberties of individuals. In responding to this objection I shall focus on the liberty of expression,[22] and shall begin by filling out a version of the objection which I put in the words of an imagined critic.[23]

"You embrace the ideal of a democratic order. The aim of a democratic order is to maximize the *power of the people* to secure its wants. To defend the liberty of expression you will argue that that power is diminished if the people lack the information required for exercising their will. Since expression provides information, you will conclude that abridgments of expression ought to be barred. The problem with your argument is that preventing restrictions on expression also restricts the power of the people, since the citizens may collectively prefer such restrictions. And so it is not at all clear as a general matter that the protection of expression will maximize popular power. So while you will, of course, not want to prevent everyone from speaking all the time, you cannot defend the claim that there is even a presumption in favor of the protection of expression. And this disregard for fundamental liberties is unacceptable."

This objection has force against some conceptions on which democracy is a fundamental ideal, particularly those in which the value of expression turns exclusively on its role as a source of information about how best to advance popular ends. But it does not have any force against the deliberative conception, since the latter does not make the case for expression turn on its role in maximizing the power of the people to secure its wants. That case rests instead on a conception of collective choice, in particular on a view about how the "wants" that are relevant to collective choice are formed and defined in the first place. The relevant preferences and convictions are those that arise from or are confirmed through deliberation. And a framework of free expression is required for the reasoned consideration of alternatives that comprises deliberation. The deliberative conception holds that free expression is required for *determining* what advances the common good, because what is good is fixed by public deliberation, and not prior to it. It is fixed by informed and autonomous judgments, involving the exercise of the deliberative capacities. So the ideal of deliberative democracy is not hostile to free expression; it rather presupposes such freedom.

But what about expression with no direct bearing on issues of public policy? Is the conception of deliberative democracy committed to treating all "nonpolitical expression" as second-class, and as meriting lesser protection? I do not think so. The deliberative conception construes politics as aiming in part at the formation of preferences and convictions, not just at their articulation and aggregation. Because of this emphasis on reasoning about preferences and convictions, and the bearing of expression with no political focus on such reasoning, the deliberative view draws no bright line between political speech and other sorts of expression. Forms of expression that do not address issues of policy may well bear on the formation of the interests, aims, and ideals that citizens bring to public deliberation. For this reason the deliberative conception supports protection for the full range of expression, regardless of the content of that expression.[24] It would violate the core of the ideal of free deliberation among equals to fix preferences and convictions in advance by restricting the content of expression, or by barring access to expression, or by preventing the expression that is essential to having convictions at all. Thus the injustice objection fails because the liberties are not simply among the topics for deliberation; they help to comprise the framework that makes it possible.[25]

### Irrelevance

The irrelevance objection is that the notion of public deliberation is irrelevant to modern political conditions.[26] This is the most important objection, but also the one about which it is hardest to say anything at the level of generality required by the present context. Here again I shall confine myself to one version of the objection, though one that I take to be representative.

The version that I want to consider starts from the assumption that a direct democracy with citizens gathering in legislative assemblies is the only way to institutionalize a deliberative procedure. Premising that, and recognizing that direct democracy is impossible under modern conditions, the objection concludes that we ought to be led to reject the ideal because it is not relevant to our circumstances.

The claim about the impossibility of direct democracy is plainly correct. But I see no merit in the claim that direct democracy is the uniquely suitable way to institutionalize the ideal procedure.[27] In fact, in the absence of a theory about the operations of democratic assemblies—a theory which cannot simply stipulate that ideal conditions obtain—there is no reason to be confident that a direct democracy would subject political questions to deliberative resolution, even if a direct democracy were a genuine institutional possibility.[28] In the absence of a realistic account of the functioning of citizen assemblies, we cannot simply assume that large gatherings with open-ended agendas will yield any deliberation at all, or that they will encourage participants to regard one another as equals in a free deliberative procedure. The appropriate ordering of deliberative institutions depends on issues of political psychology and political behavior; it is not an immediate consequence of the deliberative ideal. So, far from being the only deliberative scheme, direct democracy may not even be a particularly good arrangement for deliberation. But, once we reject the idea that a direct democracy is the natural or necessary form of expression of the deliberative ideal, the straightforward argument for irrelevance no longer works. In saying how the ideal might be relevant, however, we come up against the problem I mentioned earlier. Lacking a good understanding of the workings of institutions, we are inevitably thrown back on more or less speculative judgments. What follows is some sketchy remarks on one issue that should be taken in this spirit.

At the heart of the institutionalization of the deliberative procedure is the existence of arenas in which citizens can propose issues for the political agenda and participate in debate about those issues. The existence of such arenas is a public good, and ought to be supported with public money. This is not because public support is the only way, or even the most efficient way, of ensuring the provision of such arenas. Instead, public provision expresses the basic commitment of a democratic order to the resolution of political questions through free deliberation among equals. The problem is to figure out how arenas might be organized to encourage such deliberation.

In considering that organization, there are two key points that I want to underscore. The first is that material inequalities are an important source of political inequalities. The second point—which is more speculative—is that deliberative arenas which are organized exclusively on local, sectional or issue-specific lines are unlikely to produce the open-ended deliberation required to institutionalize a deliberative procedure. Since these arenas bring together only a narrow range of interests, deliberation in them can be expected at best to produce coherent sectional interests, but no more comprehensive conception of the common good.

These two considerations together provide support for the view that political parties supported by public funds play an important role in making a deliberative democracy possible.[29] There are two reasons for this, corresponding to the two considerations I have just mentioned. In the first place, an important feature of organizations generally, and parties in particular, is that they provide a means through which individuals and groups who lack the "natural" advantage of wealth can overcome the political disadvantages that follow on that lack. Thus they can help to overcome the inequalities in deliberative arenas that result from material inequality. Of course, to play this role, political organizations must themselves be freed from the dominance of private resources, and that independence must be manifest. Thus the need for public funding. Here we arrive back at the second point that I mentioned in the discussion of Rawls's view— that measures are needed to ensure manifest equality—though now as a way of displaying a shared commitment to deliberative decisions, and not simply as an expression of the commitment to fairness. Second, because parties are required to address a comprehensive range of political issues, they provide arenas in which debate is not restricted in the ways that it is in local, sectional, or issue-specific organizations. They can provide the more open-ended arenas needed to form and articulate the conceptions of the common good that provide the focus of political debate in a deliberative democracy.

There is certainly no guarantee that parties will operate as I have just described. But this is not especially troubling, since there are no guarantees of anything in politics. The question is how we can best approximate the deliberative conception. And it is difficult to see how that is possible in the absence of strong parties, supported with public resources (though, of course, a wide range of other conditions are required as well).

## IV

I have suggested that we take the notion of democratic association as a fundamental political ideal, and have elaborated that ideal by reference to an ideal deliberative procedure and the requirements for institutionalizing such a procedure. I have sketched a few of those requirements here. To show that the democratic ideal can play

Deliberation and Democratic Legitimacy

the role of a fundamental organizing ideal, I should need to pursue the account of fundamental liberties and political organization in much greater detail and to address a wide range of other issues as well. Of course, the richer the requirements are for institutionalizing free public deliberation, the larger the range of issues that may need to be removed from the political agenda; that is, the larger the range of issues that form the background framework of public deliberation rather than its subject matter. And, the larger that range, the less there is to deliberate about. Whether that is good news or bad news, it is in any case a suitable place to conclude.

## Notes

I have had countless discussions of the subject matter of this paper with Joel Rogers, and wish to thank him for his unfailingly sound and generous advice. For our joint treatment of the issues that I discuss here, see Cohen and Rogers (1983), ch. 6. The main differences between the treatment of issues here and the treatment in the book lie in the explicit account of the ideal deliberative procedure, the fuller treatment of the notions of autonomy and the common good, and the account of the connection of those notions with the ideal procedure. An earlier draft of this paper was presented to the Pacific Division Meetings of the American Philosophical Association. I would like to thank Alan Hamlin, Loren Lomasky, and Philip Pettit for helpful comments on that draft.

1. I originally came across the term "deliberative democracy" in Sunstein (1985). He cites (n. 26) an article by Bessette, which I have not consulted.

2. For some representative examples, see Sunstein (1984, 1985, 1986), Michelman (1986), Ackerman (1984, 1986).

3. I have in mind, in particular, criticisms which focus on the ways in which material inequalities and weak political parties restrict democracy by constraining public political debate or undermining the equality of the participants in that debate. For discussion of these criticisms, and of their connections with the ideal of democratic order, see Cohen and Rogers (1983), chs. 3, 6; Unger (1987), ch. 5.

4. In the discussion that follows, I draw on Rawls (1971, esp. sections 36, 37, 43, 54; 1982).

5. This rejection is not particularly idiosyncratic. Sunstein, for example, argues (1984, 1985) that ideal pluralism has never been embraced as a political ideal in American public law.

6. Officially, the requirement of fair value is that "everyone has a fair opportunity to hold public office and to influence the outcome of political decisions" (Rawls 1982, p. 42).

7. Whatever their stringency, these distributional requirements take priority over the difference principle, since the requirement of fair value is part of the principle of liberty; that is, the first principle of justice (Rawls 1982, pp. 41–42).

8. The importance of democratic politics in the account of the acquisition of the sense of justice is underscored in Rawls (1971), pp. 473–474.

9. The principle of participation states that "all citizens are to have an equal right to take part in, and to determine the outcome of, the constitutional process that establishes the laws with which they are to comply" (Rawls 1971, p. 221).

10. I assume that the principle of participation should be understood here to include the requirement of the fair value of political liberty.

11. The reasons for the phrase "in the first instance" are clarified below at pp. 74–75.

12. Since writing the first draft of this section of the paper, I have read Elster (1986) and Manin (1987), which both present parallel conceptions. This is especially so with Elster's treatment of the psychology of public deliberation (pp. 112–113). I am indebted to Alan Hamlin for bringing the Elster article to my attention. The overlap is explained by the fact that Elster, Manin, and I all draw on Habermas. See Habermas (1975, 1979, 1984). I have also found the discussion of the contractualist account of motivation in Scanlon (1982) very helpful.

13. For philosophical discussions of the importance of manifestness or publicity, see Kant (1983), pp. 135–139; Rawls (1971), p. 133 and section 29; Williams (1985), pp. 101–102, 200.

14. The distinction between the ideal procedure and an initial-choice situation will be important in the later discussion of motivation formation (see pp. 76–77) and institutions (pp. 79–80).

15. There are of course norms and requirements on individuals that do not have deliberative justification. The conception of deliberative democracy is, in Rawls's term, a "political conception" and not a comprehensive moral theory. On the distinction between political and comprehensive theories, see Rawls (1987), pp. 1–25.

16. For criticism of the reliance on an assumption of unanimity in deliberative views, see Manin (1987), pp. 359–361.

17. Note the parallel with Elster (1986) indicated in note 12. See also the discussion in Habermas (1975), p. 108, about "needs that can be communicatively shared," and Habermas (1979), ch. 2.

18. For an interesting discussion of autonomous preferences and political processes, see Sunstein (1986 pp. 1145–1158; 1984, pp. 1699–1700).

19. Whitney *vs.* California, 274 US 357 (1927).

20. For contrasting views on sectarianism, see Rawls (1987); Dworkin (1985), part 3; MacIntyre (1981); Sandel (1982).

Deliberation and Democratic Legitimacy

21. See Riker (1982); for discussion of Riker's view see Coleman and Ferejohn (1986); Cohen (1986b).

22. For discussion of the connection between ideals of democracy and freedom of expression, see Meikeljohn (1948), Tribe (1978; 1985, ch. 2) and Ely (1980, pp. 93–94, 105–116). Freedom of expression is a special case that can perhaps be more straightforwardly accommodated by the democratic conception than liberties of conscience, or the liberties associated with privacy and personhood. I do think, however, that these other liberties can be given satisfactory treatment by the democratic conception, and would reject it if I did not think so. The general idea would be to argue that other fundamental liberties must be protected if citizens are to be able to engage in and have equal standing in political deliberation without fear that such engagement puts them at risk for their convictions or personal choices. Whether this line of argument will work out on the details is a matter for treatment elsewhere. See "Procedure and Substance in Deliberative Democracy," below.

23. This objection is suggested in Dworkin (1985), pp. 61–63. He cites the following passage from a letter of Madison's: "And a people who mean to be their own Governors, must arm themselves with *the power which knowledge gives*" (emphasis added).

24. On the distinction between content-based and content-neutral abridgments, the complexities of drawing the distinction in particular cases, and the special reasons for hostility to content-based abridgments, see Tribe (1978), pp. 584–682; Stone (1987), pp. 46–118.

25. I am not suggesting that the deliberative view provides the only sound justification for the liberty of expression. My concern here is rather to show that the deliberative view is capable of accommodating it.

26. For an especially sharp statement of the irrelevance objection, see Schmitt (1985).

27. This view is sometimes associated with Rousseau, who is said to have conflated the notion of democratic legitimacy with the institutional expression of that ideal in a direct democracy. For criticism of this interpretation, see Cohen (1986a).

28. Madison urges this point in the *Federalist Papers*. Objecting to a proposal advanced by Jefferson which would have regularly referred constitutional questions "to the decision of the whole of society," Madison argues that this would increase "the danger of disturbing the public tranquillity by interesting too strongly the public passions." And "it is the reason, alone, of the public that ought to control and regulate the government . . . [while] the passions ought to be controlled and regulated by the government" (*Federalist Papers* 1961, pp. 315–317). I endorse the form of the objection, not its content.

29. Here I draw on Cohen and Rogers (1983), pp. 154–157. The idea that parties are required to organize political choice and to provide a focus for public deliberation is one strand of arguments about "responsible parties" in American political-science literature. My understanding of this view has been greatly aided by Perlman (1987), and, more generally, by the work of my colleague Walter Dean Burnham on the implications of party decline for democratic politics. See, for example, Burnham (1982).

# References

Ackerman, B. 1984: The Storr Lectures: Discovering the Constitution. *Yale Law Journal* 93: 1013–1072.

Ackerman, B. 1986: Discovering the Constitution. Unpublished manuscript.

Burnham, W. D. 1982: *The Current Crisis in American Politics.* Oxford: Oxford University Press.

Cohen, J. 1986a: Autonomy and democracy: reflections on Rousseau. *Philosophy and Public Affairs* 15: 275–297.

Cohen, J. 1986b: An epistemic conception of democracy. *Ethics* 97: 26–38.

Cohen, J. 1988: The economic basis of deliberative democracy. *Social Philosophy and Policy* 6/2: 25–50.

Cohen, J., and Rogers, J. 1983: *On Democracy.* Harmondsworth: Penguin.

Coleman, J. and Ferejohn, J. 1986: Democracy and social choice. *Ethics* 97: 6–25.

Dworkin, R. 1985: *A Matter of Principle.* Cambridge, Mass.: Harvard University Press.

Elster, J. 1982: Sour grapes. In A. Sen and B. Williams (eds), *Utilitarianism and Beyond,* Cambridge: Cambridge University Press, 219–238.

Elster, J. 1986: The market and the forum: three varieties of political theory. In J. Elster and A. Hylland (eds), *Foundations of Social Choice Theory.* Cambridge: Cambridge University Press, 103–132. Also this volume, chap. 1.

Ely, J. H. 1980: *Democracy and Distrust: a theory of judicial review.* Cambridge, Mass.: Harvard University Press.

*Federalist Papers* 1961: ed. C. Rossiter. New York: New American Library.

Habermas, J. 1975: *Legitimation Crisis,* tr. T. McCarthy. Boston: Beacon Press; London: Heinemann.

Habermas, J. 1979: *Communication and the Evolution of Society,* tr. T. McCarthy. Boston: Beacon Press.

Habermas, J. 1984: *The Theory of Communicative Action,* vol. 1, tr. T. McCarthy. Boston: Beacon Press.

Kant, I., tr. T. Humphrey 1983: Toward perpetual peace: a philosophical essay. In *Perpetual Peace and Other Essays.* Indianapolis: Hackett, 107–143.

MacIntyre, A. 1981: *After Virtue.* Notre Dame: University of Notre Dame Press.

Manin, B. 1987: On legitimacy and political deliberation. *Political Theory* 15: 338–368.

Meikeljohn, A. 1948: *Free Speech and Its Relation of Self-Government.* New York: Harper and Row.

Michelman, F. I. 1986: The Supreme Court, 1985 Term—Foreword: Traces of Self-government. *Harvard Law Review* 100:4–77.

Perlman, L. 1987: Parties, democracy and consent. Unpublished.

Rawls, J. 1971: *Theory of Justice.* Cambridge, Mass.: Harvard University Press; also Oxford: Clarendon Press, 1972.

Rawls, J. 1982: The basic liberties and their priority. *Tanner Lectures on Human Values.* Salt Lake City: University of Utah Press, vol. III.

Rawls, J. 1987: The idea of an overlapping consensus. *Oxford Journal of Legal Studies* 7: 1–25.

Riker, W. 1982: *Liberalism against Populism: A Confrontation between the Theory of Democracy and the Theory of Social Choice.* San Francisco: W. H. Freeman.

Sandel, M. 1982: *Liberalism and the Limits of Justice.* Cambridge: Cambridge University Press.

Scanlon, T. M. 1982: Contractualism and utilitarianism. In A. Sen and B. Williams (eds.), *Utilitarianism and Beyond.* Cambridge: Cambridge University Press, 103–128.

Schmitt, C. 1985: *The Crisis of Parliamentary Democracy,* tr. E. Kennedy. Cambridge, Mass.: MIT Press.

Stone, G. 1987: Content-neutral restrictions. *University of Chicago Law Review* 54: 46–118.

Sunstein, C. 1984: Naked preferences and the constitution. *Columbia Law Review* 84: 1689–1732.

Sunstein, C. 1985: Interest groups in American public law. *Stanford Law Review* 38: 29–87.

Sunstein, C. 1986: Legal interference with private preferences. *University of Chicago Law Review* 53: 1129–1184.

Tribe, L. 1978: *American Constitutional Law.* Mineola, N.Y.: Foundation Press.

Unger, R. 1987: *False Necessity.* Cambridge: Cambridge University Press.

Williams, B. 1985: *Ethics and the Limits of Philosophy.* Cambridge, Mass.: Harvard University Press; London: Fontana, Collins.

# 4

## The Idea of Public Reason

*John Rawls*

A political society, and indeed every reasonable and rational agent, whether it be an individual, or a family or an association, or even a confederation of political societies, has a way of formulating its plans, of putting its ends in an order of priority and of making its decisions accordingly. The way a political society does this is its reason; its ability to do these things is also its reason, though in a different sense: it is an intellectual and moral power, rooted in the capacities of its human members.

Not all reasons are public reasons, as there are the nonpublic reasons of churches and universities and of many other associations in civil society. In aristocratic and autocratic regimes, when the good of society is considered, this is done not by the public, if it exists at all, but by the rulers, whoever they may be. Public reason is characteristic of a democratic people: it is the reason of its citizens, of those sharing the status of equal citizenship. The subject of their reason is the good of the public: what the political conception of justice requires of society's basic structure of institutions, and of the purposes and ends they are to serve. Public reason, then, is public in three ways: as the reason of citizens as such, it is the reason of the public; its subject is the good of the public and matters of fundamental justice; and its nature and content is public, being given by the ideals and principles expressed by society's conception of political justice, and conducted open to view on that basis.

John Rawls

That public reason should be so understood and honored by citizens is not, of course, a matter of law. As an ideal conception of citizenship for a constitutional democratic regime, it presents how things might be, taking people as a just and well-ordered society would encourage them to be. It describes what is possible and can be, yet may never be, though no less fundamental for that.

## 1 The Questions and Forums of Public Reason

1. The idea of public reason has been often discussed and has a long history, and in some form it is widely accepted.[1] My aim here is to try to express it in an acceptable way as part of a political conception of justice that is broadly speaking liberal.[2]

To begin: in a democratic society public reason is the reason of equal citizens who, as a collective body, exercise final political and coercive power over one another in enacting laws and in amending their constitution. The first point is that the limits imposed by public reason do not apply to all political questions but only to those involving what we may call "constitutional essentials" and questions of basic justice. (These are specified in section 5.) This means that political values alone are to settle such fundamental questions as: who has the right to vote, or what religions are to be tolerated, or who is to be assured fair equality of opportunity, or to hold property. These and similar questions are the special subject of public reason.

Many if not most political questions do not concern those fundamental matters, for example, much tax legislation and many laws regulating property; statutes protecting the environment and controlling pollution; establishing national parks and preserving wilderness areas and animal and plant species; and laying aside funds for museums and the arts. Of course, sometimes these do involve fundamental matters. A full account of public reason would take up these other questions and explain in more detail than I can here how they differ from constitutional essentials and questions of basic justice and why the restrictions imposed by public reason may not apply to them; or if they do, not in the same way, or so strictly.

Some will ask: why not say that all questions in regard to which citizens exercise their final and coercive political power over one another are subject to public reason? Why would it ever be admissible to go outside its range of political values? To answer: my aim is to consider first the strongest case where the political questions concern the most fundamental matters. If we should not honor the limits of public reason here, it would seem we need not honor them anywhere. Should they hold here, we can then proceed to other cases. Still, I grant that it is usually highly desirable to settle political questions by invoking the values of public reason. Yet this may not always be so.

2. Another feature of public reason is that its limits do not apply to our personal deliberations and reflections about political questions, or to the reasoning about them by members of associations such as churches and universities, all of which is a vital part of the background culture. Plainly, religious, philosophical, and moral considerations of many kinds may here properly play a role. But the ideal of public reason does hold for citizens when they engage in political advocacy in the public forum, and thus for members of political parties and for candidates in their campaigns and for other groups who support them. It holds equally for how citizens are to vote in elections when constitutional essentials and matters of basic justice are at stake. Thus, the ideal of public reason not only governs the public discourse of elections insofar as the issues involve those fundamental questions, but also how citizens are to cast their vote on these questions (section 2.4). Otherwise, public discourse runs the risk of being hypocritical: citizens talk before one another one way and vote another.

We must distinguish, however, between how the ideal of public reason applies to citizens and how it applies to various officers of the government. It applies in official forums and so to legislators when they speak on the floor of parliament, and to the executive in its public acts and pronouncements. It applies also in a special way to the judiciary and above all to a supreme court in a constitutional democracy with judicial review. This is because the justices have to explain and justify their decisions as based on their understanding of the constitution and relevant statutes and precedents. Since acts of the legislative and the executive need not be justified in this way, the court's special role makes it the exemplar of public reason (section 6).

## 2 Public Reason and the Ideal of Democratic Citizenship

1. I now turn to what to many is a basic difficulty with the idea of public reason, one that makes it seem paradoxical. They ask: why should citizens in discussing and voting on the most fundamental political questions honor the limits of public reason? How can it be either reasonable or rational, when basic matters are at stake, for citizens to appeal only to a public conception of justice and not to the whole truth as they see it? Surely, the most fundamental questions should be settled by appealing to the most important truths, yet these may far transcend public reason!

I begin by trying to dissolve this paradox and invoke a principle of liberal legitimacy as explained in *Political Liberalism* (PL) IV:1.2–1.3. Recall that this principle is connected with two special features of the political relationship among democratic citizens:

First, it is a relationship of persons within the basic structure of the society into which they are born and in which they normally lead a complete life.

Second, in a democracy political power, which is always coercive power, is the power of the public, that is, of free and equal citizens as a collective body.

As always, we assume that the diversity of reasonable religious, philosophical, and moral doctrines found in democratic societies is a permanent feature of the public culture and not a mere historical condition soon to pass away.

Granted all this, we ask: when may citizens by their vote properly exercise their coercive political power over one another when fundamental questions are at stake? Or in the light of what principles and ideals must we exercise that power if our doing so is to be justifiable to others as free and equal? To this question political liberalism replies: our exercise of political power is proper and hence justifiable only when it is exercised in accordance with a constitution the essentials of which all citizens may reasonably be expected to endorse in the light of principles and ideals acceptable to them as reasonable and rational. This is the liberal principle of legitimacy. And since the exercise of political power itself must be legitimate, the ideal of citizenship imposes a moral, not a legal,

The Idea of Public Reason

duty—the duty of civility—to be able to explain to one another on those fundamental questions how the principles and policies they advocate and vote for can be supported by the political values of public reason. This duty also involves a willingness to listen to others and a fair-mindedness in deciding when accommodations to their views should reasonably be made.[3]

2. Some might say that the limits of public reason apply only in official forums and so only to legislators, say, when they speak on the floor of parliament, or to the executive and the judiciary in their public acts and decisions. If they honor public reason, then citizens are indeed given public reasons for the laws they are to comply with and for the policies society follows. But this does not go far enough.

Democracy involves, as I have said, a political relationship between citizens within the basic structure of the society into which they are born and within which they normally lead a complete life; it implies further an equal share in the coercive political power that citizens exercise over one another by voting and in other ways. As reasonable and rational, and knowing that they affirm a diversity of reasonable religious and philosophical doctrines, they should be ready to explain the basis of their actions to one another in terms each could reasonably expect that others might endorse as consistent with their freedom and equality. Trying to meet this condition is one of the tasks that this ideal of democratic politics asks of us. Understanding how to conduct oneself as a democratic citizen includes understanding an ideal of public reason.

Beyond this, the political values realized by a well-ordered constitutional regime are very great values and not easily overridden and the ideals they express are not to be lightly abandoned. Thus, when the political conception is supported by an overlapping consensus of reasonable comprehensive doctrines, the paradox of public reason disappears. The union of the duty of civility with the great values of the political yields the ideal of citizens governing themselves in ways that each thinks the others might reasonably be expected to accept; and this ideal in turn is supported by the comprehensive doctrines reasonable persons affirm. Citizens affirm the ideal of public reason, not as a result of political compromise, as in a modus vivendi, but from within their own reasonable doctrines.

John Rawls

3. Why the apparent paradox of public reason is no paradox is clearer once we remember that there are familiar cases where we grant that we should not appeal to the whole truth as we see it, even when it might be readily available. Consider how in a criminal case the rules of evidence limit the testimony that can be introduced, all this to insure the accused the basic right of a fair trial. Not only is hearsay evidence excluded but also evidence gained by improper searches and seizures, or by the abuse of defendants upon arrest and failing to inform them of their rights. Nor can defendants be forced to testify in their own defense. Finally, to mention a restriction with a quite different ground, spouses cannot be required to testify against one another, this to protect the great good of family life and to show public respect for the value of bonds of affection.

It may be objected that these examples are quite remote from the limits involved in relying solely on public reason. Remote perhaps but the idea is similar. All these examples are cases where we recognize a duty not to decide in view of the whole truth so as to honor a right or duty, or to advance an ideal good, or both. The examples serve the purpose, as many others would, of showing how it is often perfectly reasonable to forswear the whole truth and this parallels how the alleged paradox of public reason is resolved. What has to be shown is either that honoring the limits of public reason by citizens generally is required by certain basic rights and liberties and their corresponding duties, or else that it advances certain great values, or both. Political liberalism relies on the conjecture that the basic rights and duties and values in question have sufficient weight so that the limits of public reason are justified by the overall assessments of reasonable comprehensive doctrines once those doctrines have adapted to the conception of justice itself.[4]

4. On fundamental political questions the idea of public reason rejects common views of voting as a private and even personal matter. One view is that people may properly vote their preferences and interests, social and economic, not to mention their dislikes and hatreds. Democracy is said to be majority rule and a majority can do as it wishes. Another view, offhand quite different, is that people may vote what they see as right and true as their comprehensive convictions direct without taking into account public reasons.

the same point. For example his "Give us the Ballot" (ibid., pp. 197–200), his address of May 1957 on the third anniversary of *Brown,* and "I Have a Dream" (ibid., pp. 217–223), his keynote address of the March on Washington for civil rights, August 1963, both given in Washington before the Lincoln Memorial. Religious doctrines clearly underlie King's views and are important in his appeals. Yet they are expressed in general terms, and they fully support constitutional values and accord with public reason.

39. It seems clear from n. 30 that Channing could easily do this. I am indebted to John Cooper for instructive discussion of points in this paragraph.

40. This suggests that it may happen that for a well-ordered society to come about in which public discussion consists mainly in the appeal to political values, prior historical conditions may require that comprehensive reasons be invoked to strengthen those values. This seems more likely when there are but a few and strongly held yet in some ways similar comprehensive doctrines and the variety of distinctive views of recent times has not so far developed. Add to these conditions another: namely, the idea of public reason with its duty of civility has not yet been expressed in the public culture and remains unknown.

41. I am indebted to Robert Adams for instructive discussion of this point.

42. Think not of an actual court but of the court as part of a constitutional regime ideally conceived. I say this because some doubt that an actual supreme court can normally be expected to write reasonable decisions. Also, courts are bound by precedents in ways that public reason is not, and must wait for questions to come before them, and much else. But these points do not affect the propriety of the check suggested in the text.

## Postscript

[This postscript is adapted from the introduction to the paperback edition of Rawls's *Political Liberalism.* In the previous section, Rawls had explained that his book *Theory of Justice* presupposed that citizens agree on Kantian liberalism as a comprehensive doctrine; consequently, it did not take adequate account of the fact of pluralism.—Eds.]

A main aim of *Political Liberalism* (PL) is to show that the idea of the well-ordered society in *A Theory of Justice* may be reformulated so as to take account of the fact of reasonable pluralism. To do this it transforms the doctrine of justice as fairness as presented in *Theory* into a political conception of justice that applies to the basic structure of society.[1] Transforming justice as fairness into a political conception of justice requires reformulating as political conceptions the component ideas that make up the comprehensive doctrine of justice as fairness.[2] Some of these components may seem in *Theory* to be religious, philosophical, or moral, and indeed may actually be so, since *Theory* does not distinguish between comprehensive doctrines and political conceptions. This transformation is done in all of part I of PL and in lecture V of part II. A political conception of justice is what I call freestanding when it is not presented as derived from, or as part of, any comprehensive doctrine. Such a conception of justice in order to be a moral conception must contain its own intrinsic normative and moral ideal.

One such ideal can be set out this way. Citizens are reasonable when, viewing one another as free and equal in a system of social cooperation over generations, they are prepared to offer one another fair terms of social cooperation (defined by principles and ideals) and they agree to act on those terms, even at the cost of their own interests in particular situations, provided that others also accept those terms. For these terms to be fair terms, citizens offering them must reasonably think that those citizens to whom such terms are offered might also reasonably accept them. Note that "reasonably" occurs at both ends in this formulation: in offering fair terms we must reasonably think that citizens offered them might also reasonably accept them. And they must be able to do this as free and equal, and not as dominated or manipulated, or under the pressure of an inferior political or social position. I refer to this as the criterion of reciprocity.[3] Thus, political rights and duties are moral rights and duties, for they are part of a political conception that is a normative (moral) conception with its own intrinsic ideal, though not itself a comprehensive doctrine.[4]

For an example of the difference between the moral values of a comprehensive doctrine and the (moral) political values of a political conception, consider the value of autonomy. This value may take at least two forms. One is political autonomy, the legal independence and assured political integrity of citizens and their sharing with other citizens equally in the exercise of political power. The other form is moral autonomy expressed in a certain mode of life and reflection that critically examines our deepest ends and ideals, as in Mill's ideal of individuality,[5] or by following as best one can Kant's doctrine of autonomy.[6] While autonomy as a moral value has had an important place in the history of democratic thought, it fails to satisfy the criterion of reciprocity required of reasonable political principles and cannot be part of a political conception of justice. Many citizens of faith reject moral autonomy as part of their way of life.

In the transformation from the comprehensive doctrine of justice as fairness to the political conception of justice as fairness, the idea of the person as having moral personality with the full capacity of moral agency is transformed into that of the citizen. In moral and political philosophical doctrines, the idea of moral agency is discussed, along with agents' intellectual, moral, and emotional powers. Persons are viewed as being capable of exercising their moral rights and fulfilling their moral duties and as being subject to all the moral motivations appropriate to each moral virtue the doctrine specifies. In PL, by contrast, the person is seen rather as a free and equal citizen, the political person of a modern democracy with the political rights and duties of citizenship, and standing in a political relation with other citizens. The citizen is, of course, a moral agent, since a political conception of justice is, as we have seen, a moral conception. But the kinds of rights and duties, and of the values considered, are more limited.

The fundamental political relation of citizenship has two special features: first, it is a relation of citizens within the basic structure of society, a structure we enter only by birth and exit only by death; and second, it is a relation of free and equal citizens who exercise ultimate political power as a collective body. These two features immediately give rise to the question of how, when constitutional essentials and matters of basic justice are at stake, citizens so related can be bound to honor the structure of their constitutional regime and to abide by the statutes and laws enacted under it. The fact of reasonable pluralism raises this question all the more sharply, since it means that the differences between citizens arising from their comprehensive doctrines, religious and nonreligious, are irreconcilable and contain transcendent elements. By what ideals and principles, then, are citizens as sharing equally in ultimate political power to exercise that power so that each of them can reasonably justify their political decisions to each other?

The answer is given by the criterion of reciprocity: our exercise of political power is proper only when we sincerely believe that the reasons we offer for our political action may reasonably be accepted by other citizens as a justification of those actions.[7] This criterion applies on two levels: one is to the constitutional structure itself, and the other is to particular statutes and laws enacted in accordance with that structure. Political conceptions to be reasonable must justify only constitutions that satisfy this principle. This gives what may be called the liberal principle of legitimacy as it applies to the legitimacy of constitutions and statutes enacted under them.[8]

In order to fulfill their political role, citizens are viewed as having the intellectual and moral powers appropriate to that role, such as a capacity for a sense of political justice given by a liberal conception and a capacity to form, follow, and revise their individual doctrines of the good,[9] and capable also of the political virtues necessary for them to cooperate in maintaining a just political society. (Their capacity for the other virtues and moral motives beyond this is not of course denied.) . . .

I now consider the idea of public reason and its ideal, and supplement what is said in sections 4, 7, 8 of "The Idea of Public Reason." The reader should be careful to note the kinds of questions and forums to which public reason applies—for example, the debates of political parties and those seeking public office when discussing constitutional essentials and matters of basic justice—and distinguish them from the many places in the background culture where political matters are discussed, and often from within peoples' comprehensive doctrines.[10] This ideal is that citizens are to conduct their public political discussions of constitutional essentials and matters of basic justice[11] within the framework of what each sincerely regards as a reasonable political conception of justice, a conception that expresses political values that others as free and equal also might reasonably be expected reasonably to endorse. Thus each of us must have principles and guidelines to which we appeal in such a way that the criterion of reciprocity is satisfied. I have proposed that one way to identify those political principles and guidelines is to show that they would be agreed to in what in PL is the original position

(PL I:4). Others will think that other ways to identify these principles are more reasonable. While there is a family of such ways and such principles, they must all fall under the criterion of reciprocity.

To make more explicit the role of the criterion of reciprocity as expressed in public reason, I note that its role is to specify the nature of the political relation in a constitutional democratic regime as one of civic friendship. For this criterion, when citizens follow it in their public reasoning, shapes the form of their fundamental institutions.[12] For example—I cite easy cases—if we argue that the religious liberty of some citizens is to be denied, we must give them reasons they can not only understand—as Servetus could understand why Calvin wanted to burn him at the stake—but reasons we might reasonably expect that they as free and equal might reasonably also accept. The criterion of reciprocity is normally violated whenever basic liberties are denied. For what reasons can both satisfy the criterion of reciprocity and justify holding some as slaves, or imposing a property qualification on the right to vote, or denying the right of suffrage to women?

When engaged in public reasoning may we also include reasons of our comprehensive doctrines? I now believe, and hereby I revise section 8 in "The Idea of Public Reason," that such reasonable doctrines may be introduced in public reason at any time, provided that in due course public reasons, given by a reasonable political conception, are presented sufficient to support whatever the comprehensive doctrines are introduced to support.[13] I refer to this as the proviso[14] and it specifies what I now call the wide view of public reason. It is satisfied by the three cases discussed at pp. 120ff. Of special historical importance are the cases of the Abolitionists and the civil rights movement. I said that they did not violate what in section 8 I had called the inclusive view of public reason. Both the Abolitionists' and King's doctrines were held to belong to public reason because they were invoked in an unjust political society, and their conclusions of justice were in accord with the constitutional values of a liberal regime. I also said that there should be reason to believe that appealing to the basis of these reasons in citizens' comprehensive doctrines would help to make society more just. I now see no need for these conditions so far as they go beyond the proviso and drop them. The proviso of citizens' justifying their conclusions in due course by public reasons secures what is needed.[15] It has the further advantage of showing to other citizens the roots in our comprehensive doctrines of our allegiance to the political conception, which strengthens stability in the presence of a reasonable overlapping consensus. This gives the wide view and fits the examples in section 8.

It is crucial that public reason is not specified by any one political conception of justice, certainly not by justice as fairness alone. Rather, its content—the principles, ideals, and standards that may be appealed to—are those of a family of reasonable political conceptions of justice and this family changes over time. These political conceptions are not of course compatible and they may be revised as a result of their debates with one another. Social changes over generations also give rise to new groups with different political problems. Views raising new questions related to ethnicity, gender, and race are obvious examples, and the political conceptions that result from these views will debate the current conceptions. The content of public reason is not fixed, any more than it is defined by any one reasonable political conception.

One objection to the wide view of public reason is that it is still too restrictive. However, to establish this, we must find pressing questions of constitutional essentials or matters of basic justice that cannot be reasonably resolved by political values expressed by any of the existing reasonable political conceptions, nor also by any such conception that could be worked out. PL doesn't argue that this can never happen; it only suggests it rarely does so. Whether public reason can settle all, or almost all, political questions by a reasonable ordering of political values cannot be decided in the abstract independent of actual cases. We need such cases carefully spelled out to clarify how we should view them. For how to think about a kind of case depends not on general considerations alone but on our formulating relevant political values we may not have imagined before we reflect about particular instances.

Public reason may also seem too restrictive because it might seem to settle questions in advance. However, it does not, as such, determine or settle particular questions of law or policy. Rather, it specifies the public reasons in terms of which such questions are to be politically decided. For example, take the question of school prayer. One might suppose that a liberal position on this would reject their admissibility in public schools. But why so? We have to consider all the political values that can be invoked to settle this question and on which side the decisive reasons fall. The famous case of the debate in the Virginia House of Delegates in 1785 between Patrick Henry and James Madison over the establishment of the Anglican Church and involving religion in the schools was argued almost entirely by reference to political values alone.[16]

Perhaps others think public reason is too restrictive because it may lead to a stand-off[17] and fail to lead to agreement of views among citizens. It is alleged to be too restrictive since it doesn't supply enough reasons to settle all cases. This, however, happens not only in moral and political reasoning but in all forms of reasoning, including science and common sense. But the relevant comparison for public reasoning is to those cases in which some political decision must be made, as with legislators enacting laws and judges deciding cases. Here some political rule of action must be laid down and all must be able reasonably to endorse the process by which it is reached. Public reason sees the office of citizen with its duty of civility as analogous to that of judgeship with its duty of deciding cases. Just as judges are to decide cases by legal grounds of precedent and recognized canons of statutory interpretation and other relevant grounds, so citizens are to reason by public reason and to be guided by the criterion of reciprocity, whenever constitutional essentials and matters of basic justice are at stake.

Thus, when there seems to be a stand-off, that is, when legal arguments seem evenly balanced on both sides, judges cannot simply resolve the case by appealing to their own political views. To do that is for judges to violate their duty. The same holds with public reason: if when stand-offs occur, citizens invoke the grounding reasons of their comprehensive views,[18] then the principle of reciprocity is violated. The reasons deciding constitutional essentials and basic justice are no longer those that we may reasonably expect that all citizens may reasonably endorse, particularly those whose religious liberties, or rights to vote, or rights to fair opportunity are denied. From the

John Rawls

point of view of public reason citizens should simply vote for the ordering of political values they sincerely think the most reasonable. Otherwise we fail to exercise political power in ways that satisfy the criterion of reciprocity.

However, disputed questions, such as that of abortion, may lead to a stand-off between different political conceptions, and citizens must simply vote on the question.[19] Indeed, this is the normal case: unanimity of views is not to be expected. Reasonable political conceptions of justice do not always lead to the same conclusion, nor do citizens holding the same conception always agree on particular issues. Yet the outcome of the vote is to be seen as reasonable provided all citizens of a reasonably just constitutional regime sincerely vote in accordance with the idea of public reason. This doesn't mean the outcome is true or correct, but it is for the moment reasonable, and binding on citizens by the majority principle. Some may, of course, reject a decision, as Catholics may reject a decision to grant a right to abortion. They may present an argument in public reason for denying it and fail to win a majority.[20] But they need not exercise the right of abortion in their own case. They can recognize the right as belonging to legitimate law and therefore do not resist it with force. To do that would be unreasonable: it would mean their attempting to impose their own comprehensive doctrine, which a majority of other citizens who follow public reason do not accept. Certainly Catholics may, in line with public reason, continue to argue against the right of abortion. That the Church's nonpublic reason requires its members to follow its doctrine is perfectly consistent with their honoring public reason.[21] I do not pursue this question since my aim is only to stress that the ideal of public reason does not often lead to general agreement of views, nor should it. Citizens learn and profit from conflict and argument, and when their arguments follow public reason, they instruct and deepen society's public culture.

## Notes

1. By the basic structure is meant society's main political, constitutional, social, and economic institutions and how they fit together to form a unified scheme of social cooperation over time. This structure lies entirely within the domain of the political.

2. Not very much of the content of the doctrine of justice as fairness needs to be changed. For example, the meaning and content of the two principles of justice and of the basic structure are much the same except for the framework to which they belong. On the other hand, as I note later in the text above, PL stresses the difference between political autonomy and moral autonomy (II:6) and it is careful to emphasize that a political conception of justice covers only the former. This distinction is unknown to *Theory*, in which autonomy is interpreted as moral autonomy in its Kantian form, drawing on Kant's comprehensive liberal doctrine (*Theory*, sections 40, 78, 86).

3. See PL, pp. 49–50, 54; in emphasizing that "reasonably" occurs at both ends, so to speak, the criterion of reciprocity is stated more fully than in PL, as it needs to be.

4. See, for an example, the third view described in PL, p. 145.

5. See *On Liberty*, ch. 3, esp. paras. 1–9.

6. Recall here what was said in note 2 concerning Kant's doctrine of autonomy.

7. I note that there is, strictly speaking, no argument here. The preceding paragraph in the text simply describes an institutional context in which citizens stand in certain relations and consider certain questions, and so on. It is then said that from that context a duty arises on those citizens to follow the criterion of reciprocity. This is a duty arising from the idea of reasonableness of persons as characterized at pp. 49f. A similar kind of reasoning is found in T. M. Scanlon's "Promises and Practices," *Philosophy and Public Affairs* 19:3 (Summer 1990): 199–226. Of course, the particular cases and examples are entirely different.

8. The last two paragraphs summarize PL, pp. 135ff.

9. I use the term *doctrine* for comprehensive views of all kinds and the term *conception* for a political conception and its component parts, such as the conception of the person as citizen. The term *idea* is used as a general term and may refer to either, as the context determines. Both *Theory* and PL speak of a (comprehensive) conception of the good. From here on, it is referred to as a doctrine.

10. Public reason in political liberalism and Habermas's public sphere are not the same thing. See PL, IX: 1:382n.

11. Constitutional essentials concern questions about what political rights and liberties, say, may reasonably be included in a written constitution, when assuming the constitution may be interpreted by a supreme court, or some similar body. Matters of basic justice relate to the basic structure of society and so would concern questions of basic economic and social justice and other things not covered by a constitution.

12. It is sometimes said that the idea of public reason is put forward primarily to allay the fear of the instability or fragility of democracy in the practical political sense. That objection is incorrect and fails to see that public reason with its criterion of reciprocity characterizes the political relation with its ideal of democracy and bears on the nature of the regime whose stability or fragility we are concerned about. These questions are prior to questions of stability and fragility in the practical political sense, though of course no view of democracy can simply ignore these practical questions.

13. This is more permissive than section 8, which specifies certain conditions on their introduction in what it refers to as the inclusive view. The wide view (as I call it) is not original with me and was suggested to me by Erin Kelly (summer 1993). A similar view is found in Lawrence Solum, whose fullest statement is "Constructing an Ideal of Public Reason," *San Diego Law Review* 30:4 (Fall 1993), with a summary at pp. 747–751. There is a more recent statement in the *Pacific Philosophical Quarterly* 75:3 and 4 (Sept.–Dec. 1994).

14. Many questions may be asked about satisfying this proviso. One is: when does it need to be satisfied, on the same day or some later day? Also, on whom does the obligation to honor it fall? There are many such questions—I only indicate a few of them here. As Thompson has urged, it ought to be clear and established how the proviso is to be appropriately satisfied.

15. I do not know whether the Abolitionists and King ever fulfilled the proviso. But whether they did or not, they could have. And, had they known the idea of public reason and shared its ideal, they would have. I thank Paul Weithman for this point.

16. The most serious opposition to Jefferson's "Bill for Establishing Religious Freedom," which was adopted by the Virginia House of Delegates in 1786, was provided by the popular Patrick Henry. Henry's argument for keeping the religious establishment was based on the view that "Christian knowledge hath a natural tendency to correct the morals of men, restrain their vices, and preserve the peace of society, which cannot be effected without a competent provision for learned teachers." See Thomas J. Curry, *The First Freedoms* (New York: Oxford University Press, 1986), with ch. 4 on the case of Virginia. Henry did not seem to argue for Christian knowledge as such but rather that it was an effective way to achieve basic political values, namely, the good and peaceable conduct of citizens. Thus, I take him to mean by "vices," at least in part, those actions violating the political virtues found in political liberalism (194f.), and expressed by other conceptions of democracy. Leaving aside the obvious difficulty of whether prayers can be composed that satisfy all the needed restrictions of political justice, Madison's objections to Henry's bill turned largely on whether religious establishment was necessary to support orderly civil society—he concluded it was not. Madison's objection depended also on the historical effects of establishment both on society and on the integrity of religion itself. See Madison's "Memorial and Remonstrance" (1785) in *The Mind of the Founder,* ed. Marvin Meyers (New York: Bobbs-Merrill, 1973), pp. 7–16; and also Curry, pp. 142ff. He cited the prosperity of colonies that had no establishment, notably Pennsylvania and Rhode Island, the strength of early Christianity in opposition to the hostile Roman Empire, and the corruption of past establishments. With some care in formulation, many if not all of these arguments can be expressed in terms of political values of public reason. The special interest of the example of school prayer is that it shows that the idea of public reason is not a view about specific political institutions or policies, but a view about how they are to be argued for and justified to the citizen body that must decide the question.

17. I take the term from Paul Quinn. The idea appears at section 7.1–7.2.

18. I use the term *grounding reasons* since many who might appeal to these reasons view them as the proper grounds, or the true basis, religious or philosophical or moral, of the ideals and principles of public reasons and political conceptions of justice.

19. Some have quite naturally read note 31 to "The Idea of Public Reason" as an argument for the right to abortion in the first trimester. I do not intend it to be one.

(It does express my opinion, but an opinion is not an argument.) I was in error in leaving it in doubt that the aim of the note was only to illustrate and confirm the following statement in the text to which the note is attached: "The only comprehensive doctrines that run afoul of public reason are those that cannot support a reasonable balance [or ordering] of political values [on the issue]." To try to explain what I meant, I used three political values (of course, there are more) for the troubled issue of the right to abortion, to which it might seem improbable that political values could apply at all. I believe a more detailed interpretation of those values may, when properly developed at public reason, yield a reasonable argument. I don't say the most reasonable or decisive argument; I don't know what that would be, or even if it exists. (For an example of such a more detailed interpretation, see Judith Jarvis Thomson's "Abortion: Whose Right?" *Boston Review* 20:3 [Summer 1995] 11–15; though I would want to add several addenda to it.) Suppose now, for purposes of illustration, that there is a reasonable argument in public reason for the right of abortion but there is no equally reasonable balance, or ordering, of the political values in public reason that argues for the denial of that right. Then in this kind of case, but only in this kind of case, does a comprehensive doctrine denying the right of abortion run afoul of public reason. However, if it can satisfy the proviso of the wide public reason better, or at least as well as other views, it has made its case at public reason. A comprehensive doctrine can be unreasonable on one or several issues without being simply unreasonable.

20. For such an argument, see Cardinal Bernadin's view in "The Consistent Ethics: What Sort of Framework?" *Origins* 16 (Oct. 30, 1986), pp. 345, 347–350. The idea of public order the Cardinal presents includes these three political values: public peace, essential protections of human rights, and the commonly accepted standards of moral behavior in a community of law. Further, he grants that not all moral imperatives are to be translated into prohibitive civil statutes and thinks it essential to the political and social order to protect human life and basic human rights. The denial of the right to abortion he hopes to justify on the basis of those three values. I don't assess his argument here, except to say it is clearly cast in the form of public reason. Whether it is itself reasonable or not, or more reasonable than the arguments on the other side, is another matter. As with any form of reasoning in public reason, the reasoning may be fallacious or mistaken.

21. As far as I can see, this view is similar to Father John Courtney Murray's position about the stand the Church should take in regard to contraception in *We Hold These Truths* (New York: Sheed and Ward, 1960), pp. 157f. See also Mario Cuomo's 1984 lecture on abortion at Notre Dame in *More than Words* (New York: St. Martin's, 1993), pp. 32–51. I am indebted to Leslie Griffin and Paul Weithman for discussion and clarification about points involved in this and the two preceding notes and for acquainting me with Father Murray's view.

# II

**Recent Debates and Restatements: Reason, Politics, and Deliberation**

# 5

## How Can the People Ever Make the Laws?
## A Critique of Deliberative Democracy

*Frank I. Michelman*

### I General Ideas

How, if at all, is deliberative democracy a practically pursuable objective? I intend a conceptual rather than a pragmatic question—an inquiry into the structure and coherence of a certain practical ideal, as distinguished from an invitation for proposals about what you or I ought now to do for the sake of that or some competing ideal's advancement. Inevitably, I am concerned not with just any old notion of what the deliberative-democratic ideal might be and why it might matter, but with a certain construction of the ideal and its motivations that I develop over the course of this essay. For convenience, I attribute this construction to a certain party to democratic political thought that I'll be calling the "blue party." By "political thought" I mean the general cast of one's views with regard to the question of rightness in politics, the question of what is required of a set of political arrangements in order for them to be as they morally ought to be. We blues are presumably just one party among many that join in vocal support of the proposition that the government of a country morally ought to be democratic in character. Blues have a particular set of reasons for asserting the democratic proposition, and they correspondingly have a particular set of standards for deciding when the proposition is satisfied in practice. Blues, in other words, have a particular conception of what political democracy rightly *is*.

Frank I. Michelman

In blue political thought, as I shall be portraying it below, a certain notion of deliberative democracy figures in a way that is both pivotal and problematic. Deliberative democracy is something that blues think a country must be able to institute for the sake of political rightness, but it also has the look of something that no country can possibly institute. It is in anticipation of that sort of conclusion that I have subtitled this essay a "critique" of deliberative democracy. But the essay is at the same time a critique of blue political thought. Its twofold message is that: (1) blue thought issues in a conclusion that rightness in politics consists, in indispensable part, in a political society's dedicated pursuit of deliberative democracy, but (2) the very factors in our thought that make this the case for us also make it hard to understand how deliberative democracy (as *we* mean it) is something that *can possibly* be dedicatedly, purposefully pursued by anyone.

But what is deliberative democracy, bluely understood? It is a confection—obviously—of democracy and deliberativeness.

### Democracy

In blue thought, the democratic ideal in politics straightforwardly calls for government by the governed. "Democracy" in our time certainly signifies something beyond the rule of the many or the crowd as opposed to the few, the best, or "the one." It means that a country's political practice is not right—the practice is not as it morally ought to be—unless, in the last analysis, it leaves the country's people under their own rule. I say "in the last analysis" because the blue democratic ideal does accept a large amount of rule *pro tanto* by officers—legislative, administrative, and judicial—under forms of representative government. What the ideal seemingly cannot accept is that a country's people should fail to be themselves the authors of the laws that constitute their polity; the laws, that is, that fix the country's "constitutional essentials"—charter its popular-governmental and representative-governmental institutions and offices, define and limit their respective powers and jurisdictions, and thereby express a certain political conception. Political democracy, then, or popular political self-government, is first of all the ongoing social project of authorship of a country's fundamental laws by the country's people, in some nonfictively attributable sense. That is, of course, a question-begging formulation. A groping for closure on what it so glaringly leaves open is exactly what we are headed for.

### Deliberativeness

Before proceeding, I have to say something about how I use the terms "valid," "just," and "right" in this essay, as applied to fundamental laws. I take "validity" in fundamental lawmaking, "justice" in fundamental laws, and "rightness" in a constituted political regime or practice to be distinct notions, although intricately related ones. Very roughly, "rightness" in a regime means the regime is as it morally ought to be. "Justice" in fundamental-legislative outcomes refers to a set of process-independent standards for the treatment ("concern" and "respect") that is morally due to affected persons or groups. "Validity" in fundamental lawmaking refers to features in a lawmaking ambience or procedure that are thought to warrant a certain level of confidence in the tendency-towards-justice of the resulting laws[1]—enough confidence, that is, to qualify the containing regime as right.

According to this cluster of definitions, *justice* (if there be such a thing) is unalterably what we may call a "perfectly" process-independent standard: in judging whether fundamental laws are just (if such judgments be possible at all), no reference can ever be called for to the process of their legislation. But the definitions are contrived so as to allow that *rightness,* by contrast, may be (although it does not have to be) conceived as an "imperfectly" process-independent standard. A conception of rightness is a notion of what it means for something to be as it morally ought to be. Whatever notion of political rightness we hold, it seems that notion must itself be preprocessual, its content not contingent on any political process. Yet it would be possible to hold a (preprocessual) notion of what rightness in politics consists in, such that one cannot always (or maybe ever) judge the rightness of a regime without reference to the validity-conferring characteristics—the reasonably apprehensible epistemic or veridical, or as one might say the "justice-seeking" virtues—of the fundamental lawmaking procedures that the system employs and maintains.[2] Such a notion of rightness would be one that says that a regime of lawmakings need not, in order to be right, result in perfectly just laws; rather, it need only use procedures capable of producing laws that are valid as defined above (somewhat circularly, I admit). Such a notion might further say, conversely, that a regime is *not* right—submission to it morally ought not be undertaken or imposed—*unless* inhabitants have sufficient reason for confidence in the justice-tending character of their regime's fundamental lawmaking practice (in and only in which case the outcomes are counted as valid).

In sum, I have defined the three terms—"justice," "rightness," and "validity"—in such a way that there can be a gap between the political rightness of a regime and the perfect justice of its laws; validity is what bridges or mediates the gap. Of course, no set of definitions can *mandate* such a relaxed or compromised notion of political rightness (as some may consider it to be). What the definitions can do and have been chosen to do is accommodate the possibility of such a notion—which is indeed, as we shall see, exactly the sort of notion of political rightness that blue thought is driven to uphold.

I return, then, to "deliberativeness." I take the general notion of deliberativeness in democratic politics to refer to something in a set of (broadly speaking) procedural requirements for lawmaking that demands more for full compliance than mere occasional approval of the laws by truly measured voting majorities. Such transmajoritarian demands, as we may call them, may pertain to organizational, motivational, discursive, or (in a particular sense I'll soon explain) constitutive features of the system. Various thinkers may have various reasons for imposing transmajoritarian demands on political practice as conditions of validity, or of rightness otherwise understood, and the content of the demands may vary accordingly.

Blue thought takes the notion of "the people's" authorship of the laws to mean authorship of the laws by everyone who stands to be governed by or under them. Such a view gives rise to transmajoritarian demands on democratic lawmaking. Of course, authorship of the laws by each—by "everyone" (in some nonfictively attributable sense!)—is not at all a transparently self-explanatory notion in modern nation-state conditions, or one easily translated into practice.

But the notion may be clarifiable; it does for better or for worse convey the blue view of the matter; and this view does surely lead one to make transmajoritarian demands on lawmaking practices. In the formulation offered by Seyla Benhabib, such authorship requires that a country's processes for fundamental lawmaking be so designed and conducted that outcomes will be continually apprehensible as products of "collective deliberation conducted rationally and fairly among free and equal individuals."[3] Precisely what features in a lawmaking system suffice to let it pass this sort of test is a question that we need not try to decide here, because we use the term "deliberativeness" to refer to these normatively requisite transmajoritarian features, whatever we may finally decide they are. Pending decision, any or all of the following may count provisionally as components of deliberativeness: motivational and discursive features such as public-spiritedness and reciprocity, expectations of sincerity and of "epistemic" as opposed to pure-proceduralist disposition[4] (or, in other words, the focusing of debate on the pursuit of supposedly process-independent right answers), and commitment to public reason-giving and to various other putative discourse rules of an ideal-speech situation; organizational/institutional features such as voting rules, bicameralism, federalism, and interbranch checks and balances; and constitutive features such as basic rights of (free and equal) persons[5] and a legally protected political public sphere.

"Deliberative democracy," in sum, I take to be our name for a popularly based system or practice of fundamental lawmaking that meets a threshold standard of overall deliberativeness. The term names a system or practice whose combined organizational, motivational, discursive, and constitutive attributes are such, we judge, as to qualify its legislative outputs as approvable in the right way by all who stand to be affected. In blue thought, then, deliberative democracy is a (broadly speaking) procedural ideal correlative to a bottom-line moral demand for political self-government by the people—where "by the people" is taken to mean "by everyone."

### The Problem of Deliberative Democracy

In blue thought the idea of deliberative democracy occupies a pivotally problematic position that we can call "transcendental." My sense is that blues by and large regard the idea, or ideal, of deliberative democracy as on the whole counterfactual, but not as divorced from experience. We also regard the ideal as uncertainly defined or incompletely specified, but not as unthinkable or uninterpretable. We see this ideal as part of a rational reconstruction of the actual political self-understanding of constitutional-democratic societies—an "elucidation," as Benhabib puts it, of "the already implicit principles and logic" of historic and contemporary constitutional-democratic thought and practice.[6] By the same token, though, the practical possibility of the actual pursuit and measurable achievement of this elusive ideal figures for us as a condition of the possibility of rightness in politics. If that is so, then for the sake of blue political thought there had better not be anything we build into our regulative notion of deliberative democracy that would render the practical pursuit of this ideal conceptually impossible. The worry that gnaws at the root of this essay is that there is.

But what exactly do I mean by questioning the conceptual possibility of the pursuit of a practical idea such as deliberative democracy? Of course, we would have to specify the idea much more precisely and concretely than I have done or will here attempt to do, in order to render it into a practically pursuable shape. And most likely the motivational and discursive demands of deliberative democracy as more concretely specified will be such that, realistically, we must expect that they often will not be met in practice. Definitional and empirical worries of these kinds do not, however, threaten our ability to conceive of the pursuit of deliberative democracy. They just mean that some further definitional work is required and that real-world pursuit of the ideal will very likely always fall short of full success. We might nevertheless be able to maintain a conception of rightness in politics that depends on deliberative democracy's being something that we make it our high-priority business to pursue in earnest, and thus on deliberative democracy's being a sort of objective that anyone *could* thus dedicatedly pursue. I say "*might* nevertheless be able," in order to allow for the possibility that an unavoidable shortfall from fully successful pursuit of deliberative democracy might give rise to a "second-best" objection to the pursuit of it at all. Such an objection would rest on a judgment that outright abandonment of a destined-to-fail pursuit of that objective would land us closer to some more ultimate aim—justice, as it might be, or the justified character of political coercion that we cannot do without—to which deliberative democracy, if only it could practicably be fulfilled, would stand in some secondary or supportive relation. The possibility of such a "second-best" surprise is not, however, my focal worry at the moment. Rather, the worry is that blue thought might be building something into its notion of deliberative democracy that would make the dedicated, deliberate pursuit of it a conceptual impossibility.

What I have in mind is this: A practical idea might be so framed or structured as to set going an infinite regress of imperatives, so that not only would it be an idea that could not—literally and absolutely could not—ever be carried out, but it would also be an idea for the pursuit of which no program could ever be devised that we could even launch at a first step. Now, deliberative democracy *en bleu* is going to prove, without a doubt, to be a *recursively* or *self-referentially* structured practical idea, but recursion and self-reference in a practical idea do not make the pursuit of it impossible. You can write a book about yourself writing the book. Even if you can't exactly complete the writing of it (did Proust complete the writing of his book?), you can certainly commit yourself to the undertaking, start it up, take it a long way, and get credit for all that. Infinite regress, however, is another matter. If someone told you to write a book whose every chapter begins with the terminal sentence of an immediately preceding chapter, your problem wouldn't be an inability to complete the task, but rather an inability to begin it. The assignment would immobilize you; there would be nothing at all that you could do about it. The worry is that there is something similarly immobilizing in the demand for deliberative democracy as blue thought is driven to try to conceive it.

## II   Constructing Blue Political Thought—A Beginning

Blue political thought makes political rightness depend on an ongoing process of authorship by everyone ("in some nonfictively attributable sense") of the fundamental laws—not, however, on the basis that this dependency is certified by political-moral reasoning that we already accredit as right or by political-moral authority that we already accredit as warranted, but rather on the basis that democratic procedure is itself a validity condition for political-moral reasoning or authority in the first place. No reasoning in this field is accreditable as right, and no authority is accreditable as warranted, that does not already show democratic provenance or credentials. Blue thought is in these respects what I shall call "deeply" democratic. Correspondingly, I shall call those political institutions and practices of a country whereby everyone supposedly becomes an author ("in some nonfictively attributable sense") of the most basic of a country's basic laws the country's deeply democratic institutions and practices.

Deeply democratic though it is, blue political thought nevertheless proceeds within a thoroughly deontological-liberal outlook, as opposed to one that is either teleologically or populistically inspired. The blue view is deontological and not teleological, because it subordinates any and all pursuit of a social or collective good to a prior distributive constraint of right, of doing justice to each taken severally of as many as there are to be considered of the "self-authenticating sources of claims"[7]—the entities severally possessed of basic moral entitlements to consideration and respect—that it recognizes.[8] The blue view is liberal and not populist, because only individuals, and not any supraindividual entity such as a people or a majority, figure as self-authenticating sources of claims in the view's derivations of rightness requirements for political regimes.[9]

Blue thought's combination of liberal deontology with deep democracy may be hard to fathom at first mention, in an intellectual milieu where it has long been axiomatic that one must ultimately make one's choice between (substantive) rights and (procedural) democracy as first principles.[10] When we have come to see the precise way in which blue thought bridges the two positions, we will also see precisely how and why blue democracy must be "deliberative," and why and how, in the light of that understanding, deliberative democracy *en bleu* is such a problematic notion.

### The Deontological-Liberal Wellsprings of Blue Political Thought

Somehow or other, sooner or later, liberal deontologists have to justify civil government. "Justification" here simply means what can more or less cogently be said in response to complaint, and for liberal deontologists complaint against government must always be waiting to break out. Do you not, from time to time, experience government as an external, coercive intervention in your life and are you not abidingly aware that others surely do on many if not all of the occasions when you do not? Such, at any rate, is the deontological-liberal sense of the matter, which makes a question of justification wait expectantly upon virtually every act of government.

At the times, at least, when we turn our thoughts to practical questions of political ordering, we liberal-minded devotees of deliberative democracy see our social world as populated by individual "persons" or "subjects," conscious and regardful of themselves as such. This means we then regard ourselves and others as individuals severally possessed of minds and lives of their own and severally possessed, furthermore, of worthwhile—indeed incalculably worthwhile (a deontological moment)—capacities for rational agency, for taking some substantial degree of conscious charge of their own minds and lives, making and pursuing their own judgments about what to do, what to strive for, what is good, and what is right.[11]

However scientifically challengeable may be these attributions to persons of individualized self-possession and subjectivity, they are rampant in deontological-liberal political thought—and they lead inexorably, as we'll see, to conditioning the possible rightness of deep democratic institutions and practices on the practical pursuability of a correct entrenchment into them of transmajoritarian/deliberative provisions. This view does constantly nourish in our thought a sense of politics as coercion and government as outside force, a sense that is thankfully sometimes abeyant but is nevertheless recalcitrantly recurrent, and that the idea of deliberative democracy is meant to limit or pacify. And the view furthermore shapes our notion of what it must mean to defend the governmental presence in people's lives against imaginable complaint. For to those who cannot find it in themselves to deny the existential primacy of individuals, or the overriding value or dignity attached to the rational agency of each, or the correlative primordial claim of everyone to the same concern and respect, political justification *must* mean consent by everyone affected (another deontological moment), at least in principle (please note carefully this qualification). In other words,

Frank I. Michelman

a justification must show that all of the persons subject to the range of governmental actions in question severally have what are actually, for them as individuals (whether they appreciate this at the moment or not), good reasons to consent to the fundamental laws that constitute the system of government.

Perhaps we needn't demand such a showing for every single political act as it comes along. Perhaps for most such acts it suffices to show that they have followed properly from a prior, government-chartering (fundamental lawmaking) political act that itself can supposedly claim everyone's agreement. A division of laws into the fundamental and the ordinary perhaps allows us to concentrate our demands for universal reasonable acceptability on the fundamental laws while allowing ordinary-level political acts to be justified derivatively—to inherit justification—by showing how they issued from a universally acceptable set of fundamental, constitutive laws. The division of laws into fundamental/constitutive and ordinary caters to deontological-liberal striving, in the face of inauspicious social conditions, to preserve a sense of the justified character of political government. The inauspicious conditions are facts of modernity: societal immensity, complexity, and anonymity combined with irreducible plurality and conflict of considered political opinions. These facts evidently preclude the possibility of countrywide agreement on the political merit—the practical utility, ethical suitability, and responsiveness to everyone's interest—of the sundry, compromised legal-policy choices that day-to-day government must make. By positing a "higher" (or deeper) legal tier of relatively abstract, regulative rules and standards for the conduct of ordinary government, we may hope to have opened the possibility of countrywide rational agreement or agreement-in-principle—or something approaching it or standing in for it (an echo, there, of "nonfictively attributable" universal authorship of the laws)—on the political merit, including the fairly arguable consonance with everyone's interests, of at least these fundamental rules and standards.[12]

### Why Deep Democracy? Or, What's Wrong with Rights Foundationalism?

Standing by itself, the liberal political deontology I have charted thus far does not—at least it does not directly and self-evidently—require deep democracy. It does not require authorship of the fundamental laws by everyone, not even in any remotely figurative, much less any "nonfictively attributable," sense. All it directly requires is consent *in principle* by everyone affected—that everyone should have, as I put it above, "what are actually, for them as individuals (whether they appreciate this at the moment or not), good reasons to consent." Liberal political deontology seems fully receptive to what I'll call, following Bruce Ackerman,[13] a "rights-foundationalist" view of rightness in politics, in which there need never arise any major vexation over deliberative democracy and the possibility of its dedicated pursuit.

Consider a class of views according to which rightness in civil affairs consists in the prevalence of justice, where (1) the requirements of justice are conceived to be accessible by right reason, (2) determinations of right reason are conceived as process-independent, that is, as standing free and apart from any democratic process,[14] and (3) popular government is not itself, at any level or in any degree, conceived to be a dictate of justice as process-independent right reason determines it. Such a view would not care in any crucial way about political-procedural democracy at all, much less about either deep or deliberative democracy.

But now suppose a right on the part of everyone to participation in government *is* found to be a part of justice as process-independent right reason determines it. And even suppose, further, that right reason's conclusion in support of popular government, as a component of justice, hinges on a favorable assessment of the possibility of deliberativeness in politics, somehow more or less concretely understood. We still wouldn't be dealing with a view of rightness in politics that makes the possibility of doing what's right depend on the possibility of the pursuit or achievement of deliberative democracy. For what we are now envisioning is a *process-independent* line of right reasoning that runs roughly as follows: "I have to determine, among other things," the right-reasoner begins,

whether a just political constitution for this country does or does not include popular government as one of its components. Reason tells me that it does include it, if and only if there is warrant in reason for a certain minimum confidence level that popular government, conducted under some institutional forms that I know how to specify, will in fact attain to a certain threshold level of deliberativeness. As it happens, I do (or I don't) judge that the requisite confidence level is warranted. Accordingly, I do (or I don't) conclude that political justice does encompass popular government.

The process-independent right reasoner has to decide whether she does or does not have the requisite level of confidence in the deliberative character of an anticipated popular political process. If she does, then political rightness would encompass popular government and if she does not, it does not. Either way, political rightness remains possible. So while an assessment of the possibility of deliberative democracy does figure crucially in this kind of process-independent right reasoning about political rightness and (individuals') political rights, this possibility could not figure as a precondition of the possibility of political rightness itself. As long as political rightness is conceived to be ascertainable in principle by process-independent reason, such rightness has to remain possible, however pessimistically the right reasoner may judge the possibility of deliberative democracy or any other social process. Thus, to complete our construction of the blue view of political rightness, which makes a practically pursuable goal of deliberative democracy both necessary and deeply problematic, we need to find out precisely what prompts resistance in blue thought to a non-deep-democratic, rights-foundationalist or process-independent-right-reason-based idea of political rightness. Before explaining in part III what I understand the source of the resistance to be, I first briefly consider and find wanting, in the two subparts below, two other possible sources that I expect will occur to some readers.

### "Full Autonomy"

Suppose you affirm an overriding moral requirement of individual freedom, somewhat demandingly understood—freedom, that is, understood "positively" (as well as, no doubt, "negatively"), so that I am not in a fully adequate state of freedom, or "fully autonomous," unless the constitutive laws of the regime that regulates my affairs are ones that *I* myself have approved as laws of justice—for the reason, let us say, that I have found them to be reasonably and rationally approvable by everyone as free and equal. (My willing submission to regulation by a regime whose fundamental laws I have *not* thus approved would be, then, a case of heteronomy.) "Full autonomy" is John Rawls's term, and he does seem to envision by it the fully autonomous person's conscious affirmance of the harmony of her political regime with true principles of justice. When Rawls writes that full autonomy "is realized by citizens when they act from principles of justice that specify the fair terms of cooperation they *would* give themselves when fairly represented as free and equal persons,"[15] he evidently means that they act from principles that *they themselves just then appreciate* would issue from such a representation of them.[16]

In Rawls's view, full autonomy corresponds to an interest, of sorts, of individuals. It is the fulfillment of individuals' "higher-order interest" in the simultaneous exercise of their capacities for public justice and for rationally conceiving and pursuing their own self-responsibly determined ideas of the good.[17] Perhaps we can get from there to a conclusion that it's a requirement of rightness in politics—for the sake of everyone's full autonomy—that a country's fundamental laws should be such as to invite continuous affirmation on the part of every inhabitant as free, equal, reasonable, and rational. But such a requirement wouldn't yet take us past rights foundationalism to deep democracy, for it wouldn't yet require actual, public, discursive engagement among inhabitants over the contents of their country's constitutive laws. Rather, this requirement would be satisfiable, in theory, by everyone's separately reading, cogitating, and considerately endorsing a single philosopher's book—*Theory of Justice,* for example—addressed to the search for a set of fundamental laws that everyone as free and equal might reasonably and rationally affirm.[18]

### The "Co-originality of Private and Public Autonomy": Enfranchisement as a Constitutive Right

Ideally, according to the blue view, fundamental laws should be understandable as outcomes of "collective deliberation[s] conducted rationally and fairly among free and equal individuals."[19] But what, for such purposes, are the freedom and equality of individuals

Frank I. Michelman

if not the manner in which we dependably regard and treat one another as coparticipants in public life? Presuppositional, then, to a deep-democratic discursive encounter among free and equal persons is a set of institutionally supported norms—one might as well call them rights—that govern the treatment of persons by one another in respects pertinent to participation in public discourse.[20] Is not this a part, at least, of what a blue partisan like Jürgen Habermas has in mind when he speaks of the "co-originality of civic and private autonomy?"[21] If so, political rightness will always require the presence on the scene of individuals already constituted by law as free and equal.[22]

Blue constitutive rights are constitutive in two respects: on one side, they are constitutive of free-and-equal persons; on the other, they are constitutive of a liberal-not-populist-yet-deep-democratic political regime. Unsurprising then would be a guess that among the constitutive rights of individuals is one to a direct voice and vote in all determinations of the fundamental laws of the regime to which one is subject. Many have maintained that political enfranchisement of that kind is every person's due just in virtue of the respect owed him or her as presumptively free and equal. Is it possible, though, to think *that*, while also deontologically-liberally maintaining that the right in politics requires fundamental legal dispensations that truly are rationally approvable by everyone as in their respective interests? Given the obvious conceptual gap between (i) a procedure designed to afford equal and adequate participation to everyone and (ii) a procedure geared to issue in a set of fundamental laws that are rationally approvable by everyone, how can one uphold simultaneously both (i) an aprioristic universal right of political enfranchisement and (ii) a rightness requirement that fundamental laws be rationally approvable by everyone as in their respective interests? If that is possible at all (a question I do not here try to resolve), it can only be by strictly conceiving the right of enfranchisement as a right of participation in an aptly constituted procedure—which is to say, a suitably deliberative procedure—for public discourse over the very question of devising laws that can meet the test of universal rational-and-reasonable approvability. And now, at last, we may see taking shape before us a requirement of deliberativeness as a precondition of democratic political rightness. The deliberativeness requirement

then would seem to result from the positing of an aprioristic universal individual right of enfranchisement within a generally deontological liberal approach to the question of political rightness.

But we aren't yet past rights-foundationalism and into deep democracy, because that "posited" right of enfranchisement didn't just
present itself for no reason. Rather it comes, it would seem, out of
some prior stage of process-independent right reasoning about political justice. And then what is before us is a case of purported right
reasoning about political justice issuing in a conclusion that the
fundamental laws of a country ought absolutely and always to make
provision—from here on in, and always subject to this very requirement of which we are now speaking—for the universal rights of
individuals to take their parts as free and equal in practical discourses over fundamental lawmaking. The absolute and ultimate
entrenchment of the enfranchisement right would itself have to
stand, though, as a dictate of process-independent right reason—
albeit reason reflecting on the presuppositions of a collective deliberation among free and equal individuals.

Now, this cannot quite be the full blue view as I am trying to
construct it in this essay, because the view as I've undertaken to
construct it is *unrestrictedly* "process-bound." It is, so to speak, process-bound "all the way down," fitting into its generally deontological-
liberal approach to political rightness a demand for democratic
procedure even at the point of deciding the *most* fundamental laws—
or principles or norms—of the regime.[23] This melding in blue
thought of unrestricted process-boundness with a universalistic commitment to equality of respect makes deliberative democracy become, in blue thought, both a necessary and deeply problematic
idea. But we still have to specify what is prompting the trouble-
making blue requirement of unrestricted process-boundness.

## III  Strong Normative Epistemic Democracy

With this question in mind, I turn now to recent writings of Jürgen
Habermas to see how he comes to endorse such a requirement.
Habermas, I am saying, remains in other respects a true blue deon-
tological liberal when it comes to the question of political rightness.
Nevertheless, his thought—which I take to be representative in this

respect of blue thought—makes political rightness dependent from the start, or dependent all the way down, on validation supposed to be obtainable only through the constant availability of broadly participatory, actual democratic political processes to take up any question whatever of fundamental law.[24]

According to Habermas, the "validity" of a legal enactment arises from a combination of two factors: the apparent "facticity" of legal enforcement (i.e., the state's readiness, using compulsion if necessary, to ensure "average compliance" with the law once enacted), and an "expectation of legitimacy." For Habermas, a law's "legitimacy" signifies the content-evaluative or "normative" aspect of the law's validity. But, in tune with our own earlier definition of validity, legitimacy-as-aspect-of-validity does not mean for Habermas a direct judgment of the law's absolute moral correctness; it rather signifies a more oblique, probabilistically mediated sort of morally inflected judgment.[25] In the words of Habermas, legitimacy (as an aspect of validity) signifies the possibility of uncoerced compliance out of "respect" for the law, born of an "expectation" that the laws altogether "guarantee the autonomy of all persons equally." But what makes "possible" such an expectation is the apparent fulfillment of certain "institutional preconditions for the legitimate genesis" of enacted legal norms. Just as we ourselves stipulated, then, the validity ("legitimacy") of a fundamental law depends on something about the provenance of the law.[26]

More specifically, Habermas declares that "the *democratic procedure* for the production of law evidently forms the only postmetaphysical source of legitimacy."[27] On his account, the legitimacy-conferring characteristic of a fundamental law—the characteristic by virtue of which the law exerts upon all within range of its coercive potential a claim to rational acceptability—is and can only be a procedurally constructed characteristic: Only those fundamental laws are legitimate, Habermas avers, that might claim the agreement of all citizens in a discursive process equally open to all.[28] Now *that* agreement may be hypothetical or in principle.[29] Nevertheless, the judgment that all do indeed have reason to agree must in his view arise against the background of an actual democratic-discursive forum to which the question is at all times submissible. Only such constant submissibility to actual democratic-discursive reexamination can sustain a "presumption" of fair results.[30]

However, we still want to know what is prompting this blue demand for unrestricted process-boundness, within an otherwise deontological-liberal view of political rightness to which a rights-foundationalist position seems so apparently congenial. For Habermas, a crucial proposition is that no political philosopher or lawgiver, or select group of them, unaided by actual live dialogic encounter with the full range of affected others, can reliably presume to see and appraise a set of proposed fundamental laws as all those others will reasonably and justifiably see and appraise them. No unaided internal effort of empathy can suffice to answer the question of universal reasonable approvability of the fundamental laws, reliably enough to pass the test of legitimacy on which the rightness of a coercion-backed political regime depends. "[I]ndividual private rights," Habermas writes in one exemplary passage,

cannot even be adequately formulated, let alone politically implemented, if those affected have not first engaged in public discussions to clarify which features are relevant in treating typical cases as alike or different, and then mobilized communicative power for the consideration of their newly interpreted needs.[31]

Only by actual democratic discourses, Habermas apparently means, can we attend to possibilities of the sort described by Nancy Fraser:

that biases might become apparent in even what have been thought to be relatively neutral forms of discourse; that such forms could themselves become stakes in political deliberation; that subordinated groups could contest such forms and propose alternatives, and thereby gain a measure of collective control over the means of interpretation and communication.[32]

These possibilities would explain why Habermas thinks that, as a condition of legitimacy, "consociates under law must be able to *examine* whether a contested norm . . . could meet with the agreement of all those possibly affected"[33]—why only an actual available process of deeply democratic scrutiny can begin to "justif[y] [a] presumption" of fair results.

We would have before us, then, what we may call a "strong normative version of an epistemic theory of democracy." By an "epistemic

Frank I. Michelman

theory of democracy" I mean a theory that cites, as one reason for favoring democratic procedures, a supposed tendency in such procedures to reach outcomes approximating to procedure-independent standards of political rightness or justice (such as that fundamental laws should conform to the Rawlsian two principles of justice as fairness; or that they should be nonrejectable by anyone who reasonably seeks a set of fundamental laws that other, similarly reasonably disposed participants could not reasonably reject;[34] or that they should be rationally acceptable to everyone as in their respective interests; or that they should be such as could in principle have been the consensus outcome of a fairly constituted democratic discourse). I call the blue version of epistemic-democracy theory a "strong normative" one because it goes beyond offering the claimed epistemic virtues of democratic-discursive procedures as a functional argument in favor of their use: it also asserts that a political system that omits them fails for that very reason to produce valid laws and fails, therefore, to be a morally defensible system. Strong normative-epistemic considerations are the only motivation I have been able to find for blue thought's attempt at the unlikely-seeming combination of a decisively deontological-liberal view of political rightness with an unrestricted binding of political right reason to democratic process "all the way down" the hierarchy of legal norms.

## IV  The Regress Problem

However, this combination harbors a serious difficulty. On the epistemic-democratic reading of the blue commitment to deep democracy, right reasoning about the right in politics is unrestrictedly bound to an adequately or properly democratic process. But the question of what *is* (for this purpose) an adequate or proper process is one that must itself fall under right reason's jurisdiction. Where but to right reason should we look for an answer? Doesn't some philosopher finally have to step forward and take responsibility here, as a putative fundamental lawgiver? For that matter, hasn't Habermas himself set the example?

Habermas has, after all, famously argued that a distinct, if abstract, idea of procedural fairness can be gathered from reflection on the

presuppositions of a discussion by which an otherwise radically diverse and divided set of participants honestly mean to find agreement on the universally, rationally, self-respectingly acceptable character of some set of norms to govern their social life.[35] In *Between Facts and Norms,* moreover, Habermas has affirmed his belief that a relatively abstract idea of procedural fairness, thus derived, can point the way toward a relatively concrete prescription for a constitutional bill of rights or body of fundamental laws. The makings of a rights-foundationalist view of political rightness seem to be there.

If Habermas does not finally and unambiguously offer such a view, is it not because he finally doubts that the rationally accessible idea of a fair democratic procedure does itself go far enough to resolve the specification of a set of fundamental laws for a given country in given times? The relatively concrete terms and conditions of a democratic debate that is *fair* and *open to all,* in the sense required for the universal rational acceptability of lawmaking occurrent in its wake (if that is what rightness demands), are themselves reasonably contestable and actually contested, and the acceptability judgments of sundry putatively free and equal persons will not be indifferent to how the contests are resolved. Is the procedure relevantly and properly democratic only in the absence (as some would claim) or only in the presence (as others would oppositely claim) of certain controls on economic inequality or of certain positive social and economic guarantees—subsistence, health care, housing, education? In the absence (or, oppositely, in the presence) of worker security, collective bargaining, or industrial democracy rights? In the absence (or in the presence) of affirmative action, or of cumulative voting or proportional representation? In the absence (or in the presence) of federalism or of intragovernmental countermajoritarian checks—bicameral legislatures, executive vetos, supermajority requirements? In the absence (or in the presence) of restrictions on "hate speech," or of controls on political spending and access to media, or of guarantees of procreational autonomy, or of barriers to religious expression in public educational and spaces? All these variables (and others) are sharply contested in our political culture, just as matters of what a democratic procedure properly is. Yet resolving them seems to be

Frank I. Michelman

quintessential grist for democracy's mill—questions for democratic resolution if any questions are.

Suppose blue thought, epistemically-democratically construed, is correct about the deep-democratic prerequisites for valid fundamental lawmaking and hence for political rightness. It follows that only in the wake of a proper democratic debate can there be valid resolutions, which can rightly be imposed on the country, of the foregoing list of arguably "procedural" questions. What validity and rightness require is that fundamental legal resolutions visibly have undergone, in the sight and minds of the legislators, the test of an actual and proper democratic debate that has not only addressed itself to the right question (is this law one to which, hypothetically, all citizens might rationally be expected to agree in an ideally democratic discourse?) but that also was itself an instance of such a discourse, or at any rate was "open to all" in some uncompromisingly normatively requisite sense.

Only in the wake of a proper democratic debate, on the epistemic-democratic reading of blue thought, can that sort of question be validly resolved. But that sort of question is exactly the sort of question presented by the contestable and contested notion of a proper democratic debate, one that is "fairly" open to all in the way required to instill the procedure with the very epistemic virtue that's supposed to make it validity-conferring and hence morally mandatory. As Habermas himself arrestingly puts the matter, a validity-conferring procedure of democratic examination of the laws must be one "that is itself legally constituted."[36] If so, and if it takes a legally constituted democratic procedure to bring forth valid fundamental laws, then the (valid) laws that frame *this* lawmaking event must themselves be the product of a conceptually prior procedural event that was itself framed by (valid) laws that must, as such, have issued in their turn from a still prior (properly) legally constituted event. And so on, it would appear, without end: "The idea of the rule of law sets in motion a spiraling self-application of law."[37]

To recapitulate: according to blue thought epistemically-democratically construed, the rational derivability of fundamental laws from the very idea of a critically self-conscious, democratic discourse directed to universal reasonable agreement is a necessary condition of rightness in politics. It is not, however, a sufficient condition, and what keeps it from being one is a circumstance of pluralism: we have not, as particular individuals and groups, sufficient reason to submit our political fates to what any given gang of savants may *say* are the true derivations of constitutional norms from the idea of democratic discourse. In these circumstances, nothing suffices for validity short of actual submissibility, at any time, of pending derivations to the critical and corrective rigors of *actual* democratic discourses. "Consociates under law" must have access at any time to civic forums of which it is true both (1) that the forums address the correct question, that of the universal, reasonable and rational acceptability of regulative norms for politics, and (2) that the forums are themselves conducted under similarly derived regulation. Thus "the citizens themselves . . . decide how they must fashion the rights that give the discourse principle legal shape as a principle of democracy. . . . [They] make an originary use of a civic autonomy that thereby constitutes itself in a performatively self-referential manner."[38] But then the question must be: Where in history can this "originary" constitutive moment ever be fixed or anchored? Granting that it is necessary, how may it be possible?

## V Democracy and Validity

That is a very hard question. Need we answer it? Here we already are, after all, living under a set of fundamental laws (those of us who luckily are) that we as denizens of this very legal culture easily construe as an intentional, if always necessarily imperfect, approximation of the deontologically-liberally inspired deep-blue-deliberative-democratic ideal. The ideal, that is, of an endlessly cycling resubmission to the critical rigors of aspirationally democratic discourses (themselves correspondingly evolving), of the very laws that for the sake of political rightness have to constitute those discourses as both democratic and autonomous,[39] their constituents as free and equal, and so on. Although, as we have now seen, no one could have ever had a blue warrant for setting this project off on its first iteration, that truth wouldn't disable *us,* in our lucky circumstances, from doing our parts to carry the project on. We could not perfectly

Frank I. Michelman

confidently pronounce our continually evolving political practice to be issuing in just results, because as blues we would know that no acculturated denizen of *this* ostensibly deliberative-democratic practice could presume that the practice had not for some time been spiraling off in a wrong direction due to some "bias" of the kind that Nancy Fraser compellingly warns that no human flesh can ever surely evade. Might our doing our parts to uphold and advance the practice nevertheless be what rightness requires?

Here is where we most tellingly see the crucial place in blue political thought of the idea of "validity"—now appearing baldly as the proposition that rightness in politics consists in making our honest best bet on the justice-tending characteristics of a fundamental lawmaking procedure. Liberal deontology tells blues that there are such things in principle as truly just (or unjust) laws. Liberal modesty tells blues that none of us knows certainly what just laws are, and that we cannot look for agreement on what they are (even after casting out all the "unreasonable" opinions) with sufficient specificity to describe a workably concrete set of constitutive laws for the country. But we do (so the blue argument goes) have "overlapping" inklings of some general contours of just institutions, and what we already have going seems to us as likely to carry us in the right direction as anything else we're capable of proposing. (It being understood, of course, that what we already have going includes an array of intentionally inbuilt autocritical capacities.)

To take validity to be the key to political rightness is to be ready, sometimes, to accept as morally binding—as a kind of "political" but not "comprehensive" truth—fundamental-law resolutions that *we now honestly* judge to be in some material degree deviant from justice, just because those resolutions came out of a democratic procedure that (i) is in force and (ii) we judge to be reasonably defensible as justice-seeking. We cannot here try to settle whether proceeding in that way truly is what anyone morally ought to do. What we can say, though, is that for the sake of deep-blue-democratic political thought, it had better be. Deep-blue-democrats have to believe that it is so, and 'twere better for us (I take it) that what we believe is so, is so. Blues have to believe it, because if at some level of awareness we believe the contrary—that not validity but justice (as best we

severally can make it out from time to time) is the key to rightness—
then we are really just a sect of rights-foundationalists *malgré nous.*

## Notes

1. Perhaps such features must exist in conjunction with nonprocedurally appraised
characteristics of the run of legislative outcomes, such as high average formal generality and high average respect for core liberties, and perhaps in further conjunction
with experience-justified expectations of the state's regular effectuation of the laws
its procedures enact.

2. "Justice-seeking" is due, I believe, to Lawrence Gene Sager. See, for example,
Sager, "The Birth Logic of a Democratic Constitution," paper presented to the N.Y.U.
Colloquium on Constitutional Theory, February 1995; Sager, "The Domain of Con-
stitutional Justice," paper presented to the N.Y.U. Colloquium on Constitutional
Theory, February 1996. See also Anthony J. Sebok, "Justice-Seeking Constitutional
Theory and the Problem of Fit," paper presented to the N.Y.U. Colloquium on
Constitutional Theory, March 1996.

3. Seyla Benhabib, "Deliberative Rationality and Models of Constitutional Legitimacy," *Constellations* 1 (1994): 26, 31.

4. See David Estlund's paper, this volume.

5. These would be rights of *private* correlative to *civic* "autonomy"—see Jürgen
Habermas, *Between Facts and Norms: Contributions to a Discourse Theory of Law and
Democracy,* tr. William Rehg (Cambridge, MA: MIT Press, 1996) 118–130—or rights
of (deliberative) *autonomy* correlative to (deliberative) *democracy*—see James E.
Fleming, "Securing Deliberative Autonomy," *Stanford Law Review* 48 (1995): 1–71. On
the idea of individuals' rights as "constitutive" of democracy, as justified for that
reason and interpretable in light of it, see Ronald Dworkin, *Freedom's Law: The Moral
Reading of the American Constitution* (Cambridge, MA: Harvard. University Press, 1996):
200–202.

6. Benhabib, "Models of Constitutional Legitimacy," 42–43.

7. John Rawls, *Political Liberalism* (New York: Columbia University Press, 1993), 32.

8. My use of the "deontological"/"teleological" opposition is also found in Rawls. See
*Theory of Justice* (Cambridge, MA: Harvard University Press, 1971), 24–26.

9. In drawing the distinction between "liberal" and "populist" outlooks, I assume the
tendency of thought to apply critical standards of moral adequacy to political arrangements, and furthermore to judge the arrangements morally adequate or not,
according to whether they do or do not honor elementary entitlements to some kind
of consideration that the thought in question attributes to entities in some class. By
"liberal" I mean thought that attributes whatever such elementary political-moral
entitlements-to-consideration it posits to individuals taken severally, whereas popu-
lists, to the contrary, begin with the proposition that among requirements of rightness in political arrangements the most basic is the entitlement of the people of a
country, somehow conceived as a single situs of political agency or "energy," to decide

Frank I. Michelman

the country's laws. See Richard D. Parker, *"Here the People Rule": A Constitutional Populist Manifesto* (Cambridge, MA: Harvard University Press, 1994).

Perhaps it's worth noting the presence in contemporary American debates of what appear to be two distinct strains of populist thought. One strain attributes the right to rule to a collective consisting of the entire population of the country, and then arrives at majority-voting as the only procedure yet discovered by which the political will of such an entity could defensibly and practicably be ascertained, constructed, or imputed. See Akhil Reed Amar, "The Consent of the Governed: Constitutional Amendment Outside Article V," *Columbia Law Review* 94 (1994): 457–508, p. 503. The other populist strain attributes the right to rule not to the whole populace (acting *faute de mieux* by majority vote) but rather to a somehow meritorious or for some other reason privileged fraction of the populace, perhaps a main or modal fraction, that is called "the majority" and that manifests itself and its will through majoritarian political processes. For example, Parker, *"Here the People Rule,"* 96–97:

> [T]he goal inspiring argument about "interpretation" of the Constitution ought to be government of, for, and—to the extent it is feasible—by the majority of the people. Of course this is simply an ideal. There is no such entity as "the majority." Yet as an ideal, . . . [the notion of the majority] conveys a powerful claim: that "common" people, ordinary people—not their "betters," not somebody else's conception of their supposed "better selves"—are the ones who are entitled to govern our country.

The quoted passage suggests resistance on Parker's part to any suggestion that political rightness might hinge on a tempering of majority rule by some further call for deliberativeness. According to Amar, by contrast, "majority rule popular sovereignty presupposes a deliberate majority of the collective 'people,' not a mere mathematical concatenation of atomized 'persons'"—meaning that "the People must . . . be exposed to and must engage opposing ideas; the majority should attempt to reason with and persuade dissenters, and vice versa." See Amar, "The Consent of the Governed," pp. 501–503. We need not here try to decide how or whether a deliberativeness standard of some kind becomes a prerequisite of political rightness in one or another form of populist thought, given that our concern is with how this occurs in a certain variant—the blue variant—of decidedly nonpopulist, deontological-liberal thought.

10. See, for example, Bruce Ackerman, *We the People: Foundations* (Cambridge, MA: Harvard University Press, 1991), 6–16.

11. To avoid suspicion that I've attributed too atomized a notion of subjectivity to blue thought, I append here "a list of attributes of persons as liberally conceived" from Frank I. Michelman, "The Subject of Liberalism," *Stanford Law Review* 46 (1994): 1807, 1812:

> Liberal subjects are [conceived as being] all of the following: ethically several, interest-bearing, self-activating, communicative, and self-conscious (or self-reflective). This means:
>
> *Ethically several:* Each subject leads a life of its own that is conceptually distinct from the lives of other subjects, and each of these several lives is a conceptually distinct field of value. ("Conceptually distinct" means that in contemplating the values of lives we take them one by one. This does not rule out causal linkages or require that the values assigned to any one subject's actions or experiences be held independent of values assigned to others' actions or experiences.)

*Interest-bearing:* Each subject stands to be differentially affected for better or worse by various events, so that the events can be judged to enhance or detract from the thriving or well-being of subjects taken one by one. (Again, this does not rule out empirical linkages between the interests of one subject and the interests of others.)

*Self-activating:* Each subject is able to contemplate its interests, to discover and present to itself corresponding reasons for action, and to act or alter its state accordingly. (This does not rule out joint, coordinated, reciprocal, or otherwise coresponsive reasons and actions.)

*Communicative:* Each subject is capable of intentionally affecting other subjects' perceptions of reasons for action and of having its own perceptions intentionally affected by others.

*Self-conscious (reflective):* Each subject is aware of itself as an ethically several, interest-bearing, self-activating, communicative subject. (This does not rule out that individual self-consciousness may depend on reciprocal awareness by subjects of each other.)

12. See, for example, Habermas, *Between Facts and Norms,* 30: "generally the legal system as a whole has a higher measure of legitimacy than individual legal norms." Compare Habermas, "Three Models of Democracy," *Constellations* 1 (1994): 1, 5. For discussion of John Rawls's version of this strategy, see Frank I. Michelman, "The Subject of Liberalism," 1807, 1827–1828.

13. See Ackerman, *Foundations,* 10–13.

14. Contrast the deep-democratic commitment of blue political thought as I rendered at pp. 151–152, above.

15. Rawls, *Political Liberalism,* 77 (emphasis supplied).

16. For this reason, I disagree in part with Habermas's complaint against Rawls's political constructivism in Habermas, "Reconciliation Through the Public Use of Reason: Remarks on John Rawls's *Political Liberalism*," *Journal of Philosophy* 92 (1995): 109, 124. See Frank I. Michelman, "Book Review," *Journal of Philosophy* 93 (1996): 307–315, 314. That Rawls's meaning is as I have suggested is confirmed by his adjacent sentences. Fully autonomous citizens, he writes,

not only comply with the principles of justice, but they also act from those principles as just. Moreover, they recognize these principles as those that would be adopted in the original position. It is in their public recognition and informed application of the principles in their political life, and as their effective sense of justice directs, that citizens achieve full autonomy. (*Political Liberalism,* 77)

17. Rawls carefully specifies that full autonomy is a "political" not an "ethical" value, one that is specific to the public aspect of a person's life, her life as citizen which is less than her whole life. See Rawls, *Political Liberalism,* 77–78. The good of full autonomy in any person's whole life—the worth in or fit with her whole life of this political value—is presumably left to determination by and in accord with the person's own comprehensive view. But Rawls must be understood to claim that affirmance *in some way* of the good or worth or fit of (political) full autonomy in or with a whole life will indeed be a part of a political-liberal overlapping consensus among reasonable comprehensive views.

Frank I. Michelman

18. Partly for this reason, Habermas finds Rawlsian political constructivism not sufficiently deeply democratic to meet the demands of validity or, hence, of political rightness on his (blue) view of what that is. By ultimately grounding the law in the conditions that the philosopher writes into the original position, Habermas objects, the Rawlsian construction places the grounds of law, in principle, beyond reach of democratic-discursive validation. See Habermas, "Reconciliation Through the Public Use of Reason," 128.

19. See Benhabib, "Deliberative Rationality," and text accompanying note 3 above, p. 149.

20. See Robert C. Post, *Constitutional Domains: Democracy, Community, Management* (Cambridge, MA: Harvard University Press, 1995), 299–300.

21. See, for example, Habermas, *Between Facts and Norms*, 127.

22. Compare Habermas, *Between Facts and Norms*, 408–409, 417, 437:

> A well-secured private autonomy helps "secure the conditions" of public autonomy just as much as, conversely, the appropriate exercise of public autonomy helps "secure the conditions" of private autonomy. . . . A legal order *is* legitimate to the extent that it equally secures the co- original private and civic autonomy of its citizens; at the same time, however, it *owes* its legitimacy to the forms of communication in which alone this autonomy can express and prove itself. (408–409)

> According to the discourse-theoretic reading of the system of rights, positive law . . . must split up the autonomy of legal persons into the complementary relation between private and public autonomy, so that the addressees of enacted law can at the same time understand themselves as authors of lawmaking. . . . [E]nfranchised citizens must, in exercising their public autonomy, draw the boundaries of private autonomy in such a way that it sufficiently qualifies private persons for their role as citizen. This is because communication in a public sphere that recruits private persons from civil society depends on the spontaneous inputs from a lifeworld whose core private domains are intact. (417)

> [T]he *discourse theory of law* conceives constitutional democracy as institutionalizing—by way of legitimate law (and hence by also guaranteeing private autonomy)—the procedures and communicative presuppositions for a discursive opinion- and will- formation that in turn makes possible (the exercise of political autonomy and) legitimate lawmaking. (437)

23. See again pp. 151–152, above.

24. In summarizing Habermas's view here and below, I draw in part from my review of *Between Facts and Norms, Journal of Philosophy* 93 (1996): 307–315.

25. Compare above pp. 147–148.

26. See Habermas, *Between Facts and Norms*, 447–448.

27. Ibid. (emphasis supplied).

28. Ibid., 107.

29. See, for example, Michel Rosenfeld, "Law as Discourse: Bridging the Gap Between Democracy and Rights," *Harvard Law Review* 108 (1995): 1163–1189, 1169, 1175.

30. See Habermas, *Between Facts and Norms*, 33, 296.

31. Habermas, *Between Facts and Norms*, 450. See Thomas McCarthy, "Kantian Constructivism and Reconstructivism: Rawls and Habermas in Dialogue," *Ethics* 105 (1994): 44–63, 45–46, 49.

32. Nancy Fraser, "Toward a Discourse Ethic of Solidarity," *Praxis International* 5 (1986): 425–429, esp. 425–426.

33. Habermas, *Between Facts and Norms*, 104 (emphasis supplied).

34. See T. M. Scanlon, "Utilitarianism and Contractarianism" in Amartya Sen and Bernard Williams, eds., *Utilitarianism and Beyond* (Cambridge: Cambridge University Press, 1982), 103–128.

35. On the close connection between Habermasian treatments of "discourses oriented to understanding [or agreement]" and legitimacy conditions for political institutions, see Seyla Benhabib, *Critique, Norm, and Utopia* (New York: Columbia University Press, 1986), 283.

36. Habermas, *Between Facts and Norms*, 110. See also Habermas, "Reconciliation Through the Public Use of Reason," 130–131.

37. Habermas, *Between Facts and Norms*, 39.

38. Ibid., 127, 128.

39. Autonomous, that is, as a "communicative power" vis-à-vis a correlative "administrative power." For the relation between these, see Habermas, *Between Facts and Norms*, 147–150.

# 6

## Beyond Fairness and Deliberation: The Epistemic Dimension of Democratic Authority

*David Estlund*

It is with the first thing he takes on another's word without seeing its utility himself, that his judgment is lost.

—*J.-J. Rousseau, Emile, Book II*

Each man, in giving his vote, states his opinion on this matter, and the declaration of the general will is drawn from the counting of votes. When, therefore, the opinion contrary to mine prevails, this proves merely that I was in error, and that what I took to be the general will was not so.

—*J.-J. Rousseau, On The Social Contract, Book IV*

Assume that for many choices faced by a political community, some alternatives are better than others by standards that are in some way objective. (For example, suppose that progressive income tax rates are more just than a flat rate, even after considering effects on efficiency.) If so, it must count in favor of a social decision procedure that it tends to produce the better decision. On the other hand, there is wide disagreement about what justice requires, and no citizen is required to defer to the expertise or authority of any other. Thus, normative democratic theory has largely proceeded on the assumption that the most that can be said for a legitimate democratic decision is that it was produced by a procedure that treats voters equally in certain ways. The merits of democratic decisions are held to be in their past.

One sort of theory treats every voter's views as equally valid from a political point of view and promises only the procedural value of

David Estlund

equal power over the outcome. A distinct approach urges that citizens' existing views should be subjected to the rational criticism of other citizens prior to voting. In both cases, the legitimacy of the decision is typically held to lie in facts about the procedure and not the quality of the outcome by procedure-independent or epistemic standards.

This contrast between procedural and epistemic virtues ought to be questioned. Certainly, there are strong arguments that some form of proceduralism must be preferable to any theory in which correctness is necessary and sufficient for a decision's legitimacy. Democratic accounts of legitimacy seek to explain the legitimacy of the general run of laws (though not necessarily all of them) under favorable conditions. However, even under good conditions many laws are bound to be incorrect, inferior, or unjust by the appropriate objective standard. If the choice is between proceduralism and such correctness theories of legitimacy, proceduralism is vastly more plausible. Correctness theories, however, are not the only form available for approaches to democratic legitimacy that emphasize the epistemic value of the democratic process—its tendency to produce outcomes that are correct by independent standards. Epistemic criteria are compatible, at least in principle, with proceduralism. Thus, rather than supposing that the legitimacy of an outcome depends on its correctness, I shall suggest that it derives, partly, from the epistemic value, even though it is imperfect, of the procedure that produced it. Democratic legitimacy requires that the procedure is procedurally fair and can be held, in terms acceptable to all reasonable citizens, to be epistemically the best among those that are better than random.

After preliminaries, then, two classes of nonepistemic proceduralist accounts will be scrutinized. I will criticize several variants and relatives of Fair Proceduralism and Deliberative Proceduralism in support of a subsequent sketch of Epistemic Proceduralism.[1]

Why suppose that there is any kind of legitimacy for a political decision other than whether it meets some independent standard such as justice? Why not say that it is legitimate if correct, and otherwise not? Call this denial of proceduralism a *correctness theory* of legitimacy.

One thing to notice about a correctness theory of legitimacy is that in a diverse community there is bound to be little agreement on whether a decision is legitimate, since there will be little agreement about whether it meets the independent standard of, say, justice. If the decision is made by majority rule, and voters address the question whether the proposal would be independently correct, then at least a majority will accept its correctness. However, nearly half of the voters might deny its correctness, and on a correctness theory they would in turn deny the legitimacy of the decision—deny that it warrants state action or places them under any obligation to comply.

This potential instability makes it tempting to seek a proceduralist standard of legitimacy that might become widely accepted, so that the legitimacy of a decision could be accepted even by many of those who believe it is incorrect. It is important, though, to ask whether there is anything more to this impulse than the temptation to capitulate to the threat of the brute force that could be unleashed by large numbers of dissident citizens. Without something more, the correctness theory of legitimacy would be undaunted; those dissidents, for all we have said, might be simply in the wrong—renouncing their genuine political obligations.

So leave aside the brute fact of controversy and the potential for instability. Rather, the morally deeper concern is that much of the controversy is among conscientious citizens, rather than merely unreasonable troublemakers. We are far less timid about insisting on, and even enforcing, decisions whose legitimacy is rejected only on unreasonable grounds. Consider someone who rejects the legitimacy of our laws because he insists on being king; or someone who rejects the legitimacy of any laws that are not directly endorsed by the pope. I believe we would not, or at least should not, see any significant moral objection to the correctness theory in the fact that such people might be numerous. We ought to be led by such reflections as these to a general criterion of legitimacy that holds that the legitimacy of laws is not adequately established unless it can be defended on grounds it would be unreasonable to object to. Legitimacy requires the possibility of reasons that are not objectionable to any reasonable citizens. This criterion is liberal in its respect for

David Estlund

conscientious disagreement, and I will call it the *liberal criterion of legitimacy,* following Rawls.[2] The aim here is not to defend this particular criterion of legitimacy, but to use it as a well worked out and demanding liberal constraint on political justification. I accept that some such demanding version of liberalism is appropriate, and note that this is the greatest obstacle to an epistemic theory of democratic legitimacy. I hope to show that, at least in this form, it is not insuperable.

## Beyond Fairness and Deliberation

A critical taxonomy will allow the argument for Epistemic Proceduralism to develop in an orderly way.

### Fair Proceduralism

Fair Proceduralism is the view that what makes democratic decisions legitimate is that they were produced by the fair procedure of majority rule. A problem for this approach is that, while democratic procedures may indeed be fair, the epitome of fairness among people who have different preferences over two alternatives is to flip a coin. Nothing could be fairer. Insofar as we think this is an inappropriate way to decide some question, we are going beyond fairness. Of course, if there is some good to be distributed, we would not think a fair distribution to be one that gives it all to the winner of a coin toss or a drawing of straws.[3] This reflects our attention to procedure-independent moral standards applying to this choice. Since we think some of the alternative distributions are significantly more appropriate than others, we are not satisfied that mere procedural fairness is an appropriate way to make the decision. A fair procedure would be a fair way to make the decision. But if making the decision in a fair way (as in a coin flip) is insufficiently likely to produce the fair or just or morally required outcome, it may not be good enough.

I assume that making political decisions by randomly selecting from the alternatives, as in a coin flip, would not provide any strong moral reason to obey or any strong warrant for coercive enforcement. I conclude from this that the procedural fairness of democratic procedures does not lend them much moral legitimacy.

A second problem is that in this pure, spare form, Fair Proceduralism allows nothing to favor one citizen's claims or interests over another's—not even good reasons. It entails that no one should be favored by any reasons there might be for treating his or her claims as especially important. Robert Dahl apparently endorses such a view when he "postulate[s] that the goals of every adult citizen of a republic are to be accorded equal value in determining governmental policies."[4] In this way, Fair Proceduralism is insensitive to reasons. This does not, of course, mean that it simply favors brute power over reason or morality. The partisan of brute power has no interest in equalizing individuals' power over outcomes, nor in giving any reasons for his recommended arrangements. Fair Proceduralism aims to place severe constraints on the use of power; indeed, the problem is that the constraints are too strong, since effective rational argument in favor of certain outcomes is, in this context, a form of power which Fair Proceduralism is led implausibly to equalize.

It is not clear that any theorists, even those who claim to appeal only to procedural fairness, have advanced this implausible pure form of Fair Proceduralism.[5] It is widely acknowledged that the legitimating force of democratic procedures depends on conceiving them as, at least partly, procedures of rational interpersonal deliberation. "Deliberative democracy," then, is not generally in dispute. What divides democratic theorists is, rather, whether democratic deliberation improves the outcomes by independent standards (its epistemic value), or at least whether this is any part of the account of democratic authority. Two nonepistemic versions say "no," and two epistemic versions say "yes." Begin with the naysayers.

### Fair Deliberative Proceduralism

Consider Fair Deliberative Proceduralism: it makes no claims about the epistemic value of democratic deliberation, but it insists that citizens ought to have an equal or at least fair chance to enter their arguments and reasons into the discussion prior to voting. The impartiality is among individuals' convictions or arguments rather than among their preferences or interests. Reasons, as the voters see them, are explicitly entered into the process, but no particular independent standard need be appealed to in this theory. The result is held to be legitimate without regard to any tendency to be correct by independent standards; its legitimacy lies in the procedure's impartiality among individuals' convictions and arguments.[6]

This account interprets the inputs somewhat differently, but also conceives of the entire process more dynamically. Inputs are not merely to be tallied; they are first to be considered and accommodated by other participants, and, likewise, revised in view of the arguments of others. To allow this there must be indefinitely many rounds of entering inputs into the deliberative process, though of course it eventually ends in a vote.

Why does deliberation help? Perhaps the idea is that voters' convictions will be more genuinely their own after open rational deliberation. This would make it simply a more refined version of Fair Proceduralism. Fair Deliberative Proceduralism, however, cannot really explain why deliberation is important. If the outcome is to be selected from individuals' views, it can perhaps be seen as enhancing fairness if their views are well considered and stable under collective deliberation. If the goal is fairness, though, why select the outcome from individuals' views? It is true that if the outcome is not selected in this way it might be something no one would have voted for. But that does not count against the fairness of doing so. It is just as fair to choose randomly from the available alternatives.

If we add to fairness the aim of satisfying at least some citizens, we will want the outcome to be one that some would have voted for. There is still no reason, however, to let an alternative's chance of being chosen vary with the amount of support it has among the citizens. It would be perfectly fair to take the outcome randomly from the set of alternatives that at least some voters support after deliberation. Call this method a *Post-Deliberative Coin Flip*. This is importantly different from randomly choosing a citizen to decide (which I'll call *Queen for a Day*; see below on this method). That would favor the more popular alternatives. The idea here is rather to let all alternatives with any support have an equal chance of being chosen. In one respect this can look even more fair: no one's view is disadvantaged by the fact that few others support it.

The objection is not that these views are undemocratic in allowing coin flips; I leave that question aside. Rather, their allowing coin flips highlights their indifference to the epistemic value of the procedure. Post-deliberative voting probably has considerable epistemic value, but Fair Deliberative Proceduralism must be indifferent between it and a coin flip. The legitimacy of the coin flip is all the legitimacy Fair Deliberative Proceduralism can find in democratic social choice. But it is too epistemically blunt to have much legitimacy, at least if their are better alternatives.

### Rational Deliberative Proceduralism

Some authors seem to advocate a view that is like Fair Deliberative Proceduralism except that the procedure's value is primarily in recognizing good reasons rather than in providing fair access (though fair or equal access would be a natural corollary).[7] We might thus distinguish Fair Deliberative Proceduralism (FD) from Rational Deliberative Proceduralism (RD). This latter view would not claim that the procedure produces outcomes that (tend to) approximate some standard (of, say, justice or the common good) that is independent of actual procedures, and does so by recognizing better reasons and giving them greater influence over the outcome (e.g., by way of voters being rationally persuaded). That would be an epistemic view. Instead, RD insists that the only thing to be said for the outcomes is that they were produced by a reason-recognizing procedure; no further claim has to be made about whether the outcomes tend to meet any independent standard of correctness. The outcomes are rational only in a procedural sense, not in any more substantive sense. This claim would be analogous to Fair Proceduralism's claim that outcomes are fair in a procedural but not a substantive sense.

This procedural sense of rational outcomes is not available to the advocate of this reason-recognizing procedure, however. If the procedure is held to recognize the better reasons, those reasons are being counted as better by procedure-independent standards. Then to say that the outcome reflects the better reasons can only mean that the outcome meets or tends to meet that same procedure-independent standard. By contrast, in the case of Fair Proceduralism, the procedure is never held to recognize the more fair individ-

David Estlund

ual inputs. If that were the basis of its claim to fairness, then it too would be an epistemic view. The space held out for a nonepistemic Rational Deliberative Proceduralism has disappeared. Deliberative democracy, as a theory of legitimacy, then, is either an inadequate refinement of Fair Proceduralism, or it is led to base its recommendation of democratic procedures partly on their performance by procedure-independent standards.

This is a good place to recall what is meant here by "procedure-independent standards." This does not mean that the standards are independent of any possible or conceivable procedure, but only that they are independent (logically) of the actual procedure that gave rise to the outcome in question. Fair Proceduralism's standard of fairness is defined in terms of the actual procedures producing the decision to be called fair, and so Fair Proceduralism admits no procedure-independent standard in this sense.

Consider, in light of this point, a view that says that democratic outcomes are legitimate where they (tend to) match what would have been decided in a certain hypothetical procedure, such as the Rawlsian original position, or the Habermasian ideal speech situation, or some ideal democratic procedure. Joshua Cohen writes, "outcomes are democratically legitimate if and only if they would be the object of an agreement arrived at through a free and reasoned consideration of alternatives by equals."[8] This may seem not to require recognizably democratic institutions at all, but he also says, "The ideal deliberative procedure provides a model for institutions, a model that they should mirror, so far as possible."[9] The combination of these two claims implies that actual procedures that mirror the ideal procedure will tend to produce the same results as the ideal, though not necessarily always. This would be an epistemic view as defined here, since the ideal procedure is logically independent of the actual procedures. For this reason, I interpret Cohen as developing one kind of epistemic theory. This implication is in some conflict, however, with his claim that "what is good is fixed by deliberation, not prior to it."[10] That may be misleading, since on his view, it is fixed by ideal, not actual, deliberation, and actual deliberation is held to this logically prior and independent standard. Within the class of epistemic theories there will be a number of important distinctions, such as that between standards defined in terms of hypothetical procedures and those defined in other ways. Those are not the distinctions at issue here, for all such views invoke procedure independent standards in one important respect: the standards are logically independent of the actual procedures.[11]

Without any space for the view that democratic outcomes are procedurally, even if not substantively, rational, deliberative conceptions of democracy are forced to ground democratic legitimacy either in the infertile soil of an impartial proceduralism, or in a rich but combustible appeal to the epistemic value of democratic procedures.

### Two Epistemic Theories: Three Challenges

Turning then to epistemic theories of democratic legitimacy, there is a fork in the road. Three challenges for epistemic theories are helpful in choosing between them: the problem of *deference,* the problem of *demandingness,* and the problem of *invidious comparisons.* Epistemic Proceduralism, I will argue, can meet these challenges better than non-proceduralist epistemic approaches, which I am calling correctness theories of democratic legitimacy. The latter sort of theory holds that political decisions are legitimate only if they are correct by appropriate procedure-independent standards, and adds the claim that proper democratic procedures are sufficiently accurate to render the general run of laws and policies legitimate under favorable conditions. This was Rousseau's view. Having pushed things in an epistemic direction, I now want to prevent things from getting out of hand. Existing epistemic conceptions of democracy are, in a certain sense, too epistemic. (See figure 6.1.)

### *Deference*

It is important to appreciate the reasons many have had for resisting epistemic accounts of political authority. Some seem to have thought that if there existed epistemic standards then it would follow that some know better, and that the knowers should rule, as in Plato's elegant and repellent Republic. In order to reject what we might call

David Estlund

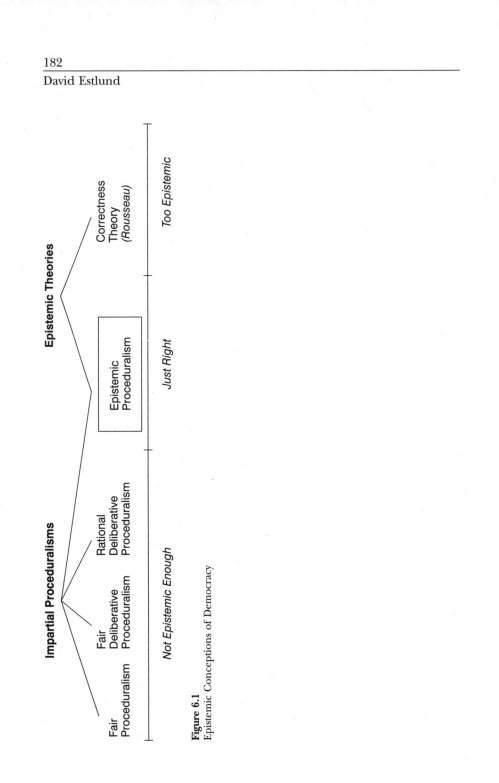

**Figure 6.1**
Epistemic Conceptions of Democracy

"epistocracy," or rule of the knowers, some think it is necessary to deny that there are any procedure-independent epistemic standards for democratic decisions. An adequate answer to this worry, I believe, is to argue that sovereignty is not distributed according to moral expertise unless that expertise would be beyond the reasonable objections of individual citizens. But reasonable citizens should (or, at the very least, may) refuse to surrender their moral judgment on important matters to anyone. Then, unless all reasonable citizens actually agreed with the decisions of some agreed moral/political guru, no one could legitimately rule on the basis of wisdom. So there might be political truth, and even knowers of various degrees, without any moral basis for epistocracy.[12]

The moral challenge for any epistemic conception of political authority, then, is to let truth be the guide without illegitimately privileging the opinions of any putative experts. Experts should not be privileged because citizens cannot be expected or assumed (much less encouraged or forced) to surrender their moral judgment, at least on important matters—to say, "that still doesn't seem right to me, but I shall judge it to be right because I expect this person or that thing to indicate reliably what is right." Rousseau proposed an epistemic conception of democracy which was sensitive to this danger, but yet violated it in the end. This is of some independent interest since Rousseau is perhaps the originator of the strong conception of autonomy that is at stake.

Rousseau argued that properly conducted democratic procedures (in suitably arranged communities) discovered a procedure-independent answer to the moral question, "what should we, as a political community, do?" The correct answer, he held, is whatever is common to the wills of all citizens, this being what he called every citizen's "general will." In this way, citizens under majority rule could still "obey only themselves,"[13] securing autonomy in a way in which under Locke's theory, for example, they could not. (For Locke, the minority simply loses, since the majority determines the direction of the whole group.)[14] For Rousseau, democratic procedures discover the general will when citizens address themselves to the question of the content of the general will, though they often use the process illegitimately to serve more particular ends. The key point, for our

David Estlund

purposes, is that according to Rousseau, outcomes are legitimate when and because they are correct, and not for any procedural reason. When they are incorrect, they are illegitimate, because nothing but the general will can legitimately be politically imposed.

Rousseau, uncharacteristically, asks the citizen to surrender her judgment to the properly conducted democratic process. "When, therefore, the opinion contrary to mine prevails, this proves merely that I was in error, and that what I took to be the general will was not so."[15] The minority voter can, of course, conclude instead that the process was improperly conducted, and that others have not addressed the question that was put to them. But she must decide either that it is not even a legitimate collective decision, or that it has correctly ascertained the general will—the morally correct answer. In a well-functioning polity, where she has no grounds to challenge the legitimacy of the procedure, she must not only obey it but also surrender her moral judgment to it. She must say to herself "while it doesn't seem right to me, this proves merely that I was in error."

One problem with Rousseau's expectation of deference is suggested by a passage in John Rawls's doctoral dissertation. In chastising appeals to exalted entities as morally authoritative, he writes,

The kinds of entities which have been used in such appeals are very numerous indeed. In what follows I shall mention some of them very briefly. The main objection in each case is always the following: how do we know that the entity in question will always behave in accordance with what is right[?] This is a question with [sic] which we always can ask, and which we always do ask, and it shows that we do not, in actual practice, hand over the determination of right and wrong to any other agency whatsoever.[16]

Here, Rawls generalizes one of Rousseau's central teachings, that no one's reason should be subordinated to anyone else's.[17]

In *Theory of Justice,* Rawls applies the idea to democratic choice:

Although in given circumstances it is justified that the majority . . . has the constitutional right to make law, this does not imply that the laws enacted are just. . . . [W]hile citizens normally submit their conduct to democratic authority, that is, recognize the outcome of a vote as establishing a binding rule, other things equal, they do not submit their judgment to it.[18]

This is the problem of deference faced by epistemic approaches to democracy. The objection is not to Rousseau's requirement that the outcome be obeyed. I believe (and will argue below) that something much like Rousseauian voting can perhaps justify this requirement. Rousseau goes wrong, I believe, in resting this case on the fact— when it is a fact—that the outcome is the general will, the morally correct answer to the question faced by the voters.[19]

Here we can see the promise of an epistemic form of proceduralism, one that holds that the outcome is legitimate even when it is incorrect, owing to the epistemic value, albeit imperfect, of the democratic procedure. Such an account would not expect the minority voter to surrender her judgment to the procedure in any way, since she can hold both that the process was properly carried out, and that the outcome, while morally binding on citizens for procedural reasons, is morally mistaken.

What if a correctness theory can support the claim that the majority is overwhelmingly likely to be correct? Wouldn't it be sensible to expect deference to the outcome in that case? Recent discussions of the epistemic approach to democratic authority have usually invoked the striking mathematical result of Rousseau's contemporary, Condorcet, known as the *Jury Theorem:* roughly, if voters are better than chance on some yes/no question (call this their *individual competence*), then under majority rule the group will be virtually infallible on that question if only the group is not too small.[20,21]

Plainly, this result is important for the epistemic approach to democratic authority. It promises to explain, as fairness alone cannot, why majority rule is preferable to empowering randomly chosen citizens: under the right conditions majority rule is vastly more likely than the average individual to get the morally correct answer. But the Jury Theorem's very power ought to raise a warning flag. Is this really an instrument to which we can comfortably surrender our moral judgment on certain matters?

One objection to the surrender of judgment is that there is, perhaps, never sufficiently good reason for thinking the supposedly expert person or procedure really is so reliable. Applying this caution to the Jury Theorem, we notice that one cannot think majority rule is nearly infallible unless one thinks individual voters are (at least on average) better than random. But why ever substitute the outcome of majority rule for one's own moral judgment, if all that is required in order to stick with one's own judgment is to believe that the voters must probably have been, on average, worse than random? A voter has no more solid basis for the probabilities the theorem requires than she has for her moral judgment that the outcome of the voting procedure is morally mistaken. It is doubtful, then, that the Jury Theorem can ever give a person good reason to defer in her moral judgment to the outcome of a majority vote. This objection to correctness theories says that the minority voter's disagreement with the outcome is a perfectly good reason for doubting that the procedure is highly reliable.

There is also a deeper point. Suppose there were no good reason to challenge the overwhelming likelihood that the procedure's outcome is correct, and never mind whether the basis for this likelihood is the Jury Theorem or something else altogether. Since correctness theories treat outcomes as legitimate because they are correct, the reason, given to the minority voter, for obedience is the correctness of the outcome, something the minority voter is on record as denying. So correctness theories go on to say to the minority voter that it is overwhelmingly probable that the outcome is correct. This might be supported by the Jury Theorem or in some other way. Correctness theories need this claim for two reasons: first, to supply legitimacy in the vast majority of cases; second, to give the minority voter in any given case reason to change her opinion to match that of the outcome of a majority vote and so to accept its legitimacy. Correctness theories, then, apparently rely on the following premise:

**Probability Supports Moral Judgment:** One who accepts that all things considered the correctness of a given moral judgment is extremely probable has good reason to accept the moral judgment.

Epistemic Proceduralism does not rely on any such assumption since it does not rest the minority voter's acceptance of an outcome's legitimacy on the outcome's correctness. This is an advantage for Epistemic Proceduralism, since the claim that probability supports moral judgment is deeply problematic. It may be false; at least it is not something all reasonable citizens can be expected to accept, as the following thought experiment suggests.

Suppose there is a deck of 1,000 cards, and each has written on it a moral statement about which you have no strong opinion either way. Suppose further that you accept on some evidence that exactly 999 of these contain true statements, and 1 is false. Now you cut the deck and the card says, "Physician-assisted suicide is sometimes morally permissible" (or some other moral statement about which you are otherwise uncertain). It is not clear that you have been given very good reason to accept that physician-assisted suicide is sometimes permissible. Of course, you might doubt the reliability of the deck of cards (or the "expert"), but suppose you do not. There is nothing inconsistent in holding that "While there is almost no chance that this is incorrect, still, that doesn't make physician-assisted suicide seem permissible to me, and so I do not accept that it is. The expert is almost certainly correct, and yet I am not prepared to share in the expert's judgment." This attitude may make sense for moral judgments even though it apparently does not for factual judgments.

Correctness theories assume that probabilistic considerations support moral judgment in expecting the minority to come around to the majority judgment on the basis of the procedure's reliability. Epistemic Proceduralism has the advantage of avoiding this commitment. There is no expectation that the minority voter will conform her opinion to that of the majority, since the reason given to the minority voter for obedience does not depend on the correctness of the outcome in question.[22]

### Demandingness

Epistemic Proceduralism does not require democratic procedures to be as epistemically reliable as correctness theories do. More precisely, Epistemic Proceduralism generates more legitimacy out of a given level of the procedure's epistemic value, because unlike correctness theories it allows that there can be legitimacy without correctness.

David Estlund

This might be questioned in the following way: the Jury Theorem does not support moderate epistemic value except in cases where it also supports strong epistemic value. Therefore, if Epistemic Proceduralism relies on the Jury Theorem for its moderate epistemic claims on behalf of the procedure, then it is committed to just as much epistemic value as correctness theories are.

The Jury Theorem seems to imply that, in groups of much size, if it is correct more often than not then it is also virtually infallible. Majority rule is only better than random if voters are better than random; but if they are, then in large groups majority rule is virtually infallible. In that case, the minority voter would have no basis for thinking the procedure tends to be correct which was not an equally good basis for thinking it is almost certainly correct every time. To accept this is to surrender one's judgment to the process. The proceduralist version would seem to provide no advantage on this score.

In reality, however, the fates of proceduralist and non-proceduralist epistemic accounts are not as closely linked as this suggests. It is possible to have majority rule perform better than .5 (random) even if voters are on average worse than .5, so long as individual competences are arranged in a certain way. For majority rule in a given society to be correct more often than not, all that is required is that, more often than not, voters have, for a particular instance of voting, an average competence only slightly better than .5. Then the group is almost certain to get it right in every such instance, and so more often than not. After that, it does not matter how low voter competence is in other instances, and so they could drag the overall average competence, across instances of voting, well below .5.[23]

Certainly non-proceduralist epistemic conceptions can weaken their own competence requirements by using the same device: letting average competence vary from one voting instance to another. But this will not change things much.[24] The view still depends on the outcome being correct almost all the time, and so the minority voter who accepts this account will have to believe she is most likely mistaken. This consequence can only be avoided by requiring less credulity of the voters. A non-proceduralist epistemic theory can only do this by counting fewer decisions as legitimate.

The weaker use of the Jury Theorem, as presented here, still depends on that model's applicability to real contexts of democratic choice. This cannot be confidently maintained, owing to at least the following two difficulties. First, there are still many questions about what kinds and degrees of mutual influence or similarity among voters are compatible with the Jury Theorem's assumption that voters are independent. Independence is not automatically defeated by mutual influence as has often been thought,[25] but whether actual patterns of influence are within allowable bounds is presently not well understood.

Second, the Jury Theorem assumes there are only two alternatives. In some contexts it does look as if there are often precisely two alternatives. Consider the choice between raising the speed limit or not raising it, or forbidding abortion or not. These are genuine binary choices even though the "not" in each case opens up many further choices. Of course, they have been somehow selected from a much larger set, and we would want to know how the choice came down to these.

For these and other reasons, the Jury Theorem approach to the epistemic value of democratic procedures is less than trustworthy. Epistemic Proceduralism needs some basis for its epistemic claims, though it need not be seen as wedded to the Condorcetian device. If the Jury Theorem is applicable, then it is worth worrying whether whenever it supports moderate epistemic value of the procedure it also supports strong epistemic value, vitiating Epistemic Proceduralism's claim to be less demanding. I have argued that a weaker use of the Jury Theorem can solve the problem. If the Jury Theorem is not applicable after all, then there is little reason to think, even initially, that the problematic entailment might hold.

### Invidious Comparisons

Just as moral experts will be too controversial, even if they exist, to figure in any justification of authoritarian political arrangements, any particular set of criteria for determining whether the average voter is better than random (as, for example, the Jury Theorem requires) will be just as controversial. If the qualifications of an alleged moral expert will always be subject to reasonable disagreement, then so will any list of qualifications itself. So, even if (as I doubt) we might sometimes have good reason to think the requirements of the Jury Theorem are met, and so have good reason to surrender our moral judgment to the majority outcome when we disagree with it, there will always be reasonable grounds for others to deny this by rejecting the criteria of moral competence that we have used. It would violate the liberal criterion of legitimacy, then, to employ any such claims in political justification. This is a third challenge faced by epistemic approaches to democracy; call it the problem of *Invidious Comparisons*.

I propose to answer this objection indirectly. I shall sketch an account of social and structural circumstances that might suffice for the weaker kind of epistemic value required by Epistemic Proceduralism. Of course, a social/structural account might be employed in support of a correctness theory's strong epistemic claims as well, and if successful it could meet the challenge of avoiding invidious comparisons. I assume, however, that showing a procedure to have higher epistemic value requires more appeal to the epistemic capacities of the participating individuals. If so, a social/structural basis for the procedure's epistemic value has a better chance of supplying the moderate epistemic value required by Epistemic Proceduralism than the strong epistemic value required by correctness theories. There is no intention of showing that these considerations suffice for moderate epistemic value, nor of showing that they could not suffice for strong epistemic value. The point is only that the need, stemming from the problem of invidious comparisons, to stay with a social/ structural account favors the more moderate needs of Epistemic Proceduralism. I propose the following conditions as examples drawn from familiar ideas:

1. Every adult in the society is permitted to participate.

2. Participants sincerely address questions of justice, not of interest group advantage, and it is common knowledge that this is so.

3. Participants accept and address a shared conception of justice, and this is common knowledge.

4. Participants evaluate arguments fairly, irrespective of the identity of the person, or the size of the group offering the argument.

5. Each participant's views are easily available to the others (at least via some other proponent of the views, and at least those views that would have any chance of gaining adherents).

6. Participants represent a personal, educational, and cultural variety of life experiences.

7. Participants' needs for health and safety are sufficiently well met that it is possible for them to devote some time and energy to public political deliberations, and in general all are literate.

No individual experts are involved in the way they are in the case of epistocracy, but the epistemic needs of Epistemic Proceduralism cannot be met without the voters having a certain decent level of competence. The thing to avoid is using any considerations that would also imply specific conclusions about which individuals are likely to be morally wiser than others. First, there are the situational assumptions, that all are allowed to participate, all are sincere, all address a shared conception of justice, and so on. Then we must add a claim about the usual power of interpersonal deliberative procedures under such conditions. This, too, leaves aside any claims about which kind of person is morally wisest. In this way, the account avoids what appears to be the main threat of reasonable disagreement.

**Queen for a Day**

Having laid out the epistemic needs of Epistemic Proceduralism, the question arises whether certain non-voting procedures might also meet all the criteria. If so, is this a defect in Epistemic Proceduralism? The challenge I have in mind is the one I have called Queen for a Day: Suppose a voter is picked at random to make each decision. So long as most voters are better than random[26] this is bound to perform better than a random selection from alternatives, even after deliberation.

Justifying this procedure on the basis of its better performance already goes beyond procedural fairness. But, assuming it is still fair, it poses a possible challenge to the case I am presenting for

David Estlund

Epistemic Proceduralism. Queen for a Day meets several criteria urged here for accounts of democratic legitimacy. First, it is procedurally fair. Second, it can be held to perform better than a random selection from the alternatives in a way that is acceptable to all reasonable citizens. But is it the best among the procedures that meet these conditions? The case for voting comes down, then, to whether it performs better than Queen for a Day (or any other fair procedure).

Good performance should take into account more than just how likely it is to get the correct answer, but also *how far* it is likely to deviate from the best outcome. The existence of a small number of evil voters is literally no threat to a majoritarian procedure's performance, but they would occasionally, or at least with some chance, be Queen for a Day. This counts against that method. On the other hand, a small number of esoteric moral experts is no benefit to a majoritarian procedure, but they will have some chance of being Queen for a Day. These two considerations appear to balance out.

The Jury Theorem, if it can be applied to real social choices, would show just what is needed: majority rule is more competent than the average voter, which is the exact competence of Queen for a Day.[27] However, we have noted that it is unclear whether the Jury Theorem is applicable, and so it is not available here as an argument for majority rule over Queen for a Day.

Should we be disturbed that Epistemic Proceduralism does not have a more decisive way to reject Queen for a Day? Can it really come down to the difficult question of whether majority rule voting performs better? Is Epistemic Proceduralism otherwise indifferent between democratic and undemocratic modes of social choice?

This objection would need to defend its assumption that Queen for a Day is undemocratic. If it were stipulated that a social choice procedure is not democratic unless it involves voting, then of course Queen for a Day is not democratic. But then the question becomes why this should matter morally? Unless it fails to treat voters equally in some morally important way, or leaves them all entirely out of social choice, we should regard it as democratic whether or not it involves voting. Certainly, historically the selection of some decision makers by lot rather than by election (as in ancient Athens and Renaissance Florence) has often been regarded as entirely democratic.[28]

Would Queen for a Day deprive citizens of power they would have if there were voting? What power does a voter have? It is not the power to choose outcomes, so that is not lost under Queen for a Day. Each voter faces a choice only between ways of voting. The outcome is largely out of the voter's control, since it depends on how others choose to vote. Does a voter influence the decision in a way the uncrowned citizens do not in Queen for a Day? A voter, by voting, has no influence on the decision unless she is decisive, which almost no one ever is. Each voter has an equal initial chance of being decisive, but a vote's influence on the social choice stops there. Queen for a Day offers citizens an equal chance of being decisive too. Moreover, it can add the guarantee that there will always be a decisive citizen; in voting usually no voter is decisive.

In voting, there is a margin of victory, and every vote influences that. That is not, strictly, part of the outcome of the vote, in that it does not affect the social choice. Still, margin of victory can be very important. Again, though, there is no fundamental difference between voting and Queen for a Day. In both cases, the social choice can be made without paying any attention to any further facts about the number of supporters for each alternative. If such further information is important, it can be gotten under either system. In Queen for a Day, citizens could become eligible to be chosen as monarch for a certain issue by disclosing in advance the decision they would make, with the decision to take effect only if it is drawn by lot. Then all other advance declarations could be counted and publicized for whatever value this has.

One begins to see how much like voting Queen for a Day is, or could be. I know of no strong moral argument against it as compared with ordinary voting. Insofar as it is distasteful, bear in mind that none of the approaches to democratic legitimacy canvassed in this essay has any reason to reject it. It is fair, and it can take place after individual views are shaped by public deliberation. Only Epistemic Proceduralism has even a potential reason to reject it: First, it must at least be better than a random selection from alternatives (the other approaches don't require this); second, it might not be as epistemically valuable as another fair procedure, such as voting. But if it is epistemically better than voting, Epistemic Proceduralism would not be embarrassed to recommend it as the appropriate procedure for democratic social choice. In offering an account of democratic legitimacy in terms of other values it is impossible to avoid the implication that other methods that meet the other values at least as well would be at least as legitimate. The question is whether this conclusion is so implausible as to defeat the general account. Without knowing whether Queen for a Day does meet the proposed conditions as well as voting, it appears in any case that this would not be a morally unacceptable conclusion.

### Why Obey Bad Laws?

What moral reason is there to obey the decisions of the majority, when they meet the criteria of Epistemic Proceduralism, even if they are incorrect? I know of no moral principle, widely accepted, from which this obligation can be derived. It finds support, however, in the limitations of the idea of procedural fairness. Procedural fairness is a way of being impartial among individuals' competing interests, even while producing a command or directive that suits the interests of some and not of others. Procedural fairness is designed for the case where the only standards of evaluation are first, each individual's interests, and second, the moral principle of impartial treatment. It is not well suited to cases where there is a procedure-independent standard of moral correctness that applies to the decision that must be made.

Begin, then, with a case where it is granted that each individual is under an obligation to abide by the outcome of a fair procedure. The question "What should we do?" is treated as answered by aggregating what each of us wants to do in some impartial way. But now suppose it is known that the choice we make will be morally better or worse, and we do not all agree on which choices are morally better. First, it would be odd to use a procedure that operated solely on our individual interests, ignoring our moral judgments. I assume that there would be little obligation to obey the outcome of such a procedure despite its procedural fairness. Second, it still seems an insufficient ground of obligation merely to use a procedure that chose the alternative in accord with the moral judgments of a majority for reasons of fairness. There is no point in attending to moral judgments rather than interests if they are simply to be counted up on the model of procedural fairness. Why should this produce any stronger sort of obligation than the straight procedurally fair aggregation of interests? The reason for moving to the moral judgments could only be to apply intelligence to the moral issue at hand.

I propose, as the counterpart of the idea of procedural fairness in cases where there is an independent moral standard for the outcome, the idea of Epistemic Proceduralism: procedural impartiality among individuals' opinions, but with a tendency to be correct; the impartial application of intelligence to the cognitive moral question at hand.

Why does one have any obligation to obey such a procedure when one firmly believes it is mistaken? The question is produced by supposing that the epistemic dimension is meant to make the procedure's outcome also the individual's best guess as to the answer, as if the goal of the procedure were epistemic reasons.[29] But that is not the role of the epistemic dimension in Epistemic Proceduralism. That would be roughly like supposing the role of majority rule in Fair Proceduralism is to make the outcome conducive to one's own interests. Thus, one would ask, why obey a fair procedure when it doesn't accord with one's own best interests? I am taking as a starting assumption that the fairness of the procedure is a fully adequate reason to obey in simple nonepistemic cases. The problem is to stay as close to this model as possible, while making adjustments to fit the case where there is a procedure-independent moral standard for the outcome. In neither case will the reason to obey be based on any substantive feature of the outcome—both are pure proceduralist accounts of the reason or obligation to obey.

Mere procedural fairness is a very weak reason to obey when I believe the outcome is morally mistaken. It may seem, then, that my own moral judgment about the outcome is supreme in my own deliberations. That is not, however, the only reason for thinking procedural fairness is insufficient in such cases. A different reason is that procedural fairness is not equipped to address cognitive

David Estlund

issues—it is not a cognitive process. This can be remedied without making my own moral judgment supreme, if fair proceduralism can be adapted to cognitive purposes. This is what is accomplished by a process that is impartial among individual opinions, yet has some tendency to be correct. It is suited to the cognitive task and is impartial among participants. Thus, there is a moral reason to abide by its decisions quite apart from their substantive merits, just as there is reason to abide by a procedure that fairly adjudicates among competing interests quite apart from whether it serves one's interests. Epistemic Proceduralism is proposed as a conservative adaptation of the idea of procedural fairness to cases of morally evaluable outcomes. It is conservative in requiring no more epistemic value than necessary (just-better-than-randomness so long as it is the best available)—while still fitting the cognitive nature of the cases.[30]

The case for a moral reason to obey Epistemic Proceduralist outcomes is, as I have said, not derived from any more basic moral principles. Still, it can be made compelling in other ways, and I have just attempted one. A second supporting stratagem is to suggest a metaphor that triggers roughly the right inferences and associations. It is instructive, I believe, to see Epistemic Proceduralism as an account of the public view of justice and its authority.

**The Public View**

The idea of a public view fits Epistemic Proceduralism in a number of ways. For one thing, it signals the application of cognitive intelligence to the moral question collectively faced. Another connection is the explanation this metaphor yields of the obligation to abide by the public view even when one believes (and even correctly believes) that it is mistaken. One's own belief is one's personal view, and it conflicts with one's view as member of the public, or as citizen. (This parallels Rousseau's doctrine of public vs. private will, only this is about opinion, not will.) Just as each agent has a duty to do what he believes to be right, the agency of the public—and each person qua public citizen—has a duty to do what seems right from the public point of view. The public, like any agent, has a duty to do what it believes to be right, even when it happens to be mistaken.[31] There is such a duty only if the agent's judgment meets some epistemic criteria; for example, the person with utterly distorted moral judgment may get no moral credit for being conscientious. This qualification is reflected in Epistemic Proceduralism's account of the public view by the requirement that the procedure be better than random.[32] In these ways, Epistemic Proceduralism's outcomes produce obligations to obey in much the way that they would if they were conceived as the public view of justice, by analogy to an individual's view of what is right.

It may be suspected that Epistemic Proceduralism relies on this being more than a metaphor, and actually posits a collective social entity with intentional states of its own. Many would object to this (though I leave aside the question whether it should be thought to be objectionable). To test this suspicion, consider whether Fair (NB: not Epistemic) Proceduralism would have to be seen as positing a spooky subject, the public, if it turned out to be useful to speak of its outcomes as constituting the public interest. This might be useful because it is indeed constructed out of interests, even though no individual's or group's particular interest is privileged by the procedure. So it is interest-like, and yet there is no ordinary subject who owns it. Clearly the usefulness of treating it as the interest of the public has no metaphysical implications. The usefulness of treating Epistemic Proceduralism's outcomes as the public view of justice is no less metaphysically innocent. No opinion is taken here even on the intermediate question whether these outcomes constitute a collective opinion about justice, where this idea might be analyzed without collectivist metaphysical commitments. Epistemic Proceduralism's democratic outcomes are view-like in certain respects, and the right inferences are produced by this heuristic device only if the subject of the view is imagined to be an entity called the public rather than any single citizen or subset of citizens. The public point of view is no more committed to an additional collective subject than is the traditional idea of the moral point of view.

Even without controversial metaphysical implications, the very idea of an obligation to do what is thought just from the public point of view even where this conflicts with what seems just from one's personal point of view may seem objectionable. Plainly I cannot be morally required (or even permitted) to do what it is morally wrong to do, but I might yet be morally required to abide by laws that are unjust.[33] Granted there are limits to the degree of injustice that can coexist with a moral obligation to comply. Still, within limits, the injustice of a directive is not generally thought to settle the question of whether one must obey it. If classrooms are assigned to professors in what I believe to be an unjust way—say, by seniority rather than by instructional needs—this is not immediately grounds for disobedience. So the fact that Epistemic Proceduralism would require citizens often to obey laws and policies they believe not to be just does not mean that it calls for some abdication of moral responsibility.

It may seem that Epistemic Proceduralism goes back on its critique of deference, since in the end it requires citizens to defer to the public point of view. But it doesn't; it requires obedience, not any surrender of moral judgment. There is no intention here of showing that political authority is possible without requirements to obey.

**Rousseau Revisited**

Looking at Epistemic Proceduralism from the standpoint of Rousseau's view, the authority of the public view takes the place of the authority of the general will. The Rousseauian will object that if the general will is replaced in this way political obedience will no longer be obedience to oneself, and political society cannot be reconciled with freedom. The Rousseauian argument that legitimacy requires correctness is based on a respect for the ultimate authority of the individual will. Only if the political decision is willed by each citizen can required compliance be reconciled with autonomy. The general will is that part of each citizen's will that all have in common, and so only decisions in conformity with the general will can be legitimately required of everyone.

If this were a good argument, then the authority of the majority decision would not depend, as it does in Rousseau, on majority rule having been agreed upon in an original social contract.[34] By positing a previous unanimous authorization of majority rule, Rousseau undermines the idea that majority decisions are only legitimate because they correctly ascertain the general will. If the procedure must be previously authorized, this could only be because obedience to the general will is not straightforwardly obedience to one's own will. This is because a person's general will is not simply the person's will, but the part of his will that is also a part of every other citizen's will. The authority of the general will is the authority of all over the behavior of each. Even if this is conceived as compatible in a certain way with freedom, morality is not simply freedom to do as one wills, since each person's private will is morally subordinated to the general will. Thus, Rousseau thinks the legitimacy of majority rule depends on unanimous contractual acceptance (apparently hypothetical). Once this is admitted, we see that even Rousseauian democracy does not avoid every kind of subjection of the individual to external authority, rhetoric notwithstanding. The question is how this kind of subjection can be justified, not how it can be avoided. It is not as if Rousseauian theory avoids subjection to political authority and Epistemic Proceduralism embraces it.

Epistemic Proceduralism parts company with Rousseau on the question of what it takes to justify majority rule. Rousseau apparently held, not that subjection to the general will was simply unproblematic, but rather that majority rule would not be contractually accepted unless or insofar as it reliably discovered the general will. Since the minority voter is expected to conclude that she is mistaken, the initial acceptance of majority rule is an agreement to surrender one's judgment on the general will to the procedure. Without rehearsing the objections to this sort of deference, suffice it to say that we should not believe Rousseau's claim that it would be agreed to in an appropriate initial contractual choice. Epistemic Proceduralism offers a different account of the authority of majority rule. It is indebted to Rousseau insofar as it acknowledges the cognitive nature of the moral questions political communities face, and the need for an epistemic dimension to the account of democratic authority. But strongly epistemic accounts such as Rousseau's expect citizens to stop thinking for themselves so long as the procedure has been carried out correctly. Ironically, it is Rousseau who so influentially taught that no person or thing is owed that sort of deference.[35]

David Estlund

## Acknowledgment

I have benefited from discussion of these issues with Arthur Applbaum, Victor Caston, Tom Christiano, Jamie Dreier, Alon Harel, Jerry Gaus, Andy Levine, Tim Lytton, Martha Nussbaum, Bill Rehg, Henry Richardson, Tim Sommers, Ernie Sosa, Lewis Yelin, and audiences at Brown University, the University of Wisconsin, and the conference on Deliberative Democracy at St. Louis University, April 1996. Much of this work was supported by a sabbatical from Brown and by the fellowship (in both senses) at the Program in Ethics and the Professions at Harvard University during 1993–94.

## Notes

1. I am indebted to Jules Coleman and John Ferejohn, "Democracy And Social Choice," and to Joshua Cohen, "An Epistemic Conception of Democracy," both in *Ethics,* October 1986, pp. 26–38. They discuss an epistemic approach, though they do not clearly distinguish between proceduralist and non-proceduralist versions.

2. Rawls, *Political Liberalism* (New York: Columbia University Press, 1993), p. 137. This approach to political legitimacy is richly motivated as well in Charles Larmore, *The Morals of Modernity* (Cambridge: Cambridge University Press 1996), especially chapters 1, 6, and 7.

3. I take up the special case of giving the power of decision all to one citizen (chosen randomly for each decision) below in the section on "Queen for a Day."

4. *A Preface to Democratic Theory* (Chicago: University of Chicago Press, 1956). Dahl explicitly opposes this to postulating that "the goals of some particular set of individuals are inherently right or good, and the process of making decisions should ensure maximization of these goals" (p. 31). It is not clear whether his motive for rejecting such favoritism is liberal or skeptical.

5 See Cohen, "Pluralism and Proceduralism," *Chicago-Kent Law Review,* vol. 69 (1994). Of theorists who reject using independent standards to judge democratic outcomes, few offer any clear account of the basis of democratic legitimacy. Thomas Christiano is more clear in defending a version of Fair Proceduralism in "Social Choice and Democracy," in Copp et al., eds., *The Idea of Democracy* (Cambridge: Cambridge University Press, 1993), pp. 183–186. He develops the view in detail in *The Rule of the Many* (Boulder, CO: Westview Press, 1996). Stuart Hampshire also endorses Fair Proceduralism quite explicitly in his review of Rawls's *Political Liberalism.* See *New York Review of Books,* August 12, 1993, pp. 43–47, esp. p. 46.

6. Bernard Manin provides a clear statement of Fair Deliberative Proceduralism: "Because it comes at the close of a deliberative process in which every one was able to take part, . . . the result carries legitimacy." See "On Legitimacy and Deliberation," *Political Theory* (August 1987), p. 359. Cass Sunstein's deliberative theory of democ-

racy is less clear on this score. He associates deliberative democracy with "a process through which rejection will encourage the emergence of general truths." See *The Partial Constitution* (Cambridge, MA: Harvard University Press, 1993), p. 253. And yet there is his ambiguous "association of truth in politics with what emerges from a well-functioning political process." See *Democracy and the Problem of Free Speech* (New York: Free Press, 1993), p. 243. Putting these together, he writes, "There are frequently correct answers to political controversy. Answers are understood to be correct through the only possible criterion, that is, agreement among equal citizens" (*The Partial Constitution*, p. 137). I argue, in "Who's Afraid of Deliberative Democracy?" *Texas Law Review* (June 1993), pp. 1437–1477, that Frank Michelman's deliberative theory of democracy also rejects the evaluation of outcomes by procedure independent standards. See, for example, "Conceptions of Democracy in American Constitutional Argument: The Case of Pornography Regulation," *Tennessee Law Review*, 56 2 (1989), pp. 291–319.

7. See, for example, Seyla Benhabib, "Toward a Deliberative Model of Democratic Legitimacy," in *Democracy and Difference* (Princeton: Princeton University Press, 1996), pp. 67–94: "It is not the sheer numbers which support the rationality of the conclusion [under majority rule], but the presumption that if a large number of people see certain matters a certain way as a result of following certain kinds of rational procedures of deliberation and decision-making, then such a conclusion has a presumptive claim to being rational until shown to be otherwise" (p. 72). James Fishkin also seems to hold to a view of this type. See my review in *Ethics* (October 1994), pp. 186–188, of his book *The Dialogue of Justice: Toward a Self-Reflective Society* (New Haven: Yale University Press, 1992).

8. "The Economic Basis of Deliberative Democracy," *Social Philosophy and Policy* 6:2 (1989), p. 32.

9. "Deliberation and Democratic Legitimacy," in Hamlin and Pettit, eds., *The Good Polity* (Oxford: Blackwell, 1989), p. 26.

10. Ibid., p. 29.

11. That they all involve procedure-independent standards of something like justice or the common good does not determine whether or not they involve procedure-independent standards of legitimacy. Epistemic Proceduralism, for example, does not. Cohen's view apparently does. See note 20 below.

12. I make this case at length in "Making Truth Safe For Democracy," in Copp, Hampton, Roemer, eds., *The Idea of Democracy* (Oxford: Oxford University Press, 1993), pp. 71–100.

13. *On the Social Contract*, Book I, chapter iv, paragraph 4. (Hereafter, SC I.iv.4.)

14. *The Second Treatise of Civil Government*, chapter VIII, section 96.

15. SC IV.ii.8.

16 John Rawls, *A Study in the Grounds of Ethical Knowledge*, Ph.D. dissertation, Princeton University (1950; available from University Microfilms International, Ann Arbor, Michigan), p. 319. Rawls goes on to identify the proper source of moral authority as the collective sense of right. This raises interesting questions that cannot be pursued here.

David Estlund

17. This is a running theme in Rousseau's *Emile,* trans. Allan Bloom (New York: Basic Books, 1979). It emerges explicitly at, e.g., pp. 84, 111–112, 120, 125, 148, 168, 207, 215. It may provide a clue to the puzzling role of the wise legislator in the *Social Contract.* Jason Maloy fruitfully compares the legislator to Emile's teacher in *The Mind of Utopia,* Honors Thesis, Brown University, 1996.

18. John Rawls, *Theory of Justice* (Cambridge, MA: Harvard University Press, 1971), pp. 356–357.

19. Notice that Cohen's definition of democratic legitimacy ("if and only if [the outcomes] would be the object of an [ideal] agreement," in "The Economic Basis of Deliberative Democracy," p. 32) commits him, with Rousseau, to a correctness theory rather than a proceduralist criterion of legitimacy; when actual procedures fail to match the answer of the hypothetical ideal procedure, they are not democratically legitimate, even though (as he seems to think) they are reliable evidence, to some degree, about that ideal standard. This is a crucial difference from Epistemic Proceduralism.

20. Condorcet's Jury Theorem has often been treated as identifying an epistemic engine that might drive an epistemic conception of democracy. For an introduction in this context, see Grofman and Feld, "Rousseau's General Will: A Condorcetian Perspective," *American Political Science Review* 82:2 (1988), pp. 567–576. See also Duncan Black, *The Theory of Committees and Elections* (Cambridge: Cambridge University Press, 1958); Brian Barry, *Political Argument* (Berkeley: University of California Press, 1965); and Cohen, "An Epistemic Conception of Democracy."

21. The result is so striking, and the proof of it so straightforward, that it is worth pausing a moment to consider. Begin with the fact that while a fair coin flipped a few times is not likely to produce a very equal head/tail ratio, with more tosses the ratio becomes more even. With just a few tosses, an outcome of, say 70% heads, 30% tails, would not be shocking. But with many tosses of a fair coin, a 70/30 split is almost out of the question. With enough tosses it becomes certain that the division will be almost exactly 50/50. This "Law of Large Numbers" is the core of the proof of the Jury Theorem.

Let us proceed in several small steps: first, change the coin from a fair one, to one weighted slightly in favor of heads, so in each toss it has a 51% chance of being heads. Now with enough tosses the percentage of heads is certain to be almost exactly 51%. The more tosses, the closer to exactly 51% it is likely to be. Now obviously the same would be true if instead of one coin flipped repeatedly, we considered many coins, all weighted the same way, each having a 51% chance of coming up heads. The more coins we flipped, the closer the frequency of heads would come to exactly 51%. Now, the same obviously would be true if we had individual voters instead of coins, where each will say either "heads" or "tails" but each has a 51% chance of saying "heads." The more such voters, the closer the frequency of "heads" answers would come to exactly 51%. Here is the payoff: if the frequency of "heads" is bound to be almost exactly 51%, then, of course, it is even more certain to be over 50%. So the chance that at least a majority will say "heads" is astronomical if the group is large, and it gets higher with the size of the group. It is also plainly higher if instead of 51%, each voter (or coin) has an even higher chance of saying "heads," say 55% or 75%.

So if voters each have an individual likelihood above 50% (call it [50+n]%) of giving the correct answer (whatever it is) to a dichotomous choice (heads/tails, yes/no, true/false, better/worse, etc.), then in a large group the percentage giving the correct answer is bound to be exceedingly close to (50+n)%. Therefore, the

# Beyond Fairness and Deliberation

chance that it will be at least 50% is even higher, approximating certainty as the group gets larger or the voters are better. In summary, if voters are all 51% likely to be correct, then in a large number of voters it is almost certain that almost exactly 51% will be correct, and so even more certain that more than 50% will be correct.

The results are very much the same if we weaken the assumption that all voters have the same competence, but assume only an average competence above 50%, so long as the individual competences that produce this average are distributed normally around the average. Abnormal distributions change the results significantly, sometimes for better, sometimes for worse.

22. While this probabilistic case is more intuitively compelling, I believe the same results are obtained even if it is accepted that all 1,000 cards are correct. The more general question then is whether epistemic authority (probabilistic or not) supports moral judgment.

23. Here is just one example, devised to be somewhat extreme: If in 51% of voting instances the average individual competence was .525, and if there are 10,000 voters, in those 51% of voting instances majority rule would be correct more than 99.99% of the time. Thus, overall, majority rule will almost certainly be correct more often than not, regardless of the competence of the voters in the other 49% of cases. Now suppose in the other cases voter competence was very low, say .10. The average voter competence would then be $(.10 \cdot 49\%) + (.525 \cdot 51\%)$, or about .32, well below .5. This shows that group competence can be better than .5 even if individuals do not have a competence over .5.

24. If such a view needs outcomes to be correct almost all the time, say at least 95% of the time, then it needs average individual competence to be over .5 slightly more than 95% of the time. In a very large group, this could be as close as you please to .5. Then voters in the other instances could be bad enough to bring the overall average below .5, but only slightly, because there cannot be very many of them. In this specific case the overall average competence must remain about .475. 95% at .5 = .475, so that's what the average competence would be if in the other 5% of cases voter competence were zero.

25. David Estlund, "Opinion Leaders, Independence, and Condorcet's Jury Theorem," *Theory and Decision*, vol. 36, no. 2 (1994).

26. This is not about the average competence. That could still be almost as low as .25, if half the voters had competence of 0.

27. Queen for a Day will be correct as often as it happens to pick a correct voter. The fraction of correct voters across instances of voting will equal the average voter competence.

28. Rousseau writes, "Elections by lot would have few disadvantages in a true democracy." (SC IV.iii.7). Notice that I have not criticized coin flips as undemocratic but only as epistemically random.

29. This is the epistemic conception of democracy defended in Carlos Santiago Nino, *The Ethics of Human Rights* (Cambridge: Cambridge University Press, 1991), pp. 245–255. For example, he claims "the democratic origin of a legal rule provides us with a reason to believe that there is good reason to accept its content and to act accordingly" (p. 255). This is deference to the expertise of the procedure with a vengeance.

David Estlund

30. Availability is understood, of course, to be constrained by which considerations can be accepted by all reasonable citizens.

31. There is some controversy whether there is a duty to do what you believe right. But it is perfectly obvious that in normal cases it is blameworthy not to *try* to do what is morally required, and you cannot try except by doing what you believe is morally required. Therefore, it is blameworthy not to do, and so morally required to do, what you believe is morally required. This does not deny that there could be especially perverse people whose moral beliefs are so distorted that we cannot count it in their favor that they are true to them.

32. This requirement is probably too high in the case of personal agents. You get moral credit for trying to do the right thing unless your judgment is much worse than random, perhaps because there is, in the personal case, a phenomenology of seeming right that is not present in the collective case, and that provides on its own some reasons for action.

33. This is puzzling to some, though it is not an uncommon view among political philosophers. Socrates had this view in Plato's *Crito*, and Rawls defends it in *Theory of Justice*, as have many others.

34. SC IV.ii.5–7.

35. I reply to criticisms of my view by Gerald Gaus and William Rehg in an addendum to a shorter version of the present paper in *The Modern Schoolman* (1997) 74:4. The shorter version is entitled "The Epistemic Dimension of Democratic Authority."

# 7

# Reason, Justification, and Consensus: Why Democracy Can't Have It All

*Gerald F. Gaus*

## 1   Three Ideals of Deliberative Democracy

My concern in this essay is the relation between three ideals that characterize a familiar version of deliberative democracy. The first, the *Ideal of Reason,* is at the heart of deliberative democracy. As Joshua Cohen observes, "[t]he notion of a deliberative democracy is rooted in the intuitive idea of a democratic association in which the justification of the terms and conditions of association proceeds through public argument and reasoning among citizens."[1] According to the Ideal of Reason, then,

Deliberation is *reasoned* in that the parties to it are required to state their reasons for advancing proposals, supporting or criticizing them. They give reasons with the expectation that those reasons (and not, for example, power) will settle the fate of their proposal.[2]

In itself, embracing the Ideal of Reason is hardly an innovation. Aristotle and his followers present us with an ideal of collective political choice based on reasoned deliberation; and to Frederick Watkins, the "distinguishing feature" of modern liberal thought is its emphasis on reasoned political deliberation.[3] Contemporary deliberative democracy is distinctive, however, in making two further claims. Deliberative democrats insist that deliberation must be public in a radical sense—only reasons that can be embraced by all of us are truly public, and hence justificatory. As Gerald Postema has put

Gerald F. Gaus

it, a public reason must be a shared reason.[4] So according to *the Ideal of Public Justification,* a policy or principle *P* is justified only if it can, in some way, be embraced by all members of the public.

Now many deliberative democrats maintain that, together, the Ideals of Reason and Public Justification lead to what I will call the *Regulative Ideal of Real Political Consensus.* Gerald Postema expresses this ideal when he tells us that "[a]greement among members of the community is set as the open-ended task or project of . . . [the] exercise of practical reason and judgment," and that "the aim of the regulative idea is agreement of conviction on the basis of public reasons uttered as assessed in public discourse. . . . "[5] While this basic idea seems clear enough, the Regulative Ideal of Real Political Consensus is difficult to characterize precisely. Deliberative democrats are well aware that complete actual consensus is not a reasonable aim "even under ideal conditions;" Postema is clear that the deliberations of citizens may not yield a consensus, and so we may have to cut the discussion off by taking a vote.[6] But, he says, no such closure can ever be final: *"public discussion must remain open until common conviction is reached."*[7] But although the regulative goal is not complete political consensus here and now, the Regulative Ideal of Real Political Consensus is more than the claim that ideally, all rational people should agree. Achieving actual common conviction is the ideal that should regulate political institutions and processes. As Postema stresses, this notion that public discourse can reach consensus is

not meant merely as a heuristic device, like Rawls' "original position," describing the reasoning of a hypothetical congregation of abstract, representative, rational beings whose choice under restricted conditions is supposed to tell us something about the principles we have reason to endorse. Rather, it is intended as a model for real moral discourse in concrete, historical, social conditions. It is an idealization, to be sure, but it is an ideal to which we can demand real social and political institutions to approximate.[8]

One way of expressing this ideal is to insist that healthy democratic political institutions should generate wide, though of course not complete, actual consensus on political outcomes. This, I think, is true to Rousseau, in whose footsteps many deliberative democrats follow. Recall that to Rousseau the breakdown of actual consensus into "contradictory views and debates" indicates the corruption of the body politic.[9] As he puts it, "[t]he more concert reigns in the assemblies, that is, the nearer the opinion approaches unanimity, the greater is the dominance of the general will. On the other hand, long debates, dissensions, and tumult proclaim the ascendancy of particular interests and the decline of the state."[10]

I shall argue in this essay that, far from leading us toward the Regulative Ideal of Real Political Consensus, The Ideals of Reason and Public Justification point us away from it.[11] Common conviction, I shall argue, is not a regulative ideal of political discourse aimed at sincere public justification. I begin in section 2 by further characterizing the Ideals of Reason and Public Justification; I then argue that these two ideals do not endorse the pursuit of actual political consensus. Sections 3 and 4 examine prominent attempts to unite the Ideals of Reason and Public Justification with the Regulative Ideal of Real Political Consensus; I argue that these important proposals fail to insulate politics from our broader disagreements and for that reason fail to show how actual political consensus can arise in a pluralistic society. I close in section 5 by sketching an alternative, adjudicative, conception of democracy which retains the Ideals of Reason and Public Justification but rejects the pursuit of actual political consensus. On this conception the quintessentially political is the practical resolution of intractable disputes, not the search for consensus.

## 2   Reason, Public Justification, and Disagreement

### 2.1   Sincerity as Part of the Ideal of Reason

As indicated above, according to the Ideal of Reason "[d]eliberation is *reasoned* in that the parties to it are required to state their reasons for advancing proposals, supporting or criticizing them. They give reasons with the expectation that those reasons (and not, for example, power) will settle the fate of their proposal."[12] To say that parties are giving "their reasons" supposes that they are giving what they believe to be *good* reasons. Postema insists that "[p]articipants regard themselves as bound by a principle of *sincerity* to present proposals and evidence, arguments, and interpretations that they can fully endorse."[13] This, I think, is actually too restrictive. Postema's principle would seem to imply that Betty, who is trying to convince Alf to accept her proposal $P$, can appeal to reason $r$ in support of $P$ only if Betty actually accepts $r$ as a good reason for *her* to endorse $P$.[14] But suppose that Betty proposes the policy that children's health care should be funded by the state. And suppose that Betty, an atheist and a feminist, supports this policy because she believes it will help empower women. But when deliberating with Alf, a Roman Catholic who supports right-to-life groups and believes that the proper place for women is in the home, she rightly believes that he will be unmoved by her reason. But suppose she says to Alf "Your religious beliefs about the sanctity of life justify your supporting children's health care." It certainly seems as if this would violate Postema's principle of sincerity, as Betty cannot fully endorse this reason. But, if (1) Betty really does have good reasons of her own to endorse state-funded children's health care, (2) she believes that Alf is justified in holding his religious beliefs, and (3) she believes that Alf's religious beliefs really ought to lead him to support state-funded children's health care, then her appeal to them doesn't seem objectionably insincere.[15] After all, she believes that she has good reasons to support the policy and that Alf is justified in entertaining reasons that should lead him to endorse the policy. In this case they have *convergent* reasons for supporting the policy.[16] I propose, then, a more modest Principle of Sincerity:

**S:** A reasoned justification must be sincere. Betty's appeal to reason $r$ justifying $P$ to Alf is sincere if and only if (1) she believes that she is justified in accepting $P$; (2) she believes that Alf is justified in accepting $r$; and (3) she believes that $r$ justifies $P$ in Alf's system of beliefs.

### 2.2  *Rational Consensus and the Pursuit of Actual Political Consensus*

Distinctive of contemporary deliberative democracy is the conjunction of this Ideal of Reason with an Ideal of Public Justification, or the giving of uniquely public reasons. One does not simply utter reasons that one finds sound, but one's arguments must be directed at what others can see as good reasons. As Kant said, to reason publicly is to "think from the standpoint of everyone else."[17] Now taken together, the Ideals of Reason and Public Justification lead us to seek a "rationally motivated consensus—to find reasons that are persuasive to all who are committed to acting on the results of a free and reasoned assessment of alternatives. . . . "[18] If (1) I am committed to giving good reasons for my political proposals and (2) I am also committed to the idea that these reasons must (in some sense) be seen as good reasons by every member of the public, I seem committed to the further claim that (3) my proposal P is justified only if, supposing all members of the public were rational, all would accept it. For if any rational member of the public does not have a good reason to accept my proposal, it appears that I have not lived up to the Ideal of Public Justification. And although the notion of a rationally motivated consensus is by no means the same as that of the Regulative Ideal of Real Political Consensus, it seems, at least on the face of it, that if the Ideals of Reason and Public Justification support the former they may well carry over to endorse the latter. My basic claim is that this is not so. That is, although it is indeed the case that the Ideals of Reason and Public Justification do commit us to an ideal of rationally motivated consensus, the same ideals prevent us from embracing the Regulative Ideal of Real Political Consensus.

In order to see why this is so, we must consider the relation between public justification and rational consensus. Three notions of public justification are worth considering. None, we shall see, combines all three elements of deliberative democracy: The Ideals of Reason, Public Justification, and the Regulative Ideal of Real Political Consensus.

The most obvious way to articulate the idea that public justification aims at rational consensus is:

**PJ(1):** Principle or policy P is publicly justified if and only if, supposing everyone reasoned in good faith, reasoned perfectly and had perfect information, everyone would accept P [or, alternatively, no one would reject P].[19]

Manifestly, this is consistent with **S,** the Principle of Sincerity. The "public" addressed in **PJ(1)** is composed solely of purely rational deliberators—they are perfectly rational, well informed and argue in good faith in the sense that they accept all, and only, what they have good reason to accept. But while **PJ(1)** expresses an ideal of sincere public justification, it does not ground the pursuit of actual political consensus. What would be done by fully rational and informed people with unlimited ability to process information does not seem an appropriate benchmark for *our* practice. That demigods would agree hardly seems a reason for us to aspire to actual political consensus. Ours is a condition of scarcity of cognitive resources and information, in which the pursuit of minimal rationality is challenging enough, without seeking to model our practices on what we would do if we had such semidivine status.[20] And because we know that actual people fall far short of cognitive perfection, one who accepts **PJ(1)** should not expect anything even approaching actual consensus on policy *P.*

**PJ(1)** supports the pursuit of actual consensual politics only if we can suppose—as I think Rousseau did—that the pursuit of actual consensus is the best way to track what perfectly rational agents would all accept. But a contrary hypothesis seems equally plausible: that actual consensus is better obtained by advancing arguments that do not meet **PJ(1).** For example, a large body of evidence indicates that most reasoners rely on what Amos Tversky and Daniel Kahneman describe as "heuristics"; of special interest here are the "vividness" and "availability" heuristics.[21] According to the former, people draw on the most vivid or psychologically salient bit of information, typically discounting or altogether ignoring better information; the latter concerns the way in which people base their judgments on the most readily retrievable information. Thus, for example, one reason that racial or ethnic stereotypes persist is that they focus on vivid and available information. People find these false but simple images compelling and attractive. Consequently, it seems a reasonable conjecture that the political judgments of cognitively imperfect people are more apt to converge (though of course incompletely) on stereotypical characterizations of some groups than are fully-informed understandings. A political style that sought to move as far as possible down the road of actual consensus may well employ stereotypes, thus embracing arguments that violate **PJ(1)**. A comparison of the deep cleavages in the democracies of the 1930s with the seemingly widespread consensus in authoritarian states, which made extensive appeal to ethnic stereotypes to vilify minority groups, suggests that this may well be more than an interesting possibility suggested by psychological research.

It might be responded that, although cognitively flawed arguments could perhaps gain wide approval, they could never be the objects of total consensus. But that seems quite beside the point, for we are never going to achieve complete actual consensus on any interesting constitutional or political issue. Our options are always between conditions of imperfect consensus. Given this, and given the wide attractiveness of heuristics that can lead to results that would be rejected by perfectly rational creatures, there is no compelling reason to suppose that the path to the most justified position according to **PJ(1)** is the same path as that which seeks the widest possible consensus among citizens in the actual political world.[22]

Perhaps the problem is with the thoroughly rationalistic conception of public justification expressed by **PJ(1)**. And, indeed, many deliberative democrats and political liberals[23] seem to offer a much less demanding conception:

**PJ(2)**:   Principle or policy *P* is publicly justified if and only if it would be accepted by every reasonable person reasoning in good faith [or, alternatively, it would not be rejected by any reasonable person reasoning in good faith].

"Liberal public justification," says Stephen Macedo, "properly seeks principles and arguments that can be widely seen to be reasonable."[24] Indeed, for Rawls the fundamental claim of political liberalism is not that it is true (something about which he is agnostic), but that it is "reasonable."[25] In a similar vein, Charles Larmore believes that respect for persons demands that political principles be justifiable to all reasonable people.[26] By "reasonableness," Larmore tells us, he means "thinking and conversing in good faith and applying, as best as one can, the general capacities of reason which belong to every domain of inquiry."[27] On this view, a principle or policy is justified if and only if it is accepted by every—or not rejected by any—reasonable person.

If we explicate "rationally motivated consensus" along the lines of **PJ(2)**, the jump from "rationally motivated consensus" to the Regulative Ideal of Real Political Consensus seems a short one; and thus it seems as if, after all, a deliberative democrat might be able to unite all the ideals. To be sure, **PJ(2)** does not require the actual consent of everyone before a principle or policy can be justifiably imposed; Larmore is quite right that requiring the actual assent of everyone would render politics impossible.[28] Unreasonable objections need not stop the coercive imposition of law. Clearly, though, those who adopt **PJ(2)** believe that, overwhelmingly, ordinary reasoners are— or usually are—reasonable in the requisite sense: they are free from gross cognitive defects and typically reason in good faith according to well-known and widely-accepted canons of thought. Consequently, a practice modeled on this conception of public justification would seem committed to some fairly broad-based actual political consensus; if almost everyone is reasonable (at least most of the time), and if a justified policy must be accepted by every reasonable person (or not rejected by any reasonable person), it is clearly a sign that things are amiss if policies are imposed in the face of actual widespread dissent.

**PJ(2)**, however, suggests an unacceptable notion of a rationally motivated consensus. It will be recalled that the notion of a rationally motivated consensus seems to derive from the Ideals of Reason and Public Justification. However, **PJ(2)** is inconsistent with the Ideal of Reason, as it sanctions arguments inconsistent with the Principle of Sincerity. To see this, consider again Betty's proposal that children's health care be provided by the government; suppose again that her atheist and feminist beliefs give her good reason to support the proposal. Alf is a reasonable person—he is cognitively normal and reasons in good faith according to widely embraced canons of thought; once again, he has religious beliefs that lead him also to endorse state-provided health care. According to **PJ(2)** the proposal would seem to be justified (in the public restricted to Alf and Betty). But let us now suppose that, in Betty's considered opinion, Alf's religious beliefs are not justified: she thinks religious beliefs are nonsense. In this case **S** implies that she has not engaged in reasoned justification if she appeals to Alf's religious beliefs; but according to **PJ(2)** the appeal would be justificatory. So, according to **PJ(2)** an imposed policy of state-supported children's health care would be justified, but Betty's commitment to reasoned justification insists that it is not. **PJ(2)** thus allows that what Betty sees as bad reasons may be justificatory.[29]

Of course this problem would not arise if it was the case that Alf thinking that $r$ is a good reason when it is not implies, ipso facto, that he is unreasonable. But this would essentially drive us right back to **PJ(1)**. And, as a matter of fact, it seems that quite reasonable people have a large number of unreasonable beliefs. Consider, for example, the famous belief perseverance experiments of Lee Ross and his associates, which induced subjects to develop theories and opinions on the basis of information that was later shown to them to be false.[30] In one experiment, subjects were given false feedback when sorting authentic suicide notes from fictitious ones. Based on their "successes" and "failures," subjects developed beliefs about their own competency at the task, and their future ability to make such discriminations. Afterwards, subjects were extensively debriefed, and each subject acknowledged that his or her "performance" was strictly an artifact of the experimenters' manipulation. Nevertheless, even after the experimenters discredited the evidence upon which their beliefs were based, subjects showed marked belief perseverance—subjects tended to believe they were competent at the task even after the evidence for their competency was undermined. Similar results were achieved in an experiment in which subjects were induced, by being given false evidence, to develop theories about the relation between firefighters' professional performance and the firefighters' scores on a test for risk taking. Once again, despite being later informed that the scores were fictitious, subjects showed significant perseverance in their theories. The subjects were above normal in intelligence, and their beliefs were subject to far more rigorous criticism than are most of our political beliefs. In spite of all this, subjects continued to hold beliefs that seem manifestly unjustified.[31] Since the evidence in favor of their beliefs was shown by the experimenters to be illusory, the belief that they do not know whether they possess these skills is strikingly more credible than the belief that they do. The subjects have all the information they need to draw that conclusion, yet they do not. The results of this experiment are consistent with a large body of evidence showing that reasonable people often have strikingly unreasonable beliefs.[32]

More promising for an account of public justification is to focus on reasonable beliefs rather than reasonable people:

**PJ(3):** Principle or policy *P* is publicly justified if and only if everyone has reasonable grounds for accepting it [or, alternatively, no one has reasonable grounds for rejecting it].[33]

The focus here is not on what reasonable *people* accept (or reject) but whether principles or policies would be accepted or rejected on the basis of reasonable beliefs. A theorist of deliberative democracy relying on **PJ(3)** could respond to the above case by insisting that Betty's argument is not justificatory, even though reasonable Alf accepts it because his acceptance of it is not based on a reasonable belief.

Explications of **PJ(3)** must avoid collapsing into either **PJ(1)** or **(2).** If we characterize a reasonable belief as one that a fully rational, perfectly well-informed person would accept, we move back to **PJ(1).** Even an articulation of "reasonableness" in terms of what is fully justified (where one can have a fully justified belief that is not what a fully informed person would believe)[34] would seem to share the problem of **PJ(1):** there is no compelling reason to suppose that the pursuit of actual political consensus is the best way to track what would be accepted by beings who always had fully justified beliefs. On the other hand, to hold that "[a]n understanding . . . is fully reasonable just in case its adherents are stably disposed to affirm it as they acquire new information and subject it to critical reflection"[35] drives us back to **PJ(2):** a reasonable belief seems very much whatever a reasonable person is disposed to affirm.[36] To avoid these sorts of collapses an explication of **PJ(3)** must, I think, appeal to something like a minimally credible belief or reason. A reasonable belief, let us say, is one that is sufficiently credible to justify acceptance, assuming that a belief that violates clear maxims of logic or is based on manifestly bad evidence cannot be sufficiently credible. The notion of a sufficiently credible belief is, I think, fundamental to justification. Analyses of cognitive complexity show that human belief systems are far too vast, and processing time much too precious, for us to accept the rule "Only believe what is best justified."[37] In order to efficiently cope with such complexity, cognizers typically evaluate beliefs just long enough to decide whether they are sufficiently credible—that is, they pass some threshold of reasoning or of evidence that is sufficient to show that they merit acceptance. And this threshold will be far below what is required to obtain the best (i.e., most justified) belief.[38]

Although attractive—and I believe ultimately correct—this sort of explication of reasonable public justification requires appeal to people's epistemic judgments about what constitutes a minimally credible belief. Although we can expect more consensus on what is a sufficiently credible belief than we can on what is the correct or best justified belief, there is nevertheless bound to be considerable dispute. To some all religious beliefs are unreasonable. Recall here Freud's characterization of religion: "[t]he whole thing is so patently infantile, so foreign to reality, that to anyone with a friendly attitude to humanity it is painful to think that the great majority of mortals will never be able to rise above this view of life."[39] On the other hand, many committed Christians insist that appeals to their religious convictions in political choice are entirely reasonable (as indeed do many liberal philosophers);[40] it is Freudianism, they say, that is preposterous. The same can be said by, and about, Marxism, eco-feminism, deconstructionism, libertarianism and fascism. This is not the point that many claim that whatever they believe to be false they also believe to be unreasonable.[41] The point, rather, is that for any one of these doctrines, a large number of citizens firmly believe that they are more than a little crazy; they are not just wrong, but unreasonably so.[42] The problem is that we do not simply live in a society with plural understandings of the good life, but with diverse and conflicting ideologies that insist their competitors are *deeply* misguided. None of this is to say that political life in an ideologically fractured society is impossible. It does, however, strain beyond plausibility the claim that politics ought—even ideally—to aim at actual consensus. If I believe that eco-feminism is an unreasonable doctrine, then even

Gerald F. Gaus

accepting **PJ(3)**, I will not see myself as having a reason to obtain the assent of an eco-feminist, nor see her rejection of my proposal as showing it is not publicly justified.

## 3 Consensus and the Political Point of View

### 3.1 Political Reasonableness

Deliberative democrats who accept the notion of public justification as explicated by **PJ(3)** need to show that, notwithstanding these debates, an actual consensus obtains as to what constitutes a reasonable belief, and thus the Regulative Ideal of Real Political Consensus is grounded in the Ideals of Reason and Public Justification. Political liberals such as Rawls and Cohen seek to do just this by insisting that public justification depends on a distinctively political conception of reasonableness. "[P]olitical liberalism," Rawls tells us, "aims for a political conception of justice as a freestanding view."[43] It is thus "expounded apart from, or without reference to, any . . . wider background."[44] For Rawls, then, political liberalism is justified from a distinctively political point of view. The political point of view, it seems, gives rise to a distinctively political conception of reasonableness. From the political point of view it would seem that a proposal is reasonable if it meets several conditions.[45] *First,* it must affirm—or at least be consistent with—the importance of achieving a fair system of cooperation, and it must support abiding by the requirements of such a system. *Second,* it will not seek to repress competing reasonable doctrines. *Third,* it must recognize that the "burdens of judgment" lead to conflicting judgments about questions of the good and the claims that others have on us. Thus we must recognize that in many of our moral and valuational disputes:

a. The evidence—empirical and scientific—bearing on the case is conflicting and complex, and thus hard to assess and evaluate.

b. Even when we fully agree about the kinds of considerations that are relevant, we may disagree about their weight and so we arrive at different judgments.

c. To some extent all our concepts, and not only moral and political concepts, are vague and subject to hard cases; and this indeterminacy means that we must rely on judgment and interpretation. . . .

d. To some extent (how great we cannot tell) the way we assess evidence and weigh moral and political values is shaped by our total experience, our whole life up to now; and our total experiences may differ. . . .

e. Often there are different kinds of normative considerations of different force on both sides of an issue and it is difficult to make an overall assessment.

f. . . . In being forced to select among cherished values, or when we hold to several and must restrict each in view of the requirements of the others, we face great difficulties in setting priorities and making adjustments. Many hard decisions seem to have no clear answer.[46]

Rawls thus advances a purely political conception of the reasonable or, we might say, a notion of what is reasonable from the political point of view. From the political point of view, then, a religious doctrine is reasonable just in case it meets these three conditions. Although Freud may think that the doctrine is unreasonable from the psychological or epistemic points of view, it is politically reasonable. And it is political reasonability that counts for **PJ(3)**. Thus, it is claimed that (1) political reasonableness can be distinguished from epistemic reasonableness and (2) disagreements about epistemic reasonableness do not lead to disagreements about political reasonableness. The fundamental challenge for political liberalism's conception of deliberative democracy is to justify these two claims; unless that can be done, there is little reason to think that **PJ(3)** provides the basis for pursuit of actual political consensus.

### 3.2 Points of View

To reply to this challenge, the political liberal-deliberative democrat must explain what is meant by a political point of view, and distinguish this point of view from an epistemic, religious or economic perspective. As an initial proposal we might, in Aristotelian fashion, identify a *telos* or end that is unique to each point of view. Thus we might, as Cohen suggests, characterize the political perspective as aiming at the common good;[47] in contrast, we might say, the economic perspective sees social life in terms of seeking the satisfaction of preferences while the religious perspective devotes itself to the end of salvation. But this proposal seems overly narrow in two ways. First, it is by no means obvious that perspectives are best understood as having a unitary end; more generally, it is far from clear that all perspectives are properly characterized simply in terms of *ends*. The religious perspective, for example, may be better understood as expressing an attitude than seeking an end. We can probably say, though, that a point of view will always be characterized by a constellation of interests, concerns and considerations. If it is too narrow to characterize the political simply in terms of the pursuit of the common good, it doesn't seem wrong to insist that the political, as the political, is not concerned with the pursuit of beauty for its own sake (or salvation?). And, we might say, the constellation of interests and concerns that characterizes the political is distinct from that which characterizes the economic perspective. If we cannot say at least that, we cannot distinguish the political from the economic point of view.

This points to a familiar debate. Marxists reject the idea that politics and economics are distinct points of view, characterized by distinct interests, concerns and problems. For them political economy forms a coherent perspective: to simplify, we can say that to the Marxist, politics and economics both view the world from the perspective of group interest and power. This contrasts with those who insist that, while related, the political and economic points of view are distinct; thus a "mainstream" economist might insist that economics views social relations in terms of preference satisfaction and efficiency while political science views society in terms of authority, power and coercion. The political, economic, religious and moral points of view are all subject to these sorts of debates. To adopt H. L. A. Hart's distinction between a concept and a conception,[48] it seems right to say that the concept of the political perspective is characterized by competing conceptions. A Marxist has very different ideas about the nature of politics than does a deliberative democrat. It is important to stress that this is not the banal point that the Marxist and deliberative democrat have different political proposals—it is the more interesting point that they entertain different conceptions of the political.

It does not seem possible to make a claim that $R$ is a reason from the political perspective that is not related to some particular conception of politics. Points of view are theoretical notions; to employ them is to rely on some more or less well developed conception of what politics is all about. Let me, then, propose the Principle of Points of View:

**PV:** $R$ can be deemed a reason from a point of view $V$ only if $C$, a conception of $V$, deems $R$ to be a reason.

An obvious objection to **PV** might be advanced by a certain sort of realist, according to whom no conception $C$ could render $R$ a reason because $R$ is a reason simply in virtue of being a fact about the world, not because it is deemed so by some theoretical construct. However, **PV** in no way claims that $R$ is an artifact of $C$, only that $R$ cannot be identified as a reason from point of view $V$ independently of some notion of what $V$ is all about.

### 3.3 The Principle of Perspectival Autonomy

Suppose we are confronted by two (and for simplicity assume only two) conceptions of the political point of view. According to $C_1$, $R$ is reasonable from the political point of view; $C_2$ denies this. Is, then, $R$ reasonable from the political point of view? **PV** suggests that it depends on which is the superior conception. If we know that $C_1$ is a truly awful conception of the political, while $C_2$ is an extremely well-justified conception, then we have excellent grounds for denying that $R$ is reasonable from the political point of view. So if we know which is the better conception, we know how to proceed. Not surprisingly, then, the question becomes: how do we adjudicate between competing conceptions?

Gerald F. Gaus

Those who take perspectival reasoning seriously, I think, are apt to be attracted to what I shall call the *Principle of Perspectival Autonomy:*

**PA:** $C_1$ is a better conception of $V$ than $C_2$ if and only if $C_1$ is better justified solely on the basis of $V$ reasons.

The basic idea here is that the proper epistemic bases for determining, say, the best conception of the political point of view are inherently political reasons. The attractiveness of this proposal to those who seek to reason from the political point of view should be manifest: it holds out the promise that we can develop a purely political conception of politics—a freestanding view of politics—and so we can insulate our understanding of the political from sectarian religious, moral and epistemic disputes.

I don't think we ought to be too worried by the obvious objection to **PA,** namely, that the epistemic base we employ to evaluate conceptions of the political cannot be determined until we possess a conception of the political. We seem caught in a circle: we cannot know what is a political reason until we have the correct conception of politics, but we only know what is the correct conception of politics by appeal to political reasons. Those who worry about circularity will be impressed by the problem. I doubt whether advocates of reflective equilibrium will be. The familiar reflective equilibrium account would maintain that we have an intuitive conception of the political, which we employ to evaluate various proposed conceptions; but these conceptions in turn are employed to refine and verify our intuitions. And so we proceed back and forth, seeking a narrow equilibrium between our political intuitions and conception of the political.[49] At the end of the process, one could affirm both **PV** and **PA:** the preferred conception is justified only by appeal to political reasons (thus satisfying **PA**), but now only considerations approved by the preferred conception count as political reasons (hence satisfying **PV**).

Let us accept this. Suppose that conception $C_1$ is in narrow reflective equilibrium with our political intuitions. Suppose further that, according to $C_1$, $R$ is reasonable from the political point of view. Does this mean that $R$ really is reasonable from the political point of view? To make the problem less abstract: suppose that a certain variety of

Machiavellianism is in narrow equilibrium with our intuitions about politics, and suppose that, according to this conception, when one assumes power by overthrowing a prince, one should immediately kill the former prince's family.[50] Would it follow that it is politically reasonable to do so? Two cases need to be distinguished.

1. The first can be set aside quickly. Assume that one has a well-justified belief that this Machiavellian conception of politics is the best justified conception, but one also has a religious ethic that instructs one never to kill humans. In this case the political point of view clashes with the religious point of view. Even if the religious perspective is the more important of the two—even if religious reasons override political reasons—it would still be the case that, from the political perspective, it is reasonable to kill the former prince's family. That it is reasonable to do something from the political point of view does not imply that it is reasonable to do it all things considered. To be sure, a theory that stressed reasoning from the political point of view would have to deal with the possibility of these sorts of conflicts, but in themselves they would not undermine the autonomy of the political.

2. The second case is more of a worry. Consider one who embraced the Machiavellian conception of politics, but who also accepted a religion according to which God always undoes the plans of murderers—He ensures that their plans always backfire. Given this religious belief, is it reasonable *from the political point of view* to kill the family of the former prince? It is hard to see how it could be. The point of killing his family is to ensure political success; but one's religious beliefs assure one that God will not allow murders to achieve success. So taking into account one's religious beliefs (which, I shall assume, are more firmly justified than the political intuitions), it is manifestly unreasonable to murder the family. This is not like the previous case in which an action is perfectly reasonable from the political point of view but is overridden by a different perspective's reasoning; rather, taking into account one's religious beliefs, one has no reason at all to murder.

This example illustrates that a rational believer cannot compartmentalize her beliefs in a way that refuses to recognize that one perspective can entirely undermine the conclusions of another. Although considerations of cognitive efficiency indicate that it will usually not be efficient to scan far-flung parts of one's belief system for such undermining reasons, it nevertheless is true that they may be relevant, and when they are known to be relevant, a rational person will take account of them. But if different parts of our belief systems interact in these ways the Principle of Perspectival Autonomy is implausible. For epistemic, economic, political and religious convictions will affect our view of what is politically reasonable; and thus the effort to insulate political reasonableness from these other disputes cannot succeed. Because notions of political reasonableness will be affected by our epistemic, religious and other commitments, there is little prospect of a consensus emerging on what is politically reasonable in a society that disagrees on what is religiously, morally and epistemically reasonable.

It might be replied here that the example simply shows that I have construed the political point of view too narrowly. If a person's religious beliefs impact on what she sees as politically reasonable, then those beliefs are part of the political point of view, and are political reasons. But to accept this interpretation undermines the point of trying to identify a political perspective: the aim, it will be recalled, is to show that there can be actual consensus on the politically reasonable in a deeply pluralistic society. If, however, we allow the identification of the political point of view to be affected by religious, epistemic and other commitments, it will no longer serve as a common perspective.

### 3.4 The Robustness of the Political

The failure of the Principle of Perspectival Autonomy calls into doubt a core idea of political liberalism, sometimes expressed by Rawls through the metaphor of a module. "To use a current phrase, the political conception is a module, an essential constituent part, that fits into and can be supported by various reasonable comprehensive doctrines that endure in the society regulated by it."[51] The notion that the political is a distinct and independent perspective that can be plugged into a variety of belief systems, and remains the same whatever system it is plugged into, points to **PA**. A somewhat different idea is suggested by Rawls's remark that the module is "supported by various reasonable comprehensive doctrines." Here the claim seems to be that the political is not so much a distinct module but that it has the quality of robustness: although it links up with and depends on other parts of the system, it retains the same characteristics in each person's belief system, and is not affected by the different epistemological, religious and economic views by which it is supported. On this view the political is not so much *freestanding* as *easily supported:* it needs legs (to slightly change metaphors), but any reasonable doctrine will provide them, and the legs will not change the character of what is supported.

Robustness is certainly a virtue in a conception of the political. If everyone's different moral, religious or epistemic beliefs lead them to adopt significantly different conceptions of politics, there will be political chaos in pluralistic societies. But that robustness of the political is something to be sought does not, of course, mean that we can achieve anything like maximum robustness. In particular, it is exceedingly difficult to see how one can articulate a conception of political reasonableness that is even roughly robust in relation to one's epistemic notions of what constitutes a reasonable belief. Consider, for example, the overall rational response of a confident atheist to arguments for religious toleration. Our atheistic humanist is likely to accept general arguments for free speech and privacy; she may well be convinced that any reasonable person will see that these liberties are essential to leading a satisfying life. But she will resist calls to constitutionally protect freedom of religion, as she is convinced that religion involves gross errors of reasoning and is based on childish superstition; any specific appeal to religion as a valuable human activity she dismisses as absurd. Consequently, although she embraces **PJ(3)**, and so accepts that any proposal to which there is a reasonable objection is not publicly justified, she concludes that there is no reasonable objection to refusing to admit specific constitutional provisions protecting religion as such. All objections are, she concludes, based on some affirmation of the value of religion, and so they are absurd. What is supported gets modified by how it is supported; the nature of the justification affects what it is that is justified. Jeremy Waldron makes this point in relation to conceptions of private property:

> To repeat: the conception of private property we adopt is not a matter of independent choice; it is the upshot of the arguments we are convinced by. . . . The same holds true of other contestable concepts in political philosophy. For example, we cannot simply opt for one conception of harm or another in the context of Mill's famous "Harm Principle." Everything depends on the arguments used to defend the "Harm Principle": for example, one set of arguments may have as its upshot a conception of harm that necessarily includes moral offence; another set of arguments may have as its upshot a conception that excludes this. Since our arguments are our connection with the considerations that ultimately *matter* to us, we should take their upshot more seriously than we take the results of any independent "conceptual analysis."[52]

### 3.5 The Two Distinct Conceptions Argument

At this point it might simply be insisted that all this rests on a confusion: epistemic and political reasonableness are simply different ideas. A view is epistemically reasonable just in case believing it is justified, while a view is politically reasonable (let us say) just in case it tolerates others. If so, then our atheist is simply confused or being ambiguous when she asserts that the religious citizen has unreasonable views; if it tolerates other views of the good life and religions it simply *is* politically reasonable, full stop.

But this won't do. I leave aside the stipulative character of this proposal—its simply insisting that "reasonable" means "tolerant." Even if we accept it, this proposal will not allow us to interpret **PJ(3),** that is, that proposal *P* is publicly justified if and only if there are reasonable grounds for everyone to accept it (or there are no reasonable grounds for anyone to reject it). If we strip the concept of reason to simply mean "tolerant" we cannot apply **PJ(3),** for we can no longer explain what is a reasonable ground for accepting or rejecting a proposal. The only thing that is politically reasonable is toleration and the only thing that is politically unreasonable is intolerance; so what constitutes a reasonable objection or acceptance? I suppose we could say that no proposal that tolerates everyone could reasonably be rejected, and so is publicly justified. But this gives us no way to evaluate the public justifiability of proposals about property rights, economic institutions, political arrangements and so on. It seems a hopelessly thin principle of public justification, unsuitable to libertarianism, much less to deliberative democracy.

## 4  Reason Socialized

The problem of identifying a common public reason in a society of diverse reasoners is central to Hobbes's political theory; the solution he proposes is worth examining. For Hobbes the conflict in the state of nature arises from conflicting private judgments;[53] people's private reasoning yields conflicting judgments of right and wrong, as well as matters of fact, and this leads to the less intellectual conflict that characterizes the state of nature. Hobbes's solution is to appoint an "arbitrator."[54] This "judge," said Hobbes, provides "public reason" to which private reason "must submit."[55] As David Gauthier observes:

The individual mode of deliberation, in which each person judges for herself what she has reason to do, is to be supplanted by a collective mode, in which one person judges what we all have reason to. . . . [O]nce they have agreed, then rationality is exercised not by the individual parties to the controversy. Someone who then acted on the basis of her own judgment would of course still exhibit the capacity for rationality, but her rationality would be deficient. She would exhibit rationality correctly only in conforming or endeavoring to conform her actions to the arbitrator's judgment.[56]

This would seem to solve the problem: the arbitrator proclaims what is politically reasonable, and so defines a single, coherent conception of political reason. And because we have authorized the judge to define public reason for us, the judge's pronouncements constitute a shared public reason on which there is consensus. In short, the sovereign defines what is reasonable, and so allows a common interpretation of **PJ(3)**. This does not seem simply a matter of *doing* what the arbitrator says to do: it is a matter of *taking his reasoning as your reasoning*. And it is a demand of reason itself that you do this.

Rationality frees us . . . from dependence on our own considered judgments, in contexts in which that dependence is disadvantageous to us. In this respect, rationality is, as it were, a remedy for ills that it itself creates. Differing from our fellows in judgments, we find controversy and conflict in our interactions with them. So long as each relies on his own judgments, only force can resolve such conflicts. If each demands that his own reason be taken for right reason, then Hobbes's war of every man against every man must result—and this is "intolerable in the society of men." By transferring the locus of deliberation from each individual to an agreed arbitrator, rationality supplants the resort to force in the resolution of conflicts.[57]

Rationality comes to have a social dimension: a shared judgment with others. Kurt Baier, also drawing on Hobbes, has advanced a similar proposal. To coordinate our actions, he argues, we require guidelines that overrule "self-anchored reasons" (which may tempt us to defect from coordinative schemes). But, he argues (following Hobbes), these coordinative guidelines are not merely another set of self-anchored reasons that defeat our self-anchored reasons to defect, they are a different sort of practical reason: "we can think of the reasons based on them as society anchored."[58] Gauthier and Baier concur in their reading of Hobbes insofar as they both understand him to be arguing that reason drives us to supplant our private judgments with shared social judgments about what reasons we have.

To evaluate this neo-Hobbesian account of political reason, we must keep before us the distinction between the following deliberative schemas:

A. Consulting his system of beliefs, Alf considers:

i. Betty knows more about situation $S$ than does he;

ii. Betty tells him that $p$ is the best thing to believe in $S$;

iii. if he had access to Betty's expertise and information, he too would believe $p$ in $S$;

iv. Alf concludes that it is reasonable for him to believe $p$.

B. Consulting his system of belief, Alf considers:

i. relying on his own (private) reasoning in situation $S$ will lead to conflict;

ii. if each believes what Betty says ($q$) there will not be conflict in $S$.

iii. because Alf's interests would be advanced by securing peace, he would benefit from believing $q$. This gives him a strong reason ($r$) to believe $q$.

iv. relying on his own (private) reasoning, Alf concludes that *not-q* is justified; he believes that this conclusion would not change in the light of further information or arguments.

v. Alf concludes that it is reasonable for him to believe *q*.

The deliberation outlined in (A) is not problematic: it sketches relying on the knowledge of experts.[59] When we recognize an expert authority we take her reasoning as a proxy for our own because we suppose that she knows more than we do (A.i) and if we had access to what she knows, we would conclude the same thing (A.iii). The neo-Hobbesian argument is fundamentally different: it insists that *r* can give me a reason to take *q* as a reasonable belief for me to embrace, even though I am convinced that given complete information and faultless reasoning I would conclude that *not-q* is the justified belief. Clause B.iv is what makes the argument interesting, for it takes the reasoning of the arbitrator not as a proxy for your own but as replacing or supplanting your own. If we delete (iv), schema (B) can be reinterpreted as at least a possible case of expert authority (i.e., schema [A]), where Alf would himself conclude *q* if he thought about it hard enough. The interesting case for the neo-Hobbesian is when Alf believes that, if left to his private judgment, he would conclude *not-q*.

An appeal by Alf to *q* in a public justification would violate the Principle of Sincerity. Ex hypothesi, Alf believes that given his system of belief, *not-q* is the justified belief; that is what is meant by saying that if he deliberated about it on his own, he would believe it. Of course he may think that if he deliberated about it on his own he would just make a mistake, and that is why he believes what Betty says—but that leads us back to schema (A). On schema (B) Alf is confident that, given his own reasons, *not-q* is the justified belief. However, Alf also has reason *r*, and *r* indicates that important interests of Alf would be secured if he accepted *q* as a reason. But even if this does give Alf a genuine reason to get himself to believe *q*,[60] it is not the belief that he thinks is justified given his system of beliefs. And given that, he cannot sincerely appeal to it in a public justification, for sincerity requires that he can only appeal to beliefs that he

Gerald F. Gaus

is justified in accepting. We see here, then, that we can unite a version of **PJ(3)** with the Regulative Ideal of Real Political Consensus if we abandon the Principle of Sincerity.

But, the neo-Hobbesian will reply, Alf *is* justified in accepting $q$: his justification is $r$. Consequently, he can sincerely appeal to it in public justification. This case is very much like one offered by Bernard Williams, which I have examined elsewhere.[61] In this famous case a man has good reason to believe that his son has been drowned at sea, though he does not know this for certain:

> Somebody might say: if he wants to believe that his son is alive and this hypnotist can bring it about that he believes that his son is alive, then why should he not adopt the conscious project of going to the hypnotist and getting the hypnotist to make him believe this; then he will have got what he wants—after all, what he wants is to believe that his son is alive, and this is the state that the hypnotist will have produced in him. But there is one sense—I think the more plausible one—of "he wants to believe that his son is alive" in which he means that *he wants his son to be alive*—what he essentially wants is the *truth* of his belief. This is what I call a truth-centred motive. The man with this sort of motive cannot conceivably consciously adopt this project, and we can immediately see that the project for him is incoherent. For what he wants is something about the world, something about his son, namely, that he be alive, and he knows perfectly well that no amount of drugs, hypnotism and so on applied to himself is going to bring that about.[62]

The neo-Hobbesian is in a similar situation: he wants it to be the case that $q$ is reasonable, but the reasonability of $q$ is determined by how well it is justified in his system of beliefs. Giving himself another reason to embrace it—that it will advance his interests to see it as reasonable—does not make it reasonable. And it clearly won't do to say to himself that, although he is not epistemically justified in accepting $q$, he is pragmatically justified in holding it, and so it is reasonable to embrace it. For, like the father in Williams's story, he could not consciously hold the belief on this ground: he must deceive himself into thinking that $q$ really is reasonable (justified). That is, the neo-Hobbesian cannot simply say to himself "I am justified in believing $q$ is reasonable because believing it is reasonable will do me good, though all my reflections about it lead me to conclude that $q$ is not reasonable."

Perhaps the problem with the neo-Hobbesian socialized account of reason is that it is not socialized *enough:* it retains the idea of private reason, which can always be used to check and criticize the pronouncements of society. Perhaps our inspiration should be not Hobbes, but Wittgenstein. Understanding rationality in terms of rule-following, Postema argues:

> Rule-following is possible, then, only if subjects are equipped with two closely related intersubjective capacities: (a) the capacity to negotiate with other subjects a conciliation and adjustment of belief and behavior; and (b) the resulting capacity to anticipate, on the basis of experience and in the practice of negotiation and mutual adjustment, the outcome in particular cases of negotiations directed toward settlement.[63]

Thus, it is argued, reasoning itself presupposes a "community," or common rules of thought. Wittgenstein, it will be recalled, argued that one could not have a private rule that one only followed once— for in such a case we could not know whether the rule was actually followed.[64] More generally, it has been argued that one cannot have a private rule, for one needs to be able to distinguish when one has correctly followed the rule and when one has gotten it wrong. But, assert Wittgensteinians such as Susan Hurley, "the difference between making a mistake and following a rule . . . and following a different rule, or none at all, is not to be found among the intrinsic, nonrelational, individualistically identified properties, movements, or states of an individual."[65] Indeed, according to the neo-Wittgensteinians, we must look to others to check and correct our performances. Thus it seems that the very idea of rule-following—and, so, of reason—supposes convergence with others. And if so, the search for reason is a search for consensus, thus uniting the Ideals of Reason, Public Justification and the Regulative Ideal of Real Political Consensus.

This is not the place to evaluate intersubjective theories of justified belief.[66] At least in its more or less basic Wittgensteinian version, however, the argument provides scant support for the Regulative Ideal of Real Political Consensus in a pluralistic society. Just as a society may be characterized by a number of languages and diverse dialects, it may be composed of diverse groups, sharing intragroup intersubjectively validated rules of reason. No reasoner would be a private reasoner, and each would check his performances by reference to intersubjective agreement within his group. But nothing in the basic Wittgensteinian account requires that the groups must themselves negotiate their differences. India need not adopt Esperanto to conform to Wittgensteinian insights. And neither must the diverse cultural, religious and philosophical groups converge on a common conception of the reasonable.

Postema has a reply. "We assume," he argues, "a *unity*" of experience:

This fundamental orientating frame of reference is expressed not only in the experience of difference as disunity or inconstancy, but also in the drive to reconcile, to achieve constancy. Thus unity, taking shape as an orientating frame, makes constancy both possible and necessary. Unity is experienced, we might say, as both a *Sein* and a *Sollen* (that is, as both a fact about us and a rational demand on us). This orientating idea commissions us—it empowers and obligates us—to seek conciliation.[67]

This supposition of the unity of experience would thus seem to drive us toward a "reconciliation" and "negotiation" of our differences with others. This, though, leads us back to the differences between **PJ(1)** and **(3)**. Even granting the supposition of the unity of experience, this would give us a strong push toward actual consensus only if we were thoroughly rational creatures; for actual cognizers, a plausible hypothesis for difference of belief is that one of the parties is simply wrong, and will continue to be wrong, since reasonable people are known to persist in unreasonable beliefs. Given the plausibility of this hypothesis, a reasoner devoted to sincerity would often have excellent grounds to resist "negotiating" differences. If you have excellent grounds for believing that your group is right, and that the other is persisting in unreasonable error (recall here Freud's view of the religious), a commitment to sincere reason-giving would block negotiated settlement. In negotiations one gives up something of value to achieve agreement; sincere reasoners will not give up good reasons to nail down the deal.

## 5  Adjudicating Reasonable Disagreement

### 5.1  Sincerity: Splitting Hairs, Not the Difference

The problem, then, is that a commitment to sincere reasoning often, perhaps typically, prevents us from securing agreement. Sincere reasoners will find themselves in principled disagreements. The metaphor of a "negotiation" is appropriate when interests or preferences are at stake, but not in discussions aimed at the truth.[68] And just as one must be guided by one's own understanding of the truth, so too must one be guided by one's own understanding of reasonableness when applying a principle of public justification. My efforts to sincerely give what I believe to be good arguments that will not be rejected on reasonable grounds inevitably calls on my own understanding of what constitutes reasonableness. Among the political liberals, Charles Larmore stands out, not only grasping but stressing this central truth:

Here has arisen the great dilemma pointed out by Habermas's critics. If we imagine that under ideal conditions others continue to hold their own view of the world, and that that view is significantly different from our own (imagine them to be the Bororo, or Tutankhamen and Li Po), we cannot expect that they could come to agree with us about the justification of some substantial claims of ours. And if, as Habermas seems to prefer, we imagine the supposedly ideal conditions as detached from our general view of the world as well as from theirs, we have no good notion of what would take place, if anything, and it is certainly unclear what sense there would be to saying that it is with the Bororo that we would be conversing. The quandary can be avoided, however, if the ideal conditions in which someone supposes his claim would be vindicated to others are understood as *including what he considers to be the correct general view of the world and of ways of acquiring knowledge about it.*[69]

Because this is so, we will inevitably have competing judgments about what is publicly justified. To be sure, on some matters we may converge: on basic constitutional matters dealing with abstract rights, for example. And even in normal politics we can expect significant agreement about many matters. Without some wide and deep agreement a viable political order cannot be attained. But this sort of consensus is a matter of sociology, not philosophy. Just how much consensus is required, and how it is to be achieved, are questions that, at least ideally, a political sociologist could tell us. Political consensus, though, is not a test for justification; indeed, I have tried to show here that it is not even usually a good thing to seek.

Sincere reasoners offering public justifications will constantly differ. They will arrive at conflicting judgments about the notion of reasonableness, about what has met the test of reasonableness, about what is sincere and much else. That is, a political order that embraces the Ideals of Reason and Public Justification will be one of constant arguments and disputes about what is justified, and there is no reason to think that anything remotely like actual consensus will emerge on these issues. Indeed, efforts to give the best justification—to live up to the Principle of Sincerity and **PJ(3)**—may well lead one to put forth arguments that block consensus. One can often achieve consensus by splitting the difference, giving something to everyone. However, as philosophers know better than most, this often leads to blurring the dispute and confusing the issue. Philosophers excel at splitting hairs—sharpening differences and making fine distinctions; that is an excellent way to seek the truth (or, that which is best justified), but it is not a particularly good way to achieve consensus.

### 5.2 The Lockean Solution

The situation of agents devoted to sincere public justification has two critical features. On the one hand, such agents are committed to justifying themselves to others, but they cannot escape evaluating their success or failure to live up to this commitment by their own standards. They thus reason sincerely but inevitably differ. On the other hand, although constant lively debate and disagreement is the philosopher's ideal, it suits less well the demands of most citizens who need to get on with their lives. For them, argument is often important, but less a part of the good life than a necessary cost. And the reason we argue about matters such as economic justice, abortion and environmental regulation is that we need to *act: something must be done*. But (and this brings us back to our first commitment), we do not just want to do anything, but that which is best justified. But we cannot agree what that is. What are we to do?

Locke, not Hobbes, provides the model for adjudicating public reason among private reasoners who arrive at conflicting judgments. Hobbes would have our private reason supplanted by the sovereign's, but we have seen that sincere reasoners cannot accept that. Locke, of course, argued that in order to escape the inconveniences of each relying on his own moral judgment, we appoint an "Umpire" to adjudicate our disagreements.[70] The ideal of an umpire helps us to reconcile the two features of our practical situation: to sincerely justify and to act. The umpire does its best to track the best arguments. In baseball, for example, the umpire seeks to provide the correct ruling based on shared rules and concepts.[71] His decisions are not mere Hobbesian acts of will, proclaiming that his reason is definitive; rather, his authority is partially based on his claim to be at least competent—to be good at getting the answers right. This makes the umpire appear to be something of a sage. But players typically do not, and nothing about accepting an umpire requires that they must, see the umpire as a sage. Players certainly may, but usually do not, take the umpire's decisions as reasons to believe. Seldom do they reason as in schema (A) (in section 4 above): they do not typically take his judgment as a proxy for theirs. Players often enough continue to believe what they did before the umpire decided—they accept his judgment as a resolution of the practical dispute even if they think he is wrong. Yet, again, the participants expect the umpire to deliberate about what to do on the basis of the rules and the facts. Although the problem is essentially a practical one, the umpire's resolution is to be based on his determinations concerning the facts and the rules of the games, both epistemological matters.

Umpiring, then, is based on the supposition that (1) there is an intractable difference of opinion; (2) to proceed with practice, there must be a practical resolution of the dispute; (3) this practical resolution need not be accepted by all the parties as the correct solution; but (4) the authority of the umpire's decision requires that it seeks to arrive at the best answer. Sincere reasoners committed to public justification who also wish to get on with their lives require precisely this sort of umpiring of their disputes. *It honors their commitment to sincerity* since it never requires anyone to abandon what she thinks is the best reason. It also *honors their commitment to public justification* because no one simply imposes her will, or even her reasoning, on another: she submits her reason to the umpire, who provides an impartial resolution of the dispute. Lastly, the umpire *honors their commitment to deliberation,* for the umpire always seeks to act on the basis of the best possible reasons, and considers the merits of the opposing views.

Democracy, I have argued, can itself be understood as an umpiring mechanism.[72] In his or her deliberations each citizen presents what he or she believes is the best public justification; the voting mechanism constitutes a fair way to adjudicate deep disagreements about what is publicly justified. It does not seek political consensus, but reasoned debate about what is best justified, and procedures that do a tolerable job in tracking justification. Adjudicative democracy recognizes that our commitment to sincere public justification is precisely what produces principled disagreement; *democracy is required just because even rough consensus is not a plausible political ideal.* Thus the everyday institutions of democratic rule such as voting are, on the adjudicative conception, the heart of democracy, for they define how the umpire operates.

### 5.3 Three Types of Disagreements

On the adjudicative conception, then, actual consensus is not even a regulative ideal. The normal condition of politics is that we disagree. We need, though, to distinguish three types of political disagreement. The adjudicative theory of democracy focuses on *reasonable disagreement,* that is, where Alf and Betty disagree about what principle or policy is publicly justified, but understand the position of the other as reasonable (though erroneous). The adjudicative conception supposes that most of the disagreements between most of the people most of the time are of this sort: people have different political views, but do not dismiss the views of most other citizens as unreasonable. This, I have argued, is just the sort of case in which our commitment to public justification leads us to submit to the democratic umpire: I believe my proposal is correct, but I also see your objection as reasonable.[73] If we are to arrive at a common policy, we need some way to adjudicate our dispute.

The second sort of disagreement is more troubling: *one party sees the competing position of the other as unreasonable.* Suppose Alf believes that *P* is publicly justified, and is entirely convinced that Betty's support of *not-P* is unreasonable. It is hard to see why Alf should submit the dispute to an umpire. Why submit to arbitration when the other's position is, in your view, manifestly unreasonable? It may thus seem that the adjudicative view has the same fatal flaw as the deliberative conception: we do not have consensus on the reasonable. Two considerations, however, indicate that the adjudicative conception can admit this lack of consensus without undermining the justification of the democratic order: (1) In complex communities we do not have simply dyadic disagreements. Alf may believe Betty's opposition to *P* is unreasonable, but there are also Charlie's and Doris's objections to consider. If Alf believes that the democratic umpiring procedure is justified, he will still have reason to submit the justifiability of *P* to the umpire. (2) Indeed, assuming Alf has faith in the reliability of the umpire, he may even agree, for purely pragmatic reasons, to adjudicate his dispute with Betty. To revert to the baseball example, suppose that Betty claims a right to a fourth strike. If we understand umpiring simply as a way to resolve reasonable disputes, Alf has no reason to submit the dispute to adjudication as it is manifest that she has no case, and it would be outrageous for the umpire to rule in her favor. It is not a question open to reasonable dispute. Nevertheless, Alf may indeed refer the claim to the umpire for purely pragmatic reasons. If Betty also has faith in the umpire, it will be a quick way to resolve the conflict and get on with the game. *If he has faith in the reasonability of the umpire,* then he has good reason to appeal to the umpire even in the face of what he sees as an unreasonable proposal. Now, interestingly, both parties may be in the same position. Alf may believe that Betty's position is unreasonable, while she may view his as beyond the bounds of plausibility, yet each may view the umpire as a reasonable way to decide their disputes. They may do so because they may believe it is impartial, and that it generally yields reasonable answers. What is of interest here is that political life is possible even in the face of mutual conviction of the unreasonability of others if each party has grounds for accepting the reasonability of the umpiring mechanism.

It may seem that all this at least supposes a basic consensus on the justifiability of the umpire. What if citizens disagree about *that*? It is here that philosophical questions of justification must be distinguished from questions of efficacy. The justification of the umpiring mechanism does not depend on widespread actual consensus on its justifiability. Perhaps a large group of anti-democratic citizens wish to overturn democracy. This certainly does not show that democracy is unjustified. If, given all his cognitive resources, Alf concludes that there are no reasonable objections to the democratic method of resolving disputes—reasonable given his own epistemic standards—then he will conclude that democracy is justified, even in the face of its rejection by many. However, if for whatever reasons many citizens reject the democratic method, it will no longer serve its practical function of resolving disagreements. Alf may well conclude that, however justified the democratic state, his fellow citizens are so irrational or immoral that it cannot perform its task of resolving disputes, and so appeals to it are pragmatically pointless.

Of course if his fellow citizens are thoroughly irrational or immoral, Alf himself may reject democracy on deeper grounds: when placed in the hands of his fellow citizens it yields consistently unreasonable results. As I argued in section 5.1, an umpire has an epistemological task at which it must be competent. One's commitment to the umpire is thus contingent on one's evaluation that it does a reasonable job tracking the merits of the disputes. If Alf concludes that the umpire is incompetent, he will not see it as conforming to the Ideals of Reason and Public Justification, and so will conclude that it is not justified. If many believe this, again, democracy will not be efficacious. But whether or not democracy is a justified way to adjudicate disputes does not depend on how many people think it is justified, but whether it does indeed conform to the Ideals of Reason and Public Justification.

## 6 Conclusion

I have made a number of claims in this essay; it may help to summarize the main steps in the argument. The point of departure was the claim made by one familiar variety of deliberative democracy that (1) the Ideal of Reason conjoined with the Ideal of Public Justification leads to the Regulative Ideal of Real Political Consensus. My main aim has been to show that (1) is not the case. I began by arguing that (2) the Ideal of Reason implies the Principle of Sincerity; (3) together, the Ideals of Reason and Public Justification underwrite the idea that justified principles and policies should express a rational consensus: all rational citizens should be able to embrace them. (4) This seems to provide the basis for the Regulative Ideal of Real Political Consensus; however, I have argued that (5) a commitment to a political life based on rational consensus does not support the pursuit of actual political consensus. To show this, I examined several different interpretations of a public justification. I claimed that (6) the Principle of Sincerity conjoined to **PJ(1)** does not lead to the Regulative Ideal of Real Political Consensus; (7) **PJ(2),** on the other hand, seems to easily lead to the Regulative Ideal of Real Political Consensus, but it is inconsistent with the Principle of Sincerity. Further, (8) **PJ(3)** plus the Principle of Sincerity does not lead to the Regulative Ideal of Real Political Consensus, because we disagree about what constitutes reasonable beliefs and so disagree about the demands of **PJ(3).** Sections 3 and 4 considered and rejected several attempts to show that, since we do (or can) agree about political reasonableness, the Principle of Sincerity coupled with **PJ(3)** does after all endorse the pursuit of actual political consensus; because these attempts fail, my conclusion in (8) stands. Having tried to show that claim (1) is dubious, I closed in section 5 by arguing that devotion to the Ideals of Reason and Public Justification leads us away from a consensual understanding of democracy to an adjudicative conception, according to which the point of democracy is to umpire our inevitably conflicting judgments about what is publicly justified. Pace Rousseau, "contradictory views and debates," and "dissensions, and tumult" are the very heart of a healthy democracy.

Gerald F. Gaus

## Acknowledgment

An early version of this essay was delivered as the Presidential Address to the International Economics and Philosophy Society, Brisbane, July 1996. I would like to thank Jim Bohman, Fred D'Agostino, Christi Favor, and Loren Lomasky for their comments and criticisms. My special thanks to Julian Lamont for his detailed and too often sound criticisms. My thanks also to the participants in the Henle Conference on Deliberative Democracy at Saint Louis University, whose deliberations led me down this path.

## Notes

1. Joshua Cohen, "Deliberation and Democratic Legitimacy" in Alan Hamlin and Philip Pettit (eds.) *The Good Polity: Normative Analysis of the State* (Oxford: Blackwell, 1989): 17–34, 21.

2. Ibid., 22.

3. Frederick Watkins, *The Political Tradition of the West: A Study in the Development of Modern Liberalism* (Cambridge, MA: Harvard University Press, 1948): 244. See also my *Modern Liberal Theory of Man* (New York: St. Martin's Press, 1983): 205ff.

4. Gerald J. Postema, "Public Practical Reason: An Archeology," *Social Philosophy & Policy*, vol. 12 (Winter 1995): 43–86, 70.

5. Gerald J. Postema, "Public Practical Reason: Political Practice" in Ian Shapiro and Judith Wagner DeCrew (eds.) *Nomos XXXVII: Theory and Practice* (New York: New York University Press, 1995): 345–385, 356.

6. Ibid.

7. Ibid., 359. Emphasis added.

8. Ibid., 360.

9. Jean-Jacques Rousseau, *The Social Contract* in *The Social Contract and Discourses*, G.D.H. Cole. (trans.) (London: Dent, 1973): 248 (Bk V. ch. i).

10. Ibid., 249 (Bk. V, ch. ii). Cf. Cohen: "When properly conducted, then, democratic politics involves public deliberation focused on the common good . . . " in "Deliberation and Democratic Legitimacy," 19.

11. Throughout the essay, "the pursuit of actual political consensus" is equivalent to the Regulative Ideal of Real Political Consensus.

12. Cohen, "Deliberation and Democratic Legitimacy," 21.

13. Postema, "Public Practical Reason: Political Practice," 369.

14. See Postema, "Public Practical Reason: An Archeology," 70ff.

15. I argue this point more fully in *Justificatory Liberalism: An Essay on Epistemology and Political Theory* (New York: Oxford University Press, 1996): 138ff.

16. See Fred D'Agostino, *Free Public Reason: Making It Up As We Go* (New York: Oxford University Press, 1996): 30ff. Cf. Postema, "Public Practical Reason: Political Practice," 350.

17. Immanuel Kant, *Critique of Judgment*, Werner S. Pluhar (trans.) (Indianapolis: Hackett, 1987): 160 (sec. 40).

18. Cohen, "Deliberation and Democratic Legitimacy," 23.

19. I shall not consider the question of whether justification should be characterized in terms of acceptability or rejectability. For a characterization stressing rejectability, see Thomas Scanlon, "Contractualism and Utilitarianism" in Amartya Sen and Bernard Williams (eds.), *Utilitarianism and Beyond* (Cambridge: Cambridge University Press, 1982): 103–128.

20. See Christopher Cherniak, *Minimal Rationality* (Cambridge, MA: MIT Press, 1986). See also Herbert Simon, *Reason in Human Affairs* (Stanford: Stanford University Press, 1983).

21. See Amos Tversky and Daniel Kahneman "Availability: a Heuristic for Judging Frequency and Probability" in Daniel Kahneman, Paul Slovic, and Amos Tversky (eds.), *Judgments under Uncertainty: Heuristics and Biases* (Cambridge: Cambridge University Press, 1982): 163–179. On vividness, see Richard E. Nisbett and Lee Ross, *Human Inference: Strategies and Shortcomings of Social Judgments* (Englewood Cliffs, NJ: Prentice-Hall, 1980): 55, 15.

22. It may seem that the Condorcet Jury Theorem, explored by David Estlund in his contribution to this volume, supports the contrary view, that is, that large majorities are more likely to be correct than are individual voters. The evaluation of the Jury Theorem is a complex matter, but it is important to note that the Jury Theorem supposes that each individual seeks to form her own judgment, not that each is seeking to arrive at consensus. I certainly am not claiming here that majoritarian decisions are always less likely to be correct than individual judgments; the question concerns whether a political order that embraces a regulative aim of actual political consensus is most likely to reach the most justified decisions. I explore the Jury Theorem's relation to public justification in "Does Democracy Reveal the Will of the People? Four Takes on Rousseau," *The Australasian Journal of Philosophy*, 75 (1997): 141–162.

23. The doctrines of political liberalism and deliberative democracy are closely allied. See the contributions of John Rawls and Joshua Cohen in this volume.

24. Stephen Macedo, *Liberal Virtues: Citizenship, Virtue, and Community in Liberal Constitutionalism* (Oxford: Clarendon Press, 1991): 51.

Gerald F. Gaus

25. Rawls, *Political Liberalism*, p. xx. For a criticism of Rawls's agnostic stance toward truth, see Joseph Raz, "Facing Diversity: The Case of Epistemic Abstinence," *Philosophy & Public Affairs,* vol. 19 (Winter 1990): 3–46.

26. Charles Larmore, "Political Liberalism," *Political Theory,* vol.18 (August 1990): 339–360, 340–341, 348–349. See also Thomas Nagel, "Moral Conflict and Political Legitimacy," *Philosophy & Public Affairs,* vol.16 (Summer 1987): 215–240.

27. Larmore, "Political Liberalism," 340. See also 345.

28. Ibid., 348–349.

29. It might be objected that the problem with **PJ(2)** is that it depicts the assent of—or nonrejection by—all reasonable people as sufficient for justification; perhaps it is only necessary. I have considered this possibility more fully in my "The Rational, the Reasonable and Justification," *Journal of Political Philosophy,* vol. 3 (September 1995): 234–258.

30. For summaries, see Lee Ross and Craig A. Anderson, "Shortcomings in the Attribution Process: On the Origins and Maintenance of Erroneous Social Assessments," in Kahneman, Slovic, and Tversky, *Judgments Under Uncertainty:* 129–152. See also Nisbett and Ross, *Human Inference,* ch. 8.

31. Although Ross and his colleagues certainly believed that the subjects were persisting in unjustified beliefs, some philosophers have recently risen to the defense of Ross's subjects. See for example Gilbert Harman, *Change in View* (Cambridge, MA: MIT Press, 1986): 29ff, and Stephen Stich, *The Fragmentation of Reason* (Cambridge, MA: MIT Press, 1991): 8–10.

32. I consider this evidence in more detail in my "The Rational, the Reasonable and Justification," and in my *Justificatory Liberalism.*

33. I leave aside the problem of bad-faith rejection here.

34. See my *Justificatory Liberalism,* 38ff.

35. Joshua Cohen, "Moral Pluralism and Political Consensus" in David Copp, Jean Hampton, and John E. Roemer (eds.), *The Idea of Democracy* (Cambridge: Cambridge University Press, 1993): 270–291, 281–282. Cohen attributes this view to Mark Johnston.

36. See my "The Rational, the Reasonable and Justification."

37. See Cherniak, *Minimal Rationality.*

38. More needs to be said to fully explicate the idea of "the best belief"—best relative to what constraints? For here, however, the crucial idea is that Betty's belief can be sufficiently credible even if she believes that further reflection would lead her to some different belief (though she does not know what different belief).

39. Sigmund Freud, *Civilization and its Discontents,* James Strachey (trans.) (New York: W.W. Norton, 1961): 21.

40. See, for example., Kent Greenawalt, *Religious Convictions and Political Choice* (New York: Oxford University Press, 1988).

41. See Cohen, "Moral Pluralism and Political Consensus," 283ff.

42. "My sister Louise . . . attended the [1992 National Woman's Studies] conference with me. . . . Having spent several hours with the . . . conferees, she had doubts about their competence and reasonableness." Christina Hoff Sommers, *Who Stole Feminism? How Women Have Betrayed Women* (New York: Simon and Schuster, 1994): 53.

43. Rawls, *Political Liberalism,* 10.

44. Ibid., 12.

45. Rawls characterizes reasonableness in terms of the virtues of persons (*Political Liberalism,* 48), which leads us back to **PJ(2).** I revise Rawls here so as to be consistent with **PJ(3).**

46. Rawls, *Political Liberalism,* 57.

47. See Cohen, "The Economic Basis of Deliberative Democracy," *Social Philosophy and Policy,* vol. 6 (Spring 1989): 25–50, 34ff.

48. See H. L. A. Hart, *The Concept of Law* (Oxford: Clarendon Press, 1961): 155ff; Rawls, *Theory of Justice* (Cambridge, MA: Harvard University Press, 1971): 5; Ronald Dworkin, *Law's Empire,* (Cambridge, MA: Harvard University Press, 1986): 71; D'Agostino, *Free Public Reason,* 15–17.

49. See further my *Justificatory Liberalism,* 101–108.

50. See Machiavelli, *The Prince,* Peter Bondanella and Mark Musa (trans.) (New York: Oxford University Press, 1979): 17.

51. Rawls, *Political Liberalism,* 12.

52. Jeremy Waldron, *The Right to Private Property* (Oxford: Clarendon Press, 1988): 433. Citation omitted.

53. See R. E. Ewin, *Virtues and Rights* (Boulder, CO: Westview, 1991): ch. 2.

54. Thomas Hobbes, *Leviathan,* Michael Oakeshott, ed. (Oxford: Blackwell, 1948): 102 (ch. 15). See also Ewin, *Virtue and Rights,* 34.

55. Hobbes, *Leviathan,* 291 (ch. 37). See also Lawrence B. Solum, "Constructing and Ideal of Public Reason," *San Diego Law Review,* vol. 30 (Fall 1993): 729–762, 754.

56. David Gauthier, "Public Reason," *Social Philosophy & Policy,* vol. 12 (Winter 1995): 19–42, 25–26.

57. Ibid., 26.

58. Kurt Baier, *The Rational and the Moral Order: The Social Roots of Reason and Morality* (Chicago: Open Court, 1995): 189.

Gerald F. Gaus

59. See Richard B. Freidman, "On the Concept of Authority in Political Philosophy" in Richard E. Flathman (ed.), *Concepts in Social and Political Philosophy* (New York: Macmillan, 1973): 121–146.

60. I have questioned this in "The Rational, the Reasonable and Justification."

61. Ibid.

62. Bernard Williams, "Deciding to Believe" in his *Problems of the Self* (Cambridge: Cambridge University Press, 1973): 136–151, 150.

63. Postema, "Public Practical Reason: An Archeology," 48. Postema is following here Philip Pettit's *Common Mind* (Oxford: Oxford University Press, 1993).

64. Ludwig Wittgenstein, *Philosophical Investigations,* 3rd ed., G. E. M. Anscombe (trans.) (London: Macmillan, 1958), sec.199.

65. Susan Hurley, *Natural Reasons* (Oxford: Oxford University Press, 1989): 91.

66. See my *Justificatory Liberalism,* 116–120.

67. Postema, "Public Practical Reason: An Archeology," 50.

68. Cf. James Bohman's notion of a "moral compromise" between divergent cultural frameworks, "Public Reason and Cultural Pluralism," *Political Theory,* vol. 23 (May 1995): 253–279, 268ff.

69. Larmore, *Patterns Of Moral Complexity* (Cambridge: Cambridge University Press, 1987): 57–58, citation omitted. Emphasis added.

70. John Locke, *Second Treatise of Government* in Peter Laslett (ed.), *Two Treatises of Government* (Cambridge: Cambridge University Press, 1960), sec. 7. See my *Justificatory Liberalism,* 184ff.

71. It is worth pointing out that an umpire in baseball does not merely apply clear rules or make judgments of fact; the calling of balls and strikes is an exercise in the application of an abstract concept—the strike zone.

72. See my *Justificatory Liberalism,* chs. 13–15 and my "Public Justification and Democratic Adjudication," *Constitutional Political Economy,* vol. 2 (1991): 251–281.

73. Ibid.

# 8

# The Significance of Public Deliberation

*Thomas Christiano*

A number of theorists have recently put forth and defended a conception of democracy called *deliberative democracy*. Their thesis is that democratic decision making ought to be grounded in a substantial process of public deliberation, wherein arguments for and against laws and policies are given in terms of whether they advance the common good of citizens and the justice of the political society. This conception is to be understood by contrast with interest-group pluralist and elitist conceptions of democracy. While many have proclaimed adherence to the idea that public deliberation ought to play a major role in a democratic society, few have offered a clear account of the significance that deliberation has for democracy. This paper provides an account of the value and significance of public deliberation in democracy. Its main aim is to establish that while public deliberation per se has an exclusively instrumental value in enhancing the quality of decisions in democracy, equality in the process of public deliberation has an intrinsic worth grounded in the requirements of justice. In the second part of this paper, I argue that one main opposing view of the significance of public deliberation to democracy, the justificatory view articulated by Joshua Cohen, fails to provide a cogent account of the importance of public deliberation to democracy.

First, I outline three different kinds of value that public deliberation might have in political decision making. Second, I describe three principal theses about the importance of public deliberation

Thomas Christiano

to democratic processes. Third, I argue for the claim that public deliberation has essentially an instrumental value for democratic decision making: it makes an important contribution to the ability of democracies to produce just outcomes. Fourth, I argue that equality in the process of public deliberation is intrinsically just. So while public deliberation is instrumentally valuable, a just process of public deliberation ought to be structured in an egalitarian way. This is the mixed account of the worth of public deliberation. Fifth, I argue that Cohen's attempt to account for the value of public deliberation cannot be sustained and that the mixed account of the worth of public deliberation is the one that deliberative democrats ought to adopt.

**Three Kinds of Value of Deliberation**

Public deliberation transforms, modifies, and clarifies the beliefs and preferences of the citizens of a political society. When and why is this a valuable process? There are three kinds of value that public deliberation might have. First, public deliberation may be valuable because of its results. Three kinds of results are often hoped for from public deliberation. One result is that public deliberation generally improves the quality of legislation by enhancing citizens' understanding of their society and of the moral principles that ought to regulate it. Societies that experience a great deal of good-faith discussion and rational debate among all citizens on the merits of alternative proposals tend to be more just or to protect liberty better. Here, the *justice* of laws and social institutions may be increased by the process of discussion. A second result is that the laws of these societies may tend to be rationally justified more often in the eyes of their citizens than those of societies that do not undergo intensive processes of deliberation on legislation. Deliberation, it is often said, leads to reasoned agreement among citizens on the merits of legislation. In this case, the *legitimacy* of the society is increased by the process of deliberation. A third result is that certain desirable qualities in citizens are enhanced when they must participate in the process of deliberation. People who participate frequently in deliberation as free and equal citizens are more likely, many think, to develop traits of autonomy, rationality, and morality. In this instance, the *virtues* of citizens are increased by the process.[1]

It is important to emphasize the independence of the values of justice, legitimacy, and virtue from the deliberative process that is thought to be causally responsible for their realization. Rousseau seems to have thought that these values were less likely to arise in a society where public deliberation plays a role in the passage of legislation.[2] Others argue that public discussion only diminishes agreement on matters of principle and policy and undermines the legitimacy of the social institutions. I do not mean to endorse these claims, but to emphasize the point that the values discussed above are at most contingent results of public deliberation. They support only an *instrumental* value of public deliberation.

Second, public deliberation might have intrinsic value so that it is worthwhile in itself that a person or a society go through a well-conducted process of deliberation before making a decision. One such view is that participation in public deliberation is an essential part of the good life for an individual. This value is independent of the results of deliberation.[3] A second version of the intrinsic value approach, which will receive the most attention in this paper, is the idea that a society in which individuals deliberate publicly before making decisions embodies a kind of mutual respect and concern among citizens. To the extent that mutual respect and concern is demanded by justice, it is intrinsically important that a group of people treat each other in this way. The idea is that each has a right to participate in a process of deliberation among free and equal persons. I will defend a particular version of this idea in what follows. One point to note, however, is that while these intrinsic values may confer some worth on the outcomes of the decision making (the decision is made in an egalitarian way), their presence is compatible with there being independent standards for the worth of outcomes that compete with the procedural values involved in the particular way of bringing about the outcomes. Hence it is possible to ascribe both instrumental and intrinsic worth to the process of public deliberation.

A third way in which deliberation might be thought to be valuable is as a condition of political justification. In this account, a process

Thomas Christiano

of deliberation, suitably constrained, is necessary and sufficient for the justification of the outcomes of the process. The outcomes are justified because they are brought about in a certain way. There are no independent standards for assessing outcomes on this approach: the standards for assessing institutions are entirely elaborated within the process of deliberation among free and equal and citizens.

## Three Theses about the Importance of Public Deliberation to Democracy

There are three theses about the significance of public deliberation to democracy. Each of them can apply to the three ways in which deliberation is valuable. I list them in the order of increasing strength. First, we might simply say that public deliberation can contribute to the worth of democratic institutions. Public deliberation may not be necessary for the worth of those institutions and it may not be sufficient either. Call this the *contribution thesis*. The second thesis is that deliberation is a necessary condition for the worth of democratic institutions. That is, a democratic society that makes decisions without public deliberation is an undesirable form of political society.[4] Call this the *necessity thesis*. The third thesis is that public deliberation is the only value in democracy. The only reason why democracy matters is that it involves public deliberation among equals. This is the *exclusivity thesis*.

Notice that the instrumentalist account of the value of deliberation is compatible with the contribution thesis as long as we hold that there are other important values (intrinsic or instrumental) associated with democracy. It is compatible with the necessity thesis to the extent that the deliberative aspect of democracy is instrumentally important. The exclusivity thesis coupled with the instrumental approach to deliberation would entail a kind of instrumentalist account of democracy. The view that public deliberation has intrinsic value is similarly compatible with all three theses, as is the mixed view. The justificatory view, which is compatible with the necessity thesis and may entail the exclusivity thesis, may be incompatible with the contribution thesis since it requires that there be no value to democracy other than the process of deliberation.

While not all logically possible ways of talking of these values have been listed, these three values and three theses are exhaustive of the space of plausible things one can say about the significance of public deliberation to democracy. We are now ready to assess the various positions that are taken on the question regarding the significance of deliberation to democracy. I use the three kinds of value that deliberation can have to classify views and assess the three theses for each of these categories of value.

## The Instrumental Value of Deliberation

Is it the case that public deliberation enhances the outcomes of democratic decision making? The justice and virtue effects of public deliberation on democratic outcomes would appear to be reasonably likely outcomes of democracy, at least if the public deliberation takes place in a political context free of fear and intimidation or ridicule and a wide variety of points of view can be expressed and heard in the public forum. Discussion and deliberation promote greater understanding of the interests of the members of society, as well as how the common features of the society relate to those interests. They allow us to submit our understandings to the test of critical scrutiny. John Stuart Mill states the reason forcefully:

The whole strength and value then of human judgment, depending on the one property, that it can be set right when it is wrong, reliance can be placed on it only, when the means of setting it right are kept constantly at hand. In the case of a person whose judgment is really deserving of confidence, how has it become so? Because he has kept his mind open to criticism on his opinions and conduct. Because it has been his practice to listen to all that could be said against him; to profit by as much of it as was just, and expound to himself, and upon occasion to others, the fallacy of what was fallacious. Because he has felt that the only way in which a human being can make some approach to knowing the whole of a subject, is by hearing what can be said about it by persons of every variety of opinion, and studying all modes in which it can be looked at by every character of mind.[5]

Under the assumption that minds informed in this way will often make better decisions and that a society wherein all its members participate in this process of discussion and debate will at least be able to root out policies based on unsubstantiated prejudices, we

Thomas Christiano

have reason to think that a society that promotes public deliberation will make better decisions. It is likely to be more sensitive to and understanding of the interests of a broader portion of the population than one where citizens do not have the opportunity to express and discuss their interests. Its decisions will be informed by a better knowledge of the facts that are important to the realization of the aims of the society, since a wide variety of people and groups have the opportunity to examine the facts and test each others' views on these matters. The ideas of justice and the common good that provide the ultimate justification for many policies will usually avoid egregious forms of arbitrary treatment that arise when a decision-making group is not aware of other groups in the society. The more fallacious and superstitious forms of reasoning about these matters will generally be undermined. In short, the process of public deliberation will serve as a kind of filtering device, taking out the egregious forms of ignorance regarding interests and justice.

These are modest claims that appeal to our common sense, but we ought to remember that empirical evidence for such large-scale effects of public discussion is fairly thin and not all of it is positive. Most of the supporting research has been done only on small groups, and so its generalization to the context of democratic societies must be treated with caution.[6] So we can only give a tentative endorsement to these claims. They call for more empirical research. In addition, the virtue effect of deliberation is endorsed by common sense. In a society where public deliberation is the norm, having traits by which one can contribute to public deliberation is highly functional for individuals, or at least for groups. Where one is unable to make a contribution to the public discussion that informs policy making and one has distinctive interests and points of view, those interests and points of view are not likely to be accommodated in the policies that are chosen. At the same time, in a society where public discussion is ignored or suppressed, individuals are not likely to have reason to discuss their views with others, and they will have less reason to think carefully about many of their views. To the extent that participation in discussion on a regular basis enlists the abilities necessary for that participation, it is likely to enhance the character traits of citizens. And to the extent that public deliberation calls

upon a set of morally important qualities such as rationality, autonomy and respect for others, there is some reason to think that these
traits which are important in politics will be promoted more in a
society that encourages deliberation among all of its citizens. Here
too, the empirical evidence for this kind of commonsensical claim is
scanty, and more research is called for. Moreover, we can see some
ways in which public deliberation might promote poor character
traits in some circumstances as well. For instance, a capacity for
pandering and manipulation may prove to be superior to the more
desirable traits in some contexts. Or perhaps indecisiveness will also
result in some societies that greatly value public deliberation.

Does public deliberation increase the tendency among citizens to
agree on political matters and thereby increase the legitimacy of the
actions of the state? This outcome is unlikely in a large pluralistic
society. Discussion and debate increase the diversity of opinions on
many matters. While discussion may eliminate some disagreements
such as those that are the result of mere prejudice and superstition,
it is likely to generate disagreements also. If discussion is set in an
egalitarian context, then many more points of view will have to be
debated to the extent that previously neglected sectors of society
come to the fore. One need not be a skeptic about knowledge of
matters in politics to see that debates about these matters are extremely hard to resolve. Differing points of view cannot be eliminated when there are participants with differing social and
economic backgrounds and experiences in life and when the evidence always falls short of proof. His highly speculative developmen-
tal moral psychology notwithstanding, what Rawls has called the
"burdens of reason" weigh against achieving agreement on matters
that are of great importance in politics, including issues relating to
the common good and social justice.[7]

Would it be desirable for deliberation to increase the tendency
toward agreement? While agreement may contribute to the stability
of society, disagreement and diversity of view are among the most
fertile conditions for the realization of the justice and virtue effects.
Some might say that reasoned agreement among citizens is a good
since they live under a scheme of social institutions that accords with
their sense of what is right. But this is not a desirable state of affairs

unless what they believe to be right is in fact right or close to it. Mere agreement on principles adds only a little value (viz., some stability) to the institutions on which there is agreement and may make matters worse if those institutions are unjust. Furthermore, given the likelihood that egalitarian institutions will in fact produce a lot of disagreement, the idea that we will in fact achieve agreement on the right principles of justice if and only if we structure our democratic institutions in the right way is clearly false.[8] The best we can do toward achieving an understanding of justice and the common good is by means of a trial and error process wherein a diversity of points of view is always present to test any particular view. Hence, we ought not to be aiming at consensus on moral and political matters. As long as public discussion acts as a process of trial and error for excluding forms of ignorance, it serves a useful purpose for individuals as well as for society while increasing the amount of disagreement in the community.

Are these instrumental values of public deliberation the only values in democracy? Clearly the exclusivity thesis is false with regard to instrumental values. Democratic societies include mechanisms that are instrumentally important aside from their encouragement of deliberation. First and foremost is the power-checking mechanism of majority voting. Majority rule helps ensure that a small elite cannot tyrannize the rest of the population. Majority voting diffuses power throughout the population and thereby substantially disables anyone from seriously abusing his or her fellow citizens. In addition, voting is an informational mechanism. A vote for or against a candidate or policy sends a signal that, relative to the alternatives, there is something desirable or undesirable about the candidate or policy. This signal is not always a very clear one, but it is clearer than most that are available in society. Hence, majority voting has a function in ensuring justice, and we have reason to think that voting also has an effect on character since it requires one to think for oneself and make choices that have some impact on the world one lives in.

The power-checking and signaling functions of voting are greatly enhanced when they are coupled with public deliberation among equals in a society. But they have value independent of the worth of public deliberation and can play an important role even when public deliberation is absent. Moreover, the function of public deliberation cannot be realized without voting power being distributed widely. First, a logical point: one does not deliberate unless one is making a choice, and *we* do not deliberate unless each one of us participates in making the choice. For example, a prosecutor does not deliberate with a jury; she merely tries to persuade and advise the jury which in turn deliberates about the verdict. Second, it is because citizens have voting power that they have reason to contribute to public deliberation. A citizen's incentive to listen to another's opinion with which he disagrees strongly diminishes when that other has no power. So a citizen's incentives to express her opinions and supporting reasons, as well as to think about political matters, correspondingly decline when she has no power. Hence, it is because voting power is widely distributed that public deliberation on a wide scale exists at all. Thus the mechanism of voting has an independent impact on the justice of society (through power checking and signaling) as well as on the characters of citizens, and it is a necessary condition for the efficacy and even the existence of public deliberation. The exclusivity and necessity theses with regard to instrumental values are false.

## Why Public Deliberation Per Se Is Only Instrumentally Valuable

Turning to the intrinsic value of deliberation, there are two ways in which public deliberation is thought to have intrinsic value. First, it may have intrinsic value to the extent that participating in discussing matters of great moral importance is an essential or at least irreducible component of the good life. Second, public deliberation may have intrinsic value to the extent that the presence of public deliberation is an expression of a kind of mutual respect among citizens in the society.

When I submit my views and my arguments to you for your evaluation and response and I listen to your ideas and arguments with an eye to learning something from you, I express a kind of respect for you. I am treating you as a kind of rational and intelligent being who has something to offer. If I am discussing some topic with you or someone else and you say something germane to the discussion which I simply ignore, I express a kind of contempt for you. To the extent that respect is due you, I have acted in a way that is not fitting in my relation to you. I have treated you unjustly.

Politics adds another dimension to this mutual respect argument. When I think about mathematics, say, and I do not ask you for your opinion even though you know a lot about it, I am not necessarily expressing contempt for you. I may be shy or I may not wish to take the time to discuss the matter with you. These are sufficient reasons for my not coming and talking to you about the subject. I may display imprudence by not discussing matters with you but I am not thereby treating you unjustly. Of course if there is a general expectation that I discuss topics with those who are knowledgeable and you are the only such person around, then my failing to discuss the matter may be taken as a slight without some stronger explanation. In general, though, in ordinary discussion, we express contempt for someone only when we ignore or dismiss a legitimate contribution they make.

In politics, by contrast, the matters up for discussion have to do with decisions that affect people's lives. If, even if as a result of shyness, I fail to discuss with you my ideas about how our lives should be lived together and I attempt to realize these ideas without consulting you, I express a kind of contempt and lack of concern for you. This contempt is what characterizes all forms of nondemocratic political decision making. Not only do you not have a vote, I do not consult with you in my private deliberation. In democratic politics, of course, decisions are not imposed in this way even when there is no public deliberation. A decision is imposed only when there has been a vote. What decision is made is uncertain until the vote, and so it is not the case that individuals simply impose their views on others. Nevertheless, democratic politics without *widespread* public deliberation does seem to express a failure of respect for those fellow citizens who are not included in the deliberation. In politics, expressing respect for persons who will be affected by a decision involves, in addition to giving them a vote in the decision, seeking out their views and engaging them in discussion on the matter. In addition to the duty of not ignoring the expressed opinions of equals, there is the duty of seeking out their opinions.

What is the central intrinsic value appealed to in this latter case? In my view the central intrinsic concern is that individuals have equal access to the cognitive conditions necessary to making good decisions regarding their lives together. The cognitive conditions of decision making are those conditions that enable a person to understand better what is at issue in a decision as well as better to discern the right decision. Participation in the process of public deliberation is one of the main cognitive conditions. The idea here is that the mere fact of talking together about politics is not the central intrinsic concern; what is of central importance is that individuals have *equality* in the cognitive conditions of democratic decision making. This latter requirement, as we shall see, is a requirement of justice. Where there is a process of public deliberation and some have no opportunity to have a say, they are being treated as inferiors in the decision-making process because they have been denied equality of access to the cognitive conditions of democratic decision making. To be sure, deliberation and discussion also generally have instrumental value, as was argued in the previous section, but there need not be any injustice in the mere fact that a society makes decisions without a process of public deliberation.

This claim is quite complex, and I shall explain it in what follows. It accounts for a series of considered judgments on the intrinsic importance of deliberation. In one scenario, one person makes a decision that affects another's life without consulting that other person; in addition to the inequality of power in the decision making itself, there is an inequality in the fact that only the deliberations of the decision maker will affect the decision. Ultimately, the person who has no say is likely to have his interests neglected even by a benign decision maker. This implies that the political decision-making process fails to treat the members as equals. Notice here that the deliberator is deliberating privately about political matters. The other, by contrast, is not deliberating at all since no decision is being made by him. The injustice here, I contend, is the fact that a decision affecting all is made from the private deliberation of only one.

Now consider a second scenario of a democratic society in which no one discusses the merits of policy and law with one another. Either each person simply reflects on his or her own on what the

Thomas Christiano

best policy is, as Rousseau recommended citizens do, or everyone engages in bargaining and coalition building without discussing the merits of the preferences from which they begin. Here I suggest that there is nothing *intrinsically* wrong with either situation. No one is treating anyone else unjustly or with contempt. No one's interests or points of view are privileged. Note that the citizens' preferences need not be unreflective. They may all be revising their preferences on their own and may continue to be willing to do so on the basis of their own subsequent reflections. They may engage in private deliberation and not public deliberation. Furthermore, citizens in such a situation need not be concerned with merely their own interests or with the interests of some part of the society. They may all be concerned with the common good and with justice. Hence the deliberation about political matters, while being entirely private, can be both reflective as well as morally driven. Indeed, citizens may even attempt to choose an alternative on the basis of reflection on considerations they believe others can reasonably accept. All of these are possible without public deliberation.

Clearly there is something amiss in this situation: citizens fail to go through the learning process that discussion among differently situated persons with different points of view affords. But it is not intrinsically problematic; as long as each person's deliberations take place against the background of equality of access to the conditions of decision making, there is no injustice.

There are other situations, in which issues are framed in terms of self-interest alone, where the absence of discussion does not detract from the intrinsic value of the democratic process. For example, suppose that a group of people must decide where to do their sightseeing together. While there is no more at stake in the decision for one than for anyone else, they have different desires. Each prefers that the group remain together even if that means going to the less desired place. No matter which of the two places they visit, they prefer to remain a group despite the fact that they have different desires. They respect each other as equals. Surely, the best way for them to decide where to go is by majority rule. In this context, each is encouraged to vote on the basis of his or her own interests and no one is much inclined to discuss the alternatives with others. Each person is engaged in private deliberation about how to vote and they vote mostly on self-interest; as long as each has roughly equal access to the cognitive conditions for decision making, there is nothing intrinsically wrong with the process. To be sure, there may be some loss of information resulting from the fact that they do not discuss the matter with each other, but there is no injustice in how they make their decision. The situation is not an oppressive one.

I do not want to claim that all or even most issues are framed in terms of self-interest alone. The vast majority of issues must be framed in some mixed way where the interests of the participants are at stake but they are asked to give their views on what the common good or justice demands. And no matter how issues are framed, it seems that the presence of public discussion will probably improve the quality of the outcome.

Both judgments on this second set of scenarios suggest that the value of having a scheme of public deliberation is essentially instrumental. Let me suggest another consideration. Suppose that for some reason we know that discussion among a group of people is not likely to lead to any new understanding or information and that any change of mind will arise due to nonrational processes such as those described by social psychologists as *social comparison effects* (i.e., individuals change opinions merely because selected others have those opinions).[9] Does the process in this kind of context have much worth? It appears not to. Or suppose that the topic under deliberation is of extremely limited significance to the community. Of what significance is a process of public deliberation in this context? Its significance is very small. Or, suppose that the topic under discussion is very important but that even a minimally effective discussion of it would be incompatible with making the decision in a timely manner. Surely in this kind of context, the worth of the deliberations would be nil. In my view, these observations, along with those cited above, suggest that we regard public deliberation as primarily of instrumental value. It is an instrument for the making of high quality decisions. If public deliberation does not serve that purpose, it does not have value.

Thomas Christiano

## A Mixed Approach to the Value of Public Deliberation

Consider a situation in which individuals are unequally placed with regard to the cognitive conditions for decision making. This occurs in a democratic society where each has a vote and wherein there is a process of public deliberation, but where some do not have the means or the educational background necessary for participation or are simply not listened to in the process of deliberation for reasons not having to do with the content of what they have to say. They are being treated as inferiors. It also occurs where there is no public deliberation but where the private deliberations of citizens are based in unequal cognitive conditions. Though each has a vote, some do not have the basis on which to make informed or thoughtful decisions due to poverty and poor education. These too are being treated as inferiors and their interests are not being given equal consideration in the process of discussion. The injustice in situations of private deliberations against a background of inequality of cognitive conditions is quite similar to that of a society where there is public deliberation among unequally situated citizens.

Now consider a scenario in which all the citizens participate as equals in the process of discussion. Each has the resources to make a contribution and others are at least willing to listen to what each has to say. I shall not go into the nature of this equality right now.[10] What I want to argue here is that equality in the process of democratic discussion has two main merits. First, as argued above, it improves the quality of the outcomes of democratic decision making. Public deliberation generally improves the quality of the outcomes, and equality in the process of deliberation should enhance this effect since it permits the points of view and interests of all the participants in the society to be given a hearing and to be accommodated to the extent that they can be.

A second merit of such a process is that it treats all the members of society as equals. Institutions of discussion and deliberation affect the *distribution* of the cognitive conditions of understanding among the citizens. This is where the principle of political equality comes in. Egalitarian institutions are charged with the task of distributing the cognitive conditions of understanding widely so that individuals have the means of enhancing their understanding of their interests, and of reflecting on the grounds and merits of their politically relevant moral convictions and the best way to advance them.

How does wide distribution of the conditions of understanding promote equality? Those who do not know what policies will advance their interests or their conception of what is best are not likely to have much real power compared with those who do know. Compare a person who does not know how to drive but is at the wheel of an automobile, with someone who has a car and who does know how to drive. The first person is powerless because of his ignorance of how to use the resources at his command; the second, who has the same resources, does have control. This parallels the comparison between those who vote on the basis of some real understanding of politics and those who have little. There is a considerable differential in power, because while the ignorant might sometimes be able to block the knowledgeable from getting what they prefer, the ignorant will never get what they prefer except by accident.

Furthermore, confused or distorted conceptions of one's interests or moral aims can undermine one's ability to advance ends. Compare the person who has a car and knows how to use it, but has only confused and contradictory ideas of where he wants to go, with the person who knows where she wants to go. The first person is at a considerable disadvantage in power compared with the second. He will drive around aimlessly without achieving any end, while the second person will be able to achieve some end that she desires. This is a real difference in power.

Finally, a person whose conception of his interests and aims is more or less arbitrarily arrived at is at a disadvantage in relation to a person who has thought about her aims and has some basis for pursuing the ends she does. The person who has a poorly reasoned or unreflective conception of his or her aims is a person who is unlikely to achieve much of worth to himself. He will be easily subject to confusion, arbitrary changes in opinion as well as manipulation by others. Since it is important to advance the interests of a person, as well as morally worthy aims, it is important for him to have some reasoned grasp of his interests and aims.

Thomas Christiano

To sum up, democratic institutions and in particular institutions of discussion and deliberation have a large impact on whether individuals have the opportunities to reflect on and come to a better understanding of their interests and to arrive at a more reasoned point of view. Public discussion and deliberation thus contribute importantly to egalitarian democratic institutions and the principle of equality provides a rationale for distributing the resources for deliberation equally.

## Equal Consideration of Interests and the Importance of Public Deliberation

This twofold account of the significance of deliberation can be grounded entirely in a principle of equal consideration of interests. The argument, which I have laid out extensively elsewhere, proceeds along the following lines.[11] Justice requires that the interests of individuals be given equal consideration when there is conflict of interests. In a political society, where there is considerable disagreement about what the interests of individuals are as well as what kinds of policies and legislation embody equal consideration of interests, the ultimate public embodiment of equal consideration of interests is in institutions that ensure that each has an equal say in the collective decision making. This generates a principle of one person, one vote on collective matters, and it requires that other relevant forms of social power be distributed in accordance with a principle of equality. Contrary to what many critics have to say, the above argument shows that the principle of political equality gives a powerful account of the significance of public deliberation for a just political society. Equality in the cognitive conditions for decision making, I have argued above, is a necessary condition for political equality. Hence, justice requires such equality. Although public deliberation itself is not a requirement of justice on this account, when there is public deliberation, justice requires that each be able to participate as equals.

Here we must deal with a potential objection to the foregoing account. Because the principle of equality in public deliberation is justified as a solution to conflicts of interest, it may be unclear how the principle applies to controversies over civil and economic justice. Someone might object to my account on the grounds that since everyone has the same interests in these cases—to find the right conception of justice—there is apparently no conflict of interest. The objector might conclude that equality in public deliberation is not required in this context; and since this is one of the contexts in which public deliberation seems most desirable, one might worry that the principle of equal consideration of interests cannot provide an adequate account of the intrinsic importance of equality in public deliberation. I respond to such worries by showing that important interests do conflict when citizens advance opposed conceptions of justice and the common good. There are really four such interests. First, there is the interest in recognition. Each person has an interest in being taken seriously by others. When an individual's views are ignored or not given any weight, this undermines his sense of self-respect in which he has a deep interest. Each has an interest in having his conception of justice heard and taken into account in the process of discussion on these matters. These interests in recognition conflict to the extent that individuals advance opposing conceptions of justice. Second, conceptions of justice often reflect disproportionately the interests of those who hold them. There is a tendency to cognitive bias in elaborating and publicly defending conceptions of justice particularly in contexts of actual political conflicts. Cognitive bias is natural given that individuals are likely to be more sensitive and understanding toward their own interests than those of others. In a complex community where individuals' positions in society are quite different, this tendency to bias is increased. If many advance conceptions of justice in public discussion that reflect their interests, those who lack opportunities to advance their own will lose out. It will be clear to every excluded or underrepresented person that the process is treating his or her interests and point of view as less worthy of a hearing. Thus serious conflict of interest is likely to accompany controversies on justice, and each has an interest in having the conditions for articulating and defending his or her own views on the matter. A third interest associated with advancing a conception of justice is that a person will most likely experience a sense of alienation and distance from a social world that does not accord with any part of her sense of justice. She will have a sense of nonmembership. That individuals have these kinds of difficulties can be seen from the experience of indigenous peoples in societies that are radically different from theirs. But this sense of alienation can be experienced to lesser degrees when there are lesser disagreements. The interest in a sense of membership is a source of conflict as well, to the extent that individuals differ in terms of the kinds of communities that give them a sense of membership. A fourth interest is related to the interest in coming to have the right conception of justice. If persons are to be rationally persuaded, the arguments that lead them to the new belief must start by appealing to their initial beliefs. Persons are not persuaded by arguments based on premises they do not believe. As a consequence, the views of each person in a process of social discussion must be taken seriously if each is to have the opportunity to learn from that discussion. But a person's views will not be taken seriously in such a process if that person does not possess the power to affect political decision making, or if that person does not have the means to develop his or her understanding of the common good, or if that person's views lack coherence or consistency or any reasoned basis. Finally, a person will not be taken seriously if that person does not have the means to have his or her views heard in the public forum. Why should others try to convince someone who has no impact on the decision, or who is unable to articulate her views, or who is unlikely to hold the views for more than a short period of time, when there is so little time to persuade those who do have power and the understanding of what is at stake? So each person has an interest in having his or her own view taken into account in discussion, and citizens' interests conflict to the extent that there is a limited space in which to discuss all views. The only way to treat these interests equally is to give them equal shares in political authority, and one essential component of having such equal shares is having equal shares in the process of public deliberation.

To avoid misunderstanding, when I say that individuals have interests in advancing their own conceptions of justice, I do not mean to say that their conceptions of justice are mere masks for their own interests or that individuals' conceptions of justice are mere tools for pursuing their own interests. It is a fundamental fact that human beings are deeply concerned with matters of civil and economic justice and are concerned with having the most accurate understandings of these matters.[12] Conflict in political society is often generated by pervasive but sincerely based disagreement on these matters. The four kinds of interests described above are not interests that individuals strive to realize when advancing conceptions of justice; the realizations of those interests are by-products of a process wherein each is assured an opportunity to advance his or her own conception of justice in a world where there is uncertainty about the truth of any particular conception.

One final note here shows how the instrumental and the intrinsic merits of public deliberation among equals fit together in this context. It is precisely because the conflicting interests in advancing opposed conceptions of justice are not all that is at stake in democratic decision making that there is room for an instrumental evaluation of democratic institutions in addition to the intrinsic value that we have found. Each has an interest in seeing justice being done in his or her society, and so the process of decision making and public deliberation must be partly evaluated in terms of whether the aim of justice is achieved. On the other hand, given the opaqueness of social justice and the consequent disagreements about what it is and whether it is realized as well as the four conflicting interests described above, each person has a just claim to an equal share of the resources for making decisions and contributing to the public deliberations.

With these remarks in mind we can now see what the mixed account of the significance of deliberation says. First, public deliberation increases the chance that the decision making in a democratic society will lead to good outcomes. Public deliberation among equals may well do this job better than public deliberation *simpliciter* since it increases the information about the interests of all the different groups of people in society, and it brings in a greater variety of perspectives on justice and the common good with which to test and compare any particular conception of these matters. While public deliberation per se is only instrumentally valuable, equality in the process of public deliberation is a requirement of a just process of

Thomas Christiano

public deliberation; equality is a kind of side constraint on how the process of public deliberation is to be organized. Finally, we can see from these arguments that public deliberation and equality in this process are only some among a number of important values that democratic decision making can embody.

### Deliberation as the Context for Political Justification

The account I have provided so far provides the best understanding of the significance of public deliberation as most of its current defenders see it. It remains for us, however, to look at the one main competing conception of the significance of public deliberation. On this account public deliberation is thought to be valuable as a condition of the justification of the social institutions that are decided upon with the help of that deliberation. Joshua Cohen's characterization of deliberative democracy aptly captures this view: "The notion of deliberative democracy is rooted in the intuitive ideal of a democratic association in which the justification of the terms and conditions of association proceeds through public argument and reasoning among equal citizens." In addition, he says that "the appropriate terms of association provide a framework for or are results of their deliberation."[13] The idea is that democratic deliberation and its conclusion in reasoned agreement are not intrinsically valuable, nor are they instrumentally worthwhile; rather, they justify the outcome. On this account, there are no independent standards for evaluating outcomes, in terms of which one might criticize the deliberative process. This is in stark contrast to the account defended above, which permits that a piece of legislation can have a certain worth because it has been chosen in a democratic way while being nevertheless unjust. The justificatory view of democratic deliberation does not permit this complex kind of assessment.

A way of illustrating the contrast between these two views is to compare a criminal trial procedure to a game. In a criminal trial procedure, there are often two distinct ways of evaluating the institution. We evaluate the trial process in terms of whether it correctly determines who is guilty and who is innocent with a preference for erring on the side of innocence. This is an instrumental evaluation of the trial process. We also evaluate the trial process in terms of how it treats citizens. Does it protect the rights of the accused? Does it properly protect the rights of victims? Does it treat all the participants as equal citizens? These are intrinsic values of the trial procedure. A trial procedure that adheres to norms of just treatment of victims and defendants confers some worth on the outcomes of the use of that procedure even if we know that the outcomes are not correct. Thus we have both intrinsic methods of assessing these procedures and independent standards. The relation between democracy and desirable outcomes, on the justificatory account, is not like that of a trial procedure to guilt or innocence; it is more like the relation between the rules of a game and the winner of the game. The rules of the game do not help us discover the winner of the game as if that were an independent fact; the rules define who is the winner. The winner of the game logically cannot be determined by any other method. Similarly, the idea is that the democratic process justifies the outcomes: they constitute what an "appropriate" outcome is. The appropriate outcome logically cannot be brought about by any other procedure.

Cohen's fuller exposition of this view can be summarized in the following proposition: "Outcomes are democratically legitimate if and only if they could be the outcome of free and reasoned agreement among equals."[14] Very briefly, the process by which legitimate outcomes are brought about is called the *ideal deliberative procedure*. This procedure is one in which citizens deliberate with each other about the just terms of association under specific conditions of freedom and equality. Each citizen attempts to advance certain terms of association on the grounds that these latter serve the common good or are just. They aim to achieve consensus and the issues on which people disagree are to be settled by the force of the better argument alone. We need not review the details of this account except to observe that while the aim of public deliberation is consensus, in the absence of consensus citizens will make choices by majority rule. The idea is that outcomes of this process are politically justified to its participants.

Thomas Christiano

## Problems of Coherence in the Justificatory View

The ideal deliberative procedure is a *model* for institutions of collective decision making; it is not an initial situation wherein idealized agents define the principles for just institutions of society. Actual democratic institutions are justified to the extent that they resemble or approximate the ideal deliberative procedure. Hence Cohen attempts to allow for disagreement even in the ideal deliberative procedure. This is a proper concession to a basic reality of politics since an ideal model of the democratic process must tell us how to decide when disagreement remains. Discussion only rarely eliminates differences of opinion on matters of politics. It often produces more disagreement and diversity of opinion even while it filters out egregious forms of ignorance and arbitrary conceptions of justice. There are many problems with trying to work out how the relation of approximation to the model is to be worked out, but I will not focus on that here.[15] My concern here is with the ideal itself. For it appears to fall into a kind of incoherence.

The central puzzle with this ideal can be expressed in four propositions that are given in Cohen's account of the ideal deliberative procedure:

1. the outcomes of the ideal deliberative procedure are politically justified terms of association to its members;

2. each member presents proposals and decides on the basis of what he or she thinks is the politically justified account of justice and the common good for that association;

3. the members often end up disagreeing about what is politically justified even in the ideal case and must conclude their deliberations with a majority vote;

4. there is nothing especially important about majority rule except as a way of avoiding gridlock.

These propositions are all expressed in Cohen's account and yet it appears that they cannot all be true together. For if citizens disagree about what is politically justified and vote on the basis of majority rule then those who are in the minority cannot think that the outcome chosen by the majority is politically justified. The consequence of this is that the members of the minority cannot regard going through the ideal deliberative procedure as definitive of political justification. They must be evaluating the democratic process in terms of standards that are independent of that process. They elaborate their own minority view as an account of what is politically justified.

Of course, we could defeat this conclusion in one of four ways: either the procedure does not determine what is politically justified (denial of 1); or the members do not try to come up with views that are politically justified—this must be left to the procedure itself (denial of 2); or the ideal deliberative procedure must always end up in a kind of agreement that is somehow powerful enough to legitimate outcomes despite disagreement (denial or refinement of 3); or finally, the members see majority rule as having by itself some kind of legitimating function, for example, on the grounds of a Rousseauian account of the epistemic value of majority rule (denial of 4).

Assume for the moment that we are trying to arrive at a notion of political justification and that at least strong agreement on outcomes is impossible. So we will start by denying 2. We could distinguish between justification and political justification in the following way. Members justify their proposals to each other when they give reasons to the others for accepting the proposals. The reasons need not be conclusive or persuasive and so when one member gives a reason for his proposal to another, the other need not be persuaded. Political justification, by contrast, consists in the members successfully persuading other members of the worth of their proposals by means of reasoned argumentation. I might think of a policy as justified because I can give what I take to be good reasons for that policy. Nevertheless, I may not think that a policy ought to be chosen for the association unless others have been rationally persuaded that it is a good policy, in other words, unless it has been politically justified. Using this distinction, we can see that the minority can think that their proposals are justified but not politically justified. And they may think that their policies ought to be politically justified before they are enacted.

Thomas Christiano

The question that arises is whether the majority's views are politically justified. They think of themselves as being justified in the same way that the minority think of themselves as being justified. Yet they have not persuaded the minority. It follows that they have failed to politically justify their position. The minority must think of themselves as not participating in a process that results in political justification. The only way in which a policy can be politically justified to them is if they have been rationally persuaded.[16]

A second option is that the defender of the justificatory view can deny or refine 3 and say that the ideal deliberative procedure must lead to agreement, but of a weak kind, and that it is in virtue of weak consensus that the process results in political justification.[17] A third option is that the defender can say that political justification only requires that a majority be rationally persuaded and that some effort to persuade the others is made. As a fourth option, the defender can appeal to necessity as a means of justifying imposing a decision on a dissenting minority.

**Weak Consensus and Reasonableness**

Let us examine each of these options in turn. First, then, suppose that though public deliberation does not achieve consensus on matters of detail; it generates consensus on more general matters. There are two kinds of weak consensus here. One is that somehow everyone comes to agree on the basic principles and values that ought to ground the political association, but they disagree about the proper priority relations among these values. So, for instance, two groups might come to agree as a result of public deliberation that liberty construed in a certain way and equality construed in some other way are the central values that ought to be embodied in political institutions. Suppose the agreement here is on quite specific conceptions of these values. Call this a *consensus on the list of values*. What they end up disagreeing on is the relative worth of these values. For example, suppose one group places liberty before equality and the other reverses the order. The implication for policy in this case, let us say, is that one group favors a laissez-faire economy with few constraints on competition and few guarantees of minimum well-being; the other favors a social democratic society that has highly regulated markets in certain areas and state control in others, and a system of redistributive taxation coupled with a strong welfare state apparatus that guarantees a decent life for all whether employed or not. The idea here is that the majority has been persuaded of the worth of one of the orderings of equality and liberty and consequently views one of these different kinds of institutions as justified. But the minority, though not persuaded of the majority's view, can see that it derives from values similar to their own, albeit in reverse order of priority and with different strengths assigned to each. The minority, though it disagrees on the matter of policy and even on matters of principle to some extent, considers that the policy has been politically justified to them because it has been justified on the basis of the list of values they accept.

Consider a second kind of weak consensus. Here suppose that everyone comes to agree as a result of public deliberation that equality and liberty are the chief values of a political society. But they do not agree on interpretations of these values. Call this *abstract consensus*. Indeed, suppose that two camps form and these camps favor, in one case, the laissez-faire state that I described above, and in the other, the social democracy I described above. Once again, since the losing group sees that the policies of the victor are based on the same values in the abstract, they regard the outcome as politically justified to them.

These two approaches have a number of severe difficulties as defenses of the justificatory view. First, it is false that public deliberation can be generally expected to bring about or sustain either one of these kinds of consensus. We see a broad array of values in contemporary democratic societies and there appears to be no consensus on which list of values is best. In addition to the values of equality and liberty, and sometimes instead of them, we see the values of community, getting what one deserves, mutual advantage, virtue, efficiency, religious homogeneity, nationalism and various kinds of multiculturalism touted as political values. These values cannot be said to arise merely because the process of public deliberation is insufficiently open or reasoned. On the contrary, they result from an open and reasoned system of deliberation. They arise not only in ordinary political discourse but also in academic discussions, which are about as free as one can get from the pressures of intimidation, ignorance, irrationality, etc. The system of public deliberation in contemporary democratic societies can undoubtedly be made more egalitarian, reasoned, and open, but it is hard to believe that such a system would produce less diversity of views. To say otherwise would presuppose the truth of a deeply speculative hypothesis to which we cannot reasonably express our allegiance. The idea that weak consensus will arise or is in existence flies in the face of our common experience of liberal democratic political societies.

A second worry about this approach is that it is not clear what the boundaries are for political justification. Presumably some kinds of abstract agreement are not sufficient for political justification. For instance, everyone might agree that justice ought to be the chief concern of the legal institutions of the society, but such an abstract consensus is compatible with an extremely wide divergence of view. In many of these cases it is clear that a consensus on a list or an abstract principle cannot ground any political justification. It is hard to see how the idea of political justification can get off the ground without a serious criterion demarcating the kinds of agreement that can serve as the basis of political justification. Or at least we need a criterion that distinguishes those cases of disagreement on interpretation or ordering that defeat political justification from those that do not.

One possible criterion that makes sense states that though members of the minority disagree with the majority about the particular interpretation or ordering of the values on which there is consensus, they can see how the majority got to their interpretation in a reasonable way. They can see how someone could *reasonably* accept the view that the majority accepts. And so, they might see how, in turn, they could reasonably accept the position of the majority. This may be sufficient for political justification to them. This is at least in part a psychological claim about the minority. It does not require that the minority assess the majority position by means of the correct conception of reasonableness (including standards of evidence and inference). They assess the majority view by using their own standards of reasonableness. The trouble with this criterion, however, is that it is quite unreliable as a way of assessing political justification. What people see in this respect is likely to vary quite a bit from one to the other. The standards they apply in making these assessments of reasonableness are likely to vary. As a consequence it is highly likely that many of the members of the minority will think that the majority has not reached its conclusion in a reasonable way. Therefore they will not think that they can reasonably accept what the majority has done and they will not see the majority as having politically justified its interpretation or ordering of the common political values to them.

Another criterion suggests itself here. The defender of the justificatory view can require that the minority assess the majority view by appeal to the correct standards of reasonableness. One possibility here is to appeal to standard theories of evidence and inference offered by epistemologists.[18] A member of the minority might see that given the premises that the majority accepts and given the general claims that are agreed on, the majority is justified (in accordance with the right epistemology) in accepting what they accept. Of course, the premises too would have to be at least defensible. We might extend this reasoning by saying that even if the minority does not see this, they ought to, and so they could reasonably accept the majority choice even if they don't think so.

The trouble here should be obvious by now. If we accept the claim that people disagree on matters relating to the interpretation of the weak consensus, then we will most likely find some disagreement on whether the disputed premises from which the alternative interpretations are defended are indeed defensible, or on whether the arguments from the agreed upon principles and the disputed premises really do provide support for the alternative interpretation or the ordering of the principles that the majority accepts. In this case it is either because the epistemology is controversial or because there is disagreement over whether the epistemological criterion of justification has been met in supporting the disputed premises or the alternative view. What constitutes, in other words, a *reasonable* acceptance of a different position is likely to be a subject of controversy itself. Thus, some will see that others have come to their alternative views by reasonable means and some will not. To the latter, the result is not politically justified.

If the defender of the justificatory view says that the minority has not assessed the views by the right epistemological standards (i.e., standards of evidence and inference), then we must ask why their assessment should be evaluated by reference to standards they do not accept. Under the supposition that a plurality of epistemologies can be defended, albeit inconclusively, it is hard to see why the minority must accept the results of an epistemology they do not accept. The idea behind the justificatory view is that people ought not to have political ideals imposed on them when they cannot reasonably assent to them, because such imposition would be oppressive. As a consequence, it is hard to see how it can permit epistemological standards to be imposed on citizens when these too are open to dispute.[19] Furthermore, to require that citizens adhere to certain standards of evidence and inference when they reject these standards and when their own standards are defensible would appear to be specially oppressive on the justificatory view. This is because such a requirement would in effect take the assessment of political ideas out of their hands by denying them the use of their own defensible standards of assessment. If standards of assessment of conceptions of political values are not to violate the basic animating ideal behind the justificatory view, they must be standards that are held in common.[20] Unfortunately, however, agreement on such standards is not to be found. Hence, it appears that the weak consensus approach cannot provide an account of political justification even when it is supplemented by a conception of reasonableness.

Another difficulty with the use of correct standards of reasonableness as a way of assessing whether the majority position has been politically justified is that the majority may fail on those standards and the minority may succeed in satisfying those standards when they elaborate their interpretations. In this case, the minority would have politically justified their position to the majority (on this account) but the majority would not have politically justified their view to the minority. Another possible outcome of this approach is that no group succeeds in justifying their view to others on the basis of the correct standards of reasonableness. And this may happen even when all believe that political justification has occurred. We seem to be getting farther and farther away from a society in which "the appropriate terms of association provide a framework for or are the results of the deliberation of citizens."

## Majority Rule as a Source of Political Justification

The third way to reconcile disagreement on what is politically justified with the idea that the outcomes of the ideal deliberative procedure are politically justified is to say that justification to a majority is sufficient for political justification. On its own, this does not appear to be very promising. Why should the mere fact that a majority is persuaded constitute political justification of terms of association for those who are not persuaded? It appears that the only way that this can happen is if the persuasion of the majority communicates some information to the minority about the justification of the view the majority has adopted. Such a view has been expressed by a number of theorists called *epistemic theorists* of democracy.[21] The essential bridge between the majority and political justification to the minority is expressed by Rousseau:

> When in the popular assembly a law is proposed, what the people is asked is not exactly whether it approves or rejects the proposal, but whether it is in conformity with the general will, which is their will. Each man, in giving his vote, states his opinion on that point; and the general will is found by counting votes. When therefore the opinion that is contrary to my own prevails, this proves neither more nor less than that I was mistaken, and that what I thought to be the general will was not so.[22]

Why should this be so? Probably the most succinct account of this is given by Bernard Manin: "The relative force of [a norm's] justification can only be measured by the amplitude and the intensity of the approval it arouses in an audience of reasonable people."[23] And from this he argues that "the approval of the greatest number reflects, in that context, the greater strength of one set of arguments compared to others."[24]

We need here to distinguish two closely related claims. The first claim is that the fact that the majority has agreed to a piece of legislation gives the minority a reason, sufficient for political

Thomas Christiano

justification, to think that they were wrong and that the alternative the majority chose is right. The second is that in general and in the long run, the majority will make better decisions on the whole than the minority. The first claim is much stronger than the second. Indeed it may rely on the truth of the second but, in addition, it relies on the claim that the minority agrees with this truth in this context. The account of political justification is founded on the idea that a person must be given a reason that is acceptable by his or her own lights for a policy in order for that policy not to be oppressive. But the claim that the minority really does have reason by their own lights to think that the majority is more likely to be right than the minority about the disputed question is deeply questionable. The context in which such an improbable eventuality might take place is described by the basic axioms of the Condorcet Jury Theorem. Suffice it to say for present purposes that those axioms are not thought by anyone to hold in complex democratic societies.[25] There are two ways in which the first claim cannot hold. One, the first claim requires that the majority be more likely to be right in particular decisions or at least in particular sets of decisions. Two, the claim requires that the minority have good reason to see that the majority is right in each of the particular decisions or sets of decisions. But, if it is true that the majority's decisions are more often right than the minority's, this can only be empirically established in the long run and it would be unreasonable to expect members of the minority to see this. In addition since the superiority holds only in the long run, the minority may reasonably think that it is right more often than not. Hence, we must reject the claim that majority rule can provide the minority with political justification for the decisions of the minority.

We have come full circle to the instrumentalist account of the worth of deliberation and its association with majority rule. Though it seems reasonable to think that deliberation has beneficial effects on the outcomes of political decision making, it seems quite hard to accept the particular claims that Manin and Rousseau assert here. The beneficial impact of particular public, political deliberations must be long-term ones and ones which will often not be experienced by those who have engaged in that deliberation. Hence the deliberative account, if it is to appeal to the kinds of considerations given immediately above, must abandon the idea that the procedure is itself the source of political justification. This is because the procedure must be evaluated and endorsed in terms of its being able to bring about outcomes that satisfy an independent standard, one which can be satisfied only for the most part by a reliable process of discussion and voting. Hence the procedure is not itself the source of political justification; rather, the justification results from the fact that the procedure's outcomes approximate some independent standard.

## The Appeal to Necessity

Defenders of the justificatory view might argue that since it is often necessary to make decisions despite disagreement, it is reasonable for members of the minority to accept the outcome of majority rule in situations where a decision must be made. They might argue that these facts, when apprehended by the minority or when they ought to be apprehended by the minority, constitute a kind of political justification of the result to the minority even when that minority is not persuaded that the result is acceptable or that it could reasonably be accepted. This is, I suppose, the last line of defense of the justificatory view.[26]

There are two basic problems with this view. First, it assumes that everyone will accept the claim of necessity. Notice that we must ask when the appeal to necessity is made, necessary to what purpose? Surely logical, physical, or psychological necessity are not being invoked here. What is being invoked is the idea that if a decision is not made, some good result will not occur. But, clearly, there may be quite a bit of disagreement about whether the proposed good outcome is really good. Someone might argue, for instance, that some health care proposal for helping the indigent must be passed (otherwise, the indigent will not be helped) and so even if there is disagreement about which proposal is best, it is reasonable for everyone to accept the proposal of the majority even though on its own, it falls short of political justification. But, surely some will reject the appeal to necessity in this case. They may argue that the indigent do

Thomas Christiano

not have to be helped. Or they may argue that the indigent will not be helped by any program more than they are when there is no program. Presumably, they could argue such claims on the basis of the ideals of liberty and equality. Hence the appeal to necessity will be controversial.

The final difficulty of the appeal to necessity is that it appears to give up entirely on the ideal of political justification of laws or policies to each and every person. For by hypothesis, it allows explicitly that such political justification of the law or policy to each person cannot be had in the circumstance. Instead it says that in the absence of political justification, the majority is the right group to make the decision. But here we can see that the majority rule is not being invoked because it is supplying political justification. It is being invoked because it is a fair or just way of making decisions when a decision has to be made and disagreement on the merits of alternative proposals cannot be resolved. But such an explanation of the worth of majority rule is explicitly ruled out by the justificatory view. The only defense of majority rule along these lines is that it embodies equality. Hence, once again, we come to the second part of the view defended in this paper.

**Conclusion**

These results reflect a feature of the deliberative account that we have been tracking throughout this chapter. Given the fact of persistent disagreement on political matters, political justification cannot be seen by the members of an association to be merely a function of the ideal deliberative procedure. Each member of the association must be participating in deliberation with the view that his or her own approach is politically justified. And though they will hopefully often improve their views, citizens will end up presumably with views that they regard as politically justified and that the others in the association do not regard as politically justified. This implies two important propositions: each member must think that the ideal procedure does not produce outcomes that are politically justified to each of its members, and each member must be thinking of what is politically justified in terms of standards that are independent of the ideal procedure and understands that everyone else is thinking in the same terms. In short, the ideal deliberative procedure cannot be the source of political justification. The justificatory view cannot explain the significance of public deliberation to democracy.

What explains the readiness of citizens to attempt to justify their proposals to others? What explains their participation in the process of deliberation? And why do we think that this process is so important? We can answer these questions fully with the account of the instrumental and intrinsic worths of public deliberation I provide in this paper.[27]

## Notes

1. See John Stuart Mill, *Considerations on Representative Government* (Buffalo: Prometheus Books, 1985), ch. 2–3, and *On Liberty* (Buffalo: Prometheus Books, 1990), ch. 2, for this kind of view. See also Cass Sunstein, *Democracy and the Problem of Free Speech* (New York: Free Press, 1993), ch. 8, for this kind of view. And see my *The Rule of the Many* (Boulder, CO: Westview Press, 1996), ch. 2, for a development of these instrumentalist claims.

2. Jean-Jacques Rousseau, *The Social Contract and Discourses,* ed. G. H. D. Cole (London: J. M. Dent, 1973), p. 185, and Bernard Manin, "On Legitimacy and Political Deliberation," *Political Theory* (August 1987), pp. 338–368, esp. p. 345.

3. This view is sometimes attributed to Aristotle in his *Politics.* See also Hannah Arendt, *On Revolution* (Harmondsworth: Penguin Books, 1963). See Jon Elster, *Sour Grapes* (Cambridge: Cambridge University Press, 1983), for an argument to the effect that such a value is incoherent. I have argued that such a view is coherent in "Is the Participation Argument Coherent?" *Philosophical Studies* (April 1996), pp. 1–12.

4. I will not consider here the thesis that a society that makes decisions without public deliberation is not democratic at all. This is either a conceptual claim stating that the concept of democracy contains in some way the idea of public deliberation or it is a claim about the proper conception of democracy, where the idea of democracy is understood in a normative way. Democracy would be a notion much like justice or goodness; it is normative. Hence to say that democracy is essentially deliberative is to state a conception of democracy.

5. Mill, *On Liberty,* p. 108. See Philip Kitcher, "The Division of Cognitive Labor," *Journal of Philosophy* (January 1990), pp. 5–22, for an epistemic defense of diversity in scientific theorizing.

6. See James R. Larson, Jr., Pennie G. Foster-Fishman, and Christopher B. Keys, "Discussion of Shared and Unshared Information in Decision Making Groups," *Journal of Personality and Social Psychology* vol. 67, no. 3 (1994), pp. 446–461, esp. 459, on the sharing of unshared information and how this contributes to the qualities of outcomes. See also Herbert Blumberg, "Group Decision Making and Choice Shift,"

Thomas Christiano

in *Small Group Research: A Handbook,* eds. A. Paul Hare, Herbert Blumberg, Martin Davies, and Valerie Kent (Norwood, NJ: Ablex, 1994), pp. 195–210, esp. p. 200.

7. See John Rawls, *Theory of Justice* (Cambridge, MA: Harvard University Press, 1971), p. 473, for a discussion of the moral psychological impact of institutions regulated by the two principles of justice, and his *Political Liberalism* (New York: Columbia University Press, 1993), pp. 54–58, for a discussion of the burdens of judgment. Rawls thinks that the burdens of judgment only afflict comprehensive conceptions of the good and not conceptions of justice.

8. It is important to distinguish views (such as those of Habermas and Rawls) that claim that justice is defined in terms of what reasonable people agree to in idealized conditions from those that claim that consensus in the process of democratic deliberation is possible and desirable. The former views can be entered into the process of public deliberation as alternatives to be considered, though they are unlikely to receive unanimous consent even among reasonable people in any actual democratic society.

9. See Blumberg, "Group Decision Making and Choice Shift," p. 201.

10. See my *The Rule of the Many,* chs. 2 and 8, for an extensive examination of the nature and importance of equality in the process of public deliberation. For other discussions of equality in the process of deliberation, see the essays by Jack Knight and James Johnson and by James Bohman in this volume, as well as the essay by Harry Brighouse in *Social Theory and Practice* 1996, and Charles Beitz, *Political Equality* (Princeton: Princeton University Press, 1989), chs. 8–9.

11. For the full argument for the intrinsic justice of political equality on the basis of equal consideration of interests, see my *The Rule of the Many,* ch. 2.

12. In *The Rule of the Many,* ch. 4, I argue that not only is concern with justice and the common good a fact about human beings but also that it ought to be a concern if the society they live in is to have a chance to embody any kind of political ideal at all.

13. Joshua Cohen, "Deliberation and Democratic Legitimacy," in *The Good Polity,* eds. Alan Hamlin and Philip Pettit (Oxford: Blackwell, 1989), p. 21.

14. Ibid., p. 22.

15. For a critique of this account, see *The Rule of the Many,* ch. 1, pp. 37–43.

16. We can enter a qualification here to the effect that if the minority is not persuaded because they are irrational or unreasonable, then this too does not count against political justification. See Gerald Gaus, *Justificatory Liberalism: An Essay in Epistemology and Politics* (Oxford: Oxford University Press, 1996), for a defense of a qualification of this sort. I do not think that this qualification affects the argument I am giving.

17. Gaus, in *Justificatory Liberalism,* describes what he calls "nested inconclusive justification" on p. 189. See also Joshua Cohen, "Liberty, Equality, and Democracy," unpublished lectures given at Stanford University, August 1996, pp. 26, 105. See also Cohen's "Procedures and Substance in Deliberative Democracy" in this volume.

18. See Gaus, *Justificatory Liberalism*, p. 4, for an attempt to ground a conception of political justification in an epistemological theory, although he does not use it in this context.

19. For some parallel considerations, see Jean Hampton, "The Moral Commitments of Liberalism," in *The Idea of Democracy*, eds. David Copp, Jean Hampton, and John Roemer (Cambridge: Cambridge University Press, 1993).

20. As Rawls argues in *Political Liberalism*, p. 224.

21. See Bernard Grofman and Scott Feld, "Rousseau's General Will: A Condorcetian Perspective," *American Political Science Review* (June 1988), pp. 567–576. See also Joshua Cohen, "An Epistemic Conception of Democracy," *Ethics* (July 1986), pp. 26–38 (Cohen has subsequently abandoned this view). See also David Estlund, "Democratic Theory and the Public Interest: Condorcet and Rousseau Revisited," *American Political Science Review* (December 1989), pp. 1317–1322, for a helpful discussion of one approach.

22. Rousseau, *The Social Contract and Discourses*, p. 278

23. Bernard Manin, "On Legitimacy and Political Deliberation," *Political Theory* (August 1987), p. 354.

24. Ibid., p. 359.

25. See my "Freedom, Consensus and Equality in Collective Decision Making," *Ethics* (October 1990), pp. 151–181, for a critique of the application of the theorem to democracy. The theorem states that when a group faces a choice between two alternatives and each member of the group has on average better than .5 probability of choosing the best alternative, then groups with large numbers will have a probability nearing 1 of arriving at the best choice when they choose by a majoritarian method. The troubles are that political issues never come packaged in dichotomous choices and it is not clear that voters are independent of each other or even what this axiom means. In addition, it is hard to see why one would assign a better than 50% chance of being right to another when one disagrees with that other person about what the right answer is.

26. See Cohen, "Liberty, Equality, and Democracy," p. 74; see also Thomas Nagel, "Moral Conflict and Political Legitimacy," *Philosophy and Public Affairs* (1987), 215–240, especially pp. 233–234.

27. I wish to thank John Armstrong, James Bohman, and William Rehg for their helpful comments on a previous draft of this paper.

# 9

## What Sort of Political Equality Does Deliberative Democracy Require?

*Jack Knight and James Johnson*

### I Democracy and Equality

Democracy means rule by the people, where "the people" are understood to be heterogeneous across multiple dimensions, that is, where they are characterized not only by divergent material interests but by diverse cultural attachments and ethical commitments as well.[1] For present purposes we take democracy in a narrow sense to be an institutional arrangement for making binding political decisions.[2] A democratic institutional arrangement will consist in both formal or official decision-making forums and an extensive environment of secondary associations (Cohen and Rogers 1993).

The pluralist character of "the people" in our understanding requires that a democratic institutional arrangement generate binding political decisions through processes that are open to participation and where, from the perspective of participants, outcomes are not known ex ante. This uncertainty derives from two sources. First, in principle at least, the material interests, cultural attachments, or ethical commitments of particular participants are not privileged in advance. So outcomes depend on the actions of participants, not on their prior position or characteristics. Second, the outcomes of democratic decision making reflect interdependence both in the sense that no particular individual or group can unilaterally dictate an outcome and, consequently, in the sense that the actions of any participant will, in part, be premised upon her expectations of what relevant others are likely to do (Przeworski 1991, 10–14).

Jack Knight and James Johnson

Equality, then, plays a significant role in our understanding of democracy. Its more general importance becomes clear if we consider one recent definition of democracy: "By a democratic procedure I mean a method of determining the content of laws (and other legally binding decisions) such that the preferences of citizens have some formal connection with the outcome in which each counts equally" (Barry 1991, 25).[3] Although equality appears late in this particular definition, the fact that democratic processes will generate losers as well as winners makes it essential. Yet, if democracy requires equality, an obvious, serious question remains: What sort of equality does it require?

We are not here concerned with the relation of equality and democracy per se but, rather, with the sort of equality required by *deliberative* democracy. This is an especially pressing problem insofar as we are concerned with the legitimacy or otherwise of democratic institutional arrangements. This is because, in a democracy, "a legitimate decision . . . is one that results from the *deliberation of all*" (Manin 1987, 352).[4] Indeed, most defenses of democratic deliberation insist that this criterion of legitimacy requires a strong form of equality.[5] Some critics, however, remain unpersuaded. "Explorations of deliberative or communicative democracy," one such critic observes, "often refer rather grandly to a principle of equal access to decision-making assemblies or substantive equality in resources and power, but they do not give much consistent attention to how these conditions would ever be achieved" (Phillips 1995, 154). Our aim in this chapter is to give more consistent attention to this problem.[6]

Deliberative democracy requires a particular, relatively complex sort of equality. Given our stress on the uncertainty of outcomes produced by democratic arrangements, such arrangements obviously cannot require equality of outcomes. Democracy, then, requires some version of equality of opportunity.[7] More specifically, democratic deliberation requires *equal opportunity of access to political influence*. Influence is more than mere voting. Dworkin offers the following helpful distinction between influence and impact: "The intuitive difference is this: someone's impact in politics is the difference he can make, just on his own, by voting for, or choosing, one decision rather than another. Someone's influence, on the other hand, is the difference he can make not just on his own, but also by leading or inducing others to believe or vote or choose as he does" (Dworkin 1987, 9). This emphasis on influence suggests that the sort of equality of opportunity required by democracy will have both procedural and substantive dimensions.

It is necessary to distinguish analytically between access and influence in order to identify properly the procedural and substantive aspects of equality of opportunity as we understand it. Democratic deliberation presupposes procedural guarantees that afford equal access to relevant deliberative arenas at both agenda-setting and decision-making stages.[8] This is a difficult problem of institutional design any defensible solution to which is necessary but not sufficient to establish the sort of political equality of opportunity that democratic deliberation requires.

Because deliberation revolves centrally around the uncoerced give and take of reasoned argument, it also requires a more substantive notion of equal opportunity of political influence. We distinguish two aspects of the problem. First, deliberation presupposes equality of resources needed to ensure that an individual's assent to arguments advanced by others is indeed uncoerced. Here we have in mind such factors as material wealth and educational treatment. Second, deliberation requires equal capacity to advance persuasive claims. Here we have in mind the need to accommodate and remedy the asymmetrical distribution in any political constituency of relevant deficiencies and faculties (e.g., in the ability to reason, articulate ideas, etc.).

Although we distinguish access and influence for analytical purposes, in practice the two remain intimately related. The sort of equal opportunity for political influence that we have in mind may require policies that treat individuals unequally.[9] The justification for these inequalities rests on the idea that individuals should not be unfairly disadvantaged in the democratic process by deficiencies due to conditions or circumstances beyond their control (Roemer 1993; 1995).[10] This obviously requires criteria by which to distinguish factors that are within an individual's control from those that are not and for which that individual cannot be held responsible. On our view, however, the demand for such criteria need not either raise

Jack Knight and James Johnson

metaphysical issues regarding free will and determinism or be tied to established social conventions. Instead, on our view such criteria are themselves both established and subject to revision in a deliberative process.[11] So here equal access to relevant deliberative arenas will have crucial impact on how participants establish and revise the criteria for ensuring equal opportunity of political influence, even as this latter sort of equality will crucially determine the capacities of those same participants to press claims once they enter relevant deliberative arenas.

This, in short, is the sort of political equality that democratic deliberation requires. It remains to specify both what this conception of equal opportunity of access to political influence itself entails and the sorts of obstacles that hinder efforts to implement it. We will address procedural and substantive concerns in turn. Our argument helps, we think, to respond to critics like Anne Phillips. At the same time, however, we identify what we take to be disturbing difficulties surrounding the conception of political equality presupposed by democratic deliberation.

## II Procedural Equality I

Social choice theory provides a systematic analysis of the normative and analytical properties of voting procedures.[12] No comparable analysis exists for institutions (as opposed to the ideals) of deliberative democracy. In this section and the next we take social choice analyses as a counterpoint. We state three conditions that social choice theorists impose in order to ensure procedural equality in voting. We then explore some difficulties involved in establishing analogous criteria for ensuring procedural equality in democratic deliberation.

Social choice theorists show that, under specifiable conditions, all known aggregation procedures suffer from important, unavoidable, endogenous problems. Most famously, Kenneth Arrow demonstrated that there exists no aggregation mechanism that simultaneously conforms to a set of several relatively unobjectionable normative conditions and generates coherent collective decisions.[13] Three of Arrow's conditions aim to ensure one or another aspect of procedural equality. First, *unrestricted domain* disallows any prior constraint on the content of the preferences or interests that a proposed aggregation procedure must accommodate. It simply requires that the aggregation procedure itself not impose ex ante filters on the substantive views of relevant constituencies. In this sense unrestricted domain governs what we will refer to as "conditions of entry." Second, *anonymity* requires that all voters are treated equally by the voting procedure.[14] Third, *neutrality* requires that the voting procedure not be biased toward one or another alternative.[15] So, where anonymity requires that *voters* be treated equally, neutrality requires that the *alternatives* over which they vote be treated equally. In this sense anonymity and neutrality govern different aspects of what we will call "internal workings" of democratic arrangements. In this section we argue that entry to deliberative institutions must be governed by normative criteria very much like unrestricted domain. In the next section we turn to the conditions analogous to anonymity and neutrality that govern the internal workings of deliberative institutions.

Because "the people" who populate any plausible democratic arrangement are heterogeneous across multiple dimensions, advocates of deliberation must subscribe to some principle very much like unrestricted domain.[16] Deliberative democracy requires the most expansive possible conditions of entry to formal or official political arenas.[17] As noted earlier, such entry must be available at both agenda-setting and final decision-making stages. In order to provide a sense of what such expansive conditions of entry require we explore two useful examples of how *not* to proceed here. We draw both examples from the work of John Rawls. First, Rawls insists that parties to deliberation must subscribe to "precepts of reasonable discussion" (Rawls 1989, 238–239). Second, he claims that democratic deliberation need be responsive not to "the fact of pluralism" per se but only to the less expansive "fact of reasonable pluralism" (Rawls 1993, 36–37, 58f). We examine these examples in turn.

Precepts of reasonable discussion, according to Rawls, enjoin parties to political deliberation from accusing "one another of self- or group interest, prejudice or bias, and of such deeply entrenched errors as ideological blindness and delusion." Charges such as this

Jack Knight and James Johnson

amount, according to Rawls, to "a declaration of intellectual war" (1989, 238). We must instead be prepared to countenance deep, perhaps insurmountable, disagreement while at the same time attributing to others "a certain good faith."

There are at least three reasons why one might object to Rawls's precepts. First, political actors may, in fact, be driven by self-interest, blinded by prejudice, or deluded by ideology.[18] It very plausibly is among the desirable features of democratic deliberation that it allows participants to raise this possibility, to challenge those to whom they believe the charge applies, to do so publicly and, thereby, to afford those so challenged to respond.[19] Thus, if in a deliberative decision-making process you knowingly or not press claims that are prejudiced, ideologically biased, or unjustifiably self-interested, others must be allowed not only to contest those claims but, Rawls's precepts notwithstanding, to characterize them as prejudiced, ideological or selfish as part of their reason for so doing.[20]

The risk here becomes clearer if we attend not merely to the interaction of adversaries but also to the relation between putative allies in the deliberative process. Consider, in this regard, a recent essay by Katha Pollitt entitled "Marooned on Gilligan's Island: Are Women Morally Superior to Men?"[21] There, Pollitt, herself a feminist, publicly criticizes "difference feminists" in ways that seemingly violate Rawls's precepts of reasonable discussion. She adopts a title that lampoons those feminists who celebrate the "difference" between men and women. That, however, is not all. Pollitt also bluntly charges that, because their arguments are ideologically self-serving, difference feminists threaten the political prospects of those very constituencies that feminists traditionally aspire to mobilize.[22] Such claims, if defensible, are tremendously important to feminists. Yet, Rawls's precepts would preclude parties to deliberative processes from advancing charges of the sort that Pollitt levels at difference feminism.

Second, there surely are points when seemingly "unreasonable" factors such as for instance anger, frustration, humor, fear, joy, or humiliation, quite reasonably and justifiably enter political argument. Should political actors motivated by such emotions be disallowed, for that reason, from participating in democratic deliberation?

There seems to be no good reason why we should ground our vision of deliberation on the sort of conceptual gerrymandering that draws hard and fast boundaries between reason and emotion when such boundaries likely would banish not only obstreperous demands and angry shouts but tears and laughter from the deliberative arena.[23]

Finally, Rawls's precepts in all likelihood would disallow important political practices. Civil disobedience, for example, seems, and indeed often is designed to be, paradigmatically "unreasonable." But it surely is plausible to see civil disobedience as part of an ongoing process of political deliberation. "Outrageous" and "unreasonable" acts of civil disobedience might, by demonstrating the depth of grievances or of outrage, prompt relevant political actors to reconsider and perhaps revise an otherwise binding collective decision.[24]

Consider now the claim that deliberative procedures need only accommodate the fact of "reasonable pluralism."[25] This claim prejudges in an unjustifiable way the question of which sorts of argument or value are legitimately admissible to the process of political deliberation and debate. Here, in contrast to the precepts of reasonable discussion, Rawls does not simply demand that the parties to deliberation adopt a civil demeanor. Rather, he demands some prepolitical normative criteria to which parties to deliberation subscribe and that enable them to recognize as reasonable some range of possible sorts of claim or position that they do not merely tolerate, but treat with respect.[26] Other claims and views are inadmissible.

Rawls of course claims that his "political liberalism" requires an "overlapping consensus" on the principles of justice that govern the "basic structure" of society and that such a consensus need accommodate only "the fact of *reasonable* pluralism." In this sense, his conception of justice would emerge from deliberation over "matters of constitutional essentials and basic justice" (Rawls 1993). In a democracy, however, deliberation would address more mundane policy issues as well. In recent work, Amy Gutmann suggests how deliberation informed by a concern to accommodate "reasonable pluralism" might operate at this second level. On her account, "actual deliberation" consists in "the give and take of argument that is respectful of *reasonable* differences" (Gutmann 1993, 197). Mutual respect entails in particular ways both "integrity" in advancing one's

Jack Knight and James Johnson

own position and "magnanimity" in characterizing the positions of others (Gutmann and Thompson 1990, 78f). This, however, leaves poorly defined the criteria we should use to determine what constitutes a position that is "reasonable" and hence deserving of respect.

At this juncture there are two dangers that are not simultaneously avoidable. On the one hand, any set of substantive criteria for distinguishing reasonable from unreasonable risks unwarranted arbitrariness and introduces an odd circularity into the defense of deliberation. First, imposing substantive standards of reasonableness on the sorts of views that are admissible to the deliberative arena risks being unacceptably arbitrary.[27] The same "burdens of judgment" that, according to Rawls, ensure an irreducible plurality of interests, attachments and commitments in any democratic constituency, would make it at least difficult, probably impossible, to discern with confidence whether the views advocated by any particular actor are reasonable or otherwise.[28] Second, we encounter the problem of circularity. From a deliberative perspective, political decisions are legitimate, when they are, because they have survived a process of reasoned argument. Imposing substantive criteria of reasonableness as an ex ante filter on admissibility would preempt that very process of reasoned argument. Instead of generating outcomes that are legitimate because they emerge from reasoned debate, substantive criteria would circumscribe in advance the range of views on offer in deliberative arenas. If only reasonable views enter the deliberative process how can the view that ultimately emerges be otherwise than reasonable?

On the other hand, one might adopt fairly minimalist, largely formal criteria for differentiating reasonable from unreasonable views. Cohen seems to adopt such a strategy when he asserts that "reasonable is defined . . . in terms of a willingness to entertain and respond to objections" and that "to be unreasonable" is, by contrast, to "favor institutions and policies that cannot be justified to others" (Cohen 1994a, 1537–1538). The problem is that this criteria of reasonableness may prove too weak and so generate perverse results. Consider, for example, Americans who reject the theory of evolution and subscribe instead to "creationist" views and who, moreover, wish to implement policies that mandate the teaching of "creation science" alongside of, or instead of, the theory of evolution in public schools. A minimalist approach would not exclude such views from the deliberative arena because creationists, in fact, are reasonable in precisely the sense that Cohen requires. They entertain and respond to objections and they revise their views accordingly.[29] Conversely, it is possible to view the opponents of creationism as unreasonable in precisely Cohen's sense, because they advocate policies (e.g., the teaching of evolution rather than creation science) on rigid and hence unjustifiable grounds (Laudan 1996, 223–230).[30]

In the end, both of the types of ex ante Rawlsian constraint on admissibility that we have examined seek to establish as a condition of entry into deliberative institutions what are more plausibly seen as potential products of deliberation. Thus, where Rawls makes adherence to his "precepts of reasonable discussion" a condition of entry into relevant deliberative arenas, we suspect that deliberation, governed by the sort of expansive conditions of entry that we endorse, might, where it is successful, engender "good faith" by enabling participants to develop greater understanding of and trust in both one another and the deliberative process itself. Similarly, deliberative procedures subject to the widest possible terms of entry, would make "reasonable pluralism," where it were possible, an outcome of, rather than a precondition for, democratic deliberation.[31]

## III  Procedural Equality II

It is not sufficient to ensure expansive conditions of entry to deliberative arenas. It also is necessary to ensure that, once various participants and the competing positions that they endorse have gained admission to deliberative institutions, the internal workings of those institutions not accord differential advantage to either particular participants or to their favored positions. Recall that in their analyses of aggregation mechanisms social choice theorists impose the conditions of anonymity and neutrality in order to accord equal protection to voters and alternatives respectively. In this section we explore analogous conditions for deliberative arrangements. We consider the analogues to anonymity and neutrality in turn.

Jack Knight and James Johnson

*Anonymity*. An aggregation procedure treats voters anonymously when it operates "blindly" in the sense that while (in order to identify a winner) it differentiates between the content of votes cast, it does not discriminate between voters on the basis of characteristics such as, for example, socioeconomic position or religious affiliation. This is especially important to the goal of treating political actors equally because it minimizes the chance that they can be identified as targets of coercive interference. Historically, something like this view has been institutionalized in the practice of the secret ballot.[32] Yet because deliberation centrally involves debate over social and political practices and policies, secrecy seems a particularly inappropriate condition to impose on deliberative arrangements. We want to ensure, after all, that decisions are actually informed by and result from debate rather than being simply imposed by one or a few well-placed parties. To this end deliberative procedures rely on public contest of reasons as a way of checking power and, thereby, ensuring that participants are treated equally.[33]

Deliberation justifiably discriminates between divergent views based on their content in the sense that parties to deliberation will identify some views as more defensible or justifiable than others. Deliberative arrangements, however, "do not single out individuals" (Cohen 1989a, 22). Instead, deliberative arrangements seek minimally to dampen, and optimally to eliminate entirely any arbitrary inequalities between participants to any interaction. They do so by ensuring that, in articulating and defending their views, participants rely not on asymmetries created, for example, by socioeconomic resources or political power, but instead only upon what Habermas calls "the force of the better argument."[34] This means that the procedures that govern the deliberative phase of democratic decision making protect equality by ensuring that all claims and counterclaims are subject to critical public scrutiny and that, when challenged, any participant must defend her proposal or back her objection with reasons.[35]

This portrait will come as little surprise to those familiar with the literature on deliberation even if the connection between equality and the requirement of public scrutiny typically is not drawn out in the way we depict it here. Consider two things that this common-place view of deliberation does not entail.

First, this commonplace view of deliberation does not require that individuals actually participate equally. Thus, for example, it does not prejudge the relation between deliberative democracy and representative institutions. It does not, in other words, presume that deliberation requires direct democracy. Among the "principles" which historically have animated the practice of representative government since the eighteenth century are the following: (1) representatives are elected by and therefore accountable to constituents, and they thereby must be able to defend their actions to those constituents; (2) representatives retain discretion and hence are called upon to exercise judgment where this may require that they set aside parochial interests of their constituents; (3) freedom of expression allows for constituents to prevail upon and express opinions to officials; and (4) legislation is enacted only after discussion and debate (Manin 1994, 136–147). Thus, at each point, representative institutions presuppose the sort of public debate that characterizes deliberation. The relation between deliberation and equality simply means that representative institutions must be organized in such a way that they do not single out individual representatives or their constituents in unjustifiable ways.[36]

Similarly, the commonplace view of deliberation does not presume that citizens are *literally* equal in the sense that each has the requisite interest, experience, or expertise to participate in every decision that affects her life. It does not, therefore, preclude authority relations. This is especially important in complex, functionally differentiated societies (Warren 1996, 46–48). What the egalitarian thrust of public argumentation requires is that claims to authority are subject to challenge. Thus, for example, on contested issues those who invoke special expertise can be compelled to provide reasons for a given decision when, in the standard course of events, their claim to authority might well have sufficed (Warren 1996, 58–59).

Second, the view of deliberation as consisting in a public process through which policy proposals are advanced, challenged and defended and where, at each stage of that process, participants must rely solely on reasons, does not categorically exclude either self-interested claims or the conflicts that such claims might generate from the range of topics admissible to relevant deliberative arenas. Members of previously excluded groups, for example, typically demand entry into relevant decision-making arenas precisely because, so long as they remain excluded, their *interests* are not adequately considered.[37] There is no reason to think that this should be any less true of deliberative arrangements than, for instance, of electoral systems.

Similarly, it is easy to envision situations where self-interested claims are justified even among long-established participants in deliberation.[38] Consider a common problem of public goods provision modeled in simple game theoretic terms as a "chicken" interaction. Here two or more actors are in a situation where any one of them can supply the requisite level of a public good (say maintenance of flood control levees along a stretch of river). If no one provides the good, the consequences are potentially disastrous for all (say massive flooding in the spring). Each player nevertheless prefers that someone else perform the required task. Indeed, the equilibria in such a game involve outcomes in which some actor provides the public good while others exploit her cooperative activity. Faced with a strategic situation of this sort, any party to deliberative proceedings aimed at resolving it clearly could, with justification, object to being exploited in this way.[39] This sort of objection surely represents a justifiable response to predictable demands that some particular actor simply should sacrifice in the common interest. And, if the group were to try to arrange some "fair" resolution (e.g., rotation of burdens over time), any such resolution would have normative force precisely because self-interest based claims provide, as it were, a significant part of the normative scaffolding in terms of which fairness can be defined.

*Neutrality.* An aggregation mechanism treats alternatives neutrally when it is not biased, ex ante, for or against any particular alternative. The results from social choice theory are instructive with regard to this condition. These results suggest, among other things, (i) that different methods of counting votes (e.g., simple majority, majoritarian methods such as the Condorcet rule, or positional methods such as plurality voting) can generate dramatically different out-comes from the same initial profile of preferences, and (ii) that, as a result, the outcomes of aggregation are not only especially vulner-able to manipulation, but that we typically are unable to differentiate outcomes produced by agenda control or strategic voting from those that are not (Riker 1980). Aggregative arrangements thus have a difficult time conforming to the demand for neutrality.

Unfortunately, deliberation encounters very similar problems. Al-though the literature on this issue is significantly less extensive, there is very good reason to suspect that the outcome of political debate depends heavily upon factors such as the sequence in which partici-pants speak and the point at which debate is terminated.[40] This leaves those concerned with the problem of designing plausible de-liberative institutions with an unenviable, perhaps insurmountable, task. If different procedures that might govern political argument will generate widely different outcomes from the same initial range of views, deliberation is susceptible to objections analogous to those which have been leveled at aggregation mechanisms. The outcome of deliberation is then hostage to precisely the sort of arbitrary factors for which aggregation has repeatedly been criticized.[41]

Advocates of deliberation, of course, might view this apprehension as entirely misplaced. After all, they might claim, deliberative ar-rangements are intended to prompt participants to revise their views in light of reasons that they encounter in the course of public political argument. From this perspective, whether or not delibera-tive procedures generate different outcomes from the same initial range of views is irrelevant. Yet this response is troubling. For it suggests that we have no reliable criteria for determining whether or not any given deliberative arrangement treats alternatives equally. That hardly provides a robust basis for asserting, for instance, that the "alternatives to deliberation" represent "less moral or more authoritarian ways of dealing with fundamental moral conflicts con-cerning social justice" (Gutmann 1993, 202).

In short, the condition of neutrality raises issues of institutional design about which it is difficult to say very much with any great confidence. What we do know, however, leads us to suspect (i) that the sort of procedural equality required by deliberative democracy

Jack Knight and James Johnson

may be extremely difficult to implement and (ii) that, in any case, it will be next to impossible to determine whether any particular institutional arrangement in fact embodies anything like the requisite sort of procedural equality.

## IV Substantive Equality

Deliberative democracy makes strong demands on our criterion of political equality. Participants in the deliberative process must be actively engaged in a discourse of argumentation and persuasion. The task for any participant in such a process is to develop and communicate reasons for action that will influence others to endorse her preferred collective outcomes. If she is unable, for whatever reason, to effectively accomplish this task, she will be unable to affect the collective decision-making process. Through this failure her interests and goals will most likely go unaccounted for in the democratic process. And this violates the fundamental notion that democratic outcomes are the product of the interests of equal citizens.

In this section we explicate and defend our conception of "equal opportunity of political influence." We take this idea to be a central feature of a conception of deliberative democracy. Procedural mechanisms alone will not guarantee this feature. To adequately secure this conception we must attend to the substantive aspects of political equality. Cohen defines the substantive dimension of equality for deliberative democracy as follows: "[t]he participants are substantively equal in that the existing distribution of power and resources does not shape their chances to contribute at any stage of the deliberative process, nor does that distribution play an authoritative role in their deliberation" (Cohen 1989b, 33).

This definition highlights the fundamental connection between the social distribution of power and resources and the achievement of real political equality. The connection is a complex one. To assess the requirements of political equality for deliberative democracy, we believe that we must address the various effects of this social distribution of power and resources on effective participation in the deliberative process.

Such an analysis requires us to consider three questions. What does "equal opportunity of political influence" entail? How might we measure "opportunity of influence" in order to assess whether or not it is distributed equally?[42] What is required, in terms of policies and institutions, in order to achieve equality on this dimension? We address these questions in turn.

*Equal opportunity of political influence.* "Equal opportunity of political influence" has two main components. They relate to different ways in which asymmetries in the distribution of power and resources can affect deliberation. In one sense, equal opportunity of influence requires that asymmetries not give unfair advantage to participants. Equality entails that participation and decision making be voluntary and uncoerced. From the perspective of an individual participant, this serves to guarantee that no one else will be able to use any advantage due to asymmetries in the distribution of power and resources to cause her to vote or act in any way contrary to her unconstrained preferences. This highlights the need for equality in the resources that any participant be allowed to employ in the deliberation process. In a second sense, equal opportunity of influence requires that asymmetries not place anyone in a position of unfair disadvantage. Equality entails that the possibility that a participant might influence the preferences of other deliberators be roughly the same for all participants. From the perspective of an individual participant, this serves to guarantee that no one will be unable, due to the lack of power and resources, to participate in the process of mutual influence that is at the core of democratic deliberation. This highlights the need for a distribution of power and resources in the society such that each individual citizen will have the personal resources to participate effectively in that process.

We now elaborate and defend this conception of equal opportunity of political influence. In so doing we acknowledge that there are many factors in social life that might fall within the category of powers and resources. The general question here is which of these factors are governed by the conception of equality of opportunity of political influence. To answer this question fully we must first determine which factors are politically relevant and then assess which asymmetries in the distribution of those factors warrant corrective measures to address inequalities.

*Uncoerced participation and free and voluntary decision making.* In democratic deliberation participants assess the arguments offered in

Jack Knight and James Johnson

the course of political discussion and then decide how they want to vote on the various policy questions. Political equality requires that when the time comes to make one's final decision on a question, the asymmetries in the social distribution of power and resources should not play a role in that decision. Here equal opportunity of political influence requires institutions that constrain any actor who might seek to exploit an advantageous asymmetry for the purposes of coercing other participants.

The main politically relevant factor that affects the uncoerced nature of political decision making is the possession of material resources and the social power that follows from it. Asymmetries in material resources can affect democratic deliberation in a number of ways. This issue has been the subject of substantial analysis so we will be brief. Citizens who enjoy an advantage in the distribution of material resources can affect the democratic process through both the *promises* and the *threats* that this material advantage affords them.

Promises work through the benefits that they can provide other citizens in exchange for favorable support on particular policy decisions. Explicit bribery is generally precluded by law, but more implicit forms of trading votes for benefits are the subject of standard criticisms of most modern representative democracies. These implicit trades violate the notion of equal opportunity of influence. To constrain these trades we must establish rules that prohibit the use of material advantages in the political process. Proposals range from campaign finance restrictions on private contributions to complete public financing of political competition.[43] While any constraints would diminish the effects of resource asymmetries on deliberation, equal opportunity of influence would be most enhanced by complete public financing of all features of the democratic process.

Even this form of extensive public financing, however, will not address the effects of threats supported by resource asymmetries. Threats can be either explicit or implicit. Explicit threats seek to intimidate citizens by invoking economic or social sanctions should they vote contrary to the threatener's interests. Such explicit threats are usually precluded by law. But asymmetries in material resources can have a profound effect on democratic deliberation through what might best be conceived of as implicit threats. The best example of these effects is found in Przeworski and Wallerstein's (1988) analysis of democratic capitalist societies. On their account, capitalists have a disproportionate effect on democratic policy making because of their control of the material resources that determine the ultimate success of those policies. In terms of our analysis of the deliberative process the effect identified by Przeworski and Wallerstein is manifest as an implicit threat by those who control the material resources necessary for the success of democratic outcomes. Here citizens are disproportionately inclined to endorse the interests and views of capitalists because they—the citizens—anticipate that failure to do so will elicit an economic response from capitalists that would have severe negative consequences for the broader society. To effectively diminish the effects of such implicit threats political institutions would have to place significant constraints on the nonpolitical use of material resources.[44] As we discuss below, a society that wants to offset these effects of material asymmetries on political equality may have to resolve the possible conflicts between the requirements of political equality and their commitment to freedom of action in the economic sphere.

*Equal opportunity to influence others.* Equal opportunity of political influence involves more than constraints on the adverse effects of resource asymmetries on uncoerced political decision making. Deliberative democracy envisions the active participation of citizens in a process of mutual discussion and persuasion. Such participation requires that each citizen be able to advance arguments that others might find persuasive. Thus, political equality must attend to the conditions under which all citizens would be able to engage in discussion at this level. Here we must disentangle and assess three distinct conceptions of the conditions necessary for this requirement to be met: equality of resources, equality of capacities and equality of outcomes.

Given the uncertainty inherent in the democratic process, equal opportunity of influence should not entail equality of outcome, at least insofar as equality of outcome might mean that all relevant interests are equally manifest in collective outcomes. Real equality of influence is unachievable under democratic procedures because the very nature of the process makes the outcomes uncertain and

Jack Knight and James Johnson

subject to the exigencies of political debate and deliberation (Dworkin 1987). As we state in the introduction, on our account actual equality of influence would spell the end of democratic politics.

This leaves us with a choice between equality of resources and equality of capacities.[45] Rawls (1993) proposes a resource approach to equality of opportunity in a political society. On his account, each citizen will be guaranteed a minimum threshold of primary goods that she can use to further her political and economic goals. Justice as fairness requires nothing more for political equality. Rawls accords no explicit attention to issues of equality of capacity. He assumes only that citizens "do have, at least to the essential minimum degree, the moral, intellectual, and physical capacities that enable them to be fully cooperating members of society over a complete life" (Rawls 1993, 183). He acknowledges that if this assumption about capacities is not satisfied, then the just distribution of primary goods may not accomplish the goal of political equality. Rawls emphasizes the importance of guaranteeing that political liberties be secured by their "fair value":

this guarantee means that the worth of the political liberties to all citizens, whatever their social and economic position, must be approximately equal, or at least sufficiently equal, in the sense that everyone has a fair opportunity to hold public office and to influence the outcome of political decisions. This notion of fair opportunity parallels that of fair equality of opportunity in the second principle of justice. (Rawls 1993, 327)

Rawls's account of political equality does not appear on his own interpretation to satisfy the requirements of political equality in a deliberative democracy. On the one hand, he conceptualizes the fair value of political liberties in terms of the "fair opportunity . . . to influence the outcome of political decisions." But, on the other hand, he limits analysis of fair opportunity to the ownership of the minimum threshold of primary goods and reduces the issue of whether actors possess the capacities needed to use these resources effectively to the status of an assumption.

The differences between Rawls's conception of equality and conceptions that revolve around equal capacities is made clear by his discussion of the way that justice as fairness would treat asymmetries in capacities that arise above the minimum threshold of primary goods. On the dimension of moral and intellectual capacities and skills, Rawls concludes that any variations above the minimum threshold are acceptable and consistent with the principles of justice as fairness (Rawls 1993, 184). Ultimately, Rawls treats as an assumption what equality of capacity treats as the fundamental feature of political equality.[46]

Sen distinguishes his capabilities approach from the Rawlsian focus on primary goods by differentiating between "the *means* of freedom" and "the *extent* of freedom" (Sen 1992, 8). For Sen, an adequate conception of equality must focus on "a characterization of freedom in the form of alternative sets of accomplishments that we have the power to achieve" (Sen 1992, 34). He gives priority to the size of the feasible set open to an individual rather than to the resources or means that she possesses. He argues that a Rawlsian focus on primary goods is inadequate because it fails to address the important variations in individuals' abilities to effectively use these goods.

In developing his capacities approach, Sen further distinguishes between freedom and control. On his account "effective freedom" does not imply actual control: "As long as the levers of control are systematically exercised in line with *what I would choose* and *for that exact reason*, my 'effective freedom' is uncompromised, though my 'freedom as control' may be limited or absent" (Sen 1992, 64–65). This distinction, while defensible in some spheres of social life, seems particularly inappropriate as a conception of political equality for democratic deliberation. Here a more active conception of freedom seems more consistent with the underlying premises of deliberation. Thus, Bohman (1996a) develops a capacities-based conception of political equality that retains the spirit of Sen's argument, but advances a different conception of "effective freedom."

Bohman's conception of deliberative equality is primarily concerned with the capacities relevant to participation in a deliberative process. He argues that a focus on capacities highlights the fundamental importance of effective freedom:

[F]reedom is, on this account, the capacity to live as one would choose; it is the capacity for *social* agency, the ability to participate in joint activities and achieve one's goals in them. For political liberties, the issue is effective use of public freedoms, which may be absent even in the absence of coercion or prohibitions. (Bohman 1996a, 130)

He justifies this focus on grounds similar to Sen: that equality of resources is an insufficient remedy for deficiencies in effective participation because people differ in the capacities necessary to use available resources effectively (Bohman 1996a, 128).

Bohman's capacity-based conception of political equality seems better suited than narrower resource-based conceptions to the job of capturing the effective participation requirement of democratic deliberation. But there is much work still to be done here. In order to fully justify the equality of capacities conception of political equality, we must determine which capacities are politically relevant, identify methods by which their relative distribution can be measured, and explore policy prescriptions for offsetting the effects of unequal capacities on democratic deliberation. Unfortunately, it turns out to be quite difficult to carry out each of these tasks.

*Politically relevant capacities.* What kinds of capacities are relevant to democratic deliberation and thus to a conception of political equality? There are a number of potential candidates. We want to emphasize three primary kinds. The first is the capacity to formulate authentic preferences. As we noted earlier, asymmetrical distribution of power and resources in a society undermines democratic deliberation. In part, this is because such asymmetries can induce participants to embrace "adaptive preferences" (Sunstein 1991). On this account the legitimacy of the democratic process rests on the idea that people act on free and voluntarily established preferences. To the extent that the preferences of citizens reflect adaptation to the diminished possibilities that, in turn, result from being disadvantaged by an asymmetric distribution of resources, then these preferences may undermine the idea of equal opportunity of political influence.

The second relevant capacity relates to the effective use of cultural resources. Iris Young (1994, 133–134) highlights the political problems that "cultural imperialism" poses for minorities. This concept emphasizes the fact that minorities are required to express their ideas and needs in the language of the dominant groups in society.

To the extent that these minority groups are less adept or, in the extreme, wholly ineffective in using the language and concepts of the dominant groups, they will lack an equal opportunity to influence the members of the deliberative body to adopt policies that will address their particular needs.

The third, and we think most important, kind of relevant capacity relates to basic cognitive abilities and skills.[47] In his account of capacities, Sen highlights the problems and difficulties in acquiring the information necessary to diminish uncertainty and thus to make effective decisions (Sen 1992, 148–149). We take this to be one aspect of a more general category of cognitive capacities that is central to the deliberative process. Unless each participant has the cognitive capacities and skills necessary to effectively articulate and defend persuasive claims, then there will be no real equality of opportunity for political influence.[48]

*Measuring political equality.* Each of these three factors—autonomous preferences, command of cultural resources, and cognitive capacities—are relevant to a citizen's ability to effectively influence other citizens to support her own preferred outcomes. However, an adequate account of the substantive dimension of political equality for democratic deliberation must take seriously the observation that "we cannot deduce what is politically fair from abstract principles of political equality: we have to draw on empirical judgments of what is likely to happen as well as what seems in principle to be fair" (Phillips 1995, 38). This requires that we now consider two central features of a substantive account of political equality: (i) the measures of political equality (as understood in terms of capacities) and (ii) the mechanisms by which we might institutionalize substantive political equality taking account of these measures.

Sen suggests that the analysis of equality in "freedom to achieve" relates to the available data on actual achievement (Sen 1992, 5). Thus, while he distinguishes between achievement and the freedom to achieve, he notes that any measure of such freedom rests necessarily on a consideration of the actual outcomes of relevant collective decision-making processes. To rely on other sources of information risks delving into counterfactuals about possible outcomes that are difficult at best to justify. Part of Sen's reliance on outcomes and actual achievement may be explained by his analytical focus on effective freedom and not control. Data on achievement may be sufficient to give a reliable measure of effective freedom.[49] But, for reasons given earlier, Sen's relatively simple conception of "effective freedom" does not adequately capture the active dimension of political equality. And, unfortunately, Bohman's appropriate modification of the conception of effective freedom as applied to democratic deliberation makes measurement issues even more complex.

Bohman argues that political equality requires a guarantee of a minimum threshold of "effective freedom":

A good empirical indicator of such a deliberative capacity is whether or not citizens or groups of citizens are able to initiate public deliberation about their concerns. This ability to initiate acts of deliberation thus provides a measurable threshold for political equality and reasonable cooperation. . . . Poverty in this sense is a measure of minimal political equality in a democracy: it sets the threshold requirement of publicity in deliberation in terms of the equal capacities to participate effectively. The development of such abilities is the "floor" of civic equality, since they offer citizens greater possibilities of deliberative uptake for their differing reasons, some of which may not yet be publicly recognized as worthy of consideration. (Bohman 1996a, 128)

Thus, Bohman establishes a standard that will recognize unacceptable inequalities in capacities in those cases in which citizens are completely ineffective, completely incapable of initiating public deliberation on their concerns: "[d]eliberative democracy must fulfill demands for equality in the means for effective participation at least enough so that no citizen is so poor as to fail to influence outcomes or to avoid exclusion" (Bohman 1996a, 148).

Bohman maintains that his capacities approach is not calibrated to actual outcomes. It nevertheless is hard to see how we can apply his threshold measures without reference to the causal effect of individual participation on the collective outcomes of the deliberation process. In a subsequent consideration of these issues he writes "[t]his standard does not require that particular citizens or groups of citizens can ever expect to determine the outcomes of debate and deliberation. However, it does require that whenever citizens engage in deliberation, they reasonably expect that their reasons could ultimately be adopted by their fellow citizens" (Bohman 1996b, 14).

Without reference to prior causal effect, how would they develop those expectations?

Both Sen and Bohman, then, illustrate the importance of looking at outcomes to determine the effectiveness of participation in the deliberative process. This raises two significant questions with regard to the measurement of capacity. First, does this conception risk collapsing equal opportunity of influence into equality of outcomes? For Bohman it would appear that the answer is no, but this may be because he adopts a measure of effective freedom that sets only a minimum threshold of effectiveness. With this measure he need not demand equality of influence because he uses data on the causal effects on democratic outcomes as merely one, albeit important, source of evidence of effective participation. This raises the further question—which we address below—of whether equality of capacity converges with equality of influence if we introduce a stronger measure of effective participation.[50]

Second, how do we use evidence of outcomes to establish a measure of equal opportunity of influence? This involves a determination of the causal effect of one's participation on the collective outcomes of the democratic process. This is exceedingly complicated in the analysis of deliberative processes. To appreciate why this is so, it again is helpful to compare the ideal of deliberative democracy with a purely aggregative democratic mechanism. With a purely aggregative decision-making procedure citizens vote by merely announcing their individual preference, and the collective outcome is the manifestation of the aggregation of these preferences. There is in this scheme a direct relationship between initial preferences and the preferences instantiated in the collective outcome. The greater the deviation between an individual's preferences and those of the collectivity, the lesser the presumed causal effect.

With deliberation, however, this relationship is more complex. To the extent that deliberative democracy embodies reasoned argument and rational persuasion, one is always open to the possibility of reassessing one's own position (Cohen 1989b, 34). Because of this possibility one's subsequent position as an individual member of a deliberative assembly may not be the same as one's initial position. Indeed, the final collective outcome may not reflect the initial position of *any* member of the community in a straightforward way.

Jack Knight and James Johnson

Thus, the distance measure of causal effect available under the pure aggregation approach may not be available for an analysis of deliberation. This suggests that democratic deliberation may itself undermine our ability to assess equality of opportunity of influence by reference to the outcome of deliberative processes.

Bohman's measure is sufficient to capture the most egregious consequences of unequally distributed capacities. Most people would agree, we think, that the dictates of political equality are violated in those cases in which the interests of a particular social group *never* are reflected in collective outcomes. Bohman suggests that such failure manifests the extent to which the excluded bear a disproportionate share of the costs of democratic policies: "[a]symmetrical exclusion and inclusion succeeds by constantly shifting considerable burdens on the worst off, who lack the resources, capabilities and social recognition to mount a challenge to the conditions which govern institutionalized deliberation" (Bohman 1996b, 5). But an adequate understanding of political inequality must capture more than the complete absence of influence in the deliberative process. We need a measure of equal opportunity of influence that meaningfully captures less egregious, intermediate cases.

Cohen responds to Sen by arguing that because a Rawlsian focus on primary goods makes fewer informational demands it is more tractable and hence more attractive than a capacities-based conception of equality. We might ask whether this argument could help to resolve the problem of measuring political equality. Addressing the debate in the context of considerations of social justice, Cohen argues that the capabilities approach sets excessive and unachievable information requirements in terms of assessing the nature of an individual's capabilities set. He suggests that when we take a serious look at the types of information available to us in making these determinations, we will find that the best measure that we are able to construct in most cases is the more assessable primary goods measure:

One way to make the required simplifications would be to specify certain *especially severe* and *informationally transparent* cases of limited capabilities, to focus on capability assessments in those cases, and to rely on primary goods for interpersonal comparisons elsewhere. Thus, we would rely on capabilities when we specify a minimally acceptable threshold of human functioning—basic needs in areas of nutrition and health, for example—and when we are concerned to characterize and remedy disabilities. Apart from these cases, however, we would confine interpersonal comparisons to the means required for functioning rather than capabilities themselves (keeping in mind that greater means will generally imply a more expansive capability set). (Cohen 1995, 285)

In the discussion of political equality and democratic deliberation, then, Cohen's recommendation requires that we first determine a "minimally acceptable threshold of . . . functioning" in the deliberative sphere and then identify some package of politically relevant primary goods. The former determination presumes that we can ascertain with confidence those capacities that are distributed in an "especially severe and informationally transparent" way.

Cohen's proposal will resolve our measurement problem *if* the politically relevant asymmetries in capacities that we must capture in order to assess intermediate cases match the capacities that are necessary for a "minimally acceptable threshold of . . . functioning." Otherwise, we are left with the primary goods measure for the equal opportunity of influence. For the reasons that we discussed above, we agree with Bohman that this measure is inadequate to the task of guaranteeing substantive political equality. Unfortunately, Cohen's criterion for identifying capacities that are unequal in an "especially severe and informationally transparent" way will be either controversial and difficult to satisfy or inadequate to the task of capturing the capacities for effective participation. Rawls himself acknowledges the difficulty in reaching agreement on such matters: "[w]hether the constitutional essentials covering the basic freedoms are satisfied is more or less visible on the face of constitutional arrangements and how these can be seen to work in practice. But whether the aims of the principles covering social and economic inequalities are realized is far more difficult to ascertain" (Rawls 1993, 229). In the end, there seems to be no reason to believe that Cohen's approach to issues of substantive political equality will be more tractable than the effective capacities conception.

At this point we see no easy answer to the measurement question for intermediate cases. Our pragmatist sympathies lead us to suggest that it is a question best left to the decision-making bodies of

Jack Knight and James Johnson

individual societies. But such a suggestion risks an infinite regress in terms of a determination of the conditions under which the measurement question could be legitimately resolved by such a body.[51] What we are confident in saying is that whatever form the measure ultimately takes, it will have to attend to the relationship between the social distribution of power and resources and the distribution of opportunities for political influence. Here we tend to agree with Cohen who suggests that "greater means will generally imply a more expansive capability set." But, as we suggest in the subsequent discussion of institutional mechanisms, substantive political equality requires more than a guarantee of a basic minimum of these resources.

*Mechanisms to foster equality of opportunity of political influence.* Clearly, societies must accept tradeoffs if they hope to guarantee the type of political equality that deliberative democracy requires. The desire for political equality must be weighed relative to other societal goals. For example, Sen argues that "[a]n attempt to achieve equality of capabilities—without taking note of aggregative considerations—can lead to severe curtailment of the capabilities that people can altogether have. . . . [T]he import of the concept of equality cannot even be adequately understood without paying simultaneous attention also to aggregative consideration—to the 'efficiency aspect,' broadly speaking" (Sen 1992, 7–8).

Our defense of substantive political equality identifies additional potential tradeoffs in both the private and public spheres. In the private sphere political equality might entail constraints on the use of material resources in nonpolitical realms. This draws attention to potential conflicts between political equality on the one hand and freedom of economic activity on the other. In the public sphere political equality, we now argue, might entail the acceptance of inequalities in the treatment of citizens by the state. The policy mechanisms required to induce such inequalities will be most important during the period when citizens who are disadvantaged in ways relevant to political equality are being incorporated into the deliberative process. Presumably, as remedial policies and institutional arrangements enhance the influence of such citizens in the deliberative process, the democratic outcomes in which they effectively participate will mitigate some of the societal factors that cause their disadvantages in the first place.[52] In the interim, however, when citizens are disadvantaged due to past histories of inequality, "we do not treat them equally when we treat them the same" (Sunstein 1992, 2).

Roemer provides a way of distinguishing those asymmetries in politically relevant capacities that deserve to be corrected from those that society should accept and, thus, allow to affect the deliberative process. The distinction rests on the notion of personal responsibility:

A person's actions are determined by two kinds of cause: circumstances beyond her control, and autonomous choices within her control. . . . I say that equality of opportunity has been achieved among a group of people if society indemnifies persons in the group against bad consequences due to circumstances and brute luck, but does not indemnify them against the consequences of their autonomous choices. Thus, an equal-opportunity policy must equalize outcomes insofar as they are the consequences of causes beyond a person's control, but allow differential outcomes insofar as they result from autonomous choice. When there is equality of opportunity, then, no one will be worse off than others as a result of factors beyond her control. (Roemer 1995, 4)

To extend Roemer's idea to the question of the equality of politically relevant capacities, we must assess two issues: (1) how do we determine which politically relevant capacities are beyond the control of individuals? and (2) how do we rectify the inequalities in the context of a democratic process?

In answering the first question we follow Roemer's own suggestion that questions of autonomous choice versus uncontrollable circumstances are political in nature. The determination of which politically relevant capacities are beyond the control of individual citizens will be based on societal understandings of personal responsibility. These will often be controversial questions subject to considerable debate. It is important to note here that as long as the society determines that some asymmetries in politically relevant capacities are due to autonomous choices within the control of individual citizens, equality of opportunity of influence does not converge into equality of outcomes (in terms of influence). Unfortunately, this fact does not resolve the measurement problem, but it does reinforce the idea that the measurement problem will remain in part a political question to be resolved by the members of that society.

Jack Knight and James Johnson

Roemer's proposed answer to the second question reinforces concerns about the difficulty of adequately guaranteeing equality of opportunity of influence, including attention to relevant political capacities, without requiring equality of outcomes. In addressing broader questions of social justice, he focuses on outcomes and recommends the restructuring of outcomes through indemnification as the necessary policy mechanism for achieving equality of opportunity. We propose rather to focus on two mechanisms that might affect the relationship between the social distribution of power and resources and the development of politically relevant capacities.

The first, and potentially most important, mechanism involves the relationship between material resources and cognitive capacities. The fundamental legitimacy of democratic deliberation rests on the effective contributions of individual citizens. Effective participation, in turn, is contingent on the cognitive capacities of these citizens. The standard policy recommendations relevant to the development of cognitive capacities minimally involve government support for education, especially economic guarantees for poor and materially disadvantaged citizens. Yet, while government support of education is essential it remains an insufficient policy response. This is because the effects of unequal income and wealth on asymmetries in the development of cognitive capacities extends well beyond educational opportunities. Substantial scientific evidence demonstrates that intellectual development is significantly affected by childhood poverty and malnutrition (Brown and Pollitt 1996). Recent research shows that lack of material resources has effects on diet and environment that jeopardizes in numerous ways the cognitive development of individuals from impoverished backgrounds. The detrimental effects of poverty and malnutrition on cognitive development first appear in the formative years of childhood, but their effects extend well beyond the early childhood years.[53] The main implication of these studies is that the development of cognitive capacities necessary for effective participation in democratic deliberation requires government expenditures to guarantee the social and economic prerequisites of effective participation.

These policies imply that government intervention aimed at developing effective participation must disproportionately favor socially disadvantaged groups. It is important to note that we do not here propose redistribution of income and wealth primarily as a remedy for problems posed by the efforts of advantaged actors to exploit resource asymmetries in order to coerce others.[54] Rather, we endorse such redistribution as a remedy for the more fundamental difficulty that citizens must possess a certain level of income and resources if they are to develop the basic capacities necessary to be effective participants in democratic deliberation.

A second policy mechanism aims to avert potential difficulties arising from the relation between the social distribution of power and resources and the development of both preferences and the ability to use cultural resources. Cohen and Rogers (1993) propose state intervention to create financial incentives to establish secondary associations that foster deliberative democracy. Such secondary associations, on their account, encourage the development of various capacities related to deliberative activity and, thereby, can enhance equal opportunity of influence.[55]

Cohen and Rogers argue that government resources should be distributed in ways that encourage other-regarding behavior. They thus suggest that this policy would favor groups that encompass larger segments of the population over more narrowly defined groups. This might be an appropriate standard of resource allocation in a society in which basic thresholds of effective participation have already been satisfied. However, until such levels have been attained, a more effective policy, designed with an eye toward the goal of establishing substantive political equality, would be to have the state disproportionately reward the groups least likely to have developed the capacities necessary for effective participation.[56]

These two policy proposals for mechanisms to foster substantive political equality entail that, in their implementation of economic and social policies, governments treat citizens differently. But these policies alone might not correct the adverse effects of distributional asymmetries on equal opportunity of political influence. As part of a transitional policy to incorporate politically disadvantaged groups

Jack Knight and James Johnson

into the deliberative process, governments might also implement procedural reforms that differentially favor these groups.

To the extent that deliberation will be incomplete and not result in consensus (either because of the problems of time and resource constraints emphasized by Habermas [1996] or because of irreconcilable differences in preferences [Knight and Johnson 1994]), voting will remain a necessary component of the democratic process. Can alterations in electoral rules offset some of the problems raised by inequalities in the substantive area? Here we have in mind some of the procedural mechanisms that have been proposed to assure the adequate proportionality of representation. Young (1990) and Guinier (1994) propose mechanisms that grant certain oppressed groups partial veto power over issues of particular relevance to their interests. An alternative to the veto idea might be weighted control over the agenda concerning these issues. Bohman argues that mechanisms such as these will enhance the influence of minorities: "[a]s opposed to distributing representation as a proportional resource, a cumulative voting scheme enables a minority to build up coalitions and public associations cutting across the barriers that made a particular group's inequalities persistent. In such schemes, the development of capacities is encouraged by changes in the political economy of how minorities achieve representation: these changes in incentives make it more difficult for the majority to ignore their views and interests" (Bohman 1996a, 134).

Kymlicka (1995) offers a similar justification for another procedural mechanism that treats citizens in a differential way. In the course of his argument for ensuring the adequate representation of minorities in a multicultural society, he argues for the concept of "threshold representation." On this conception, representatives in a democratic body are chosen according to a criterion that would assure that all groups have effective representation of their interests. For some groups this might entail a threshold number of seats that is lower than their proportionate numbers in the population. For others, especially disadvantaged groups, this threshold requirement might entail that the number of seats allocated to these groups exceed the number that would be required by a strict proportional scheme. This follows from the facts that (1) if there are only a few members of disadvantaged groups in a deliberative body, they can be easily ignored and (2) effective influence in a deliberative body requires, in part, the ability to coordinate one's arguments and activities with other members of the group.

It is important to note that these procedural mechanisms place the demands of procedural and substantive political equality in apparent conflict. There are instances in which a mechanism intended to foster substantive political equality may actually generate procedural inequalities within the political realm itself.

## V  Conclusion

In lieu of a reiteration of the various arguments in this chapter, we want to emphasize three main points. First, political equality is, for deliberative democracy, a complex conception, consisting of both procedural and substantive requirements. The degree of this complexity is best seen when we move from vague generalizations about free and equal participants to a more fine-grained analysis of how we might actually institutionalize political equality in a democratic society. For deliberative democracy, political equality entails a guarantee of effective participation and thus a concern with the capacity of individual participants to engage in the process of mutual persuasion. Therefore, equality of capacity becomes a central feature of the requirements of political equality.

Second, assessing the existence and extent of political equality is more difficult than has been recognized. Since political equality presupposes effective participation, such assessment presumes that we can determine with some confidence the effectiveness of participants within deliberative arrangements. Here effective participation is calibrated in complex ways to influence the outcomes of the democratic process. But in a deliberative scheme such influence is often hard to discern. Indeed, to the extent that deliberation entails the willingness of participants to revise their own views on issues, it may often be impossible to determine in a straightforward way how the interests of particular individuals relate to the collective outcome. More work needs to be done on this question, but it is difficult to resist the conclusion that, whatever form the actual mechanism

Jack Knight and James Johnson

for assessing effective participation takes, the requirements of political equality will themselves be fundamentally political questions.[57]

Third, a commitment to political equality involves potential trade-offs with other societal goals. This follows primarily from a consideration of the institutional prerequisites of the substantive dimension of political equality. In order to guarantee that each citizen will enjoy equal opportunity of political influence, society must take the steps necessary to guarantee that each citizen has the capacity to effectively participate in the deliberative arena. Under some conditions this will entail some redistribution of power and relevant material resources as well as an acceptance of inequalities in the treatment of citizens by the state. This will involve hard choices. But the dictates of political equality in a deliberative democracy require no less.

## Acknowledgment

We share equal responsibility for any errors and equal credit for any insights in this essay. We presented an earlier version of this paper at the Henle Conference on Deliberative Democracy, Department of Philosophy, Saint Louis University. We thank the organizers of that conference, Jim Bohman and Bill Rehg, for the opportunity to participate. We also thank Jim Bohman, Josh Cohen, Emily Hauptmann, Alison Jagger, Larry May, Frank Michelman, Henry Richardson, Paul Weithman, and Iris Young for particular comments on that occasion. Any remaining errors or infelicities are our own.

## Notes

1. What is more, this heterogeneity is dynamic insofar as such factors as demographic change (e.g., immigration) and political mobilization fostered by the democratic process itself generate new interests, attachments, and commitments.

2. Here we mean narrow in the sense that we treat democracy, in Dewey's words, less as a "social idea" than as a "system of government." The reason is not that the social idea is unimportant but that, again following Dewey, it "remains barren and empty save as it is incarnated in human relationships" (Dewey, 1927, 143).

3. This definition is obviously contestable. For example, critics of "democratic elitism" will balk at the Schumpeterian notion that democracy is a method. And some

will object that democratic processes do not properly act on preferences (e.g., Estlund 1990 and Christiano 1993). Such objections are largely beside the point of our present purpose which is to highlight the egalitarian implications of our views on democracy. In any case, we are happy, for now, to substitute "process" or "institutional arrangement" for "method" and "interests" or "judgments" for "preferences." For a second depiction of the egalitarian commitments of democracy, see Dahl (1989).

4. See also Cohen (1989a) and Knight and Johnson (1994).

5. Again, see Cohen (1989a; 1989b) and Knight and Johnson (1994).

6. Since we completed the first version of this essay, two relevant papers—Brighouse (1996) and Christiano (1996)—have appeared. Each directly addresses the relation of deliberation and equality. We note convergences and differences between our respective arguments at several points below. See also Bohman, this volume.

7. Roemer (1993, 146–147) lists several current versions of equality of opportunity.

8. Dahl (1989, 107,112–114) stresses the importance of ensuring access at both stages. Christiano (1996, 262–268) stresses the complexity and contestibility of deliberative agenda-setting.

9. "In some circumstances equality means differential treatment; in other circumstances it means treating people the same—there is no logical requirement to stand by just one of these two options. What prevents people from seeing this is . . . an overly rigid understanding of equality that abstracts it from any meaningful context" (Phillips 1995, 37).

10. "When there is equality of opportunity, then, no one will be worse off than others as a result of factors beyond her control" (Roemer 1995, 4).

11. On this point we agree with Roemer (1996, 278–279): "The proposal I have outlined . . . is 'political' rather than 'metaphysical' to borrow a distinction of Rawls. For I here advocate no particular set of criteria for factoring causes of choice into ones beyond a person's control and ones within it. This set of criteria is envisioned to be, for each society, a subject of political debate."

12. For a very brief survey see Sen (1987).

13. An accessible, brief statement of his argument is Arrow (1977).

14. This condition can be weakened to demand only *nondictatorship;* this ensures that there is no individual who can unilaterally determine the social choice. Arrow's result holds even with this weaker requirement.

15. This condition can also be weakened with no damage to Arrow's result. All that is required is *nonimposition* which simply means that, for any pair of alternatives X and Y, there is some array of preferences within the relevant constituency such that X defeats Y and another array such that Y defeats X.

16. For a more fully developed argument on this point see Johnson (1997). The remainder of this section draws on this essay.

Jack Knight and James Johnson

17. Note that we are here concerned with formal or official decision-making arenas. There may be good reason to restrict entry to the sort of secondary associations necessary to a robust deliberative democracy. This is because such secondary associations, if they are to afford a secure milieu within which particular, especially disadvantaged, constituencies might articulate interests and perspectives, may need to exclude nonmembers (Fraser 1992). Any such practice of exclusion, however, may be challenged and hence require justification within the formal or official institutions within which secondary associations operate and from which they derive legal standing.

18. Rawls (1993, 58) admits as much, but claims that these are "sources of unreasonable disagreement" and so, in keeping with his views on "reasonable pluralism" (which we address below) he believes they would not emerge in democratic deliberation.

19. This benefit potentially accrues to both sides in any such exchange. For deliberation on this view does not only allow participants to challenge selfishness, prejudice and ideology. It also provides a check from which any "reasonable" party to deliberation might derive, if not exactly enjoyment, at least benefit. It might prompt such parties to reexamine their views and commitments in order to ensure that the charges are unsound. Christiano (1996, 259) makes a similar point.

20. Part of the "reason" here will require that the accusing party establish why she believes that her characterization is justified.

21. This essay, originally published in *The Nation* in 1992, is reprinted in Pollitt (1994).

22. According to Pollitt, difference feminism, inspired by writers like Carol Gilligan, Nancy Chodorow, Sara Ruddick, and others, "looks everywhere for its explanatory force—biology, psychology, sociology, cultural identity—*except* economics. The difference feminist cannot say that the differences between men and women are the result of their relative economic positions, because to say that would be to move the whole discussion out of the realm of psychology and feel-good cultural pride and into the realm of tough political struggle over the distribution of resources and justice and money. Although it is couched in the language of praise, difference feminism is demeaning to women. It asks that women be admitted into public life and public discourse not because they have a right to be there but because they will improve them. Even if this were true, and not the wishful thinking I believe it to be, why should the task of social and moral transformation be laid on women's doorstep and not on everyone's—or, for that matter, on men's, by the 'you broke it, you fix it' principle? Peace, the environment, a more humane workplace, economic justice, social support for children—these are issues that affect us all and are everyone's responsibility. By promising to assume that responsibility, difference feminists lay the groundwork for excluding women again, as soon as it becomes clear that the promise cannot be kept" (Pollitt, 1994, 61).

23. For qualms regarding such gerrymandering see Rorty (1985).

24. See Habermas (1985). It should be noted that in making his case Habermas draws directly and sympathetically on Rawls's own earlier account of civil disobedience.

25. Rawls attributes the distinction between pluralism per se and "reasonable" pluralism to Cohen (1993, 281f).

What Sort of Equality Does Deliberative Democracy Require?

26. On Rawls's account "reasonable pluralism" appears as prepolitical insofar as he sees it as a way of accommodating his conception of justice "not so much . . . to the brute forces of the world but to the inevitable outcome of free human reason" (Rawls 1993, 37).

27. Thus, even Rawls concedes that his theory of justice, because it accommodates only the "fact of reasonable pluralism"—in contrast to the "fact of pluralism" per se—"runs the danger of being arbitrary and exclusive" (Rawls 1993, 59).

28. These "burdens of judgment," according to Rawls derive from six unavoidable features of political decision making. So, in the context of reaching a decision on almost any issue one or more of the following conditions will hold: (1) empirical evidence will be complex and conflicting; (2) different parties will accord differential weight to relevant considerations even when they agree on which are "relevant"; (3) moral and political concepts will be ambiguous and their range of applicability contestable; (4) different actors will bring different perspectives and experiences to bear on the assessment of evidence and arguments; (5) the multiple normative considerations adduced for or against an issue by participants will have differential force; or (6) the competing values raised in the decision-making process will not be fully reconcilable (Rawls 1993, 54–58).

29. "If the claims of modern day creationists are compared with those of their nineteenth-century counterparts, significant shifts in orientation and assertion are evident. One of the most visible opponents of creationism, Stephen Gould, concedes that creationists have modified their views about the amount of variability allowed at the level of species change. Creationists do, in short, change their minds. Doubtless they would credit these shifts to their efforts to adjust their views to newly emerging evidence, in what they imagine to be a scientifically respectable way" (Laudan 1996, 224).

30. Characterizing the ruling of Judge William Overton in *McLean v. Arkansas* which portrayed creationism as nonscientific and, on that basis, excluded it from the public school curriculum in the state, Larry Laudan remarks: "His *obiter dicta* are about as remote from well-founded opinion in the philosophy of science as creationism is from respectable geology" (Laudan 1996, 227).

31. Indeed, in comments on an earlier version of this essay, Josh Cohen and Jim Bohman independently suggested that we might interpret unrestricted domain to require simply that while all views must be admissible to relevant deliberative arenas, some admissible views might be accorded little or no weight by parties to deliberation. This is a plausible interpretation. But note that on this interpretation "reasonable pluralism" no longer operates as an *ex ante* filter. It instead emerges within the process of deliberation itself. And admissible views can only, in that context, be accorded little or no weight *for reasons*. In this sense our insistence that deliberative arrangements must meet something like the condition of unrestricted domain provides a vantage point from which to clarify the conception of reasonableness operative in defenses of democratic deliberation. Note also that this puts additional pressure on defenders of deliberation to identify the mechanisms at work in the exchange of reasons in deliberative interactions (Johnson 1997). Bohman (1996a) makes some important progress on this latter task.

32. Obviously voting does not entail such secrecy on all accounts. In his *Considerations on Representative Government*, John Stuart Mill, for example, opposes the secret ballot. He argues that in order to ensure that, when participating in an election, each citizen would "consider the interest of the public, not his private advantage," all "voting, like

Jack Knight and James Johnson

any other public duty, should be performed under the eye and criticism of the public." And he defends this view in part by claiming that secrecy no longer is needed to protect voters from powerful sources of external influence, claiming that in most countries of Europe "the power of coercing voters has declined and is declining" (Mill 1991, 355–356). Mill is not simply overly sanguine here. He arguably is also inconsistent. Just two years earlier in *On Liberty*, he had insisted that liberty most needed protection not from "political despotism" (however important that threat might be) but from the ubiquitous "social tyranny" of prevailing opinion (Mill 1991, 8–9). Contemporary critics of the secret ballot (e.g., Brennan and Pettit 1989) are no more convincing than is Mill on this score.

33. As we note below, however, the substantive demands of our conception of equal opportunity of political influence may, under some circumstances, require political institutions and policies at some variance with the sort of procedural equality depicted here. Put otherwise, the sort of substantive equality required by democratic deliberation may well demand policies that treat participants differently in ways that procedural equality seemingly prohibits.

34. Brighouse (1996, 125) "embraces the idea that when inequalities on influence have their source in the persuasive presentation of good evidence and argument they are acceptable." We would agree—with the very important caveat that we explore below—that deliberative arrangements presuppose policies to ensure that parties to democratic deliberation have the capacities they need if they are to be effective participants.

35. It is important to reiterate here that we understand democracy in the narrow sense laid out in the introduction.

36. The same, it should be noted, is true of the various secondary associations that constitute the environment for "official" deliberative institutions. There members cannot be singled out.

37. See, for example, Phillips (1995).

38. This example is taken from Johnson (1997).

39. We assume here that the relevant actors are equally endowed with the resources needed to provide the public good. That is, there is no obvious asymmetry of, for example, wealth, experience, or power. Obviously, inequalities on any of those dimensions (or others) might well justify the sort of exploitation depicted in the text.

40. For a brief review see Austen-Smith (1995). The termination point is an important parameter here insofar as we view deliberation as a form of political decision making; a decision requires that at some juncture argument will cease and a choice will be made among feasible alternatives. And although any such choice is revisable, deliberation is not merely ceaseless, aimless conversation.

41. This arbitrariness is most evident in noncooperative bargaining models. But note that it does not presuppose either that relevant agents are driven primarily by narrow interests or that the interests of parties to discussion conflict in extreme ways. As Austen-Smith (1995) makes clear, matters of sequence and termination also are important in so-called cheap talk models where communication is not directly payoff dependent and where players typically are concerned to coordinate their efforts, even if they differ on just how to attain coordination. Farrell and Rabin (1996) review

this game theoretic literature. Johnson (1993) draws some initial connections between cheap talk games and the sorts of mechanisms that might sustain the force of reasons in democratic deliberation.

42. Brighouse (1996, 119) suggests in passing a way of measuring political influence. As will become clear, we believe that issues of measurement are both central to the discussion of political equality and more difficult than Brighouse allows. In particular, measurement issues loom large in our account of why the conception of equality that he endorses is inadequate.

43. For arguments that campaign finance restrictions enhance free and equal participation in the democratic process, see Sunstein (1994) and Rawls (1993). For an example of an argument that political equality would be better encouraged if the state would assume the costs of party competition, see Cohen (1989b, 40).

44. Cohen (1989b) argues that these effects of material resources justify proposals for public ownership of the means of production. Short of that, it is possible to imagine both policies that place less sweeping constraints on capital mobility and measures analogous to current labor laws that prevent workers from being dismissed for union-organizing activities.

45. Christiano (1996, 255) explicitly endorses a resource-based conception of political equality. Likewise, although he seeks to distance himself from resource-based conceptions, Brighouse (1996, 127–131) apparently endorses resource-based remedies for political disabilities. Although we do not argue this here, we believe that our focus on the need to ensure that parties to deliberation enjoy equal capacities needed for effective participation rectifies the weakness that Brighouse (1996, 126–127) attributes to opportunity-based conceptions of political equality.

46. Note that Rawls's account of political equality allows for inequalities in politically relevant capacities and resources, but that any such inequality will operate in favor of the socially advantaged groups in society.

47. Christiano (1996, 255) notes the importance of such abilities to the discussion of political equality.

48. We also take note of Cohen's suggestion of the importance of self-worth: "[c]laims to equal political standing are fueled, too, by the connection between such standing and a sense of self-worth, a connection rooted in the public recognition associated with equal standing." (Cohen 1994b, 613) While we agree with the basic thrust of his suggestion, we think that successful attention to the three kinds of capacities we address here will most likely effectively address the question of self-worth.

49. Cohen (1995) challenges the informational requirements of Sen's capabilities approach for nonpolitical spheres. We take up his argument below.

50. We argue below that the two measures will not converge as long as the members of the society agree that certain asymmetries in capacities are not subject to correction under the criterion of political equality.

51. See Knight and Johnson (1996) for a discussion of the necessary conditions for normative legitimacy within a pragmatic approach to collective decision making.

Jack Knight and James Johnson

52. This particular claim touches on a point that Christiano (1996, 257) makes more generally. He points out that the relation between deliberation and political equality is reciprocal. While deliberation presumes equality, it also can promote equality by prompting participants to reflect on their interests and convictions and, thereby, render their participation more effective.

53. This suggests both the importance and the difficulty in distinguishing between conditions over which individuals have no control and those for which they can be held responsible.

54. Redistribution might well help mitigate such problems as a by-product.

55. Christiano discusses several problematic aspects of secondary associations. For example, he points out that claims by such associations to "represent" some broader constituency typically are contestable. And he notes that promoters of such associations risk circularity when they both see them as necessary to robust democratic deliberation *and* hold that deliberation will generate rich associational life (Christiano 1996, 265, 280–283).

56. Bohman (1996a, 138) makes a point similar to this regarding the goals of campaign finance reform and public campaign expenditures. Phillips (1995, 180–182) suggests that there is a tension between her focus on formal representation and Cohen and Rogers's focus on voluntary associations. We think that arguments such as ours in favor of substantive political equality suggest that this tension is misperceived. On these accounts, the voluntary associations advocated by Cohen and Rogers can be seen as a precondition for equality at the level of formal representation. Fraser (1992) makes a convincing case for the need, within an overarching public sphere, for relatively exclusive arenas within which disadvantaged groups can securely articulate interests and perspectives.

57. In this sense our arguments here support Christiano (1996, 256) who insists on "the inherent contestability of deliberative equality."

## References

Arrow, Kenneth. 1977. "Current Developments in the Theory of Social Choice," *Social Research* 44:607–622.

Austen-Smith, David. 1995. "Modeling Deliberative Democracy." Paper presented at the Workshop on Deliberative Democracy, University of Chicago.

Barry, Brian. 1991. *Democracy and Power.* Oxford: Oxford University Press.

Bohman, James. 1996a. *Public Deliberation.* Cambridge, MA: MIT Press.

Bohman, James. 1996b. "Capabilities, Resources and Opportunities: Which Inequalities Matter Most for Deliberative Democracy?" Typescript, St. Louis University. Revised version in this volume.

Brennan, Geoffrey, and Philip Pettit. 1989. "Unveiling the Vote," *British Journal of Political Science* 20:311–333.

Brighouse, Harry. 1996. "Egalitarianism and Equal Availability of Political Influence," *Journal of Political Philosophy* 4:118–141.

Brown, J. Larry, and Ernesto Pollitt. 1996. "Malnutrition, Poverty and Intellectual Development," *Scientific American* (February): 38–43.

Christiano, Thomas. 1993. "Social Choice and Democracy." In *The Idea of Democracy*, eds. David Copp et al. Cambridge: Cambridge University Press.

Christiano, Thomas. 1996. "Deliberative Equality and Democratic Order." In *Political Order: NOMOS XXXVII*, eds. Ian Shapiro and Russell Hardin. New York: New York University Press.

Cohen, Joshua. 1989a. "Deliberation and Democratic Legitimacy." In *The Good Polity*, eds. A. Hamlin and P. Pettit. Oxford: Blackwell.

Cohen, Joshua. 1989b. "Economic Bases of Deliberative Democracy," *Social Philosophy & Policy* 6:25–50.

Cohen, Joshua. 1993. "Moral Pluralism and Political Consensus." In *The Idea of Democracy*, eds. David Copp et al. Cambridge: Cambridge University Press.

Cohen, Joshua. 1994a. "A More Democratic Liberalism," *Michigan Law Review* 92:1503–1546.

Cohen, Joshua. 1994b. "Pluralism and Proceduralism," 69 *Chicago-Kent Law Review* 589.

Cohen, Joshua. 1995. "Review of Amartya Sen: *Inequality Reexamined*," *Journal of Philosophy* XCII:275–288.

Cohen, Joshua, and Joel Rogers. 1993. "Associations and Democracy," *Social Philosophy and Policy* 10:282–312.

Dahl, Robert. 1989. *Democracy and Its Critics*. New Haven, CT: Yale University Press.

Dewey, John. 1927. *The Public and Its Problems*. Athens, OH: Swallow Press.

Dworkin, Ronald. 1987. "What Is Equality, Part 4: Political Equality," *University of San Francisco Law Review* 22:1–30.

Estlund, David. 1990. "Democracy without Preference," *The Philosophical Review* 49: 397–423.

Farrell, Joseph, and Matthew Rabin. 1996. "Cheap Talk," *Journal of Economic Perspectives* 10:103–118.

Fraser, Nancy. 1992. "Rethinking the Public Sphere." In *Habermas and the Public Sphere*, ed. C. Calhoun. Cambridge, MA: MIT Press.

Guinier, Lani. 1994. *The Tyranny of the Majority*. New York: Free Press.

Gutmann, Amy. 1993. "The Challenge of Multiculturalism in Political Ethics," *Philosophy & Public Affairs* 22:171–206.

Gutmann, Amy, and Dennis Thompson. 1990. "Moral Conflict and Political Consensus," *Ethics* 101:64–88.

Habermas, Jürgen. 1985. "Civil Disobedience: Litmus Test for the Democratic Constitutional State," *Berkeley Journal of Sociology* 30:95–116.

Habermas, Jürgen. 1996. *Between Facts and Norms*. Cambridge, MA: MIT Press.

Johnson, James. 1993. "Is Talk Really Cheap?" *American Political Science Review* 87: 74–86.

Johnson, James. 1997. "Arguing for Deliberation: Some Skeptical Considerations." In *Deliberative Democracy*, ed. Jon Elster. Cambridge: Cambridge University Press.

Knight, Jack, and James Johnson. 1994. "Aggregation and Deliberation: On the Possibility of Democratic Legitimacy," *Political Theory* 22:277–296.

Knight, Jack, and James Johnson. 1996. "The Political Consequences of Pragmatism," *Political Theory* 24:68–96.

Kymlicka, Will. 1995. *Multicultural Citizenship*. Oxford: Oxford University Press.

Laudan, Larry. 1996. *Beyond Positivism and Relativism*. Boulder, CO: Westview Press.

Manin, Bernard. 1987. "On Legitimacy and Political Deliberation," *Political Theory* 15:338–368.

Manin, Bernard. 1994. "The Metamorphoses of Representative Government," *Economy and Society* 23:133–171.

Mill, J. S. 1991. *On Liberty and Other Essays*. Oxford: Oxford University Press.

Phillips, Anne. 1995. *The Politics of Presence*. Oxford: Oxford University Press.

Pollitt, Katha. 1994. *Reasonable Creatures: Essays on Women and Feminism*. New York: Vintage.

Przeworski, Adam. 1991. *Democracy and the Market*. Cambridge: Cambridge University Press.

Przeworski, Adam, and Michael Wallerstein. 1988. "Structural Dependence of the State on Capital," *American Political Science Review* 82:11–29.

Rawls, John. 1989. "The Domain of the Political and Overlapping Consensus," *New York University Law Review* 64:233–255.

Rawls, John. 1993. *Political Liberalism*. New York: Columbia University Press.

Riker, William. 1980. *Liberalism against Populism*. Prospect Heights, IL: Waveland.

Roemer, John. 1993. "A Pragmatic Theory of Responsibility for the Egalitarian Planner," *Philosophy & Public Affairs* 22:146–166.

Roemer, John. 1995. "Equality and Responsibility," *Boston Review* (April/May), 3–7.

What Sort of Equality Does Deliberative Democracy Require?

Roemer, John. 1996. *Theories of Distributive Justice*. Cambridge, MA: Harvard University Press.

Rorty, Amelie. 1985. "Varieties of Rationality, Varieties of Emotion," *Social Science Information* 24:343–353.

Sen, Amartya. 1987. "Social Choice." In *The New Palgrave: A Dictionary of Economics* (Volume 4). New York: MacMillan Press.

Sen, Amartya. 1992. *Inequality Reexamined*. Cambridge, MA: Harvard University Press.

Sunstein, Cass. 1991. "Preferences and Politics," *Philosophy and Public Affairs* 20:3–34.

Sunstein, Cass. 1992. "Neutrality in Constitutional Law (with Special Reference to Pornography, Abortion and Surrogacy)," 92 *Columbia Law Review* 1.

Sunstein, Cass. 1994. "Political Equality and Unintended Consequences," 94 *Columbia Law Review* 1390.

Warren, Mark. 1996. "Deliberative Democracy and Authority," *American Political Science Review* 90:46–60.

Young, Iris Marion. 1990. *Justice and the Politics of Difference*. Princeton, NJ: Princeton University Press.

Young, Iris Marion. 1994. "Justice and Communicative Democracy." In R. Gottlieb, ed., *Tradition, Counter-Tradition, Politics: Dimensions of Radical Philosophy*. Philadelphia, PA: Temple University Press.

# 10

# Deliberative Democracy and Effective Social Freedom: Capabilities, Resources, and Opportunities

*James Bohman*

Proponents of deliberative democracy defend a complex ideal of an association whose common life is governed by the public deliberation of its members. Deliberation is democratic, to the extent that it is based on a process of reaching reasoned agreement among free and equal citizens. This conception of democratic deliberation also implies a normative ideal of political justification, according to which each citizen's reasons must be given equal concern and consideration for a decision to be legitimate. Legitimate decisions demand equality in two senses: first, *citizens* must be equal; and, second, their *reasons* must be given equal consideration. The fact that neither sense of equality always obtains (even approximately) in deliberative situations raises basic questions of feasibility. What sorts of social inequalities are relevant to democratic deliberation? How large can actual inequalities be before they undermine the democratic ideal?

Rousseau, the philosopher who gives deliberative democracy its first modern formulation, seems to demand fairly minimal conditions of equality in *The Social Contract:* equality must be sufficient to maintain civil liberty and social stability. According to Rousseau, inequalities of wealth produce problems for democracy only when there are extreme differences: "No citizen should be rich enough to be able to buy another, and no poor enough to have to sell himself."[1] While Rousseau is satisfied with this relative standard of equality in the economic condition of citizens, he uses an intrinsic standard when talking about political equality itself. Political power can be unequal to a certain extent and still preserve democratic stability, so long as inequalities of power fall within the limits of the rule of law. These thresholds are, however, too minimal to serve as a norm of political equality for a vibrant, pluralistic, and deliberative form of democracy. The proper minimal conditions do not merely eliminate tyranny, but rather must reflect those distributive conditions which best ensure the effective participation of all citizens in decision making. The proper criterion for deliberative democracy is *equality of effective social freedom,* understood as equal capability for public functioning. The goal of my argument here is to show why this ideal of effective freedom best captures the demands of deliberative equality. Its main advantages are twofold: it not only elaborates a conception of equal standing in deliberation, it also makes central the fundamental diversity of human beings with regard to their public functioning.

The deliberative ideal of democracy places great demands upon citizens' abilities and willingness to express their own reasons publicly and consider the public reasons of others. For this reason, it also implies a demanding ideal of equality. In a deliberative democracy, citizens give themselves their own laws through a process of public discussion and debate. While there are conflicting accounts of the nature of deliberation (reflected in this volume), all proponents of this conception argue that the publicity of the *process* of deliberation makes the reasons for a decision more rational and its outcomes more just. The reasons given in discussion and ultimately accepted by citizens must primarily meet the conditions of publicity; that is, they must be convincing to all citizens. Given that it is even more difficult to discover the correct opinion that everyone might share after deliberation than it is to count their votes in majority rule, most defenders of deliberative democracy rely on the *procedures* of debate and discussion to ensure the rationality and legitimacy of decisions. These procedures necessarily embody ideal conditions that make it at least more likely that reasons will be more rational and outcomes more just: they give every citizen the equal opportunity to voice his or her reasons and to reject ones offered by others; and they ensure that dialogue is free and open and guided only by "the force of the better argument." Ideal proceduralism is the standard criterion of deliberative legitimacy, since it gives everyone equal standing to use their practical reason in the give and take of reasons in dialogue. Such ideal conditions form an independent standard in light of which we can judge whether the outcome of actual democratic deliberation is legitimate. This independent standard of legitimacy may be cast in terms of consensus, or, more weakly, in terms of reasonable terms of cooperation.

Even if we accept agreement or cooperation under ideal conditions as an appropriate standard of democratic legitimacy, ideal proceduralism might not provide a full account of the deliberative ideal.[2] It does not tell us much about the ways in which public deliberation is a joint enterprise and a social activity. Moreover, it tells us very little about deliberation itself, even if it tells us something about the conditions that make it free and fair. Most of all, it does not give us a full account of deliberative equality. This weakness of ideal proceduralism is best shown by its failure to capture the myriad ways in which deliberation may fail. Indeed, the difficulty can be put this way: it is possible for all ideal procedural conditions to hold and yet the decision made still not pass the test of publicity. The reason is that proceduralist accounts of deliberative democracy are guided by an inadequate and incomplete conception of political equality, namely, equality of opportunity.

Consider the following example of actual deliberation. According to the Indian Constitution's attempt to abolish the caste system, Untouchables are no longer officially restricted by the religious prohibitions of the past, especially with regard to appearing in public or holding political office.[3] They may now indeed have all the formal and procedural opportunities for input in a certain policy decision. When not simply ignored, however, their mere public support of a policy may cause it to be rejected by many and thus ultimately defeated. Even as the Untouchables are now struggling to make themselves a potent political force, the example points to social and cultural conditions that are necessary for successful public deliberation. These conditions specify the most basic ways in which equality and mutual respect must be realized in democratic practice: all citizens must be able to develop those capacities that give them effective access to the public sphere. Moreover, once in public, they must be given sufficient respect and recognition so as to be able to influence decisions that affect them in a favorable direction. Equality of access and social recognition are thus minimal requirements for effective political participation, or, as I will call it later, adequate public functioning. Below such a threshold of adequate functioning, it is less likely that citizens will develop their public capacities, have their opinions heard, and effectively use their political freedoms. An unfair distribution of the costs of decisions is a good indicator of such inadequate functioning; ineffective groups may not be able to have their concerns respected and recognized sufficiently to avoid such a result. Some philosophers think that the exclusion of the many is desirable, since it improves deliberation. Aristotle and even Madison avoided such difficulties simply by assuming that deliberation should be restricted to those who are already wise, virtuous, and well-off. Even if we reject such views, we may think that political equality ought to, but cannot, consider the standing of each and every person in such a detailed way, other than by designing procedures that give to each the same political opportunities. But not to consider differences in public capacities endorses the inegalitarian consequences of egalitarian procedures and practices.

Recent analyses of economic inequalities that challenge traditional "subjectivist" assumptions about well-being might be helpful both in demonstrating the fundamental weaknesses of deliberative proceduralism and in overcoming them. Theories of economic inequality have traditionally attempted to measure well-being or its absence, that is, poverty. Such inequalities may be measured in a number of different ways: in terms of well-being, resources, opportunities, primary goods, or more recently, capabilities. In order to develop this analogy, we need not assume that direct participation in political life is required for well-being in everyone's conception of the good life. But we may assume that institutions in a functioning democracy are designed well enough to give citizens more or less equal (and therefore *real*) opportunities to influence decisions about issues that affect them. This assumption grants proceduralism its due, while exposing the main weakness of its overly formal ideal of equal opportunity. Even in properly designed institutions, failures in public deliberation are still possible. As in the case of market failure,

Deliberative Democracy and Effective Social Freedom

disadvantaged groups may not be able to participate in the appropriate public arena at all. The same can be said for resources: resources may be redistributed without increasing the effectiveness of disadvantaged groups. Although resource equality at least raises the issue of effective freedom, (or, in Rawls's terms, "the fair value of political liberties"), only a capability-based account articulates an ideal of political equality that is appropriate to the high demands made on citizens in deliberative democracy. Citizens can neither have influence nor achieve their goals, if they are unable to function adequately in the public arena. By "adequate functioning," I mean the capability for full and effective use of political opportunities and liberties in deliberation, such as when citizens make their concerns known and initiate public debate about them.[4] In order to show the priority of capabilities in this context, similar and decisive arguments can be mounted against all other candidates for political equality in deliberative democracy.

**Equality of What? Democracy, Resources, and Capabilities**

To the extent that it is couched in terms of effectiveness or influence, a notion of political equality in some ways depends on the sort of decision-making mechanism employed in the polity. Democratic voting requires equal distribution of power to all citizens (such as one person, one vote) along with secrecy to eliminate forms of coercion and to prohibit certain exogenous influences (such as money in vote-buying). On the face of it, capability equality is easily the most appropriate for decision making via deliberation, the give-and-take of reasons in a collective process of practical judgment. Employing public reason in dialogue with others clearly requires highly developed capacities and skills related to cognition and communication. It may well be that some citizens develop particular interests in public life generally or in particular issues, acquiring special abilities and even expert knowledge. But if deliberative politics is to remain democratic, it cannot simply favor those who are most educated, who have access to special information, who possess the greatest resources and privileged social positions—its procedures ought not invariably favor the reasons of advantaged persons or groups. Capability equality therefore underwrites a fundamental feature of deliberative theories of democracy by developing an account of the minimal level of public functioning necessary for the deliberative equality of all citizens. Such a form of decision making requires equal capacities for active citizenship, and the lack of such capacities for citizenship makes it less likely that the outcomes of deliberation are either just or legitimate.

Capability equality is appropriate to the deliberative ideal in yet another, more important way. It allows us to develop a conception of equality that takes into account another value that is fundamental to a vibrant deliberative democracy: the plurality of human goods and the diversity of opinions. Indeed, according to Amartya Sen, the capability approach tries to solve the problem of how "the assessment of the claims of equality has to come to terms with the existence of pervasive human diversity."[5] Thus, capability equality not only emphasizes the importance of active citizenship and thus of effective participation in public life, it also promises to reconcile the potentially conflicting demands of diversity and equality. The question for political equality can thus be specified: which differences among people are unacceptable for the democratic ideal of equal recognition and respect in deliberation? Certainly, differences in opinions, tastes, preference are admissible, as well as differences in some resources such as knowledge. But the differences that are troubling to the democratic ideal are differences which make for disproportionate political advantages and persistent political disadvantages, such as differences in social circumstances (as in the above case of the Untouchable) and in basic public skills and abilities (such as communication in public). Deliberative democracy cannot assume that citizens are similarly situated or similarly capable of making use of their opportunities and resources. Unfortunately, ideal proceduralism makes both of these assumptions about democratic equality.

Perhaps we can judge equality in terms of the results of deliberation. But how? Satisfaction of preferences is hardly a measure of deliberative equality, since deliberation asks citizens to adjust their preferences and beliefs in light of the limits of their circumstance and the beliefs and preferences of other citizens. More importantly, differences in condition make this standard suspect even with regard to actual achievements, especially in light of the phenomenon that Elster has described as adaptive preference formation.[6] Like the happy slave, those who can achieve little often desire little, and this is particularly true given unjust background conditions of large inequalities of caste, race, gender, or class.[7] Here, too, the capabilities approach offers an ingenious solution. In order to solve the problem of adaptive preferences, it makes an important distinction between achievements and freedom to achieve.[8] The happy slave may not actually lack in achievements; that is, he may actually satisfy all of his given, but nonautonomous preferences. This is because the slave lacks the freedom to achieve; despite his satisfaction, he can only achieve these possibilities and not any others. Thus, preference satisfaction or any other measure of achievement is not a reliable indicator of well being, or even of the scope of freedom. Freedom to achieve is a better measure, so long as we can specify the relevant conditions for human functioning. These conditions in turn establish two different types of freedom: freedom relative to beings and doings. Freedoms of the former sort include the ability to avoid starvation, premature mortality, preventable morbidity, and the latter include such activities as persuading others or achieving complex and meaningful social goals and objectives.[9] Sen's favorite example shows the central role of the possibility of choosing in distinguishing between achievements and freedom to achieve: compare a person who is starving and thus lacks the very basic capacity to avoid going hungry, with a person who is voluntarily fasting and hence exercising freedom to achieve a social, political, or religious end. Similarly, there is an important difference between a person who chooses not to participate in public and one who cannot.

The satisfaction of preferences fails as a standard for other reasons as well. The causal histories of preferences make it impossible to endorse the equal satisfaction of each person's preferences. A possible response to such problems with preferences is to appeal to some objective standard of well-being or utility. Even apart from problems of measurement and interpersonal comparison, the standard of equal utility answers one objection by raising another: while preferences are as diverse as tastes, there is substantial disagreement about understandings of well-being. For some, this is an argument for resource equality. In *Rule of the Many*, Thomas Christiano puts the line of argument in this way: "egalitarian justice under the circumstances of substantial disagreement and pluralism about well-being is best understood as equality of resources."[10] Both resource and capability approaches agree that the diversity of conceptions of the good is a particularly telling objection against some utilitarian measure of a political equality of result. In accepting the force of appeals to pluralism, however, resourcists have raised a standard that they cannot meet. The capability approach turns the argument from pluralism against resource equality, arguing that it overlooks the most important feature of human diversity. It musters a similar and quite powerful argument against other definitions of equality that also reject all forms of "welfarist" equality of achievements for the sake of pluralism. These include measures such as income, opportunities or primary goods; all of these approaches focus on the distribution of the *means* to achieve ends, thus on some defined set of basic resources or goods. Whether broadly or narrowly conceived, these resource approaches cannot solve the problem of how to give each person equal political recognition and respect, especially when human beings are diverse and heterogeneous in condition, ends, means, and opportunities.

More specifically, resource equality ignores a very basic difference among persons: the difference in their capacities to transform means, resources, and opportunities into the achievement of their chosen goals. Or, to use Sen's terms, human diversity implies that agents have different capacities to transform objective conditions into human functionings and thus to choose a valuable life. Once we take such diversity into account, we have to give a different answer to the most basic question of a theory of justice: equality of what? Such things as means, resources and other objective conditions do not describe what is primary or basic to the equality of persons. Even if persons are equal in some particular way (such as income, rights, entitlements, or opportunities) and thus comparable in a particular "evaluative space," they are not necessarily equal in other, more politically significant respects. The argument against resource positions identifies the primacy of the space of capabilities to be the equal distribution not of resources related to the most basic human needs, but of capabilities, those conditions which establish the equal worth of human freedom. Equality of resources will not advantage everyone equally, nor would it correct the disadvantages of those who are most unequal. This is true even for votes as a resource and even more so for the resources relevant to deliberation.

To see why resources cannot provide the primary space for the evaluation of inequalities or an adequate metric for interpersonal comparisons, consider some examples from Sen's *Inequality Reexamined:* a woman with a parasitic disease such as malaria, or one with some special metabolic condition.[11] Assume further that both disadvantages are not easily treatable by drugs, so that the availability of this resource is not the only issue. Both of these women might require more nutrition to achieve bodily functioning and a productive life than others without such conditions; this amount could not be measured as some commodity packet of primary goods, but rather in terms of their capability to convert resources into means to achieving their ends. By analogy, such differences in capability for functioning are politically interesting especially in those cases where they are not the result of the person's own agency or responsible choices, as might be the case for a person fasting for religious or political reasons. Without taking into account such differences in capability, we cannot understand why differently situated persons cannot take equal advantage of political rights, liberties, or publicly redistributed resources.

More is at stake in this debate than the adequacy of theories. One role of the norm of political equality in deliberative democracy is to help in constructing policies that ensure that preexisting disadvantages do not enter into the deliberative process. But are these disadvantages and failures primarily due to the unequal distribution of resources relevant to deliberation? If so, specific corrective measures would be demanded. Joshua Cohen, for example, calls for public funding to ensure citizens' access to public arenas as the best corrective for certain deliberative failures.[12] The problem with resource conceptions of inequality is certainly generalizable to such political examples: increased funding, say in campaign finance reform, already presupposes the equal capacity to make effective use of such resources. It may achieve the desired result more indirectly, by permitting the establishment of contexts in which disadvantaged groups may develop their capacities and make it more difficult for their reasons to be ignored.[13] Capability equality suggests, then, that even when such redistributive measures are employed, they must have a different purpose than merely presenting disadvantaged groups with more resources. This purpose is *more*, rather than less, demanding in its policy implications.

Sen uses this same argument against John Rawls's account of the "worth of liberty" in his two, lexically ordered principles of justice, that is, the equal right of all to the most extensive basic liberty, coupled with maximizing the position of the worst off (i.e., the difference principle) as a basis for justifying inequalities above a certain minimum. The difference principle, however, presupposes basic equality with respect to "primary goods"; that is, the worth of any person's liberty is defined by the availability of certain minimal levels of basic goods, such as income, wealth, powers, and authority. Maximizing this minimal level of resources makes it possible for even the worst off in a society to make use of their equal liberties. Primary goods thus provide the basic index for the worth of liberty, even recognizing the diversity of possible positions in a distributive scheme in a well-ordered society.

Despite recognizing diverse social positions and differences in talents, Rawls has trouble dealing with examples such as the ones mentioned above. For the sick and disabled persons mentioned above, primary goods would not provide an index for the equal worth of liberty; such persons could not make use of primary goods in the same way as a person without such disadvantages. Nor do primary goods provide the proper minimum threshold for effective functioning: remedies constructed around the idea of a primary goods threshold treat freedom and the means to freedom as the same thing. Thus, primary goods not only fail to identify what is basic for effective freedom; they also give a false measure of poverty. Poverty is not the lack of certain goods, but rather the result of the failure to achieve minimum levels of capabilities. As Sen puts it: "The basic failure that poverty implies is one of having minimally adequate capabilities, even though poverty is also inter alia a matter of inadequacy of the person's economic means (the means to prevent the capability failure)."[14] Thus, the primary goods conception of equality fails on its own terms: given the facts of human diversity, it does not specify the conditions for achieving the equal worth of liberty. It is better, then, to measure poverty more directly in terms of the relative scope of a person's overall freedom, his or her achievings and doings. Such freedom is defined by that person's "capability set," which, in turn, consists of all the real options from which an agent is able to choose.[15] The greater the capability set, the wider the extent of the agent's overall freedom. Later, I consider problems with this extensional definition of the scope of freedom for any individual agent. But it does at least provide a solution to the most glaring weakness of the resource approach to political equality: it has, as Dworkin admits, "no basis for interpersonal comparisons of liberty deficits."[16]

In *Political Liberalism,* Rawls concedes the correctness of this basic argument for the priority of capabilities: his conception of equality, he admits, presupposes a more basic one and is thus not the primary evaluative space in which to measure equality of effective freedom. Although citizens do not have to have equal talent and abilities in every regard, they must have the capabilities that enable them to be fully cooperating members of a society over a complete life, "at least to the essential minimum degree."[17] Rawls may not be willing to accept all the consequences of his admission, however. At the very least, an independent conception of justice is demanded for the ideal of citizenship. But even the concession that the primary goods metric presupposes equal citizens does not take into account all the implications of Sen's criticism. Citizenship introduces new problems for effective functioning, which a scheme of equal liberties and rights cannot fully capture and solve. In political and public life, new possibilities of capability failure are introduced with a distinct structure. Just as with economic failures, the problem is two-sided. Some citizens, or more typically groups of citizens, may lack certain capabilities to make effective use of their rights and liberties; this may also mean inter alia that they lack the politically relevant resources and opportunities to prevent such failures. In this case, we must say that such citizens are politically impoverished. Put positively, such equality is not equality of result, but rather of capability to make effective use of one's opportunities or to turn deliberative resources into effective influence in the deliberative process. Indeed, impoverished citizens lack the ability to prevent such failures, which, in a democracy, are measured by their recurrent failures to influence the deliberative process or to have their reasons recognized in enacted decisions. The advantage of the capability approach is that it better captures persistent inequality as interpersonally comparable liberty deficits, thus making the principle of equal liberty useful in cases of the failure of democratic institutions to provide for common citizenship.

The persistent inequalities produced by capability failures are especially troubling for the deliberative ideal. According to the deliberative standard outlined above, decisions made under conditions of persistent inequality could not claim democratic legitimacy. Such legitimacy therefore requires not only opportunities to influence decisions, but a high degree of political capabilities for each and every citizen. Deliberative democracy should not reward those groups who simply are better situated to get what they want by public and discursive means; its standard of political equality cannot endorse any kind of cognitive elitism. In order to avoid this undesirable consequence, deliberative theories need to develop an account not only of adequate political functioning, but also a minimum threshold of shared capability, the absence of which leaves one politically ineffective and hence "impoverished." We can say at the very least that educative institutions must achieve one minimal goal: that it is possible for each and every generation to participate in and thus to perpetuate democratic life. Capability equality gives us distinct political responsibilities to the future. It is possible to impoverish whole generations as well as whole groups.

**Political Poverty and Democratic Deliberation**

According to Sen, the primary goods metric only identifies certain means necessary for effective freedom. However, the most basic measure of equality must consider the differences in the capabilities of agents to convert resources into the means to achieve their goals. Such an analysis could be extended to the political realm generally and to democracy in particular by considering the interrelated problems of diversity and capability failure. Both require establishing a basic threshold of equal freedom. *Political poverty* consists of the inability of groups of citizens to participate effectively in the democratic process. The consequences of such poverty are two-sided: public exclusion and political inclusion. On the one hand, politically impoverished groups cannot avoid public exclusion; they cannot successfully initiate the joint activity of public deliberation. On the other hand, such groups cannot avoid political inclusion either, since they are the legal addressees of the deliberative agreements over which they have no real control or influence. Because they cannot initiate deliberation, their silence is turned into consent by the more powerful deliberators who are able to ignore them. Asymmetrical exclusion and inclusion succeed by constantly shifting considerable political burdens on the worst off, who lack the resources, capabilities, and social recognition to mount a challenge to the conditions which govern institutionalized deliberation.

Below this poverty line, politically unequal citizens do not have the reasonable expectation of being able to affect decisions. Citizens who have developed the capabilities necessary for effective deliberation, however, can avoid both inclusion and exclusion: they are neither excluded from deliberation nor included in the plans devised by others. There is a good empirical indicator for such deliberative capability: it is not merely Sen's idea of "the capability to appear without shame in public"; more specifically, it is the social capacity to initiate public deliberation about their concerns. This ability to initiate acts of deliberation represents a threshold for political equality and social recognition. Above it, continued cooperation indicates democratic legitimacy, even when particular groups of citizens continue to disagree with existing decisions and policies. Persistently disadvantaged groups have no reason to recognize the legitimacy of the regime with which they disagree but cannot afford to ignore.

Poverty in this sense is a measure of minimal political equality in a democracy. It sets the threshold requirement of each citizen's being able to initiate deliberation and to participate effectively in it. The development of such public capabilities is the "floor" of civil equality. Such an analysis of political equality therefore extends Sen's criticism of resource conceptions in the political realm and is similarly skeptical of mere resource correctives. Politically impoverished groups will also suffer resource and well-being deficits: they will bear disproportionate burdens and fail to acquire appropriate means to political freedom even under democratic conditions.

Before developing the implications of this conception of political poverty for public deliberation, let me first mention several limitations to the analogies between economic and deliberative inequalities. There are large differences between political and economic functioning, as well as constant uncertainty in the exercise of public freedom concerning the attainment of common goals. In achieving adequate functioning in the public sphere, cultural resources and their specific definitions are, in the first place, more significant. Often the effectiveness of some deliberators is limited by their inability to formulate publicly convincing reasons appropriate to the specific audience of fellow citizens. Moreover, even the most effective participants in the public sphere cannot causally determine outcomes in the way that economic agents with sufficient means may achieve their ends, unless they are able to circumvent the political process entirely. By contrast, an agent with the proper combination of resources and capabilities in the economic sphere will be able to achieve those goals that she considers important to her well-being in the absence of external interference.

In the situation of public deliberation, even the proper combination of capabilities and resources does not assure an outcome; it assures only that the person is included and can avoid being excluded. Cooperation must also be the aim of any contribution to deliberation. Not only is well-being (in most cases) only a by-product of this goal; the achievement of individual goals is not even a proper measure for failure or success in the political domain. Effective *social* freedom requires a different measure, since it is not merely the capacity to convert resources and other objective conditions into achievements of the agent's goals. Rather, it is measured according to effective participation in a public process of decision making, the outcome of which often bears an indirect relationship to the goals of any of the participants. A direct relationship would suggest that an agent or group of agents have a causal, rather than a deliberative, influence over a particular decision.

Such a capability measure of agency freedom is sufficient for the economic case: given capability and resources, one can, all other things being equal, achieve adequate well-being. Nothing then stands in the way of such an agent achieving her particular goals. But this is not the case for political or public functioning. In the political sphere and most especially in democracies, even if one has the capabilities and the resources, one may fail to achieve one's public goals. That Sen is inattentive to these differences is seen in the fact that he is only interested in "social barriers" to freedom and in cases when freedoms are "restricted" by others directly.[18] Political achievings depend in direct ways on the cooperation of others. Still, given that people need both public and economic capabilities for full participation, deliberative democracies must work toward the goal of adequate "general" functioning among their citizens. Call this a measure of social equality, or of effective social freedom. Sen's approach to agency does not sufficiently articulate such differences within his standard of equal freedom overall, tied as he is to an instrumental conception of agency. In public functioning, communicative action is primary and thus a conception of effective communicative freedom must be developed. Some social actions can be instrumental; but success in communication in the context of deliberation is the uptake by others of one's reason for acting, not the achievement of a particular goal.[19] Uptake of reasons does not require that the course of action decided upon in deliberation be identical with the one supported by my reasons. Rather, uptake (or recognition) of my reasons by others only shapes and influences the process of deliberation itself, so that I can at least recognize my reasons as having shaped and influenced the outcome favorably, or at least in a way that makes it reasonable to endorse the decision.

Typically, deliberative theorists who discuss economic inequalities focus on the effects of the unequal distribution of resources on deliberation. But more relevant for deliberation is the way economic inequalities affect the development of capabilities, the shortfall of which is especially apparent relative to the freedom to achieve possessed by other agents. In those cases we may speak of "capability failure," and thus of political poverty in a nonmetaphorical sense. Cultural capabilities and resources are crucial here, since they specify the *type* of functioning that typically produces success in a given context. Thus, the political problem of capability failure often has to do with something other than the issues of the "equality of what" debate. Rather, cultural diversity makes it impossible to avoid the issue of *which* capabilities are the ones that are relevant to public functioning. The public contestation of any measure of effective public functioning leaves the impoverished in a double bind by requiring precisely what political poverty makes difficult: the capacity to challenge dominant standards in public debate and discussion. In order to be effective, persistently unequal citizens often must challenge not only the prevailing public reasons, but also the prevailing definition of adequate public functioning.

This problem identifies a major weakness in the capability approach. Sen's focus on individual agency simply leaves the question of social agency unanswered, since capability equality concerns the scope of the agents' freedom to achieve those goals that each autonomously chooses. The extent of one's agency freedom is as wide as one's capability set. The same cannot be said of one's political freedom, in which the issue is the extent to which persons or groups can initiate and shape the process and outcomes in a cooperative process of deliberation. For these reasons, effective social freedom is neither a species of agency freedom nor its substitute.

The special nature of social freedom affects how we are to conceive of correctives to political inequalities. Especially under the normative constraints of the democratic ideal, political exclusion should not be overcome by making it possible for certain groups to causally shape outcomes, say by fixing a scheme of proportional representation. Such a reform only gives to a particular excluded group a share of the means to effective freedom, a particular number of seats in a representative body. Equality does not require transforming political freedom of all citizens into the agency freedom of some group, since this solution does not in the end develop the capabilities of any group. Indeed, it even creates the possibility of new exclusions. For this reason, Joshua Cohen proposes that a resource approach suffices for all but the most severe cases of disability and destitution. Moreover, he argues that it is superior and more practical because of the severe informational demands that the capability approach requires for interpersonal comparisons.[20] For the standard of equal effective freedom, social exclusions of various kinds produce the same sorts of problems of poverty at the political level. This standard can apply in various domains and dimensions of social identity, so that it is basic to all judgments about the unequal extent of social freedom, not just to extremes of destitution and complete exclusion.

The problem of outcomes results from the fact that a capability approach is concerned with *effective* freedom. In the economic sphere, the uncertainty of outcomes, large as it is in complex interactions, is not always due to the same causal factors in every case, nor to the agents' inability to operate the levers of control directly. In particular, success in deliberation is dependent on convincing others about the cogency of one's reasons and on judging the cogency of the contributions of others. Call this effective communicative freedom; that is, the capacity to participate effectively in public activities. Such effectiveness is not necessarily measured by the agent's actually achieving his specific antecedent ends, as it is in the case of instrumental action. Even granting this degree of uncertainty, citizens must still know something about how to deliberate, how their reasons will be responded to, and how their goals may be achieved. They must know what it means to succeed in deliberation. Citizens cooperate in deliberation only if they confer upon each other the expectation that they can influence each other's deliberations.

While testable in public discussion, such an expectation does not require that citizens are able to identify a specific causal connection between someone's contribution and the final result, even if citizens are able to recognize their reasons as shaping some decisions some of the time. Rather, it is part of the capability to engage competently in the complex and temporally extended activity of public deliberation that one is able to know when one has had an influence and when one has failed for reasons other than having one's reasons seriously considered and then rejected. The key point here is that it must be common knowledge of citizens that the norm of publicity is operative in deliberation. This ability is not an added epistemic burden on citizens' public capacities, since adequate functioning requires the ability to distinguish good and convincing from bad and

James Bohman

unpersuasive reasons. Agents may also have wider freedom of agency than they do social freedom in the public arena.

Even with this distinction between forms of effective freedom, it might still be objected that the capability approach is only appropriate to extreme cases of destitution.[21] While capability-based conceptions of inequality begin with destitution and exclusion, neither is an all or nothing affair. This claim overlooks the myriad identities of persons and the variability of the scope of effective and public freedom in each of these dimensions. Hardly politically impoverished in other respects, AIDS patients were once entirely excluded from issues of experimental design for treatments and drugs; but activists were able to modify even experimental design by making the issue a public one. While in agreement with the substantive definition of equality offered here, Knight and Johnson raise a more difficult and internal objection to casting the theory of equality in terms of a measure of poverty.[22] They argue that operationalizing political poverty as the inability to initiate deliberation makes it less useful as a measure for the vast majority of "intermediate cases," in which deliberation is initiated and the reasons for deliberative failure are uncertain. I can only give the general direction of an answer here. A full answer would require determining the precise relation of agency and social freedom in public functioning.[23] The more extensive capability set relevant for public functioning would offer a wider range of public avenues through which agents may achieve their goals and thus have a greater *extent* of effective social freedom than others. Such a notion of the extent of social freedom allows at least some comparisons. One measure may be the extent to which collective action is necessary to achieve an extent of social freedom similar to other citizens, as in the civil rights movement's attempt to achieve voting rights that the majority population took for granted. Related to the need to use collective action to achieve normal functioning, another measure of capability failure in political deliberation is the disproportionate distribution of burdens among various groups, including those associated with the risks and costs of social coordination. If Przeworski and Wallerstein are right, for example, powerful economic groups attain a greater extent of social freedom by excluding many topics from public debate by implied threats and other nondeliberative means. Threats concerning declining investment are particularly important for blocking redistributive schemes, such as the burden of higher tax rates.[24] In these cases, public functioning is not required for the groups whose interests carry the day for structural reasons, since their credible threats circumvent the need to convince others of the reasons for their policies. Such groups can substitute their more direct agency freedom (or their social power) for their social freedom mediated through institutions that disperse power. In this case, powerful groups do so by limiting the extent of social freedom—for *all* those involved—by limiting the available options for deliberation for the whole polity. Political deliberation often then takes place among citizens who are diverse in yet another dimension: in the scope of their effective agency freedom or social power. The ideal of political equality must take this diversity into account as well, especially in deliberating about the maxima and minima of acceptable inequalities in the range of social freedom.

The purpose of the redistribution of resources relevant to deliberation, say in campaign finance reform, would be more oriented to the development of capabilities, through which citizens cross a minimum threshold of public functioning and have the reasonable expectation that they may influence the public decision. Even when they have crossed this threshold, citizens remain subject to decisions in which they have not directly participated for a variety of reasons. The division of labor, undetected cultural biases, and the interest in efficiency may all lead to the withdrawal of decision making from public scrutiny. The constant possibility of exclusion is a permanent problem of public life, so long as there are varying degrees in the extent of effective freedom for persons or groups. The possibility that some groups are so impoverished as to be excluded sets a "floor" of civil equality; the possibility that some groups are so powerful that they can limit the set of feasible alternatives in advance of deliberation sets a "ceiling" for too much agency freedom. In both cases, agents lack the conditions of mutual respect necessary for effective social freedom, in the first because it is not granted to them, in the second because they do not grant it to others.

A second problem concerns the status of "facts" about politically independent or "natural" differences in abilities relevant to the political arena. As a floor, political equality does not eliminate the possibility of the possible differences in publicly relevant capabilities. It does, however, establish a threshold for the possible entry of all citizens into public life: the presumption of a minimum, shared set of capabilities needed to have an influence on public life. Why then consider capabilities and functioning at all as part of a critical standard by which to judge actual political outcomes? If there are "inherent" differences in ability and in the social distribution of knowledge, distributive political equality seems an unrealistic ideal. Certainly, no ceiling of maximum permissible development should be specified in capability terms. This objection is especially plausible for complex societies and suggests why weak notions of procedural equality and equality of opportunity have their appeal. Stronger requirements of equality may also conflict with political liberty and imply some perfectionist doctrine of the good life. Such stronger norms of equality, it is claimed, cannot be consistent with the priority afforded to the liberty to pursue one's own conception of the good life. Or, it might be claimed, the need for division of labor in complex societies makes such demands for equality of capabilities unrealistic. Consider two objections of this sort put forth by such egalitarian defenders of the ideal of public reason as John Rawls and Jürgen Habermas, both of which seem to license larger inequalities of capabilities in the political domain, especially at the upper end, than I have argued for here.

In *Theory of Justice,* Rawls not only argues that differences in primary goods are the proper concern of a norm of distributive justice; differences in ability are a matter of good fortune and thus are unavoidable. Moreover, the conception of equality required by justice as fairness that is sensitive to the distribution of advantages and disadvantages cannot avoid being endowment- and ambition-sensitive. Rawls thinks that the evidence of "psychological facts" shows a strong relationship between a person's effort and the "natural abilities and skills and the alternatives open to him."[25] The better endowed, he argues, are not only more likely to achieve more; they are also more likely, other things being equal, "to strive conscientiously." From these "facts" about some citizens' endowment and ambition, it follows that "there seems to be no way to discount for their greater good fortune."[26] One salutary consequence of these facts is that rewarding desert is, for Rawls, "impracticable," since it makes many achievements matters of moral luck for which the agent cannot claim responsibility or credit. Such good fortune might also include better luck in politics, since there is no way to correct for it without unduly limiting political liberties. Although these psychological facts about effort and reward need not be built into representative institutions (as Mill thought), Rawls thinks that we would not normally regard differences in natural capacities as detracting from equality of opportunity in a well-ordered society.

The difference principle suggests that in well-ordered societies such differences in capability could even ultimately benefit the worst off. The benefits of such differences may apply to the agency freedom of the better endowed or more talented. This claim, however, cannot be true for equality in well-ordered democratic institutions; the lack of politically relevant capacities violates the standard of legitimacy for binding decisions. We cannot make use of these contingent differences for the benefit of the least fortunate or capable, as the difference principle requires.[27] Without the reasonable expectation of success and adequate voicing of their concerns, citizens would not have the common knowledge that the decision-making process is public. In addition, political incapacities, natural or otherwise, may well affect both the representation of interests and the distribution of burdens.[28] Since politically relevant capabilities include almost all higher-order cognitive and communicative abilities, there is not as much room for the difference principle to operate. It does, however, arguably apply to the cognitive division of labor and the unequal distribution of expert knowledge, so long as knowledge is nonetheless a shared and hence socially useful resource.[29]

As opposed to Rawls, Habermas bases his argument against requiring stronger norms of political equality in contemporary democracies on specifically social facts about the floor rather than the ceiling of equality.[30] Some of these facts concern unavoidable costs and resources necessary for the deliberative process itself. These include the costs of information and, particularly, that scarce resource, time. The fact that the deliberative process itself requires resources in order to function could lead to "inevitable inequalities." The list of

James Bohman

scarce resources and inevitable inequalities relevant to deliberation is potentially quite long: besides differences in natural abilities and the scarcity of time, one might include the unequal distribution of cognitive and moral information and expertise due to the division of labor and the selectivity in the distribution of information. Habermas lists a series of such "facts." They include the "fact" that "the structure of the public sphere reflects unavoidable asymmetries in the availability of information, that is, in the equal chances to have access to the production, validation, steering and the presentation of images."[31] Such distribution of resources would lead to a situation with regard to information much like Rousseau's description of large discrepancies in wealth: some citizens might be so poor in the politically necessary resource of information that they cannot effectively participate and must always defer to those who possess more information. When citizens are so unequal in capacities to acquire and use information, exclusion is a direct result of the resultant inadequacies of functioning. However, information is best understood as a resource for public deliberation. It is the capability to make use of information and convert it into convincing public reasons, and not merely to have it, that determines deliberative success. To the extent that citizens can do so, they must be able to have access to the relevant forms of communication that make deliberative success at least possible. Here again, capabilities have an advantage over resources: defining equality in terms of freedom lessens the potential for conflict. Thus, unequal distribution of information does not violate political equality in deliberation. Such social facts are not troubling for the deliberative ideal. Indeed, information and knowledge are precisely the sort of resources that can be shared, so long as all citizens have the capability to make use of them in deliberating with others in public, even when they cannot originate them or strictly speaking judge the full scope of their epistemic warrant.

**Conclusion**

The capability-based notion of political equality in deliberation permits us to broaden the scope of political rights and liberties beyond procedural opportunities or access to aggregate resources. Freedom is, on this account, the capability to live as one would choose. It includes the capability for effective *social* agency, the ability to participate in joint activities and achieve one's goals in them.[32] For political liberties, the issue is effective use of public freedoms, which may not be possible even in the absence of direct coercion or prohibitions. If "disease, hunger and early mortality tell us a great deal about the presence or absence of certain central basic freedoms," recent history shows that such basic freedoms can be quite unevenly distributed in democracies with functioning public spheres.[33] One lesson we can draw may be that citizenship and public life are too minimal in such cases to ensure effective freedom. The richer and more demanding the conception of equal citizenship that informs democratic practice, the more likely it is that persistent and large scale inequalities can be avoided within it. Persistent inequalities of race, class, and gender are thus not merely the results of the unequal distribution of resources. They are "beings" (not doings) which reduce the social agency of these groups in relation to the effectiveness of others in achieving their goals, as well as reduce such social freedom that is realized when one's reasons receive uptake from others. Without equal, effective, social freedom for all, cooperative arrangements invariably promote the goals and plans of those agents who are able to convert their opportunities and information into effective action. Thus, the measures for the floor of political poverty and the ceiling of unequal social power are essentially comparative and relational. One of the main roles of institutions is to correct for both kinds of shortfall: shortfalls of social agency and public uptake.

Given minimal democratic institutional constraints on the uses of coercive power, it is the development of public capacities, and not power or resources per se, that provides the primary measure of effective political freedom. Just as power can be delegated to representatives without the loss of equality, resources could be redistributed without necessarily improving the public functioning of groups suffering from persistent inequalities. But some distributions are so unequal as to ensure the agency freedom of the most powerful or wealthy groups, so that they causally influence and restrict the process of deliberation. Between the floor and the ceiling of political equality, and thus between exclusion from decision-making processes and causal control over outcomes, is the interplay among diverse citizens, each with a different range of effective freedom. The wider one's agency freedom, the more one may be assured of influence in deliberation. This relational and comparative aspect of the capability for public functioning still needs to be developed, so that the approach really does go beyond Rousseau's emphasis on tyranny alone.

As suggestive an alternative to resource equality as it is, thinking in terms of capabilities only gets us started on the difficult task of thinking through the sorts of reforms necessary to achieve adequate public functioning for all citizens. Differences between economic and political functioning present themselves in Sen's own appeal to a political solution for recurring famines. Since famines are typically due to breakdowns of social relations of entitlement rather than to shortfalls in supply, Sen argues that the best way to avoid such breakdowns is the democratic self-governance necessary to avoid the loss of public control over existing distributive networks.[34] No such analogous solution presents itself here, since breakdowns and failures in democratic deliberation are consistent with the imperfections of existing forms of democratic self-governance. It may well be that Sen's appeal to democracy works precisely because a well-ordered democracy already requires a high level of functioning among citizens who are able to avoid being excluded from socially available resources and from participation in broad areas of social life.

But capability equality gives us the proper way to understand the reform of democratic practice. On a practical level, procedural reforms of institutions and their design could make the political public sphere more inclusive and open. Redistribution of political resources through public funding could encourage the formation of multiple public spheres, in which disadvantaged groups develop political capabilities and public expression, as well as the advantages of organization. Certainly, collective action has been the most historically significant remedy for deep and persistent cultural biases and social exclusions. Such action, when mounted at all, often fails, especially when advantaged citizens are insufficiently committed to the ideal of equality to lessen the shortfalls of impoverished citizens. On a more theoretical level, the problems of persistent political inequalities demand a more substantive and relational account of public functioning. I can only here suggest that such an analysis would have to be more specific about the sorts of capabilities that are involved in political functioning, which are primarily communicative capacities to enlist the cooperation of others in discussion, to formulate reasons that all could accept, and thus to help to shape the course of ongoing deliberation. On a practical level, it would have to be more specific about the types of institutions in which such functioning is developed and exercised. At the very least, it suggests that we ought to be more concerned with the extent to which educational institutions ought to make it possible to continue democracy in the next generation.

The public character of these particular functionings is also important, especially in light of the ways in which distinctions between the private and the public spheres often reflect deep cultural and gender biases. Nonetheless, the capability-based analysis of political equality does allow us to set a much more precise threshold of democratic equality than those offered by Rousseau and the resourcists: that all citizens are able to make effective use of their deliberative opportunities. This standard does not require that particular citizens or groups of citizens can expect to determine the outcome of any specific deliberation. However, it does require that whenever citizens engage in deliberation, they may reasonably expect that their reasons could ultimately be adopted by their fellow citizens. This expectation motivates the ongoing reform of democratic practice. Such reform seeks to ensure legitimacy by making it a condition of deliberation that all citizens posses equal capabilities to make effective use of deliberative resources and opportunities. Such conditions will have to be part of the common knowledge of citizens about proper functioning in public deliberation. Citizens will then know when their failure to achieve their political goals has to do with their lack of convincing reasons rather than limits upon the extent of their effective social freedom or the greater freedom of others.

In a deliberative democracy, citizens must always examine the reasons for successes and failures in deliberation. Persistent failures indicate the presence of impoverished citizens. Once the degree of political poverty among citizens is assessed, a deliberative process of adjusting the floor and ceiling of political equality begins. Such an assessment now has new urgency, given the increasing pluralism of social life and the distressing facts in even affluent nations that rates of illiteracy, premature mortality, avoidable morbidity, and nutritionally caused deficits among children (that irreparably harm their cognitive development) all continue to rise. Capability analyses of political equality show that these problems could spell the end of democracy itself. Human diversity flourishes in a well-functioning democracy with a vibrant public sphere accessible to all citizens. Even then, the exact scope of mutually recognized social freedom is always uncertain, especially in light of the plurality of conceptions of the good and of justice among citizens. But the lack of such freedom can be measured by the limitations of the lives with which people are forced to live. The ideal of equal effective social freedom requires that institutions correct for disparities in the scope of freedom to choose and to achieve. There is no doubt that these disparities are quite large today. Without a commitment to equality, the very affirmation of human diversity that is at the core of the democratic experiment becomes a cause of its increasingly uncertain future.

## Notes

1. Jean-Jacques Rousseau, *The Social Contract* (New York: Pocket Books, 1967), chapter 9, especially p. 55.

2. For this criticism of ideal proceduralism, see James Bohman, *Public Deliberation: Pluralism, Complexity, and Democracy* (Cambridge: MIT Press, 1996), pp. 28–34 and chapter 4 for a discussion of deliberative inequalities.

3. I owe this example to Henry Richardson.

4. In order to avoid misunderstandings, I should emphasize that "capabilities" is used here as a technical term. It denotes that which is necessary to equalize the functionings that persons are able to achieve. It does not imply that the impoverished are less competent or capable, but that they have fewer such functionings and choices available to them and thus a more restricted scope of effective freedom.

5. Amartya Sen, *Inequality Reexamined* (Cambridge: Harvard University Press, 1992), p. 1; for the role of diversity in the criticism of Rawls, see p. 8. See also Partha Dasgupata, *An Inquiry into Well-Being and Destitution* (Oxford: Oxford University Press, 1993), pp. 42ff. We might also add that in Rawls's list "self-respect" is not a primary good like the others, since it is hardly an "all-purpose means." It is also not achievable in the same way as the outcome of rational action.

Deliberative Democracy and Effective Social Freedom

6. Jon Elster, *Sour Grapes* (Cambridge: Cambridge University Press, 1983).

7. See Cass Sunstein, "Democracy and Shifting Preferences," in *The Idea of Democracy* (Cambridge: Cambridge University Press, 1993), pp. 212ff.

8. See Sen, *Inequality Reexamined,* pp. 4–5.

9. This list comes up again and again; see, for example, Sen, "Gender Inequality and Theories of Justice," in *Women, Culture, and Development,* ed. M. Nussbaum and J. Glover (Oxford: Oxford University Press, 1995), p. 269.

10. Thomas Christiano, *Rule of the Many* (Boulder: Westview Press, 1996), p. 64.

11. Sen, *Inequality Reexamined,* p. 111.

12. Joshua Cohen, "Deliberation and Democratic Legitimacy," in *The Good Polity,* ed. A. Hamlin and P. Pettit (Oxford: Basil Blackwell, 1989), p. 31.

13. For an argument for this role of public funding in campaign and also for alternative voting schemes, see Bohman, *Public Deliberation,* pp. 134ff.

14. Sen, *Inequality Reexamined,* p. 111.

15. One of the putative advantages of the primary goods version of resource equality is that it seems to provide a clear solution to the problem of measurement. Capability equality does not have such a simple solution to the problem. For objections of this sort to my view, see Knight and Johnson in this volume; and also Joshua Cohen's review of Sen's *Inequality Reexamined.* In *Public Deliberation* I offer an argument for a simple measure of effective social freedom as the capacity to initiate public deliberation. Knight and Johnson raise the next question: Suppose that some person or group can initiate deliberation—how does the theory measure shortfalls in such a case? I accept that the capabilities approach must go beyond cases of exclusion or poverty. These cases, however, can only be discussed through an account of social agency and adequate public functioning, rather than its absence in political poverty. In such cases, we have to consider how it is that people deliberate with varying degrees of effective freedom and hence larger or smaller capability sets.

16. Ronald Dworkin has provided a significant revision of Rawls's theory, without solving this problem. See Dworkin, "What is Equality? Part 3: The Place of Liberty," *Iowa Law Review* 73 (1987), 1–54, here p. 41.

17. John Rawls, *Political Liberalism* (New York: Columbia University Press, 1993), p. 183.

18. See Sen, *Inequality Reexamined,* pp. 149, 135. In particular, restrictions of freedom are not reducible to Sen's two cases: violation of freedoms by others, or internal debilitation (p. 87). Political equality offers a third case related to effective *social* freedom.

19. Compare Jürgen Habermas's distinction between those strategic-instrumental actions, which employ language, and pure communicative action in *Theory of Communicative Action,* Vol. I (Boston: Beacon Press, 1984), p. 294. This distinction could establish different senses of freedom of action. For this reason, effective social freedom is different from what Sen calls "effective freedom." It is not a species of agency freedom more generally.

James Bohman

20. Joshua Cohen, "Review of *Inequality Reexamined," Journal of Philosophy* (1995) 92, p. 288.

21. See Cohen's review of Sen for this argument. In their essay in this volume, Knight and Johnson reject this argument, arguing that the primary goods metric has all the same problems as a capability one. I concur with this objection, since primary goods do not simplify the informational requirements of interpersonal comparisons.

22. See Knight and Johnson, this volume, pp. 298–305.

23. Jack Knight has suggested to me that this might entail comparing the result of deliberation with one determined by pure bargaining. The latter case involves *only* agency freedom and only freedom as control (or the lack thereof).

24. Adam Przeworski and Michael Wallerstein, "Structural Dependence of the State on Capital," *American Political Science Review* 82 (1988), 12–29. The problem that the "structural dependence" of the state on capital engenders for left-wing parties is not just in carrying out redistributive policies, but also in the way that the anticipation of higher taxes may itself cause a fall in investment rates. My account of this example differs from Knight and Johnson's.

25. Rawls, *Theory of Justice* (Cambridge: Harvard University Press, 1971), p. 312. In his *Considerations on Representative Government* (Toronto: Toronto University Press, 1951), Mill goes one step further. He thinks that natural differences in ability cannot be eliminated and thus must be reflected in the rules governing fair representative institutions.

26. Ibid.; for a similar criticism of Rawls on the problem of "natural" inequalities, see G.A. Cohen, "The Currency of Egalitarian Justice," *Ethics* 99 (1989): 906–944.

27. See Rawls, *Theory of Justice,* p. 102.

28. See Rawls, *Political Liberalism* (New York: Columbia University Press, 1993), p. 183. For a criticism of the limitations of Rawls's theory of justice and difference principle for primary goods as inadequate to the distinct economic realities of destitution, see Partha Dasgupta, p. 46ff.

29. For an argument to this effect, see my "Democracy and the Cognitive Division of Labor," presented at a conference on "The Political Consequences of Pragmatism," held at Washington University, September 27–29, 1996.

30. See Jürgen Habermas, *Between Facts and Norms* (Cambridge: MIT Press, 1996), pp. 325ff.

31. Ibid., p. 327.

32. See Sen, *Inequality Reexamined,* p. 63.

33. Ibid., p. 69.

34. Sen, *Poverty and Famines* (Oxford: Oxford University Press, 1981), chapter 1.

# 11

## Democratic Intentions

*Henry S. Richardson*

### I   A Tension in Deliberative Democracy

Any account of deliberative democracy gets pulled in two opposing directions. As a normative account of democracy that differs from aggregative accounts by giving an essential and not merely an instrumental role to collective deliberation, it will have to recognize a place for a conception of political truth. Serious deliberation must be *about* something—in this case, call it the *public good*—and hence implies the possibility of articulating standards for assessing alternative proposals about what to do.[1] This does not mean that the standards are available to anyone, but it does mean that the deliberation proceeds on the assumption that there are correct and incorrect views about what ought to be done. The term "public good" is the placeholder for the notion—perhaps the elusive and shifting notion—that is appealed to in normatively assessing proposals about what we ought to do. Even so loosely understood, however, this idea of the public good pulls in the direction of objectivity. A conception of democracy that makes a central place for such a cognitive standard is in danger of regarding democratic institutions merely as imperfect procedures useful for arriving at a plausible rendering of the public good. Yet, as I will be suggesting, such an interpretation of the role of democratic institutions, in turn, fails to give sufficient importance to the wishes of the individual citizens. It fails to regard citizens as self-originating sources of claims.[2] In reaction to this danger, it is natural to move to emphasize the "democracy" instead of the "deliberation" by stressing the extent that democratic institutions *constitute* the public good, which, within limits, is understood as the result of a procedure that takes citizens' wishes, duly reflected and deliberated upon, fairly into account.[3] If the procedures thus constitute the public good, however, then there is no longer any room for a cognitive interpretation of the deliberation that occurs within those procedures; for a cognitive interpretation depends, as I have just noted, upon the existence (though not the common availability) of standards logically independent of the procedures.

In this chapter, I will try to show how a truly deliberative ideal of democracy can be combined with regarding citizens as self-originating sources of claims. The cognitive commitments of deliberation will be shown to be consistent with the individualist aspect of popular sovereignty. Making this case will require three main steps. First, I will argue that the categories of will or intention, and not those of belief or preference, are the appropriate ones to use in modeling democratic deliberation. My grounds for arguing this are largely independent of the conflict sketched out above; but if this approach is accepted, then it provides a key part of the resolution of that conflict. A second step is to set out the conceptual space that lies between the notions of pure, or constituting, procedure and imperfect, or merely instrumental, procedure. If there were no such conceptual space, then it would be difficult to combine the virtues of a cognitive approach with the commitment to individualized popular sovereignty; but I will show that space exists for a normatively fruitful procedure. Third, I will set out a version of an intention-centered analysis that is meant to be open both to the cognitive aspect of deliberative democracy and to its commitment to individualized popular sovereignty. A collective popular will, such as Rousseau's often overly hypostatized "general will," might be seen to be normatively fruitful and yet subject to cognitive constraints; but it does not give adequate weight to individual wishes. In place of such a collectivist analysis of political will, I will offer an account of democratic deliberation in terms of the formation of partially joint intentions, a notion understood in terms of component individual intentions.

It will be seen that I am working out a problem that arises for theories of deliberative democracy. In doing so, I hope to be moving toward an account of what democratic deliberation is like and how it can be rational. What I offer is merely a fragment of a theory of democratic deliberation. It is democratic insofar as it grapples with the distinctively democratic commitments to regarding citizens as self-originating sources of claims and to respecting their input in cognitively oriented collective deliberation, but not yet in the further sense of arriving at any distinctive justification of majority rule. In developing this partial account of democratic deliberation, I am taking for granted that legitimate government depends upon democracy, deliberatively understood. I am also taking for granted that general justifications of democracy will have to shape any response to the problem of justifying democracy to those in the minority. If my solution to the problem internal to deliberative democracy is found acceptable, then the more general justifications could be modified accordingly. For now, I set aside the special situation of the minority voter.

Accordingly, I make no effort here to argue that legitimacy (or justice) requires democracy, let alone to give my own criterion of democratic legitimacy.[4] Developing such a criterion for judging the output of the democratic process is one important task for a normative theory of democracy; but it is not the only one. Another is to describe how the process ought, ideally, to proceed. Given its goals, how should it be conceived and designed? The second task is especially important for the nascent theory of deliberative democracy: its stress on deliberation suggests that reasoning of some kind is crucial; but how can we reason together about public policy? And how are the epistemically oriented aspects of public reasoning to be integrated, in the democratic process, with those aspects designed simply to allocate equal power to each citizen? These questions about the ideal nature of the democratic process will arise for any normative theory of democracy that takes the epistemic orientation of public deliberation seriously. While the answers that we give to them may constrain what we say about the legitimacy of outcomes of the process, they are more properly questions about political deliberation than about legitimacy. Thus, as I have said, I am concerned with how we can develop a coherent understanding of democratic deliberation, given the twin commitments to a cognitive interpretation and to individualized popular sovereignty.

## II  Political Will

A preliminary reason for thinking of political deliberation in terms of the category of will or intention is that many—I would say most—political controversies involve an ineradicable element of compromise.[5] Consider a debate between two factions over whether to continue state funding of the arts. One side, the Philistine faction, asks why it should spend the public's money on an activity of such rarefied appeal, enjoyed by only a few—mainly indeed by rich people who should just go and support the arts directly by buying paintings. The other side, the Pharisee faction, urges that the flourishing of the arts is important to the flourishing of the community as a whole, and that the free market always serves creative arts ill. "Your case is persuasive in the abstract," the Philistines retort, "but look at your recent track record of state-funded art! What you've supported lately has been offensive, antipatriotic, and generally detrimental to the flourishing of the community as we envision it!" "We'll try to do better in the future," respond the Pharisees, "to make sure that the art we fund reflects community values, which, we must admit, we have been neglecting." "But we don't trust you to do that," the Philistines reasonably answer. "Well," propose the Pharisees, fearing a complete shut-off of funds, "suppose that we allow the legislature to have some direct appointments to the boards of referees that make the decisions about which artists to fund?" "If you're sincere about giving some voice to these legislative appointees," respond the not-so-Philistines, "we agree that under those conditions state funding of the arts could promote the public good: we'll do it."

Although this little story has a not entirely unhappy ending, it does not idealize tremendously. Such compromises as this, I take it, are the bread and butter of democratic deliberation. If our theory of deliberative democracy cannot encompass such compromises, it leaves aside most of politics. Yet such compromises, I want to argue, can only be understood as reasonable, and as the product of reasoning, if we understand them in terms of the categories of goodness (or of final ends) and of will.

Now, I want to affirm that I think justice very important. I share the conviction that in some sense it is the "first" virtue of social institutions. I also agree with Habermas that the positive political liberties and the negative civil liberties are "equiprimordial," in that they arise in normative, conceptual, and empirical interdependence; and I agree with Rawls that he agrees with Habermas about this.[6] Hence, I believe that the processes of participatory democracy and the values of popular sovereignty that I will be talking about must be understood as arising within, and being constituted by, a juridical framework that provides constitutional protection for certain rights and helps establish the rule of law. (Whether this constitution is itself an expression of the popular will in some other sense is a question I leave to Frank Michelman.[7] I would just note that it would have to be a sense of the popular will other than the one I am concerned with here.)

I myself would count justice as an aspect of the public good; but even if justice is a disjoint and overriding category, it vastly underdetermines what we ought, politically, to do: what we ought to do through the state and using law. This is not an uncontroversial claim: it will be resisted, for instance, by strict libertarians. I will not try to defend this claim here; but I chose the example of funding the arts to remind you that there are many things that many of us would like to accomplish through collective action—and many things that, at least until now, we have been trying to accomplish through collective action—that do not come under the rubric of justice. We seek to promote education by funding college loan programs, knowledge by funding basic research and the space program, and environmental protection through regulations of many kinds. We have many such political ends; and these ends conflict in various ways and compete for our limited resources.

Yet we should not exaggerate the element of conflict. In a democracy, to seek a reasonable compromise among these many ends to which we are committed is to seek a way of pursuing the public good. Thus, public reasoning attempting to arrive at such reasonable compromises will, in some sense, be directed toward the public good.

Henry S. Richardson

There is nothing in the bare idea of compromise that is incompatible with the cognitive aspect of deliberative democracy. As I have already indicated, by saying that the reasoning is "directed toward the public good," I do not mean to imply that this good has any determinate prior existence, either in the minds of the citizens or as an implication of what they believe and the situation in which they find themselves. As to the first, it is plain from the example that the two factions have very different visions of the public good: they are not simply differing about means to realizing a conception of a flourishing nation that they share. As to the second, as Jack Knight and James Johnson have reminded us, the dependence of democratic results on the precise voting procedure employed undercuts any claim to the effect that the public will is already latent in a constellation of citizen preferences.[8] What I have in mind by this directedness, then, is that the parties understand themselves as disagreeing about what the government ought to do, and not just as engaged in a power struggle. Again, the term "public good" is the placeholder for the notion—perhaps the elusive and shifting notion—that is appealed to in normatively assessing proposals about what we ought to do.

I shall now argue that the notion of intention is more useful and appropriate than that of opinion or preference for the purpose of analyzing political compromise, at least where this is potentially oriented toward the public good. Opinions, being either true or false, are not subject to compromise in the right ways, as a matter of reasoned agreement between opposing parties. *Roe v. Wade* is often criticized on this ground: one opinion is that the fetus is a person, and the other is that it is not. The compromise involving distinctions among the three trimesters looked a lot more like a pragmatic way of partially satisfying the preferences of each side than a principled way of arriving at a middle opinion thought best supported by the arguments and hence most likely to be true. In this context, turning to the "pragmatic" marked a turning away from concern about the truth and toward a way of trying to smooth things out between the parties. Predictably, this has not worked very well. When what is at stake are not conflicting opinions but competing aims, however, there is less of a problem with compromises that split the difference.

In the case of competing ends or aims, by contrast, there is an intrinsic and general, though not overrideable, reason to seek and to accept a reasonable compromise. This is most obvious in the case of one person: when two of one's ends conflict, this gives one reason to look for a way of making distinctions that allow one to pursue each to some extent.[9] For instance, one can work during the day and spend the evenings with one's loved ones. Sometimes, it is not possible to find such reasonable compromises among conflicting ends; but in the case of ends, there is always reason, even apart from any special philosophical faith, to look for such a compromise. Now, in the case of two or more people engaged in democratic dialogue, I am in effect presupposing that each participant is sometimes at least generally disposed to regard the fulfillment of the ends of each of the others as worth pursuing. Each being willing to meet the other halfway, to compromise, implies this. This willingness could be a matter of solidarity, of a generalized benevolence, or more simply a result of the recognition that unless each takes that attitude, the process will be stymied. Given this kind of attitude, there will be a reciprocal willingness on the part of the deliberators, of indeterminate strength, to compromise ends. Hence, generally speaking, ends serve better to model political compromise than do opinions.

What about preferences? From the outset I have rejected preference-aggregation views of politics: we are working out a problem that arises, instead, within deliberative democracy. Still, one might use preferences as primitives in a theory of deliberative democracy. Like ends, preferences are not true or false. Yet in the case of one person, one does not make compromises among one's preferences: one ranks them and then one is supposed to pick the top-ranked alternative. Another way to put this point is that preferences do not suggest avenues of compromise that go beyond the ranking that has already been done. A state of affairs is assigned a place in a ranking, without any comment as to why it ends up there. Ends, by contrast, invite specifications that allow compromise: we aim to support the arts; but what sort of art? The point is frequently made in discussions of deliberative democracy that political deliberation *transforms* preferences.[10] Here I am suggesting that in understanding the process of reasonable preference transformation, it is more useful to use ends as the basic psychological primitive than preferences them-selves. Once one has made that step, the next natural move would be to leave preferences aside altogether. To be sure, there are many different models of interpersonal compromise that have been worked out in preference language: Nash equilibria, and in general the theory of the fair bargain, for instance.[11] In this case, the prob-lem is not with modeling a compromise, and even a reasonable compromise, but with modeling *deliberation toward* a reasonable com-promise. The preference-utility based criteria of fair bargain to which I just alluded go directly to solutions, rather than indicating what deliberation by the disputants, who seek solutions, might look like. Or rather, they imply that the deliberation would be mechani-cal: "Now, let's see; given these initial inputs, the Nash criterion indicates that our resolution would be the following:. . . ." Here there is no give and take, no seeking for a reasonable solution. And don't tell me that an economist could build agents that would "seek" a reasonable equilibrium through a *tâtonnement* process of mutual adjustment. Unless this involves the qualitative incorporation of rea-sons, it will still be too mechanical to model political compromise.

Jack Knight and James Johnson suggest a two-stage model: demo-cratic deliberation goes on for some time, and then aggregative procedures convert the resultant preferences into an outcome.[12] Now, if this just means that voting is always going to be necessary, I agree. If, however, the suggestion is that standard, preference-based models of aggregation adequately integrate the stage of democratic deliberation with the stage of will-formation, I disagree. The chal-lenge is to conceive the process of deliberation and the mechanism of its closure in an integrated way, so that the work of giving and accepting reasons that is done in the deliberative stage is not washed out by the way in which a decision is made. Habermas's frustratingly off-hand treatment of majority rule in *Between Facts and Norms* has somewhat the same problem. He characterizes democratic delibera-tion as a search for truth, and majority voting as a process whereby this search is put on hold for the sake of coming up with a decision.[13] There are both motivational and normative problems with viewing the stages of deliberation and of closure as conceptually discontinu-ous in these ways. The motivational problem is that if the decision is seen as a mere polling of individuals for their private preferences, there will be less incentive to follow through on the push toward a reasonable compromise. I can talk a good game about how much I care about the arts, all the while intending to vote for devoting no funds to them—for there is nothing in the idea of a vote whose purpose is to poll preferences to explain why the vote ought to be public. The normative problem is that the lack of connection between the two stages fails to provide a way for the result of the vote to be explicitly and mutually recognized as a reasonable compromise. Yet such explicit mutual recognition would not only be a nice thing, and a feature that would fit well with the general spirit of deliberative democracy: it also is important, as I will be suggesting, for recasting the ideal of popular sovereignty in a workable way.

There is another problem with preferences. Arrow's impossibility theorem showed that there is no fully satisfactory general way to map between individual preferences and a social choice. Thus, even the sort of minimalist conditions on such a mapping that Arrow laid out conflict with one another. As a result, from the point of view of such a mapping, there is no uniquely preferable set of democratic procedures. Some might conclude from this that the notion of the popular will is ambiguous, and is best dispensed with in a theory of deliberative democracy. I would run the argument backwards. I have no philosophical problem with the idea of a collective or institutional will, and hence I am comfortable understanding, say, legislative decisions as issuances of the legislature's will.[14] When constructing an ideal of democracy, I am comfortable talking about the popular will as the will of the government in a duly constituted democracy. Hence, by Arrow's result, if there is a popular will, then it cannot be understood as having arisen via some satisfactory mapping process from individual preferences. Hence, it must arise in some quite different way, from a different source. Individual intentions represent a different initial building block than individual preferences. It is with intentions, as I say, that I suggest we begin.

## III  Popular Sovereignty and Normatively Fruitful Procedures

Before I actually do begin to lay out the notions of intention that I think are helpful, however, I want to return to the ideal of treating persons as self-originating sources of claims—the element of democracy that creates the tension with deliberative democracy's cognitive approach. As I have said, this ideal is the individualized aspect of popular sovereignty, a commitment to respecting the voices of individual citizens in the formation of the articulate popular will. Respecting them requires not only taking individuals each to be important sources of political argument that ought to be heard, but also accepting their claims to some extent as "self-originating," or as not requiring any basis or justification. To this latter extent, it is their will that counts in a democracy: ceteris paribus, that a citizen wants a policy counts in favor of that policy being what ought to be done. We will be overreacting to preference-based analyses of democracy if we hold, for example, that what welfare mothers want from the government should count for nothing in determining welfare policy. Putting this individualized aspect of popular sovereignty to the fore will help correct for overly corporatist interpretations of the popular will. As I have indicated, I agree with those critics of Rousseau who hold that he tended to hypostatize the general will and gave it a life too independent of the wills of citizens. He either excessively weakened the links between the general will and the actual wills of each, so that the equation of obedience to law with obedience to one's own will became an insidious fiction, or else, as Habermas likes to emphasize, he expected too much from the virtue of citizens.[15] Or perhaps he did both. Either way, the flaw in Rousseau's theory is moral or normative, not conceptual. The notion of an institutional will not identical with the wills of any persons in the institution makes conceptual and methodological sense; it simply gives up the link to individual wills important in a democracy and insisted upon by the ideal of regarding citizens as self-originating sources of claims. Similarly, to expect citizens to will more civic-mindedly than they can fails to give adequate normative importance to what they actually will. Since the ideal of popular sovereignty is an intrinsically important aspect of the ideal of democracy, we need to guard against these Rousseauean errors. The best way, I believe, is to recognize the importance of regarding individual citizens as self-originating sources of claims.

I can now be more explicit than I was at the outset about how this commitment gives rise to a problem for theories of deliberative democracy. A central challenge for theorists of deliberative democracy is to find a way of conceiving of public decision-making that is at once sufficiently cognitive to make it truly deliberative and also sufficiently responsive to the positions of individual citizens to count as democratic. This problem is one that we continue to face even if Estlund and others have convinced us that truth is safe for democracy.[16] It is a question about how democratic discussion is supposed to arrive at the truth. The apparent dilemma is this: true deliberation, as opposed to interest-based bargaining, seems to require the existence of standards that are independent of the democratic process and its outcomes, as well as procedures of mutual reason-giving that are intelligible only in light of such standards.[17] Yet the existence of these standards, whether ones of justice or of what counts as a "better argument," seem to denigrate the importance of citizen input as sovereign determinants of what is "better." On a view such as Estlund's, for instance, citizens' contributions to the debate tend to be counted merely as means to the ascertainment of political truth, rather than as having even a ceteris paribus constitutive effect upon what we ought to do.[18] Conversely, views such as those of Thomas Christiano or of Jack Knight and James Johnson that resist the epistemic move see no need to understand the whole of the political process as being oriented toward external normative standards. Since they let the outcomes of a fair process wholly constitute the public good, or what ought to be done, unless some independently fixed standard of justice or morality is violated, these views can explain neither some important ways in which we actually criticize the democratic process nor how it is that the citizens can be taken to be deliberating together.[19] In other words, if the operation of the democratic process itself *constitutes* what politically ought to be done, there seems to be no room within the process for a deliberative orientation toward figuring out what ought to be done; but if there are standards of political correctness outside of the democratic process, then democracy comes to be seen merely as a means of approximating to right answers that are knowable independently of the gathering of citizen input. To use Rawls's terminology: if democracy is a pure procedure, answerable to no external standards, then it seems insufficiently epistemic to count as deliberative; but if democracy is an imperfect procedure that approximates some external standard, then it seems insufficiently respectful of the views of citizens.

This debate between the pure proceduralists and the imperfect proceduralists is an important and well-developed one; and in what I have just said I have largely been repeating the arguments that each side has made against the other. What I mean to do is not so much resolve this controversy as sidestep it by suggesting that there is a middle way that seems not to have been considered. Thus, I believe that this dilemma is only an apparent one; but I do not wish to see it resolved by giving up on either of the commitments that makes for the difficulty. To the contrary, I believe that we need to reaffirm and strengthen our conceptions of both the way in which democratic deliberation is aimed at political truth and the importance in this process of the fact that citizens are self-originating sources of claims. This means that the democratic process must be conceived both as attempting to arrive at true political views and as giving intrinsic importance to what each individual citizen thinks ought to be done. I would not get out of this dilemma by relaxing either of the aspirations that gives rise to it.

Instead, I want to suggest, we can dissolve this dilemma by conceiving of democratic deliberation as an attempt to arrive at a collective will, a joint intention, by making reasonable compromises among the various things that the individuals involved intend or propose. What I have in mind, in other words, is a kind of joint deliberation about ends.

Now, this description of deliberative democracy may seem simply mundane and noncontroversial. To suggest to you that it is not, let me indulge in some rather sketchy diagnosis of why I think that deliberative democracy has not been described in these terms. The root cause of this, I believe, is that Humean and other skeptics have made it difficult to recognize the possibility of deliberating rationally about ends. For this reason, instrumental rationality has held a grip on our normative theories as well as on our political and economic practices. In attempts to combat this skepticism, however, its legacy lives on in the tendency to think (falsely) that the only way to get beyond instrumental rationality is to rely upon a conception that is either objective or else at least strongly intersubjective. Hence, it is thought necessary to rely either on what Habermas would call the pre-existing "ethical substance" of a given community, with its shared conception of the good, or else on moral rules that are in some way universal, perhaps as grounded in the presuppositions of all communication. Civic republicans, such as Frank Michelman and Cass Sunstein, are drawn to the former option, while Habermas has developed the latter. Tellingly, when Habermas charts the types of practical reason in *The Theory of Communicative Action,* he leaves out the possibility of individual, monological reasoning about ends.[20] To reason about ends, he implies, one must immediately go dialogical. Accordingly, his writings on democracy put a strong Kantian emphasis on the framing role of justice, which he sees as grounded in universal principles. He rejects republican views of the kind elaborated by Michelman and Sunstein on the ground that ethical reasoning about the common good would have to rest upon a shared ethical substance, a deeply grounded and pre-existing common understanding of the good, if it is to get anywhere—a possibility blocked by the conditions of pluralism.[21] Cass Sunstein, by contrast, defends a version of dependence on prior ethical agreement, relying upon Elizabeth Anderson's ideas about what she calls "expressive rationality," in which substantive norms limit the appropriateness of trading off different goods as if they were all commensurable on the scale of preference-satisfaction.[22] As far as this account goes, these limiting norms must have a prior existence in the culture or in our language-games—in what Habermas would call the ethical substance of the community. Such thoughts feed the Rousseauean, cognitivist pole of our tension, as they suppose that something like a general will is there to be discovered.

What Habermas and Sunstein have in common, here, is that they concede too much to the sort of skepticism about active reasoning about ends, about the good, that Kant shared with Hume. If I thought that the only way effectively to resist preference-based understandings of democracy was to accept either Habermas's account of the unavoidable presuppositions of communication or a neo-Rousseauean reliance upon shared ethical commitments, then I would do so; but I would do so with misgivings, as this would leave us without a clear way to understand how individual citizens can make reasonable headway in the kind of compromises I have been urging are central to the work of politics. I have argued elsewhere, however, that each of us can deliberate rationally about final ends in a monological way that is not explicitly dependent upon, though it is compatible with, taking guidance either from moral principles or from communal ethical substance. It is this possibility of individual deliberation about ends that had better be harnessed by a dialogical account of democratic deliberation if we are to explain how, by starting to weave together the results of their individual deliberations about what is good, the citizens of a democracy can start to articulate a conception of the common good that goes beyond anything that already exists in the shared ethical substance of their community.[23] We need to envision how deliberation about the good can proceed from individuals, who may not begin by sharing a common conception of the public good, in a way that nonetheless begins to forge a shared conception thereof.[24] What rational dialogue can do depends in part on what monological reasoning can accomplish. We need a deeper conception of the latter to arrive at an adequate understanding of dialogical reasoning in politics.

These considerations about the possibilities of practical reasoning also provide me with the basis for side-stepping the controversy between purely procedural and imperfectly procedural versions of deliberative democracy. A correct understanding of the nature of noninstrumental practical reasoning—practical reasoning that extends to ends—will, I think, force us to recognize that Rawls's distinction between pure and impure procedures is too crude for these purposes. We can reason about our ends, I have argued elsewhere; and when we do we are both oriented (at least potentially) toward the truth about what we ought to do and responsive to our own commitments.[25] What we ought to seek and what we ought to do depend, in part, on what we affirm on due reflection.[26] This dependence can be phrased counterfactually: if we were to affirm something different on reflection, then it would be the case that we ought to do something different.[27] Because of this dependence, which is perhaps peculiar to reasoning about ends, we do not have, here, a case of perfect or imperfect procedure. The right answer about what we ought to do or seek is not settled wholly independently of what we affirm on due reflection. Yet it is also not a case of pure procedure. What we affirm on due reflection does not settle, infallibly or authoritatively, what we ought to seek or do. Our well-reasoned reflection does not constitute this answer in any sufficient way. Again, our conclusions remain open to further criticism and revision—criticism and revision that is potentially oriented, again, to arriving at a truer conclusion about what we ought to do. Nor is this a matter of core and penumbra—or of what Rawls has called "quasi-pure procedural justice."[28] It is not the case that the "external standards" set firm limits on our practical reasoning, and that the intrinsic deliberative influence on what we ought to do takes places only at the penumbra, or within the *Spielraum* left over once the external standards are satisfied. Rather, it is important that on this conception of practical reasoning, even what appear to be central standards of rationality remain in principle open to revision. (It may be that the idea of "quasi-pure procedure" will become of interest again once we think about how to implement deliberative democracy constitutionally: that was Rawls's original use for the notion. First, however, we must reconceive the abstract ideal of deliberative democracy.) What standards there are depend both on external norms and on the operation of deliberative procedures. That is, there are independent standards, but they can be modified or affected by the deliberation.[29] I shall call deliberative procedures that have this property "normatively fruitful."

Such an understanding of practical reasoning, if appropriately extended to the dialogical level, would dissolve the apparent dilemma between responsiveness to citizens and answerability to external standards. One wants both, and such a conception of practical reasoning allows for this.

## IV  Joint Intentions as the Fruit of Democratic Deliberation

The cognitivist pole of the apparent dilemma threatens the idea that each person's input is intrinsically important in a democracy. The Habermasian complaint about traditional practical reason was that it is monological. We can address both these problems at once by

Henry S. Richardson

postulating that we regard deliberative democracy as being aimed at the production of joint intentions, or partially joint intentions.

Now, at this point I must explain one caveat that I have already been making and introduce another couple of disclaimers. The first concerns the notion of a "partially joint intention." The full notion of a joint intention to which I have been alluding requires unanimity. This is not a sensible requirement for politics. Hence, I speak of a partially joint intention as one that shares the structural features of a joint intention, which I will set out shortly, but only among a subset (say, a majority) of the people. Second, as I hope to have made clear, I am concerned mainly to suggest a shift in the basic psychological categories used to understand democratic deliberation, not to oppose or revise more concrete ideas about how this deliberation is to be carried out. Accordingly, I take for granted the importance of the kind of constraints developed by others, which would help ensure equal access, the real opportunity to have one's argument heard and responded to, the publicity of reasons, and so on. My concern is how to model what goes on when equally situated deliberators compromise by taking one another's reasons into account. Third, I agree with Iris Young and others that, in modern societies, deliberative democracy cannot work without reliance upon a system of representation.[30] This fact requires complicating the story about forming political intentions. (So, too, for that matter, do Frank Michelman's points about constitutional intentions.) Since I am not able at this point to absorb these complications, I will abstract from them. Let me turn, then, to explaining the notion of joint intention that I propose to use in giving an account of deliberative democracy.

If all goes well, the process of democratic deliberation results in an agreement about what to do, which might take the form of passing legislation or electing a given slate of representatives. A distinctive feature of deliberative democracy is that the participants are to some degree responsive to the reasons offered by other people. Hence, as a result of the process of democratic deliberation, and not simply as an antecedent fact, each of the participants, or each member of the duly empowered majority, will come to have an intention to do his or her individual part, as determined by the agreement. This might mean to regard the victor as one's representative or to accept the consequences of the enacted legislation. Further, if this agreement is the result of deliberation, then we can presume that at least the winners believe that fulfilling the intention embodied in the agreement is possible, so long as enough of the citizens do their parts. Finally, if this deliberation has been democratic, it should meet certain publicity constraints.[31] In the case of the democratic decision, the publicity ought to be actual, not merely potential. That is, the individual intentions and beliefs that support the public agreement should be common knowledge among the participants.

This structure—an agreement that we do something with regard to which (1) each of us intends to do our parts as required by the joint plan, (2) each of us believes that the joint action can be carried out if enough of us do our parts, and (3) these intentions and beliefs are common knowledge—is that recently elaborated by Raimo Tuomela as an analysis of joint intention.[32] After a long period during which this topic was neglected, there are now various competing philosophical analyses of joint intention being developed. Tuomela's version has the virtue of avoiding reductionist individualism, since it builds into its analysans a notion of agreement that is already a kind of implicit joint intention ([1], the joint plan). And in the domain of deliberative democracy, at least, Tuomela's interpretation of joint intention does not compete with, but is complemented by, one of the main alternative analyses, that of Michael Bratman, as I will shortly show.

First, though, let us pause over the notion that the output of the democratic process embeds an agreement. Tuomela's analysis of joint intention builds in this element; but for that reason it may be thought to go too far.[33] It certainly goes too far for some conceptions of democracy. Imagine that democracy is conceived simply as a fair or just procedure for arriving at a social choice on the basis of individual preferences. On this conception, democracy can operate by majority rule without yielding any agreements, and the individuals who vote need not be taken to be agreeing to anything. Deliberation may play some role in airing information, and in ensuring that individuals arrive at positions that are well-informed. But on this understanding the deliberation just comes to an end at some point, and another kind of process, namely an aggregating one, takes over. In defense of understanding democratic procedures as involving underlying agreements, I have two arguments. First, more generally, agreements are necessary to fulfill the ideal of public justification implicit in deliberative democracy. In deliberative democracy, we seek not simply to aggregate individual views, but to work out in publicly acknowledged ways, and in ways that publicly recognize the reasons offered by others, what we are to do. Once we have worked this out publicly, we have agreed, in the relevant sense. Now, the operation of majority rule in itself can at best produce weak reasons for or against a policy; hence, the mutual recognition of reasons needs generally to take the form of an informal mutual agreement— albeit among an indefinite proportion of the voters—prior to a vote. Second, against the competing idea of sharply partitioning the stage of deliberation from the stage invoking majority rule, I have argued that there are strong motivational and normative reasons to insist that the means by which closure is reached must be continuous with the means of discussion. Characterizing the principle of closure as firming up and formalizing an implicit agreement is one natural way to do this. It is ironic and unfortunate, then, that, as I have already mentioned, Habermas reverts to the noncognitivists' understanding of majority rule as breaking off the process of deliberation, and of arriving at closure in precisely the same sort of way that a social-choice theorist or preference-based theorist would. At least, this would be unfortunate if there is another way of conceiving of the operation of majority rule, one more in line with deliberative democracy. I think that there is.

To bring out this alternative understanding of majority rule, I want to explain how it can be cast as yielding joint intentions, in something like Tuomela's sense.

## V  The Democratic Generation of Joint Intentions

What I would like to do, then, is give a description of the democratic process in five stages, culminating with the formation of a partially joint intention.

Where shall it begin? A narrowly instrumental, aggregative view of democracy might start with the desires or preferences of citizens; a purely cognitive view might start with their opinions and views; and a noncognitive view focusing mainly on the value of fair procedures might start with their attempts to exert their influence. By contrast, a view that sees deliberative democracy in terms of practical reasoning will naturally start with *proposals* that individuals, or their representatives, make about what the polity ought to do. Typically, but not necessarily, these proposals will arise out of the desires, preferences, or ends of the people who make them. These proposals, whether they take the form of nominating candidates for election or introducing bills for legislative consideration, are public actions in a dual sense. First, they are obviously actions essentially open to public inspection and awareness, in a way that desires or opinions may not be. Second, I am assuming that the relevant proposals are restricted as to their content: they are proposals *about* what we are to do, together.

The notion of a proposal has some simple implications that will be helpful later on in the forging of joint intentions. A proposal is a public act, whereby, among other things, one implies that one is willing to accept that some steps necessary to achieving the proposal be taken. If I propose that John be the one to carry our petition to the authorities, then I openly imply that I am willing to hand John my copies of the petition. If what I am proposing is a joint action, then I imply that I am willing to do my part, as necessary, to carry out the proposal—subject, of course, to various escape clauses, necessary largely because I cannot foresee all the difficulties that may arise in bringing the proposal to fruition. If I propose that we marry, I imply that I will get myself to the altar on time—unless I discover that you are still married to someone else. A proposal may indeed be put forward insincerely, as the study of strategic voting shows us; but an insincere proposal insincerely implies that one would undertake the necessary steps. The disappointed bride will not only feel generally jilted, but will also have special cause to complain about being stood up at the altar.

This "willingness" involved in a proposal is not yet an intention to do my part. If I propose marriage to you, it would be unusually presumptuous of me already to intend to arrive at the church on time. More normally, this willingness will still have a conditional character: I intend to do my part, as required, *if* the proposal is accepted. In politics, if I propose that we raise the tax rate, I imply my willingness to pay additional taxes—but to do so only if my proposal is accepted by the political process.

The second stage of deliberative democracy is for the proposals to be discussed on their merits. This means to assess them in terms of the public good. Yet since political rationality ought not to be understood as merely instrumental, it is important to recognize that the ends in terms of which the public good gets interpreted are themselves up for discussion. Indeed, many of the most significant political proposals will imply or suggest ways in which the public good ought to be reconceived. Thus, evaluating proposals in terms of how they serve the public good is not simply a matter of comparing them on the basis of an independent standard. In this case, too, as Rawls puts it, "there is no way to get beyond deliberative rationality."[34] Nonetheless, it remains possible to consider whether the proposal serves the public ends that, after due reflection on the proposal and what it implies, we think ought to be pursued. An ideal process of deliberative democracy would proceed in this way. Ideally, proposals should be put forward in the belief that following them will best promote the public good, understood as it ought to be.

The third stage, already implied in what I have just said, is to arrive at some informal agreement about what we ought to do. I have already explained why democratic deliberation requires mutual agreement to fulfill its ideal of the public recognition of reasons. Now, in working out an analysis of deliberative democracy in terms of practical reasoning, and in moving toward the idea that the output of the process is a joint intention, I will describe the intermediate stage of informal agreement in somewhat more practical terms, focusing on how democratic deliberation can give rise to agreements that are, *pro tanto*, normatively binding. I will also explain how Bratman's version of the idea of joint intentions here complements Tuomela's.

Let me recall the notion of joint intention that I propose to use in this account. I have suggested that Tuomela's analysis of joint intentions fits the bill, and I have described how it treats joint intentions as building, on top of a basic mutual agreement on a joint plan, the conditions that each individual intends to do his or her part, that each believes that the joint plan could be carried out if enough citizens did their parts, and that these facts are mutually known. At the core of this nonreductive understanding of joint intentions, then, is the more basic idea of a mutual agreement, an agreement on some joint plan that assigns people certain parts to play, certain duties, rights, and responsibilities. The aim of my discussion is not to show how the normative force of the resultant joint intention can arise from ultimately nonnormative facts about individual intentions; rather, it is to show how individuals' normative stances get woven together in significant ways and thereby modified, yielding a decision of collectively normative significance. Tuomela's account of joint intention makes much of the obligation inherent in the core informal agreement, using it to explain the connection to each person doing his or her part.

The idea of mutual agreement is central to my account of democratic deliberation for two reasons, each of which flows from the fact that agreements (in certain contexts, and within certain constraints) can give rise to obligations. My purpose is not, however, to sketch an account of why any individual, even a member of a majority, is obligated to obey majority-enacted legislation. Rather, my reasons for stressing the tinge of obligation involved in agreement are more modest. (1) The first is that the obligation created or implied by an agreement can bind participants to a decision, helping give rise to a seriousness of commitment that deserves to be counted as an intention (a less serious level of commitment, it will be recognized, than need be involved in a moral obligation). (2) Second, if agreements create individual obligations they can also have a direct and readily understandable influence upon what *we* ought to do. If we can see how the process of deliberation can yield obligation-creating agreements, then we can begin to explain how it partially determines what the public good is, even if that public good is thought of cognitively. We can understand this possibility in two ways. Minimally, these agreements will produce *pro tanto* obligations that at least may count for something in determining what we ought to do. More ambitiously, if we take point (1), expressing the connection between these agreements and the wills of individuals, together with the ideal of regarding individuals as self-originating sources of claims, we can see that citizens will be newly forming intentions that also ought, ceteris paribus, to affect what we ought to do.

The question thus is how the political proposals that are being discussed are forged into a political agreement whereby we form a joint democratic intention. It is being too quick simply to say that applying the principle of majority rule does it. While majority rule is part of the story of forging political agreements, it is only a part, and one that comes later in the story.

Further, the procedure of majority rule fails to give rise to mutual agreements in the relevant sense. Mutual agreements, in the sense that matters here, require the public expression of intentions and a mutual awareness of the intentions that have been expressed. Majority rule, however, can operate without either of these. That this is so is shown already by the possibility of a secret ballot, in which the votes never become publicly known.[35] Yet amending majority rule by banning secret ballots would still fail to give us the requisite sort of agreement. Applications of majority rule limited to roll-call votes do not suffice to create agreements, though of course they might fall under the clauses of a pre-existing constitutional agreement. It takes more than mutual awareness of intentions to have an agreement. Suppose you tell me that you are going to Chicago for a conference. "What a nice coincidence," I reply, "I am too." Here there is mutual knowledge of a pleasant correspondence in our intentions, but no obligation-creating agreement. Our relevant preferences were perfectly correlated from the outset, without requiring any act of agreement to bring this about. Something similar could conceivably occur in the application of majority rule. Imagine a roomful of academics, each of whom is planning, for individual reasons, to spend a given weekend either at a conference in Chicago or at one in Rome. Suppose one of the group asks for a show of hands—"How many of you were planning to go to the conference in Chicago?"—and that a majority is planning to go Chicago. "Fine," he then says, "I will therefore take the principle of majority rule as indicating that we have all agreed to go to Chicago." Now, I take it that this claim fails, not only for those in the minority, who clearly have agreed to nothing, but also for those who, by happy coincidence, ended up in the majority. The mere facts that their plans coincided and turned out to be the most common obligate none of them to go along with the results of this straw poll. Again, something besides the procedure of majority rule is needed to give rise to the normative commitment involved in mutual agreements.

We can distinguish two kinds of addition that might help convert mutual awareness of intentions into something normatively significant enough to count as an agreement: assurance and reliance.[36] If the first party desired assurance that the second would do her part, and the second deliberately took steps to reassure the first that she would, and both knew this, then this could give rise to an agreement in which the second was obligated to do her part. If the assurance was thus provided on both sides, then it can be a symmetrically binding mutual agreement. On this possibility, then, explicitly reassuring a party desiring that reassurance is what gives rise to obligation. A second route to an obligation-involving agreement, instead of arising from a pre-existing worry or desire for reassurance, looks instead to the results of an initial declaration of intention. Roughly speaking, if the first party's declaration of intention leads the second reasonably to make commitments that relied on the first party's following through, such that the second would suffer some loss if the first party did not, then that may give rise to an agreement in which the first is obligated to do his part. If the reliance is mutual, then so also may be the obligations arising out of the agreement.

Both routes to obligation involve an important kind of responsiveness between the two people involved, based on their mutual awareness of what each intends, or claims to intend. One response is to a need for reassurance, another is a result of having felt assured. In the example of arts funding with which I began, the Pharisees, relying upon the sincerity of the Philistines' avowed concerns with patriotism and national values, accepted the importance of those values and offered a compromise that departed significantly from what they considered ideal. The Philistines, in turn, admitted the importance, in the abstract, of funding the arts and accepted the Pharisees' assurances that putting legislative appointees on the relevant panels would help ensure that the funded art promoted those

Henry S. Richardson

values. This is hardly the stuff of a formal contract, but it is the kind of reliance and assurance that leads negotiators toward an agreement.

What I would now like to suggest is that Bratman's analysis of shared intention actually helps to capture the kind of responsiveness needed in forming agreements in these ways. Tuomela has criticized Bratman's account as not capturing the full notion of a joint intention. I want to suggest, however, that the very features that prevent Bratman's account from accommodating the phenomena of joint intention equip it to help us analyze the formation of the sort of agreements that Tuomela's notion of joint intention presupposes. Although this might hold generally, I will pursue this complementarity of the two analyses only for the case of democracy. While I do not think that Bratman's account will analyze the element of agreement exhaustively enough to convert the combined account into a reductionist one, it will enable me to connect my analysis of democratic deliberation with the understanding of democratic outputs as joint intentions. Admittedly, Bratman does not present his account as a theory of agreement-formation; and he actually denies that shared intentions, in his sense, always give rise to obligations. In what I have just said, however, there was no "always"; rather, what we had were two patterns that could be said generally to give rise to obligations. Other, as yet unstated, conditions would be needed to get the "always," if indeed we ever could. What I mean, then, is that the structure of Bratman's analysis provides for responsiveness of approximately the right kind to fit into these two patterns of obligation-creation I have distinguished.

Bratman's analysis of shared intention runs as follows:[37]

We intend to J if and only if

1. I intend that we J[38] and you intend that we J;

2. You and I each intend that we J in accordance with and because of our each intending that we J and having subplans for J-ing that mesh; and

3. These facts are common knowledge among us.

The responsiveness comes in, here, in the second clause, the requirement that we each intend to J "in accordance with and because of" the other's intentions, of which we are aware. Forming an intention so as to reassure another is one way to respond to the other; forming an intention in reliance upon the other's intention is another. Again, there may be more, but the point for now is just that these two bases for obligation do come under the rubric of the kind of responsiveness that Bratman has identified. Bratman's account helps us understand how mutual obligations and mutual agreements can arise together. Looked at one way, mutual responsiveness involves assurance and reliance that give rise to obligation; looked at another way, this mutual responsiveness is part of the structure of the agreement once it is formed.

In a deliberative ideal of democracy, it is above all responsiveness to the arguments and proposals of others that will be crucial in creating informal agreements. Let me briefly give another example to sketch how I see assurance and reliance phenomena arising in political debate. Some of it is pragmatic and some more cognitive. First comes the formation of shared intentions within the various competing political factions. Consider the issue of health-care reform. Various groups in the legislature would like to put forward a more free-market-oriented and less costly, albeit less comprehensive, reform package than the one proposed by the President. After much discussion of the merits of alternative proposals and much strategic jockeying back and forth, different groups of legislators will coalesce around different reform bills. In the course of debate over the merits and tactics of these alternatives, they will publicly declare themselves for one or another of these alternatives, arguing that their favorite is the one that we, as a nation, should enact. Some legislators will want to be assured that there will be enough protection for their elderly constituents built into the legislation, and they will be so assured. Sometimes this assurance is more pragmatically focused: "it will be done." Sometimes, however, the assurance is more epistemic: "we have looked into it carefully and can assure you that we have good reason for believing that the protection will be sufficient." And sometimes the assurance is cognitively normative: "we have weighed the arguments carefully and have determined that the various component values lumped under the heading of 'protection for the

Henry S. Richardson

elderly' are here being given appropriate weight and worthy interpretations." At this agreement-forging stage, deliberative democracy
depends upon a considerable degree of trust in the knowledge and
normative judgment of others. Now, once some proposals come to
be favored, other legislators will withdraw particular proposals of
their own, reasonably relying upon their faction's leaders to provide
a bill sufficiently friendly to free-marketeers. In these ways, the legislators, sometimes via open pledges, but sometimes more tacitly, will
build shared intentions (in Bratman's sense) to pursue their faction's proposal as what ought to be done. Each of them will put
forward his or her faction's bill as a proposal about what we should
do because, as he or she believes, it is in the public interest.
(Whether this implied or explicit declaration is likely to be either
cogent or sincere in actual legislatures is not now our concern.)
Some of this assurance and reliance is backward-looking, focused on
the process of judgment that leads one person or group to favor one
alternative over another: "I have looked into it." Some of it is pro-
spective, focused on the question of whether the relevant people or
groups will do their parts as required for the plan to work. Both of
these types of assurance and reliance, however, are focused on the
collective action to be taken—the proposal to be enacted—and not
just on the enacting of it. The shifts made in reliance upon others
or in response to others' assurances are shifts in what it is that
individuals think we ought to do. In this way, therefore, the types of
assurance and reliance that arise in political discussion can give rise
to informal but normatively significant agreements about what we
ought to do.

The fourth stage of the democratic process is to move from the
level of informal mutual agreement to an explicit collective decision.
Bratman's notion of shared intentions, which I have been using to
model the mutual agreements that get built in democratic deliberation, leaves out any requirement of explicit acknowledgment of
agreement. This is no accident on his part, as he means to capture
such phenomena as two people wordlessly agreeing to play "horse"
on a basketball court.[39] Thus, what we now need to turn to is the
process by which the agreement becomes explicitly acknowledged.
In a democratic body, this is the process of majority rule. Conso-

nantly with the account I have given of the first stage, that of putting forward proposals, I would describe each individual's vote as an acceptance of the proposal for which he or she votes.[40] This acceptance has two sides to it, corresponding to the two sides of citizenship that Rousseau identified: he or she accepts it as a member of the sovereign body, so that if enough of his or her peers do likewise, the measure will prevail; and he or she also accepts it as a subject, indicating his or her willingness to do his or her part, as defined by the measure, should it prevail.[41]

This process of explicit, joint acknowledgment and endorsement of an agreement via the procedure of majority rule provides all that is needed to yield a proper, partially joint intention as the outcome, and fifth stage, of the democratic process. The application of majority rule formalizes an agreement that has been forged by deliberation. It is an agreement with regard to which all those in the majority are committed to doing their parts, as defined by that agreement. Although these individual intentions were initially conditioned upon enough other people coming to agree, the application of majority rule will satisfy the antecedent in these conditional intentions. Finally, as my fanciful case of academics deciding on a conference made plain, properly applying majority rule depends upon a normative background that places it within something like a constitution and explains how it operates as part of the rule of law. As such, the operation of majority rule implies a public awareness of the commitments of each, as expressed in the vote. For this reason, then, the justified operation of majority rule will also satisfy the mutual knowledge condition of a true, partially joint intention.

## VI Conclusion

In pluralist societies such as the United States, democratic deliberation will not get very far if each citizen refuses to consider revisions in his or her conception of the good. The kind of compromises that the notion of joint intention models well need not induce dramatic shifts in individuals' conceptions of the good. They are certainly unlikely to create the solid ethical substance that a communitarian or a republican might want to have as the normative basis

Henry S. Richardson

of democracy. For one thing, it is far easier to envision reasonable compromise going forward on an issue-by-issue basis than to conceive of two competing world views becoming reconciled en bloc. I do not mean that we should give up on the attempt, urged on us by James Bohman among others, to "fuse the horizons" of disparate creeds. Even doing this, however, had best include a bottom-up, issue-by-issue effort to bring the views into alignment. Thus, whether our ambitions for reconciliation are modest or far-reaching, reasonable compromises along the lines of my arts and health care examples are essential if democratic deliberation is to make any headway at all under conditions of pluralism.

Achieving this kind of progress on a reasonable basis requires three things:

1. Individual citizens must be willing to modify their conceptions of the public good;

2. These modifications must be responsive to reasons offered by others; and

3. Citizens must openly commit themselves to acting on this modified view of the public good.

The first two conditions together make up the individual's willingness to modify his or her view on the basis of public deliberation, while the third spells out that this modification does not simply remain private, but becomes a publicly available basis for political action.

The notion of joint intention that I have put forward in this paper is intended to reflect these three conditions. In section II, I argued that compromise, understood as a willing modification of one aim in response to another, is a notion that is better understood in terms of the categories of will and goodness than in terms of the categories of opinion and correctness. We thus start with individual wills (and conceptions of the good) as the elements that require modification. My aim was to build on this basis toward an analysis of democratic decision that did not leave this basis behind, either as a mere preliminary or as transcended. Bratman's notion of shared intention helped us with the requirements of responsiveness by indicating in a general way how joint action involves a mutual adjustment of which the parties are mutually aware. To indicate how this can give rise to a serious commitment, I showed how this mutual responsiveness, because it consists largely in giving assurances and relying on the assurances given, can create obligations on the part of the participants to follow through. In this way, we show how compromises that arise from reasonable deliberation can lead to a collective commitment that is mutually recognized. We arrive at a joint intention, in Tuomela's sense, which gives explicit public recognition to an agreement to do something together. Within this joint intention, each individual will, as now modified, has its conceptually necessary place.

As I have said, I believe that this joint will is neither exempt from being normatively criticized on the basis of standards external to the democratic process nor impotent as a source of new standards. The joint will of the people has some influence upon what ought to be done, politically, that is not fully explicable on the basis of standards that existed independently of their willing. The joint will of the people, in other words, is normatively fruitful, although not normatively infallible. The notion of joint intention that I have deployed here helps explain how the joint will can be understood in a way that at the same time takes seriously the idea that each individual is a self-originating source of claims. Willing, in general, involves a kind of commitment that links motivation to normative judgment and hence to evaluative standards.[42] This is part of the reason why what one reflectively wills has some influence upon what one ought to do. The structure of joint intention transposes this effect to the level of the citizens without relying upon a fictional "general will" that belongs, potentially, to none of the citizens in particular.

By taking seriously the idea that individuals are self-originating sources of claims in a framework that shows how collective will-formation can be normatively fruitful, this conception of democratic deliberation as directed toward forging joint intentions escapes the apparent dilemma generated by the tension between cognitivism and popular sovereignty. On the one hand, the deliberations that forge joint intentions can be guided throughout by the effort, on the part of every participant, to arrive as near as possible at a reasoned consensus about what ought to be done. The deliberations can be cognitive in orientation throughout. Indeed, response to the arguments of others is a typical aspect of the mutual responsiveness

Henry S. Richardson

needed to assemble joint intentions. Thus, the cognitivist commitment of deliberative democracy is kept intact by this model. On the other hand, as we have seen, the assurance-giving and reliance-inducing features of this mutual responsiveness can shift the normative landscape so as to help determine what ought to be done. This means that individuals' considered practical judgments about what ought to be done have an effect upon what ought to be done. This is to take individual claims seriously indeed. The model reconciles cognitivism and individualized popular sovereignty by recognizing that individual claims have an appropriate place, within a cognitively oriented process of deliberation, in determining what ought to be done. I do not claim that only this model can reconcile this tension. Perhaps any normatively fruitful process of deliberation that took individual claims sufficiently seriously could do so. A model focused on joint intentions does have the distinct advantage that while its result is clearly collective, of conceptual necessity it embraces individual intentions within it, thus taking individual claims seriously in an additional way.

For these reasons, then, I commend to you the notion of joint intention as a way of thinking about the nature of democratic reasoning. If these categories are indeed appropriate, there is much work left to be done. For instance, I have not touched the question of justifying the outcome to those in a minority, nor that of how this works in a representative democracy on a large scale in which groups as well as individuals need to gain a voice. In addition, variants of the notions of joint intention and shared intention other than the precise ones put forward by Tuomela and Bratman ought to be tried out for the context of deliberative democracy. I hope simply to have done enough to suggest why the notion of joint intention is preferable to those of common opinion and of social preference for the purpose of modeling democratic decisions.

## Acknowledgments

Earlier versions of this paper were presented at the Symposium on Philosophy, Logic, and Simulation of Social Action sponsored by the Department of Philosophy of the University of Helsinki in June 1995, and at the Henle Conference on Deliberative Democracy at Saint

Louis University in April 1996. I am grateful for the comments of Raimo Tuomela on the former occasion and Thomas Christiano on the latter. I am also thankful for help received from James Bohman, Wayne Davis, David Estlund, William Rehg, and the members of my seminar on deliberative democracy (Spring 1996, Georgetown University), the Georgetown-Maryland Moral Psychology Group, and the Philamore Moralphil Group. A fellowship from the Alexander von Humboldt Foundation, for which I am most grateful, supported the initial writing of this paper.

**Notes**

1. I here endorse a point that has been developed at length by others. See, e.g, Joshua Cohen, "An Epistemic Conception of Democracy," *Ethics* 97 (October 1986): 26–38; Jürgen Habermas, *Between Facts and Norms,* trans. W. Rehg (Cambridge, MA: MIT Press, 1996); and David Estlund, "Who's Afraid of Deliberative Democracy? On the Strategic/Deliberative Dichotomy in Recent Constitutional Jurisprudence," *Texas Law Review* 71 (1993): 1437–77 and "Beyond Fairness and Deliberation: The Epistemic Dimension of Democratic Authority," this volume. The general view that these authors share—that democratic deliberation has an important epistemic element—is questioned in Jack Knight and James Johnson, "Aggregation and Deliberation: On the Possibility of Democratic Legitimacy," *Political Theory* 22 (1994): 277–296. In *The Rule of the Many* (Boulder, CO: Westview, 1996), Thomas Christiano argues for understanding the value of democratic processes mainly in terms of the equal influence they afford citizens over the outcomes.

2. I take the phrase "self-originating sources of claims" from John Rawls, "Kantian Constructivism in Moral Theory," *Journal of Philosophy* 77 (1980): 515–572, p. 543.

3. See the works by Christiano and by Knight and Johnson mentioned in n. 1, above.

4. I am attracted to the (somewhat differing) views of democratic legitimacy offered by David Estlund and Joshua Cohen in the papers cited in n. 1 and in their papers in this volume. The differences between them seem to arise from Cohen's focusing on the question of what legitimates a political result from the point of view of the holder of some comprehensive conception or other, whereas Estlund focuses on the question of when a result is really, objectively legitimate. I depart from Estlund in shifting from beliefs or opinions to intentions; but since I build in the idea that the intentions are offered with certain characteristic reasons (and hence beliefs) attached, this difference may not be crucial. I find salutary Cohen's focus on the way, under conditions of pluralism, the requirement of treating people as equals constrains the reasons it is appropriate to offer them, but I am doubtful whether one could work out in any further detail the distinction between reasons that others would find "important" or "weighty" if they are reasonable and reasons that would actually persuade them to accept a proposal, all things considered. I offer my working out of individualized popular sovereignty as a complementary route along which the ideal of treating people as equals can get specified within a deliberative conception of democracy.

Henry S. Richardson

5. As will be seen, I do not believe that the notion of a compromise rules out changes of mind that lead the compromising individuals to accept the result as justified. I think of compromise as involving changes of view that respond to others. These changes of view can encompass the ends of the parties to the compromise, leading them to accept the compromise as more than merely instrumentally justified. I elaborate the last point in a paper entitled "Democratic Deliberation about Ends" (in progress).

6. Jürgen Habermas, "Reconciliation Through the Public Use of Reason: Remarks on John Rawls's Political Liberalism," *Journal of Philosophy* 92 (March 1995): 109–131. John Rawls, "Reply to Habermas," *Journal of Philosophy* 92 (March 1995): 132–180.

7. Frank I. Michelman, "Can Constitutional Democrats Be Legal Positivists? or Why Constitutionalism," work in progress; see also his contribution to the present volume.

8. Knight and Johnson, "Aggregation and Deliberation," 278–281.

9. I argue this point in *Practical Reasoning about Final Ends* (Cambridge University Press, 1994), section 22.

10. See, e.g., Bernard Manin, "On Legitimacy and Political Deliberation," *Political Theory* 15 (1987): 338–368, and Cass R. Sunstein, "Preferences and Politics," *Philosophy & Public Affairs* 20 (1991): 3–34.

11. See, e.g., Norman Schofield, "Bargaining Set Theory and Stability in Coalition Governments," *Mathematical Social Sciences* 3 (1982): 9–31.

12. Knight and Johnson, "Aggregation and Deliberation," 286.

13. Habermas, *Between Facts and Norms,* 179.

14. My confidence in this is bolstered by an unpublished paper by Annette Baier.

15. Jürgen Habermas, "Three Normative Models of Democracy," *Constellations* 1 (1994): 1–10.

16. David Estlund, "Making the Truth Safe for Democracy," in David Copp, Jean Hampton, and John E. Roemer, eds., *The Idea of Democracy* (Cambridge University Press, 1993), 71–100; and "Who's Afraid of Deliberative Democracy?"

17. Cf. Estlund, "Who's Afraid of Deliberative Democracy?" and "Beyond Fairness and Deliberation."

18. See especially Estlund's contribution to the present volume. I am stressing the epistemic side of Estlund, rather than the side of his view that accepts the importance of impartial procedures as a working out of political equality. Perhaps my approach here could be taken as suggesting a better way to integrate the two aspects of Estlund's view. Joshua Cohen's views seem to me harder to classify, because of his reference to (at least) two layers of procedure: the hypothetical procedure of the ideal social contract, and the actual procedure of a legislature duly constituted under the principles of justice chosen at the first layer. See his "Deliberation and Democratic Legitimacy," in Alan Hamlin and Philip Pettit, eds., *The Good Polity* (London: Blackwell, 1989), 18–27; and "The Economic Basis of Deliberative Democracy," *Social Philosophy & Policy* 6 (1989): 25–50.

19. See above, n. 1. These points are Estlund's.

20. Jürgen Habermas, *The Theory of Communicative Action,* vol. I, trans. T. McCarthy (Boston: Beacon Press, 1984), 284–287.

21. Habermas, "Three Normative Models of Democracy."

22. Cass Sunstein, "Preferences and Politics," *Philosophy & Public Affairs* 20 (1991): 3–34, and "Incommensurability and Valuation in Law," *Michigan Law Review* 92 (1994), 779–861; Elizabeth Anderson, *Value in Ethics and Economics* (Cambridge, MA: Harvard University Press, 1993). I support their attacks on incommensurability; what I am criticizing is the extent to which their account seems to rely on discovering extant norms.

23. I do not mean to suggest that this would be possible unless there were *some* initial shared conception of the good, at some level of abstraction and vagueness. I believe that even a liberal view must recognize the need for this, as Rawls has. For my views on this, see "The Problem of Liberalism and the Good," in R. B. Douglass et al., eds., *Liberalism and the Good* (New York: Routledge, 1990): 1–28.

24. James F. Bohman's book, *Public Deliberation: Pluralism, Complexity, and Democracy* (Cambridge, MA: MIT Press, 1996) does an admirable job, within the Habermasian tradition, of suggesting how the problems of pluralism might be dealt with by reasonable and inclusive deliberation. What I am suggesting is that a shift of categories, away from the ones Habermas uses, will help us model how this might go.

25. Richardson, *Practical Reasoning about Final Ends,* esp. 297–304.

26. There are many deep issues, here, about the nature of normativity on such a view, and these questions are also related to the debate about whether there are "agent-relative values." Cf. Christine Korsgaard, *The Sources of Normativity* (Cambridge: Cambridge University Press, 1996).

27. This reference to what we "would affirm" points to the possibility that actual deliberation might reach different results than it does or has: it is not referring to a hypothetical standard of (idealized) deliberation.

28. John Rawls, *Theory of Justice* (Cambridge, MA: Harvard University Press, 1971), 201, 362.

29. Cf. my *Practical Reasoning about Final Ends,* 28–31.

30. Iris Marion Young, *Justice and the Politics of Difference* (Princeton, NJ: Princeton University Press, 1990), 183–191; work of hers in progress reinforces the point that representation is indispensable.

31. In *Public Deliberation,* Bohman develops the importance of publicity constraints in a deliberative context.

32. See, e.g., Raimo Tuomela, "We Will Do It: An Analysis of Group-Intentions," *Philosophy and Phenomenological Research* 51 (1991): 249–277; "Cooperation: A Philosophical Study" (unpublished MS, 1995). I am grateful to Professor Tuomela for his willingness to share this work in progress with me.

33. I am indebted to Wayne Davis for raising this issue.

34. Rawls, *Theory of Justice,* 560.

35. Here I oversimplify. The result of a secret ballot does make citizens mutually aware that a majority of them has proposed the winning course. Still, in working toward a joint intention in Tuomela's sense, I am assuming for now that what is required is a mutual awareness of what the intentions of specific people (and groups) are.

36. The assurance possibility is discussed in Michael Bratman, "Shared Intention and Mutual Obligation." *Cahiers d'épistemologie* 177 (Université du Quebec à Montreal, 1993), 16f., with reference to Thomas Scanlon's "Promises and Practices," *Philosophy & Public Affairs* 19 (1990): 199–226. The possibility of supplementing assurance with reliance as an additional element of agreement I draw from contract law. I gloss over some of the interesting complexity of Scanlon's "principle of fidelity," which Bratman discusses more fully. I am not aiming at a descriptively reductive analysis of the origins of a normative claim; rather, I am attempting to describe enough of the normatively relevant features of joint deliberation to allow us to recognize in a rough way—given some general views we share about our obligations—how obligations enter in. If we do so, I shall suggest, we shall see how a mutual responsiveness is essential to the process. I am indebted to Matthias Kettner for discussion of this question.

37. Bratman, "Shared Intention and Mutual Obligation," 16–18.

38. Bratman's use of the formula, "I intend that we J," has been objected to on the grounds that it is ill-formed, since the scope of one's intentions is limited to what one can oneself do. For a full elaboration of this view, see Tuomela, "Cooperation." This may be correct; but if for the purposes of thinking about democratic delibera-tion, at least, we substitute the locution "I propose that we J" for the offending one, then this problem will not arise. My hunch is that the assurance and reliance ac-counts of how agreements give rise to obligation will still go through with this substitution, especially given, as I have argued above, that my proposal that we J normally gives rise to the implication—and would lead a "reasonable person," as a lawyer would say, to infer—that I intend to do my part if my proposal is accepted.

39. Michael Bratman, "Shared Cooperative Activity," *Philosophical Review* 101 (1992): 327–341. While Tuomela has objected that this case rests on the specific conventions of basketball (or of horse), this seems an accidental feature. Wayne Davis has noted (in conversation) that the case of two people of different cultures wordlessly agreeing to have sex is one in which there is clearly no implicit background agreement.

40. Or, to be pedantic, each vote is what would be an acceptance if enough other people vote the same way. The vote is a performative act of communication, as Thomas Christiano notes in "Voting and Democracy," *Canadian Journal of Philosophy* 25 (1995): 395–414; but what is accomplished by it obviously depends upon what other people do.

41. Cf. Rousseau, *The Social Contract,* III.xiii.5.

42. This characterization of willing as forging a link between motivation and norma-tive judgment has both Kantian and Aristotelian manifestations. For the former, cf. Korsgaard, *The Sources of Normativity.* For the latter, cf. my "Desire and the Good in *De Anima,*" in M. Nussbaum and A. O. Rorty, eds., *Essays on Aristotle's* De Anima (Oxford: Oxford University Press, 1992): 381–399, and *Practical Reasoning about Final Ends,* section 7.

# 12

# Difference as a Resource for Democratic Communication

*Iris Marion Young*

Recently, certain liberal and New Left writers have charged the politics of difference with bringing democracy to a new crisis. By a "politics of difference" I mean social movements that make a political claim that groups suffer oppression or disadvantage on account of cultural or structural social positions with which they are associated. To combat dominant stereotypes that construct members of such groups as despised and devalued Others, these movements have expressed uniquely situated understandings of members of society as arising from their group position. The perspectives of privileged and powerful groups tend to dominate public discourse and policy, these movements have asserted, and continue to exclude and marginalize others even when law and public rhetoric state a commitment to equality. The only remedies for these disadvantages and exclusions, according to these movements, require attending to the specific situations of differentiated social groups in politics and policy.

According to the critics, such assertion of group specificity has issued in nothing but confrontation and separation, resulting in the evacuation of the public space of coalition and cooperation. In the words of Todd Gitlin, the politics of difference is "a very bad turn, a detour into quicksand,"[1] and we had better pull ourselves out and get back on the main road of general citizenship and the common good.

Critics such as Gitlin and Jean Elshtain interpret the politics of difference as identity politics. According to these critics, the politics

Iris Marion Young

of difference encourages people to give primary loyalty to identity groups rigidly opposed to one another, instead of committing themselves to a common polity that transcends the groups. People claim a victim status for these identities, and thus claim special rights for themselves without accepting any parallel responsibilities. The politics of difference produces a backlash, when those who previously thought of themselves as just "people" go looking for their group identities and then claim their own special rights. A cacophony of particular claims for recognition and redress soon fills the public sphere, and in disgust people turn away from public exchange and discussion as a means for solving problems cooperatively. So says Jean Elshtain:

> To the extent that citizens begin to retribalize into ethnic or other "fixed identity" groups, democracy falters. Any possibility for human dialogue, for democratic communication and commonality, vanishes as so much froth on the polluted sea of phony equality. Difference becomes more and more exclusivist. If you are black and I am white, by definition I do not and cannot in principle "get it." There is no way that we can negotiate the space between our given differences. We are just stuck with them in what political theorists used to call "ascriptive characteristics"—things we cannot change about ourselves. Mired in the cement of our own identities, we need never deal with one another. Not really. One of us will win and one of us will lose the cultural war or the political struggle. That's what it's all about: power in the most reductive, impositional sort.[2]

Thus these critics also reduce the politics of difference to the most crass form of interest-group politics in which people simply compete to get the most for themselves. This interest-group politics precludes discussion and exchange where people revise their claims in response to criticism and aim to reach a solution acceptable to all. For the critics, the politics of difference understood as identity politics removes both the motivation and the capacity for citizens to talk to one another and solve problems together.

Doubtless feminists, multiculturalists, and activists for gay liberation, indigenous peoples, people of color, migrants, and people with disabilities have sometimes been overly separatist, essentialist, and inward looking in their promotion of group specificity and its political claims. Attributing such excesses to the movements as a whole or to the very logic of their existence, however, and laying in their lap responsibility for an alleged crisis of democracy, in my view, greatly misrepresents their meaning. Regression and repression are the likely outcomes of a political position that dismisses these movements as a gross error, and seeks a renewed commitment to a mythic neutral state, national unity, and the proposition that we are all just human, simply individuals, and that social, cultural and economic differences among us should be ignored in politics.

In this essay I argue against the identification of a politics of difference with a politics of identity. Group differentiation is best understood as a function of structural relations rather than constituted from some common attributes or dispositions of group members. A relational interpretation of difference conceives groups less rigidly and exclusively, as more open and fluid. Individuals are not positioned as social group members because they have common identities or interests, I argue, that distinguish them entirely from others. Instead the social positioning of group differentiation gives to individuals some shared *perspectives* on social life.

The idea that social perspective arises from group differentiation, I argue, contrary to the critics, helps us think of difference as a necessary resource for a discussion-based politics in which participants aim to cooperate, reach understanding, and do justice. Aiming to do justice through democratic public processes, I suggest, entails at least two things. First, democratic discussion and decision making must include all social perspectives. Second, participants in the discussion must develop a more comprehensive and objective account of the social relations, consequences of action, and relative advantage and disadvantage, than each begins with from their partial social perspective. Neither of these conditions can occur without communication across group-differentiated perspectives. Properly understood, then, and under conditions of mutual commitment to public discussion that aims to solve collective problems, expression of and attention to social group differentiation is an important resource for democratic communication.

## I Dilemmas of Difference

Some critics of group differentiated politics write as though racial, ethnic, class, or gender conflict would not exist if it were not for the corresponding movements. Such attitudes reverse the causal story. These movements have arisen in response to experiences of oppression and disadvantage that are attached to group designation. Racist and xenophobic language positions people in groups and subjects them to invidious stereotypes. Racist and xenophobic behavior discriminates against them, treats them with disdain, avoids them, and excludes them from benefits. Culturally imperialist policies or attitudes devalue or refuse to recognize the particular practices of some people, or subject them to unfair social disadvantages because of their particular practices. Sexist assumptions about male proprietary rights over women make us vulnerable to physical, sexual, and psychological abuse and often enough to unwanted pregnancy. So it goes with many other groups of people—poor people, who are treated as lazy and stupid, people with disabilities, whose needs are often ignored and lives stereotypically misrepresented.

People speak and act as though social groups are real; they treat others and themselves as though social group affinity is meaningful. Social group designation and experience is meaningful for the expectations we have of one another, the assumptions we make about one another, and the status we assign to ourselves and others. These social group designations have serious consequences for people's relative privilege or disadvantage. The politics of difference arose from a frustration with exhortations that everyone should just be thought of as a unique individual person, that group ascriptions are arbitrary and accidental, that liberal politics should transcend such petty affiliations and create a public world of equal citizenship where no particularist differences matter to the allocation of benefits and opportunities. Oppressed groups found that this humanist ideology resulted in ignoring rather than transcending the real material consequences of social group difference, often forcing some people to devalue their own particular cultural styles and forms of life because they did not fit the allegedly neutral mainstream. Thus movements affirming group difference called for attending to rather than ignoring the consequences of such difference for issues of freedom and equality. For many, such affirmation also entailed asserting group solidarity and a positive group identity to subvert demeaning stereotypes.

We did not need to wait for recent critics of a politics of difference for its aporiae and dilemmas to surface.[3] Much of the academic and political writing of these movements of the last ten years has explored problems with a politics of difference as the positive assertion of group identity, and has often itself argued against a politics of identity. While most people would agree that categorizations such as *women, Quebecois, African-Americans, old people,* or *Muslims* are meaningful, they founder as soon as they try to define any one of these groups. Most reject an essentialism which would define a group by a particular set of attributes or dispositions that all members share and that constitutes their identity in some respect. The objections to such essentialism are fatal indeed.

Attempts to define the essential attributes of persons belonging to social groups, whether imposed by outsiders or constructed by insiders to the group, fall prey to the problem that there always seem to be persons without the required attributes but whom experience tends to include in the group. The essentialist approach to defining social groups freezes the experienced fluidity of social relations by setting up rigid inside-outside distinctions among groups. If a politics of difference entails such internal unity coupled with external borders to the concept of social group, then its critics are right to claim that such politics divides and fragments people, encouraging conflict and parochialism.

A politics that seeks to form oppositional groups on the basis of a group identity all members share, moreover, must confront the fact that many people deny that group positioning is significant for their identity. Many women, for example, deny reflective awareness of womanly identity as constitutive of their identity, and they deny any particular identification with other women. Many French people deny the existence of a French identity and will claim that being French is nothing particularly important to their personal identities; indeed, many of these would be likely to say that the search for French identity that constitutes the personal identities of individual French men and women is a dangerous form of nationalism. Even when people affirm group affinity as important to their identities, they often chafe at the tendency to enforce norms of behavior or identity that essentialist definitions of the groups entail.

Iris Marion Young

Thirdly, the tendency to conceive group difference as the basis of a common identity, which can assert itself in politics, would seem to imply that group members all have the same interests and agree on the values, strategies and policies that will promote those interests. In fact, however, there is usually wide disagreement among people in a given social group on political ideology. Though members of a group oppressed by gender or racial stereotypes may share interests in the elimination of discrimination and dehumanizing imagery, such a concern is too abstract to constitute a strategic goal. At a more concrete level members of such groups usually express divergent and even contradictory interests.[4]

The most important criticism of the idea of an essential group identity that members share, however, concerns its apparent denial of differentiation within and across groups. Everyone relates to a plurality of social groups; every social group has other social groups cutting across it. The group "men" is differentiated by class, race, religion, age, and so on; the group "Muslim" differentiated by gender, nationality, and so on. If group identity constitutes individual identity, and if individuals can identify with one another by means of group identity, then how do we deal theoretically and practically with the fact of multiple group positioning? Is my individual identity somehow an aggregate of my gender identity, race identity, class identity, like a string of beads, to use Elizabeth Spelman's image?[5] Such an additive image does not match my intuition that my life is of a piece. Spelman, Lugones and others also argue that the attempt to define a common group identity tends to normalize the experience and perspective of some of the group members while marginalizing or silencing that of others.[6]

Many conclude from these arguments and uncomfortable feelings that a discourse of group difference is incoherent and politically dangerous. Groups do not exist; there are only arbitrary categories and strategic performances, fluid and pastiche identities. Or there are only interest groups that form associations to promote certain ends, whether the legalization of same sex marriage, a raise in the minimum wage, or the right to wear a hijab to school. We are just only individuals, after all. This move, however, finds no way of accounting for or perhaps even noticing continuing patterns of privilege, disadvantage and exclusion that structure opportunity and capacity in modern societies. Group difference is a political issue because inequalities that are structured along lines of class, race, gender, physical ability, ethnicity, and relationships can usually be traced between that group specific situation of culture or division of labor and the advantages or disadvantages one has.

This, then, is one form of the dilemma of difference.[7] On the one hand, any attempt to describe just what differentiates a social group from others and to define a common identity of its members tends to normalize some life experiences and sets up group borders that wrongly exclude. On the other hand, to deny a reality to social groupings both devalues processes of cultural and social affinities and makes political actors unable to analyze patterns of oppression, inequality, and exclusion that are nevertheless sources of conflict and claims for redress. In the next section I will argue that the way out of this dilemma is to disengage the social logic of difference from the logic of identity.

## II  Disengaging Difference from Identity

Critics are right to argue against defining groups in terms of essential attributes that all members share. They are wrong, however, to reject conceptualization of group differentiation altogether. Groups should be understood in relational terms rather than as self-identical substantial entities with essential attributes.[8] A social group is a collective of persons differentiated from others by cultural forms, practices, special needs or capacities, structures of power or prestige. Social grouping emerges from the way people encounter one another as different in form of life or association, even if they also regard each other as belonging to the same same society. A group will not regard itself as having a distinct language, for example, unless its members encounter another group whose speech they cannot understand. In a relational conceptualization, what constitutes a social group is not internal to the attributes and self-understanding of its members. Rather, what makes the group a group is the relation in which it stands to others.

For political theory the relations that most matter are structural relations of hierarchy and inequality. Social structures are the relatively permanent constraints and enablements that condition people's actions and possibilities in relation to others and in relation to the natural and built environment. Hierarchical social structures denote differential relations of power, resource allocation, and normative hegemony. Class, gender, and race are some of the most far-reaching and enduring structural relations of hierarchy and inequality in modern societies. Differentiations of class or racism often rely on cultural group differentiation as a mechanism for structuring inequalities of resource allocation, power, or normative hegemony, but such structures cannot be reduced to culture or ethnicity. In some societies, age, caste, or religion also serve as the differentiating factors for structuring social relations of hierarchy and unequal access to resources, power, or prestige. Insofar as structures enable some people to have significant control over the conditions of their lives and those of others, or to develop and exercise their capacities while the same structures inhibit others, leave them less free, or deprive them of what they need, the structures are unjust. Thus groups defined by structural relations of privilege are most important for political theory because they often generate political conflicts and struggles.

So far I have aimed to disengage group difference from identity by suggesting that social groups do not themselves have substantive, unified identities, but rather are constituted through differentiated relations. The other task of this disengagement concerns the relation of individuals to groups. Some critics rightly resist a politics of identity that suggests that personal identity is determined in specific ways by group membership. This interpretation of a politics of identity suggests that members of the "same" group have a common set of group-based dispositions or attributes that constitutes them as individuals. Such a notion of personal identity as constituted by group identity fails both to give sufficient force to individual freedom and to account for the multiplicity of group affiliations that intersect with people's lives. From these failings it does not follow, however, that groups are fictions, or have no significant relation to individual possibilities.

It has been important for oppositional movements of subordinate social groups to reclaim and revalue the activities, cultural styles, and modes of affiliation associated with their social-group positions in order to subvert devaluation and negative stereotyping in dominant culture. This subversion has often encouraged cultivation of group solidarity by asserting a group identity. When the assertion of group identity is a self-conscious project of cultural creation and resistance, it can be positive and empowering, even though it corresponds to no pre-established group essence and inevitably involves only some of those associated with the group more than others. Too often, however, this political use of group identity does indeed speak as though it represents a given group identity that all associated with the group do or ought to share. The relation of individual identities to social groups, however, is more indirect than this conceptualization allows. Social groups do indeed position individuals, but a person's identity is her own, formed in active relation to that social positioning, among other things, rather than constituted by it. Individual subjects make their own identities, but not under conditions they choose.

Pierre Bourdieu theorizes the social world as a set of fields each of which is constituted by structural relations of power, resource allocation, or prestige.[9] Particular social agents can be understood in terms of their relative positions in these fields. While no individual is in exactly the same position as any other, agents are "closer" or "farther" from one another in their location with respect to the structural relations that define the field. Agents who are similarly positioned experience similar constraints or enablements as produced by the structural organization of power, resource allocation, or normative hegemony. On this view, social groups are collections of persons similarly situated in social fields structured by power and resources, but this says nothing about their particular identity as persons.

The idea that language and social processes position individual subjects in structured social fields makes this positioning process prior to individual subjectivity, both ontologically and historically.[10] Persons are thrown into a world with a given history of sedimented meanings and material landscape, and interaction with others in the social field locates us in terms of the given meanings, expected activities, and rules.[11] We find ourselves positioned, thrown, into the structured field of class, gender, race, nationality, religion, and so on, and in our daily lives we have no choice but to deal with this situation.

In an earlier essay I suggested that Sartre's concept of "seriality" can be useful for theorizing this structural positioning that conditions the possibility of social agents without constituting their identities. In Sartre's theory, to be working class (or capitalist class) is to be part of a series that is passively constituted by the material organization of labor ownership, and the power of capital in relation to labor. In the earlier essay I suggest that being a woman does not itself imply sharing social attributes and identity with all those others called "women." Instead, "women" is the name of a series in which some individuals find themselves by virtue of norms of enforced heterosexuality and the sexual division of labor.[12]

Social processes and interactions position individual subjects in prior structures, and this positioning conditions who one is. But positioning neither determines nor defines individual identity. Individuals are agents: we constitute our own identities, and each person's identity is unique. We do not choose the conditions under which we form our identities, and we have no choice but to becomes ourselves under the conditions that position us in determinate relation to others. We act in situation, in relation to the structural conditions and their interaction into which we are thrown. Individuals can and do respond to and take up their positioning in many possible ways, however, and these actions-in-situation constitute individual identity.[13] Gloria Anzaldua expresses this active appropriation of one's own multiple group positionalities as a process of "making faces."[14] We are unique individuals, with our own identities created from the way we have taken up the histories, cultural constructs, language, and social relations of hierarchy and subordination, that condition our lives.

The gendered position of women, for example, continues to put greater obstacles in the way of girls achieving recognition for technical intelligence than boys experience. One girl may react to these obstacles by internalizing a sense of incapacity, while another may take them as a challenge to overcome, and each of these reactions will differently contribute to a girl's identity. Different people may experience and act in relation to similar positional intersections in different ways.

Complex societies position individuals in multiple ways, insofar as there exist multiple structures of privilege and subordination in respect to power, resource allocation, and normative hegemony. Which structures and positions intersect in an individual's life, and how they do so, conditions her particular situation. Kimberle Crenshaw theorizes this concept of the "intersectionality" of positioning for Black women. Being located in a position where racist and sexist structures meet, she suggests, sometimes produces constraints, dilemmas, tensions, and indeed possibilities that are specific to that intersecting position, and cannot be understood simply as summing up the experiences of being female and white and and being black and male.[15] Other intersectionalities—say, of being upper class, female, and old—produce other specific conditions of structural reinforcement or weakening of privilege. This concept of intersectionality retains a generality to each social-group position without requiring a merely additive approach to the fact that individuals are multiply positioned. Each person's identity is a product of how he or she deals with his or her intersecting social positions.

Disengaging group difference from identity thus addresses many of the problems of more essentialist understandings of social group I discussed above. For many, certain social group positionings are important to their identities, and they find strong affinity with others on the basis of these relationally constituted groups. Doing so, however, is an active project of the person and does not arise from essential group attributes. The disengagement of difference from identity also addresses the "pop-bead" problem. Since groups do not themselves constitute individual identities there is no problem of how to conceive of myself as a combination of several group identities. I have only my own identity, fashioned in relation to my multiple group positionings.

### III  Social Perspective

Because they assume that giving importance to social group differentiation entails that fixed group identities make the groups entirely separate and opposed, critics claim that a politics of difference produces only division. I have argued, however, that group differentiation should be understood with a more relational logic that does not entail substantive and mutually exclusive group identities. The primary resource that structural positioning offers to democratic communication, I shall now argue, is not a self-regarding identity or interest, but rather a perspective on the structures, relations, and events of the society.

The idea of social perspective presumes that differentiated groups dwell together within social processes with history, present arrangement, and future trajectories larger than all of them, which are constituted by their interactions. Each differentiated group position has a particular experience of a point of view on those social processes precisely because each is a part of and has helped produce the patterned processes. Especially insofar as people are situated on different sides of relations of structural inequality, they have differing understandings of those relations and their consequences.

Following the logic of the metaphor of group differentiation as arising from differing positions in social fields, the idea of social perspective suggests that agents who are "close" in the social field have a similar point of view on the field and the occurrences within it, while those who are socially distant see things differently. Though different, these social perspectives may not be incompatible. Each social perspective is particular and partial with respect to the whole social field, and from each perspective some aspects of the reality of social processes are more visible than others.

Each social group perspective offers what Donna Haraway calls a "situated knowledge." Individuals in each social location experience one another, their group relations and events, and the institutions in which they move in particular ways; their cultural and material resources afford them differing assumptions from which to process their experiences or different terms in which to articulate them. Among the sorts of situated knowledge people in each social location have are: (i) an understanding of their position, and how it stands in relation to other positions; (ii) a social map of other salient positions, how they are defined, and the relation in which they stand to their position; (iii) a point of view on the history of the society; (iv) an interpretation of how the relations and processes of the whole society operate, especially as they impact on their own position; and (v) a position-specific experience and point of view on the natural and physical environment. A social perspective is a certain way of being sensitive to particular aspects of social life, meanings, and interactions, and perhaps less sensitive to others. It is a form of attentiveness that brings some things into view while possibly obscuring others. The insights each perspective carries are partial with respect to the whole society.

Thus a social perspective does not contain a determinate, specific content. In this respect perspective is different from interest or opinion. Social perspective consists in a set of questions, kinds of experiences, and assumptions with which reasoning begins, rather than the conclusions drawn. Critiques of essentialism rightly show that those said to belong to the same social group often have different and even conflicting interests and opinions. People who have a similar perspective on social processes and issues—on the norms of heterosexual interaction, for example—nevertheless often have different interests or opinions, because they reason differently from what they experience or have different goals and projects. When Senator Robert Packwood was accused of sexual harassment, for example, nearly all the women in the U.S. Congress stood together to say that this was a serious issue while many men were inclined to remain silent or even joke. The women legislators did not agree on political values or even on what course should be pursued in the Packwood case, but they nevertheless expressed a similar perspective on the meaning and gravity of the accusations.

Perspective is a way of looking at social processes without determining what one sees. Thus two people may share a social perspective and still experience their positionality differently because they are attending to different elements of the society. As sharing a perspective, however, each is likely to have an affinity with the other's way of describing what he experiences, an affinity that those differently situated do not experience. This lesser affinity does not imply that those differently positioned cannot understand the description of an element of social reality from another social perspective, only that it takes more work to understand the expression of different social perspectives than those they share.[16]

Social perspective as the point of view group members have on certain aspects of social processes because of their position in them may be more or less self-conscious, both between different individuals associated within a group and between groups. The cultural expressions of ethnic, national, or religious groups, as well as groups responding to a history of grievance or structural oppression, often offer refined interpretations of the group's situation and its relations to others. Perspective may appear in story and song, humor and word play, as well as in more assertive and analytical forms of expression.

As Linda Alcoff suggests, Paul Gilroy offers an extended example of group differentiation as providing social perspective in his book *The Black Atlantic.*[17] Gilroy accepts anti-essentialist critiques and thus denies that blacks of the diaspora are a homogenous group. He also confronts tendencies to treat social groups as unified ethnic or national groups. But he strongly rejects the suggestion that social groups are fictions. Instead, he aims to conceptualize the black experience as a particular structural location within modern history, a location initially constituted by the enslavement of Africans and their transportation across and around the Atlantic. The facts of slavery and exile produce specific experiences whose traces remain in cultural and political expression even into the present, according to Gilroy. They give black Europeans, Americans, and many Africans a distinct perspective on the events and ideas of modernity: "The distinctive historical experiences of this diaspora's populations have created a unique body of reflections on modernity and its discontents which is an enduring presence in the cultural and political struggles of their descendants today." (p. 45)

Gilroy argues that black experience and social location produce a black perspective on modernity. As with the concept of perspective I have developed here, this does not mean a fixed and self-identical set of beliefs shared by group members, but rather an orientation on the ideas and events of modern Western history.

Blacks in the west eavesdropped on and then took over a fundamental question from the intellectual obsessions of their enlightened rulers. Their progress from the status of slaves to the status of citizens led them to enquire into what the best possible forms of social and political existence might be. The memory of slavery, actively preserved as a living intellectual resource in their expressive political culture, helped them to generate a new set of answers to this inquiry. They had to fight—often through their spirituality— to hold on to the unity of ethics and politics sundered from each other by modernity's insistence that the true, the good, and the beautiful had distinct origins and belong to different domains of knowledge. . . . Their subculture often appears to be the intuitive expression of some racial essence but is in fact an elementary historical acquisition produced from the viscera of an alternative body of cultural and political expression that considers the world critically from the point of view of its emancipatory transformation. (p. 39)

Far from thinking of this black Atlantic perspective as homogeneous, self-identical and self-enclosed, Gilroy specifically articulates it as hybrid, in the sense that it consists of multiple political and cultural expressions both differentiated from and influencing one another, and influenced by their internal relation to and differentiation from white bourgeois, democratic, and imperialist culture and politics. Black intellectuals are a product of Enlightenment ideas, but they query them in specific ways. Black social movement activists are cultural hybrids of African cultural experience and the experience of racial subordination with European dominated culture and institutions which also form their experience and identities. Black diasporatic music, literature, and political rhetoric have traveled back and forth and up and down the Atlantic since the eighteenth century, proliferating hybrid differentiations. One of the purposes for theorizing a black Atlantic perspective, however, is to increase understanding of modern Western history generally, and not simply of the experience of the black diaspora.

Suppose we accept this claim that individuals positioned in similar ways in the social field have a similar group perspective on that society. What does this imply for individuals who are positioned in terms of many group-differentiated relations? Since individuals are multiply positioned in complexly structured societies, they interpret the society from a multiplicity of social group perspectives. Some of these may intersect to constitute a distinctive hybrid perspective, a black woman's perspective, perhaps, or a working class youth perspective. But individuals may also move around the social perspectives available to them depending on the people with whom they interact or the aspect of social reality to which they attend. The multiple perspectives from which persons may see society given their social-group positioning may reinforce and enhance one another, or it may be impossible to take one without obscuring another, as in a duck-rabbit figure. The perspectives available to a person may be incommensurable, producing ambiguity or confusion in the person's experience and understanding of social life; or their multiplicity may help the person form a composite picture of social processes. However experienced, the availability of multiple perspectives provides everyone with the resources to take a distance on any one of them, and to communicate in one way with people with whom one does not share perspectives. Thus understanding what is shared by members of a social group as perspective rather than identity diffuses a tendency to interpret groups as fixed, closed, and bounded.

## V  Group Difference as a Deliberative Resource

Critics of the politics of difference assume that the expression of group specificity in public life is necessarily and only the expression of a narrow and rigidly defined group interest, set against the interests of other groups in a win-lose relation. This inward-looking pressing of interests, according to them, is precisely why the politics of difference makes democracy or coalition unworkable. In contrast to this image of politics as war by other means, critics wish to promote a neo-republican image of politics as civic deliberation, oriented toward a common good in which participants transcend their particularist interests and commitments.

Thus Jean Elshtain conceptualizes genuine democratic process as one in which participants assume a public mantle of citizenship, which cloaks the private and partial concerns of local culture and familiar interaction. She is not alone among democratic theorists in setting up an opposition between the partial and differentiated, on the one hand, and the impartial and unitary, on the other. Either politics is nothing but competition among private interests, in which case there is no public spirit; or politics is a commitment to equal respect for other citizens in a civil public discussion that puts aside private affiliation and interest to seek the common good.

When confronted so starkly with an opposition between difference and civility, most must opt for civility. But a conception of deliberative politics that insists that equal respect in public discussion requires putting aside or transcending partial and particularist

Difference as a Resource for Democratic Communication

differences forgets or denies the lesson that the politics of difference claims to teach. Where there are real group-based positional differences that give to some people greater power, material and cultural resources, and authoritative voice, social norms that appear impartial are often biased. Under circumstances of social and economic inequality among groups, the definition of the common good often devalues or excludes some of the legitimate frameworks of thinking, interests, and priorities in the polity. A common consequence of social privilege is the ability of a group to convert its perspective on some issues into authoritative knowledge without being challenged by those who have reason to see things differently. As long as such unequal circumstances persist, a politics that aims to do justice through public discussion and decision making must theorize and aim to practice a third alternative to both a private interest competition and one that denies the reality of difference in public discussions of the common good. This third way consists in a process of public discussion and decision making that includes and affirms all particular social group perspectives in the society and draws on their situated knowledge as a resource for enlarging the understanding of everyone and moving them beyond their own parochial interests.[18] In this section I articulate this alternative meaning of politics as public discussion and decision making and argue that the particular social perspectives groups bring to the public are a necessary resource for making the wisest and most just decisions.

Gitlin mocks the perspectivism he sees to be typical of postmodernism. He interprets an account of social difference as positionality with perspective as a form of crass relativism and subjectivism:

How you see is a function of who you are—that is, where you stand or, in clunkier language, your "subject position," the two nouns constituting an unacknowledged gesture toward an objective grid that prescribes where you stand whether or not you know it. (p. 201)

Perspective may lead to falsity or to truth, may be conducive to some truths and not to others. Perspective may be conducive to accurate observations or distorted inferences, may lead to promising notions or idiotic ideas—but to elevate the observations, inferences, or ideas, we need to do more than inquire into their origins. . . . To know whether the science is good or bad requires a perspective different from all other perspectives: a commitment to truth-seeking above all else. (p. 205)

Iris Marion Young

This interpretation of a theory of social perspective as relativist begs the question. For just what is truth in social knowledge, what is the truth about social justice, and how do we achieve them? Gitlin correctly suggests that perspectives can only be starting points and not conclusions, and that by itself no perspective is "objective." Political discussion and debate can sort out the more from the less true, the better from the worse political judgments, however, only by encouraging the expression of all the particular social groups perspectives relevant and salient to an issue. This is the argument I shall now make.

With the neo-republican position, I assume that the democratic process ought not properly to be an adversarial process of competition among self-regarding interests, in which each seeks only to get the most for himself, whatever the costs to others. Instead, democracy should be conceived and as far as possible institutionalized as a process of discussion, debate, and criticism that aims to solve collective problems. Political actors should promote their own interests in such a process, but must also be answerable to others to justify their proposals. This means that actors must be prepared to take the interests of others into account. With theorists of deliberative democracy, I define the democratic process as a form of practical reason for conflict resolution and collective problem solving. So defined, democratic process entails that participants have a commitment to cooperation and to looking for the most just solution. These conditions of openness are much weaker, I believe, than what many thinkers mean by seeking a common good or a common interest.

If we understand democracy as a process of practical reason, then democracy has an epistemic as well as a normative meaning. Democracy is not only a process where citizens aim to promote their interests knowing that others are doing the same, though it is that. It is also a method for determining the best and most just solution to conflicts and other collective problems. Though there is not necessarily only one right answer to political problems, some proposals and policies are more just and wise than others, and the democratic task is to identify and implement the best solutions. Ideally, this epistemic function of democracy requires a political equality that includes the expression of all perspectives equally and neutralizes the ability of powerful interests to distort discussion with threats or coercion.[19] Especially in the absence of such ideal conditions, acquiring the social knowledge needed to formulate the best solutions to conflict and collective problems requires learning from the social perspectives of people positioned differently in structures of power, resource allocation, or normative hegemony.

Elshtain correctly evokes a special status for democratic publicity. She rightly claims that workable democratic politics entails that people look beyond their own parochial and private concerns. She is wrong, however, to suggest that adopting a public-spirited stance entails leaving particular group interests and perspectives behind. On the contrary, decision making takes place under conditions of publicity only if it explicitly includes critical dialogue among the plurality of socially differentiated perspectives present in the social field. For this understanding of publicity as entailing group-differentiated social perspective I rely on recent interpretations of Hannah Arendt's idea of the public.

For Arendt, the defining characteristic of a public is plurality. The public consists of multiple histories and perspectives relatively unfamiliar to one another, distant yet connected and irreducible to one another. A conception of publicity that requires its members to put aside their differences in order to uncover their common good destroys the very meaning of publicity because it aims to turn the many into one. In the words of commentator Lisa Disch,

The definitive quality of the public space is particularity: that the plurality of perspectives that constitute it is irreducible to a single common denominator. A claim to decisive authority reduces those perspectives to a single one, effectively discrediting the claims of other political actors and closing off public discussion. Meaning is not inherent in an action, but public, which is to say, constituted by the interpretive context among the plurality of perspectives in the public realm that confer plurality on action and thereby make it real.[20]

The public is not a comfortable place of conversation among those who share language, assumptions, and ways of looking at issues. Arendt conceives the public as a place of *appearance* where actors stand before others and are subject to mutual scrutiny and judgment from a plurality of perspectives. The public is open in the sense of being both exposed and inclusive; a genuinely public discussion is in principle open to anyone.

If differently positioned citizens engage in public discussion with the aim of solving problems with a spirit of openness and mutual accountability, then these conditions are sufficient for transformative deliberation. They need not be committed to a common interest or a common good; indeed, their stance of openness and mutual accountability requires them to attend to their particular differences in order to understand the situation and perspective of others. They share problems to be solved, to be sure; otherwise they would have no need for discussion. It does not follow, however, that they share a good or an interest beyond that.

Public critical discussion that includes the expression of and exchange between all relevant differentiated social perspectives transforms the partial and parochial interests and ideas of each into more reflective and objective judgment. By "objective" I do not mean a neutral point of view outside of and transcending those particular social perspectives. I mean only the contrary of subjective, that is, a reflective stance and substantive understanding that is not merely self-regarding. Judgment is objective in this sense when it situates one's own particular perspectives in a wider context that takes other perspectives into account as well. Objectivity in this sense means only that judgment has taken account of the experience, knowledge, and interests of others. Such objectivity is possible only if those particular perspectives are expressed publicly to everyone.[21]

If citizens participate in public discussion that includes all social perspectives in their partiality and gives them a hearing, they are most likely to arrive at just and wise solutions to their shared problems. Group difference is a necessary resource for making more just and wise decisions by means of democratic discussion due to at least three functions dialogue across such difference serves.

1. Plurality of perspectives motivates claimants to express their proposals as appeals to justice rather than expressions of mere self-interest or preference. Proposals for collective policies need not be expressed in terms of common interest, an interest all can share. Especially where there are structural injustices—and these are everywhere today—at least some claims that correctly appeal to justice are

likely not to express a common interest. Even without rectifying injustices, just solutions to many political problems can entail obligations on the part of the public to recognize and provide for some unique needs of uniquely situated persons. The presence of a plurality of social perspectives in public discussion helps frame the discourse in terms of legitimate claims of justice. Because others are not likely to accept "I want this" or "this policy is in my interest" as good reasons for them to accept a proposal, the need to be accountable to others with different perspectives on collective problems motivates participants in a discussion to frame their proposals in terms of justice.

2. Confrontation with different perspectives, interests, and cultural meanings teaches individuals the partiality of their own, and reveals to them their own experience as perspectival. Listening to those differently situated than myself and my close associates teaches me how my situation looks to them, what relation they think I stand to them. Such a contextualizing of perspective is especially important for groups that have power, authority, or privilege. Too often those in structurally superior positions take their experience, preferences, and opinions to be general, uncontroversial, ordinary and even an expression of suffering or disadvantage. Having to answer to others who speak from a different, less privileged perspective on their social relations exposes their partiality and relative blindness. Where such exposure does not lead them to shut down dialogue and attempt to force their preferences on policy, it can lead to a better understanding of the requirements of justice. Nor does the perspective of those less socially privileged carry unquestionable "epistemic privilege." They also may need the perspectives of others to understand the social causes of their disadvantage or to realize that they lay blame in the wrong place.

3. Expressing, questioning, and challenging differently situated knowledge adds to social knowledge. While not abandoning their own perspectives, people who listen across differences come to understand something about the ways that proposals and policies affect others differently situated. They gain knowledge of what is going on in different social locations and how social processes appear to connect and conflict from different points of view. By internalizing

Iris Marion Young

such a mediated understanding, participants in democratic discussion and decision making gain a wider picture of the social processes in which their own partial experience is embedded. Such a more comprehensive social knowledge better enables them to arrive at wise solutions to collective problems to the extent that they are committed to doing so.

This account of democratic communication, which uses the differences in group perspectives as a resource for enlarging the understanding of everyone to take account of the perspectives of others, is of course an ideal. This ideal extrapolates from real elements and tendencies in public communication across differences present within the unjust and power-oriented politics we usually experience. This ideal can serve at least three functions: to justify a principle of the inclusion of specific group perspectives in discussion; to serve as a standard against which the inclusiveness of actual public communication can be measured; and to motivate action to bring real politics more into line with the ideal.

## Acknowledgment

I am grateful to Linda Alcoff, David Alexander, Bill Rehg, and Steve Seidman for comments on earlier versions of this paper.

## Notes

1. Todd Gitlin, *Twilight of Common Dreams* (New York: Henry Holt, 1995), p. 36.

2. Jean Elshtain, *Democracy on Trial* (New York: Basic Books, 1995), p. 74.

3. For some examples of critiques of essentialism and a politics of identity from within theories and movements that support a politics of difference, see Elizabeth V. Spelman, *Inessential Woman* (Boston: Beacon Press, 1988); Anna Yeatman, "Minorities and the Politics of Difference," in *Postmodern Revisionings of the Political* (New York: Routledge, 1994); Michael Dyson, "Essentialism and the Complexities of Racial Identity," in David Theo Goldberg, ed., *Multiculturalism* (Cambridge: Blackwell, 1994), pp. 218–229.

4. Compare Anne Phillips, *The Politics of Presence* (Oxford: Oxford University Press, 1995).

5. Spelman, *Inessential Woman*, pp. 15; 136.

6. Ibid.; Maria Lugones, "Parity, Imparity, and Separation: Forum," *Signs* (14), 458–477.

7. See Martha Minow, *Making All the Difference* (Ithaca: Cornell University Press, 1990), chapter 1, for the phrase "dilemma of difference," and for some formulations of the dilemma.

8. Martha Minow proposes a relational understanding of group difference in *Making All the Difference*, especially in part II; I have introduced a relational analysis of group difference in *Justice and the Politics of Difference* (Princeton: Princeton University Press, 1990), chapter 2; in the earlier formulation, however, I do not distinguish group affiliation from personal identity as strongly as I do in this essay.

9. Pierre Bourdieu, "Social Space and the Genesis of Groups," *Theory and Society*, 14 (1985), 723–744.

10. See Rosalind Coward and John Ellis, *Language and Materialism* (London: Routledge and Kegan Paul, 1977), pp. 49–60. See also Diana Fuss, *Essentially Speaking: Feminism, Nature and Difference* (New York: Routledge, 1989); Bill Martin, *Matrix and Line* (Albany: SUNY Press, 1993).

11. I refer here to Heidegger's concept of "thrownness," as the existential condition of not being one's own origin, of the facticity of history. See *Being and Time* (New York: Harper & Row, 1965), division one, chapter V. I have developed a more extended discussion of being "thrown" into group membership in *Justice and the Politics of Difference*, p. 46.

12. Young, "Gender as Seriality: Thinking about Women as a Social Collective," *Signs: Journal of Women in Culture and Society*, vol. 19, no. 3, 1994, pp. 713–738.

13. I mean here to evoke Sartre's concepts of facticity and situation. In Sartre's early existentialism, agents are always free insofar as they choose to make of themselves what they are, but they always must do so within an unchosen historical and social situation.

14. Gloria Anzaldua, "Haciendo Caras, una entrada/an Introduction," in *Making Face, Making South/Haciendo Caras*, ed., Gloria Anzaldua (San Francisco: Aunt Lute Foundation, 1990).

15. Kimberle Crenshaw, "Mapping the Margins: Intersectionality, Identity Politics, and Violence Against Women of Color," *Stanford Law Review*, vol. 43 (July 1991), pp. 1241–1299.

16. I develop this point more in my essay, "Asymmetrical Reciprocity: On Moral Respect, Wonder, and Enlarged Thought," *Constellations*, 3 (1997), 340–363.

17. See Linda Alcoff, "Philosophy and Racial Identity," *Radical Philosophy*, 75 (January–February 1996), pp. 5–14; Paul Gilroy, *The Black Atlantic* (Cambridge: Harvard University Press, 1993).

18. James Bohman develops a version of this third alternative between the parochial and the unitary in *Public Deliberation: Pluralism, Complexity, and Democracy* (Cambridge, MA: MIT Press, 1996), especially in chapters 2 and 3.

19. For statements of this epistemic function of democracy, see Hilary Putnam, "A Reconsideration of Deweyan Democracy," *Southern California Law Review*, vol. 63, no. 6, Sept. 1990, pp. 1671–1697; Joshua Cohen, "An Epistemic Conception of Democracy," *Ethics*, 97 (October 1986), pp. 26–38; David Estlund, "Making Truth Safe for Democracy," in Coop, Hampton, Roemer, eds., *The Idea of Democracy* (Cambridge: Cambridge University Press, 1993); and Estlund, "Beyond Fairness and Deliberation: The Epistemic Dimension of Democratic Authority," this volume.

20. Lisa Disch, *Hannah Arendt and the Limits of Philosophy* (Ithaca: Cornell University Press, 1994), p. 80.

21. For such a meaning of objectivity I draw on feminist epistemologies. See, for example, Sandra Harding's notion of "strong objectivity," which relies on oppositional theories produced from the perspective of historically marginalized groups to produce objectivity in science, especially social science, in *Whose Science? Whose Knowledge? Thinking from Women's Lives* (Ithaca: Cornell University Press, 1991). See also Ismay Barwell, "Towards a Defence of Objectivity," in Kathleen Lennon and Margaret Whitford, eds., *Knowing the Difference: Feminist Perspectives in Epistemology* (London: Routledge, 1994), pp. 79–94.

# 13

## Procedure and Substance in Deliberative Democracy

*Joshua Cohen*

### Substance, Procedure, and Pluralism

The fundamental idea of democratic legitimacy is that the authorization to exercise state power must arise from the collective decisions of the members of a society who are governed by that power.[1] More precisely—and stated with attention to democracy's institutional character—it arises from the discussions and decisions of members, as made within and expressed through social and political institutions designed to acknowledge their collective authority. That is an abstract statement of the concept of democracy, and deliberately so. Democracy comes in many forms, and more determinate conceptions of it depend on an account of membership in the people and, correspondingly, what it takes for a decision to be *collective*—made by citizens "as a body."

Take a political community in which adherence to a comprehensive moral or religious doctrine,[2] perhaps rooted in national tradition, is a condition of full membership. Authorization, then, will require congruence with that view, and only decisions exhibiting such congruence can properly be deemed "collective." For that reason, the test for democratic legitimacy will be, in part, substantive—dependent on the content of outcomes, not simply on the processes through which they are reached.

What happens, though, when the idea of collective authorization is set against a different background: where there is no shared comprehensive moral or religious view, members are understood as free and equal, and the national project, such as it is, embraces a commitment to expressing that freedom and equality in the design of institutions and collective choices?[3] Does this shift in background drive us to an entirely procedural view of democracy and collective decision? I think not. But before explaining why, I want to say something about the interest of the question, and the terms in which it is stated.

My question about the effects of a shift in background is prompted by the aim of formulating a conception of democracy suited to the kind of human difference captured in the "fact of reasonable pluralism"[4]—the fact that there are distinct, incompatible understandings of value, each one reasonable, to which people are drawn under favorable conditions for the exercise of their practical reason. The good-faith exercise of practical reason, by people who are reasonable in being concerned to live with others on terms that those others can accept, does not lead to convergence on one particular philosophy of life.

The claim about reasonable pluralism is suggested by persistent disagreement about, for example, the values of choice and self-determination, happiness and welfare, and self-actualization; disputes about the relative merits of contemplative and practical lives and the importance of personal and political engagement; and disagreements about the religious and philosophical backgrounds of these evaluative views. Apart from the sheer fact of disagreement, there is, moreover, no apparent tendency to convergence generated by the exercise of practical reason; furthermore, we have no *theory* of the operations of practical reason that would lead us to predict convergence on comprehensive moralities, nor can I think of any marginally attractive social or political mechanisms that might generate such agreement.

This fact of reasonable pluralism gives shape to the conception of citizens as free and equal that constitutes part of the conception of democracy I want to explore here. To say that citizens are free is to say, inter alia, that no comprehensive moral or religious view provides a defining condition of membership or the foundation of the authorization to exercise political power. To say that they are equal is to say that each is recognized as having the capacities required for participating in discussion aimed at authorizing the exercise of power.

What, then, are the implications of reasonable pluralism for a conception of democracy? It is natural to suppose that by excluding a comprehensive consensus on values the fact of reasonable pluralism leads to a procedural conception of democracy. According to such a conception, the democratic pedigree that lies at the source of legitimacy can be settled by looking exclusively to the processes through which collective decisions are made and to values associated with fair processes: for example, values of openness, equal chances to present alternatives, and full and impartial consideration of those alternatives. The fact of reasonable pluralism appears to require a procedural conception because it deprives us of a background of shared moral or religious premises that could give determinate content to the idea of popular authorization or constrain the substance of genuinely collective choices. Without that background, we are left, it may seem, with no basis for agreement on anything more than fair procedures—and perhaps not even that.

I think this conclusion is not right, and I will sketch a view that combines an assumption of reasonable pluralism with a more substantive conception of democracy. Moreover, I will argue that this combination is a natural result of a particular way of thinking about democracy—a "deliberative" understanding of the collective decisions that constitute democratic governance. Before discussing the deliberative conception, though, I need first to fix the concerns about procedure and substance more precisely, distinguish a deliberative from an aggregative conception of democracy, and show how aggregative conceptions lead to proceduralism.

## Liberties, Ancient and Modern

Consider a familiar dilemma associated with the idea of tracing legitimacy to popular authorization.[5] On the one hand, democracy may seem too much a matter of procedure to provide a basis for an account of legitimacy; some democratic collective choices are too execrable to be legitimate, however attractive the procedures that generate them. On the other hand, the idea of democracy appears to exclude any competing basis of legitimacy. Democracy appears to be the form of collective choice mandated by the fundamental idea that citizens are to be treated as equals. So democracy is commonly thought to be the way we must decide how other political values are to be ordered, not simply one political value to be combined with others.

This dilemma is familiar from discussions of democracy and the "liberties of the moderns"—religious liberty, liberty of conscience more generally, liberty of thought and expression, and rights of person and personal property. Lacking any evident connection to conditions of democratic procedure, such liberties are commonly understood as constraints on democratic process. Not so with political liberties. A constitution disabling government from restricting political participation or regulating the content of political speech can be interpreted as safeguarding, rather than constraining, democratic process. Assurances of such political liberties help to preserve the connection between popular authorization and political outcome—to preserve the continuing authority of the people, and not simply the majority of them.[6] These liberties—the liberties of the ancients—are constitutive elements of democratic process.

Things are different when it comes to abridgments of religious liberty, or restrictions on expression whose content can be construed as political only on a uselessly capacious construal of "political." In these cases, disabling provisions in a constitution appear simply to limit democracy, not to be among its preconditions, either implicit or explicit.

The liberties of the moderns appear, then, to be founded on values entirely independent from the values of democracy. And that appearance may prompt one of two undesirable conclusions. The first is that the political liberties are merely instrumental, of value just insofar as they protect the liberties of the moderns; when they fail to ensure such protection, an authority external to the people ought to do so. Here, a conflict between democracy and other political values is easily translated into a conflict between democratic and nondemocratic procedures of political decision making.[7]

A second view holds that the liberties of the moderns have no standing deeper than contingent popular consensus. Although abridgments of nonpolitical liberties that emerge from a fair democratic process may be unjust, then, they face no problems of democratic legitimacy.[8]

We are pushed into this dilemma by a particular understanding of democracy, which I will call "aggregative"—as distinct from deliberative.[9] According to an aggregative conception, democracy institutionalizes a principle requiring equal consideration for the interests of each member; or, more precisely, equal consideration along with a "presumption of personal autonomy"—the understanding that adult members are the best judges and most vigilant defenders of their own interests.[10] To criticize processes as undemocratic, then, is to claim that those processes failed to give equal consideration to the interests of each member. The natural method for giving such consideration is to establish a scheme of collective choice—majority or plurality rule, or group bargaining—that gives equal weight to the interests of citizens in part by enabling them to present and advance their interests. And that requires a framework of rights of participation, association, and expression.

Arguably, the aggregative view can be extended beyond such straightforwardly procedural rights to some concerns about outcomes. For it might be said that collective choices that depend on discriminatory views—on hostility or stereotyping—do not give equal weight to the interests of each who is governed by them. And when we face outcomes that disadvantage people who are the likely targets of such views, we have strong evidence of a failure of the process to give equal consideration to the interests of each.[11]

This procedural reinterpretation of important political values can, however, go only so far. Religious liberty, for example, has no apparent procedural basis. To be sure, abridgments of freedom of worship are sometimes troubling because they result from discriminatory (anti-Catholic, anti-Semitic) attitudes. When they do, protections of religious liberties will emerge from the requirement of equal consideration. But the failure to give appropriate weight to religious convictions need not reflect hatred, discrimination, or stereotyping of the person—nor must it depend on any other of the conventional ways of demeaning a person or failing to treat her as an equal. The problem may have a different source: it may trace to a failure to take seriously the stringency or weight of the demands placed on the person by her reasonable moral or religious convictions—not the intensity with which she holds those convictions, which does figure in aggregative views—but the stringency or weight of the demands imposed by the convictions, given their content.[12] It is precisely this stringency that compels reasons of especially great magnitude for overriding those demands. But such considerations about the relative stringency of demands are absent from the aggregative conception; so, therefore, is the need to find reasons of great weight before overriding those demands. That is a fundamental deficiency, and it lies at the source of the dilemma I sketched earlier.

A deliberative conception of democracy does not face the same troubles about reconciling democracy with nonpolitical liberties and other substantive, nonprocedural requirements. While accepting the fact of reasonable pluralism, it is attentive to the stringency of demands to which agents are subject, and therefore does not present its conception of democracy or collective decision in an exclusively procedural way. To make this case, I will first sketch the main ideas of a deliberative view; then I will show how, on the deliberative conception, we can accommodate the fact of reasonable pluralism without endorsing a wholly procedural conception of democracy. In particular, I will show how the liberties of the moderns and other substantive conditions are themselves elements in an institutional ideal of deliberative democracy.

## Deliberative Democracy

The deliberative conception of democracy is organized around an ideal of political justification. According to this ideal, to justify the exercise of collective political power is to proceed on the basis of a free public reasoning among equals. A deliberative democracy institutionalizes this ideal. Not simply a form of politics, democracy, on the deliberative view, is a framework of social and institutional conditions that facilitates free discussion among equal citizens—by providing favorable conditions for participation, association, and expression—and ties the authorization to exercise public power (and the exercise itself) to such discussion—by establishing a framework ensuring the responsiveness and accountability of political power to it through regular competitive elections, conditions of publicity, legislative oversight, and so on.[13]

I will come back later to the conditions for institutionalizing deliberation in greater detail. First, though, I want to say more about the idea of deliberative justification itself.

A deliberative conception puts public reasoning at the center of political justification. I say "public reasoning" rather than "public discussion" because a deliberative view cannot be distinguished simply by its emphasis on discussion rather than bargaining or voting. Any view of democracy—indeed any view of intelligent political decision making—will see discussion as important, if only because of its essential role in pooling information against a background of asymmetries in its distribution. Nor is it marked by the assumption that political discussion aims to change the preferences of other citizens. Though a deliberative view must assume that citizens are prepared to be moved by reasons that may conflict with their antecedent preferences and interests, and that being so moved may change those antecedent preferences and interests,[14] it does not suppose that political deliberation takes as its goal the alteration of preferences. Nor is it distinguished by its endorsement of an epistemic conception of voting, according to which votes are interpreted as expressions of beliefs about the correct answer to a political question, rather than as preferences about what policy is to be implemented.[15]

The conception of justification that provides the core of the ideal of deliberative democracy can be captured in an ideal procedure of political deliberation. In such a procedure participants regard one another as equals; they aim to defend and criticize institutions and programs in terms of considerations that others have reason to accept, given the fact of reasonable pluralism and the assumption that those others are reasonable; and they are prepared to cooperate in accordance with the results of such discussion, treating those results as authoritative.

Which considerations count as reasons? A suitable answer will take the form not of a generic account of reasons but of a statement of which considerations count in favor of proposals in a deliberative setting suited to free association among equals, where that setting is assumed to include an acknowledgment of reasonable pluralism. This background is reflected in the kinds of reasons that will be acceptable. In an idealized deliberative setting, it will not do simply to advance reasons that one takes to be true or compelling: such considerations may be rejected by others who are themselves reasonable. One must instead find reasons that are compelling to others, acknowledging those others as equals, aware that they have alternative reasonable commitments, and knowing something about the kinds of commitments that they are likely to have—for example, that they may have moral or religious commitments that impose what they take to be overriding obligations. If a consideration does not meet these tests, that will suffice for rejecting it as a reason. If it does, then it counts as an acceptable political reason.

To be sure, the precise characterization of the acceptable reasons, and of their appropriate weight, will vary across views. For that reason, even an ideal deliberative procedure will not, in general, produce consensus. But even if there is disagreement, and the decision is made by majority rule, participants may appeal to considerations that are quite generally recognized as having considerable weight, and as a suitable basis for collective choice, even among people who disagree about the right result: when participants confine their arguments to such reasons, majority support itself will commonly count as reason for accepting the decision as legitimate.

To underscore this point about the importance of background context in the account of acceptable political reasons, I want to highlight a difference between the idea of reasonable acceptance at work here, and the idea of reasonable rejection in Scanlon's contractualism.[16] Scanlon characterizes the wrongness of conduct in terms of the idea of a rule "which no one could reasonably reject," and he advances this characterization as part of a general account of the subject matter of morality and the nature of moral motivation. So his account of reasonableness—of reasonable grounds for rejecting principles—is required to work quite generally, even in settings with no ongoing cooperation, institutional ties, or background of equal standing as citizens.

My concern is not with reasons generally, or morality generally, or with political deliberation generally, or with the reasons that are suited to democratic discussion quite generally, but with a view about the implications of democracy given a specific background. And that background constrains what can count as an acceptable reason within a process of deliberation. For if one accepts the democratic process, agreeing that adults are, more or less without exception, to have access to it, then one cannot accept as a reason within that process that some are worth less than others or that the interests of one group are to count for less than those of others. And these constraints on reasons will limit the substantive outcomes of the process; they supplement the limits set by the generic idea of a fair procedure of reason giving.

I am not here raising an objection to Scanlon's view. He has a different topic—morality generally, as distinct from democratic legitimacy. Instead, I am urging that this difference in background makes a difference to the kinds of reasons that are suited to the two cases.

To conclude these general remarks about the deliberative view, I want to emphasize that its virtues are allied closely with its conception of binding collective choice, in particular with the role in that conception of the idea of reasons acceptable to others who are governed by those choices, and who themselves have reasonable views. By requiring reasons acceptable to others, the deliberative view suggests an especially compelling picture of the possible relations among people within a democratic order.

To see the character of those relations, notice first that the deliberative conception offers a more forceful rendering than the aggregative view of the fundamental democratic idea—the idea that decisions about the exercise of state power are *collective*. It requires that we offer considerations that others (whose conduct will be governed by the decisions) can accept, not simply that we count their interests in deciding what to do, while keeping our fingers crossed that those interests are outweighed. Thus the idea of popular authorization is reflected not only in the processes of decision making but in the form—and we will see later, the content—of political reason itself.

This point about the force of the deliberative view and its conception of collective decisions can be stated in terms of the idea of political community. If political community depends on sharing a comprehensive moral or religious view, or a substantive national identity defined in terms of such a view, then reasonable pluralism ruins the possibility of political community. But an alternative conception of political community connects the deliberative view to the value of community. In particular, by requiring justification on terms acceptable to others, deliberative democracy provides for a form of political autonomy: that all who are governed by collective decisions—who are expected to govern their own conduct by those decisions—must find the bases of those decisions acceptable. And in this assurance of political autonomy, deliberative democracy achieves one important element of the ideal of community. This is so not because collective decisions crystallize a shared ethical outlook that informs all social life, nor because the collective good takes precedence over the liberties of members, but because the requirement of providing acceptable reasons for the exercise of political power to those who are governed by it—a requirement absent from the aggregative view—expresses the equal membership of all in the sovereign body responsible for authorizing the exercise of that power.

To explain the deliberative ideal more fully, I want now to explore some of its implications: the conditions that need to be met by social and political arrangements that, within the setting of a modern state, institutionalize deliberative justification. What conditions will such arrangements need to satisfy, if they are to sustain the claim that they establish the conditions for free reasoning among equals, and root the authorization to exercise state power in those conditions?

As a partial answer, I will indicate why deliberative democracy needs to ensure the liberties of the moderns. Then I will connect the deliberative view to conceptions of the common good and political equality.

### Three Principles

The aggregative conception of democracy promises the protections required for a fair process of binding collective choice, including protections against discrimination that would undermine the claim of the process to ensure equal consideration. I said earlier that the deliberative view will provide a basis for wider guarantees of basic liberties. It is time to make good on that claim. The main idea is that the deliberative conception requires more than that the interests of others be given equal consideration; it demands, too, that we find politically acceptable reasons—reasons that are acceptable to others, given a background of differences of conscientious conviction. I will call this requirement the *principle of deliberative inclusion.*

Consider, for example, the case of religious liberty. Religious views set demands of an especially high order—perhaps transcendent obligations—on their adherents; moreover, if we see these requirements from the believer's point of view, then we cannot think of them as self-imposed. Instead, the requirements are fixed by the content of the convictions, which the agent takes to be true. Reasonable adherents, then, cannot accept, as sufficient reasons in support of a law or system of policy, considerations that would preclude their compliance with those demands. What, then, about people who do not share those views? (I will describe the issue from the point of view of citizens who have fundamental moral convictions but no religious convictions. Broadly parallel remarks could be made from the standpoint of citizens with different religious convictions.) They might regard all religious views that impose such stringent demands, whatever their content and foundation, as unreasonable. I see no rationale for this view. Or they might treat the religious demands as intense preferences, to be given equal consideration along with other preferences of equal intensity. This reductive response indicates an unwillingness to see the special role of religious convictions from the point of view of the person who has them, an unwillingness to see how the religious view, in virtue of its content, states or implies that the requirements provide especially compelling reasons.

Alternatively, they might take seriously that the demands impose what the adherent reasonably regards as fundamental obligations, accept the requirement of finding reasons that might override these obligations, and acknowledge that such reasons cannot normally be found. The result is religious liberty, understood to include freedom of conscience and worship. It emerges as the product of the demanding character of religious requirements—which are seen, from the point of view of those who are subject to them, as matters of fundamental obligation—together with the requirement of finding reasons that those who are subject to those requirements can reasonably be expected to acknowledge, and the fact that citizens who are not religious have fundamental convictions that they take to impose especially compelling obligations.

Suppose, then, that we prevent others from fulfilling such demands for reasons that they are compelled—by the lights of a view that commands their conviction—to regard as insufficient. This is to deny them standing as equal citizens—full membership in the people whose collective actions authorize the exercise of power. And that, according to the deliberative conception, is a failure of democracy. We have failed to provide a justification for the exercise of power by reference to considerations that all who are subject to that power, and prepared to cooperate on reasonable terms, can accept. There are many ways to exclude individuals and groups from the people, but this surely is one.

These points about religious liberty—essentially about its free exercise—do not say anything about how to handle claims for religious exemption from general obligations with a strong secular justification (including obligations to educate children); or whether special provision is to be made for specifically religious convictions, as distinct from conscientious ethical convictions with no religious roots.[17] My aim here is not to resolve or even address these issues: any view that recognizes rights of free exercise will need to face those hard questions. My aim is only to show that a deliberative conception of democracy is not barred—by its structure—from acknowledging a fundamental role for rights of religious liberty; indeed it must provide a place for such rights.[18]

Finally, I emphasize that the point of guarantees of religious liberty, which fall under the requirement of deliberative inclusion, is not narrowly political: it is not to enable people to participate in politics—or to participate without fear—nor is the aim to improve public discussion by adding more diverse voices to it.[19] The idea instead is that abridgments of such liberties would constitute denials to citizens of standing as equal members of sovereign people, by imposing in ways that deny the force of reasons that are, by the lights of their own views, compelling. The reasons for abridgment are unacceptably exclusionary because they are unsuited to the ideal of guiding the exercise of power by a process of reason giving suited to a system of free and equal citizens.

The principle of deliberative inclusion extends naturally from religious liberty to a wide guarantee of expressive liberty.[20] In this respect, it contrasts with a more familiar strand of free speech theory that traces the foundations of stringent guarantees of expressive liberty to the need to assure a democratic framework of collective choice, but guarantees stringent protection only for political speech.[21] This limit is in tension with the requirement of deliberative inclusion.

Confining stringent protection to political speech seems natural, once one has decided to found rights to free expression on the importance of requiring government accountability and responsiveness to citizens as a body. But as my remarks on the religion case suggest, a deliberative conception of democracy cannot accept such a limit. To be sure, the idea of discussion aimed at reaching reasonable agreement is fundamental to the deliberative view. But it does not follow that the protection of expression is to be confined to speech that contributes to such discussion.

Consider expression that is not part of any process of discussion or persuasion—that is not "intended and received as a contribution to public deliberation about some issue"[22]—but that nevertheless reflects what a citizen takes, for quite understandable reasons, to be compelling reasons for expression.[23] This might be so in cases of bearing witness, with no expectation or intention of persuading others, or giving professional advice, with no expectation or intention of shaping broader processes of collective decision making. The deliberative view extends stringent protection to such expression, as a way to acknowledge the weight of those reasons. Given the background of reasonable pluralism, the failure to do so—to give due weight to an expressive interest that does not serve as input to political discussion—will constitute a denial of equal standing, and decisions that fail to ensure those stringent protections are not suitably collective.

The tradition that traces protections of expressive liberty to democratic ideals and then restricts stringent protection to contributions to debate in the public forum conflates the general strategy of

Joshua Cohen

providing a case for freedom of expression rooted in the idea of democracy with one element of that strategy: the need to protect inputs to a process of discussion. But as with religious liberty, so, too, with expressive liberty: the deliberative view also ties protections to acceptable outcomes of a deliberative process, outcomes, that is, that can be justified given the requirement on finding reasons acceptable to others under conditions of reasonable pluralism.

Earlier I suggested a connection between the deliberative conception and the value of community. That suggestion may now seem strained in light of the connections between the requirement of acceptable reasons and the protection of nonpolitical liberties. For such liberties are commonly represented as—for better or worse—the solvent of community.

But the deliberative view suggests a need for caution about that representation. Given conditions of reasonable pluralism, the protection of the liberties of the moderns is not a solvent of community. Reasonable pluralism itself may be such a solvent: at least if we define community in terms of a shared comprehensive moral or religious view. But once we assume reasonable pluralism, the protection of the liberties of the moderns turns out to be a necessary though insufficient condition for the only plausible form of political community. As the phrase "principle of inclusion" indicates, those liberties express the equal standing of citizens as members of the collective body whose authorization is required for the legitimate exercise of public power.

Turning now to the common good: aggregative views of democracy are conventionally skeptical about conceptions of the common good. Robert Dahl, for example, has suggested that in pluralistic societies conceptions of the common good are either too indeterminate to provide guidance, determinate but unacceptable because they lead us to "appalling results" in conditions that "are by no means improbable,"[24] or determinate and acceptable because purely procedural—because they define the common good as a democratic process.[25] On the deliberative conception, this skeptical outlook is unwarranted, yet another reflection of the absence of constraints beyond the requirement of fair aggregation.

A deliberative account of the principle of the common good begins by observing that citizens have good reason to reject a system of public policy that fails to advance their interests at all. (I say a "system of policy" because I do not wish to exclude the possibility that particular laws, regulations, or policies that are not attentive to the interests of some citizens may be justifiable as part of an overall package of laws and policies that is.[26]) This minimal constraint—of advancing the interests of each—comes out of the generic conception of a deliberative process and suffices to establish a Pareto-efficiency requirement, as one element of a conception of democracy.

But as I have emphasized, the deliberation that plays a role in the conception of deliberative democracy is not simply a matter of reason giving, generically understood. The background conception of citizens as equals sets limits on permissible reasons that can figure within the deliberative process. For suppose one accepts the democratic process of binding collective choice, agreeing that adults are, more or less without exception, to have access to it. One can then reject, as a reason within that process, that some are worth less than others or that the interests of one group are to count for less than the interests of others. That constraint on reasons will, in turn, limit the outcomes of the process, adding to the conditions set by the generic idea of deliberation. In particular, it provides a case for a public understanding about the distribution of resources that severs the fate of citizens from the differences of social position, natural endowment, and good fortune that distinguish citizens.

John Rawls's difference principle provides one illustration of such an understanding.[27] Treating equality as a baseline, it requires that inequalities established or sanctioned by state action must work to the maximal advantage of the least advantaged. That baseline is a natural expression of the constraints on reasons that emerge from the background equal standing of citizens: it will not count as a reason for a system of policy that that system benefits the members of a particular group singled out by social class, or native talent, or by any of the other features that distinguish among equal citizens. I do not wish to suggest here that Rawls's difference principle is the uniquely acceptable conception of the common good. But there is an especially strong case for it, both because it accepts the presumption of equality that emerges from the special constraints on reasons within the deliberative democratic view and because it insists, roughly

Joshua Cohen

speaking, that no one be left less well off than anyone needs to be —which is itself a natural expression of the deliberative conception.

I want finally to connect the deliberative view with rights of participation— the liberties of the ancients. More particularly, I want to show how the deliberative view accommodates a "principle of participation."[28] According to that principle, democratic collective choice—institutionalizing the tie between deliberative justification and the exercise of public power—must ensure equal rights of participation, including rights of voting, association, and political expression, with a strong presumption against restrictions on the content or viewpoint of expression; rights to hold office; a strong presumption in favor of equally weighted votes; and a more general requirement of equal opportunities for effective influence.[29] This last requirement condemns inequalities in opportunities for office-holding and political influence that result from the design of arrangements of collective decision making.[30]

Notice first that the mere fact that decisions are to be made in a generically deliberative way does not go very far toward establishing a case for the principle of participation.[31] Perhaps an ideal deliberative procedure is best institutionalized by ensuring well-conducted political debate among elites, thus enabling people to make informed choices among them and the views they represent, without any special provision for more substantive political equality, understood as requiring equally weighted votes and equal opportunities for effective influence.[32] How, then, does the deliberative view connect to concerns about participation and political equality?

Three considerations are important.

First, given the principles of deliberative inclusion and of the common good, the deliberative view can avail itself of conventional instrumental reasons in support of equal political rights. Such rights provide the means for protecting other basic rights and for advancing interests in ways that might plausibly promote the common good. Moreover, absent assurances of effective influence, such promotion seems an unlikely result. And it would be especially unlikely if inequalities in effectiveness corresponded to underlying social or economic inequalities in the society.[33]

In making this instrumental case, I may appear to be shifting to a bargaining conception of politics, with assurances of equal power working to ensure a political equilibrium with fair outcomes. But that gets the instrumental rationale and the mechanism wrong. The idea instead is that ensuring that all citizens have effective political rights serves as a reminder that citizens are to be treated as equals in political deliberation, and, by reducing inequalities of power, reduces the incentives to shift from deliberative politics to a politics of bargaining.

A second consideration is that many of the conventional, historical justifications for exclusions from or inequalities of political rights—justifications based on race and gender, for example—will not provide acceptable reasons in public deliberation. This consideration will not exclude all reasons for inequality—for example, if votes are of unequal weight because the political system relies, as in the case of the U.S. Senate, on a scheme of territorial representation in which districts correspond to political subdivisions. But it establishes a further presumption in favor of the principle of participation.

Finally, considerations analogous to those we met with in the case of religion and expression strengthen the case for equal political rights, with assurances of equal opportunities for effective influence. A characteristic feature of moral and religious convictions is that they give us strong reasons for seeking to shape our political-social environment. The comprehensive views underlying those reasons range from Aristotelian views about the central role of civic engagement in a good life, to Rousseauian claims about the connection between personal autonomy and participation, to views, founded on religious convictions, about the commanding personal responsibility to ensure social justice and the corresponding personal sin of failing in that responsibility. It is common ground, however, that citizens have substantial, sometimes compelling reasons for addressing public affairs. Because they do, the failure to acknowledge the weight of those reasons for the agent and to acknowledge the claims to opportunities for effective influence that emerge from them reflects a failure to endorse the background idea of citizens as equals.

Joshua Cohen

## Realizing Democracy

The deliberative conception of democracy captures the role of "un-democratic" as a term of criticism applying to results as well as processes: it provides common roots for the "by the people" and "for the people" aspects of the ideal of democracy. But this incorporation of important substantive requirements into the conception of democracy gives rise to a problem of its own. The concern is that if we offer an interpretation of democracy that treats all good things as ingredient in the idea of democracy—requirements of political equality, considerations of the common good, and the liberties of the moderns—then we may appear to integrate procedural and substantive values at the cost of practical guidance. What are we to do when the many elements of deliberative democracy come into conflict? Common foundations in deliberative democracy do not provide any insurance against conflict in practice. For example, the liberties mandated by the requirement of deliberative inclusion may conflict with the equal political liberties that fall under the requirement of participation. Why does it help to have all these elements ingredient within the ideal of democracy, given conflicts among them?

The answer is that by underscoring common foundations we highlight the need to find ways to accommodate the different requirements, so far as accommodation is possible. That may be more often than we are inclined to think, though how often is a function of politics. To make this point less telegraphic, I will sketch some examples. I want to focus the discussion on two cases in which the various requirements arguably conflict, and see what might be said about their reconciliation in these cases.

My first case is campaign finance. The central problem arises from a familiar dilemma: on the one hand, restrictions on political expenditures by candidates, parties, individual citizens, and organizations appear to burden expressive liberty, particularly given a background expectation that such expenditures are permissible; arguably, burdens also result from very stringent limits on contributions to political campaigns. Moreover, restrictions on candidate and party expenditures, even when they are accepted as a condition for receiving public financing, may reinforce incumbency advantages, resulting in a less competitive electoral system, less capable of holding elected officials accountable and so of ensuring public authorization of the exercise of power.[34] On the other hand, a regime of unrestricted expenditures is a regime in which political influence—chances to hold office and to effect the outcomes of political contests—reflects economic position, and that means inequalities in opportunities for effective influence.[35]

Thus the familiar conflict about restrictions on political spending. Some reject restrictions, even if they are content-neutral and motivated by a sincere desire to ensure greater equality of political influence. In an infamous sentence in the majority opinion in *Buckley v. Valeo,* the Supreme Court said that "the concept that government may restrict the speech of some elements of our society in order to enhance the relative voice of others is wholly foreign to the First Amendment";[36] as a result, they were unwilling to find any basis beyond concerns about quid pro quo corruption for regulating political spending.[37] Others, concerned to insist on the importance of fair political equality, argue that limits are essential.

The first idea—that it is impermissible to restrict the voice of some in order to enhance the relative voice of others—seems bizarre. My earlier account of the bases of rights of expression and political participation suggested a common foundation for both; so there is no basis for the subordinate role of political equality. Moreover, once we have accepted a presumption in favor of equally weighted votes—one person/one vote—we are already committed to precisely such restrictions and enhancements.[38]

Still, focusing on the permissibility of restrictions may be putting the emphasis in the wrong place. Given the bases of rights of expression in the principles of participation and deliberative inclusion, it would be desirable to promote equality of opportunity for effective influence through less restrictive means than expenditure limits, should such means be available.[39] And the natural route to such reconciliation is to establish a scheme of public financing. The idea of such a system is to rely principally on "floors" rather than "ceilings"—subsidies rather than limits—to remedy violations of the principle of participation.[40] By establishing floors, a suitable scheme of public financing helps to make office-holding more widely available; by reducing dependence of parties and candidates on private resources, it assures greater equality of opportunity for influence.[41] The effectiveness of floors in providing such assurance may depend on making the availability of support conditional on accepting spending limits. But limits of this kind may be unnecessary, given a regime with substantial public financing.

Of course a wide range of public financing schemes are possible: support can be provided to candidates or parties[42] or individual voters (as citizen vouchers[43]) or, in the case of initiatives and referenda, to nonparty organizations; funds can be made available for electoral activity or for more general party support; and support can be provided in the form of free media access. And in deciding among such schemes, it is important to consider their effects on deliberation as well as opportunities for effective influence. Citizen vouchers are especially promising, I think. But I do not propose to go into such details here. The point is to state the main principles, emphasize the importance of finding some accommodation of them in view of their common basis in the value of democracy, and indicate that the strategy of accommodation is, roughly stated, a strategy of empowerment, not of restriction.

My second case concerns possible tensions between a deliberative politics and the principles of participation and the common good—and the role of a strategy of "associative democracy" in blunting those tensions.[44] The problem here is less straightforward, as is the proposed solution. So I first need to set some background.[45]

Begin, then, with two familiar premises. First, any well-functioning democratic order satisfying the principles of participation and the common good requires a social base. Beyond the world of voters and parties, secondary associations—organized groups intermediate between market and state—are needed both to represent otherwise underrepresented interests (as in the case of trade unions or other independent worker organizations) and to add to public competence in advancing the common good (think of the role played by unions and employer associations in establishing standards on worker training in any well-functioning training system). Representing underrepresented interests helps to ensure political equality; adding to public competence helps to promote the common good.

Second, the right kinds of association do not naturally arise, either for the purposes of addressing problems of underrepresentation or for more functional tasks: there is, for example, no natural tendency for an emergence of secondary associations to correct for inequalities of political opportunity due to underlying economic inequalities or to ensure the regulatory competence needed to advance the common good.

Now put together the need for a favorable associative environment with the fact that such an environment is not naturally provided. This conjunction suggests a strategy for addressing the associative deficit: a strategy of associative democracy that would use public powers to encourage the development of the right kinds of secondary association. For example, where manifest inequalities in political representation exist, the associative strategy recommends promoting the organized representation of presently excluded interests. Where associations have greater competence than public authorities for advancing the common good, it would recommend encouraging a more direct and formal governance role for groups. So trade unions and employer associations that took on responsibility for the joint development of training curricula, for example, might be encouraged by public grants contingent on their assumption of such responsibilities.

But here we arrive at the tension. In seeking to meet the principles of participation and the common good by fostering governance roles for groups, we may heighten the role of group affiliation in defining political identity. And that may encourage a factionalized politics of group bargaining—albeit under more fair conditions— rather than a more deliberative politics.[46]

Standard responses to this problem are to encourage greater insulation of the state from groups, or to give up on egalitarian political values because no agent has the capacity to advance them. The idea of associative democracy suggests a different line of response. It begins by rejecting the implicit assumption that solidarities formed outside formal political arenas must be narrowly focused on particular groups, and proposes some institutional invention guided

Joshua Cohen

by that rejection. To explain the bases for rejecting that assumption and the relevant kinds of invention, I will make some very sketchy remarks about the idea of a deliberate use of associations in regulation.

Generally speaking, the idea of a regulatory role for associations reflects a sense of the limited capacity of the state to regulate for the common good. Those limits appear in four kinds of cases:

1. Where government has the competence to set specific regulatory terms, but the objects of regulation are sufficiently numerous, dispersed, or diverse to preclude serious government monitoring of compliance. Many workplace regulations—on appropriate wages and hours, compensation, and especially the appropriate organization of work, pertaining for example to occupational health and safety—provide instances of this monitoring problem.

2. Where government has the competence to set general standards of performance, but the objects of regulation are sufficiently diverse or unstable to preclude government specification of the most appropriate means of achieving them at particular regulated sites. Much environmental regulation is of this kind.

3. Where government may (or may not) be able to enforce standards once set, but cannot set appropriate ends itself.[47] Often, an appropriate standard can be determined only by those with local knowledge not readily available to government, or can be specified only as the outcome or in the context of prolonged cooperation among nongovernment actors. Industry standards on product or process uniformity and performance are often of this kind, as are standards on training. The appropriate norm shifts constantly; the content of the norm derives from cooperation in the process of establishing it.[48]

4. Where problems are substantially the product of multiple causes and connected with other problems, crossing conventional policy domains and processes. In such cases, the appropriate strategy requires coordination across those domains as well as cooperation from private actors within them. Urban poverty, local economic development, and effective social service delivery are among the familiar problems in this class. None can be solved without coopera-

tion across quite different institutions and groups—lending institutions, health care providers, technology diffusers, education and training establishments, housing authorities, community development corporations, neighborhood associations—operating wholly or substantially outside the state itself. These and other parties involved in the problem and its proposed solution, however, typically have distinct if not competing agendas, and different identities and interests.

To address such problems, the associative approach recommends explicitly relying on the distinctive capacity of associations to gather local information, monitor compliance, and promote cooperation among private actors. When problems are more or less *functionally specific*—corresponding roughly to the first three classes of cases described earlier, associative governance is not uncommon. As a general matter, it is best developed in the areas of workplace regulation and training, and it relies on institutions controlled by the traditional "social partners" of labor and capital. The use of plant committees to enforce occupational safety and health regulations, for example, or groupings of trade unions and employers to facilitate technology diffusion, or employer and union associations to set standards on training are all familiar. The lessons of practice in these areas might be more explicitly generalized to include nontraditional parties.

As the scope of associative efforts moves beyond functionally specific problems to issues that are decidedly more sprawling and open-ended—as in the urban poverty or regional economic development examples—models are less clear. Here the associative strategy recommends the construction of new arenas for public deliberation that lie outside conventional political arenas,[49] and whose aim is to establish the desired coordination.

Notice, however, that both the inclusion of nontraditional stakeholders and the development of deliberative arenas suggest a new possibility: that of constructing new bases of social solidarity *through* a process of defining and addressing common concerns. It is one thing for a well-funded union to be asked to participate in the design of training standards of obvious concern to it as well as the broader society. It is quite another for a nascent or underfunded community environmental organization to gain significant resources (and thus greater organizational life) if it assists in designing an environmental early warning system that is expected to take notice of emerging environmental problems before they become unmanageable. In this case, support is tied to public service. Or for a neighborhood association and economic development corporation in a poor community to receive assistance conditional on their jointly organizing a training program for parents and a child care program for trainees as part of a broader job-training effort: once more, participation and support are tied to a project of public advantage.

The solidarities characteristic of such efforts will be the bonds of people with common concerns—say, a concern to address persistent urban poverty—who treat one another as equal partners in addressing those shared concerns.[50] In short, these efforts—which could have very wide scope—have the potential to create new "deliberative arenas" outside formal politics that might work as "schools of deliberative democracy" in a special way. Deliberative arenas established for such coordination bring together people with shared concrete concerns, very different identities, and considerable uncertainty about how to address their common aims. Successful cooperation within them, fostered by the antecedent common concerns of participants, should encourage a willingness to treat others with respect as equals, precisely because discussion in these arenas requires fashioning arguments acceptable to those others. Assuming fair conditions of discussion and an expectation that the results of deliberation will regulate subsequent action, the participants would tend to be more other-regarding in their outlook. The structure of discussion, aimed at solving problems rather than pressuring the state for solutions, would encourage people to find terms to which others can agree. And that would plausibly drive argument and proposed action in directions that respect and advance more general interests. Moreover, pursuing discussion in the context of enduring differences among participants would incline parties to be more reflective in their definition of problems and proposed strategies for solution; it would tend to free discussion from the preconceptions that commonly limit the consideration of options within more narrowly defined groups.

If this is right, then a social world in which solidarities are formed in part by reference to such arenas is different from a social world whose associational life is narrower and factionalized. And that means that it may be possible to use the associative strategy to advance the principles of participation and the common good without thereby encouraging particularistic group identities that turn politics from deliberation to bargaining.

## Conclusion

The fact of reasonable pluralism does not, I have argued, mandate a procedural account of democracy and collective choice. Conjoined with a deliberative conception of justification, it is compatible with a substantive account of democracy, whose substance—captured in principles of deliberative inclusion, the common good, and participation—includes values of equality and liberty. Moreover, such a deliberative conception offers an attractive rendering of the idea of collective choice, tying that idea to a view of political community. Finally, we are not without resources for addressing possible tensions between and among the values of liberty, equality, and community built into the deliberative conception. But whether or not those resources are exploited is, of course, a matter of politics.

## Acknowledgment

I would like to thank John Rawls, Charles Sabel, T. M. Scanlon, Cass Sunstein, and Iris Marion Young for illuminating comments on earlier drafts of this essay. The "Deliberative Democracy" section draws on my "Deliberation and Democratic Legitimacy," in Alan Hamlin and Phillip Petit, eds., *The Good Polity* (Oxford: Blackwell, 1989), 17–34. The "Three Principles" section draws on my review of Robert Dahl's *Democracy and Its Critics* (New Haven: Yale University Press, 1989) in *Journal of Politics* 53, no. 1 (1991): 221–225, and on my "Pluralism and Proceduralism," *Chicago-Kent Law Review* 69, no. 3 (1994): 589–618. The "Realizing Democracy" section draws on Joshua Cohen and Joel Rogers, *Democracy and Association* (London: Verso, 1995).

Joshua Cohen

## Notes

1. "Governed by" rather than "affected by." Democracy is about justifying authority, not about justifying influence. See Michael Walzer, *Spheres of Justice* (New York: Basic Books, 1983); and Christopher McMahon, *Authority and Democracy* (Princeton: Princeton University Press, 1994). Alternatively stated, authorization must come from the popular will, where "popular will" is understood as indicating the ultimate authority and responsibility of citizens as a body, not as implying a collective ranking of alternatives that preexists institutions and seeks authentic expression through them. See William Riker, *Liberalism against Populism* (San Francisco: W H. Freeman, 1992).

2. On the notion of a comprehensive doctrine, see John Rawls, *Political Liberalism* (New York: Columbia University Press, 1993), 13.

3. American national identity is commonly tied to such a conception, as in Lincoln's claim that the nation was conceived in liberty and dedicated to the proposition that all men are created equal. Some regard this abstract national self-definition as exceptionally American. Considering the conflictual conditions under which modern nationalism evolved, I doubt that this claim can be sustained without substantial qualification. Claims about the content of national identity—like all claims about group identity—are endlessly contested: they are as much moves in social and political conflicts aimed at establishing the authority of a particular nationalist understanding as they are intellectual discoveries. For every person who will claim that the conception of people as free and equal is foreign to his particular national identity, we can always find someone who shares the national self-definition and will deny that foreignness.

4. For discussion of this fact, see Joshua Cohen, "Moral Pluralism and Political Consensus," in *The Idea of Democracy,* eds. David Copp, Jean Hampton, and John Roemer (Cambridge: Cambridge University Press, 1993), 270–291; John Rawls, *Political Liberalism;* and Joshua Cohen, "A More Democratic Liberalism," *Michigan Law Review* 92, no. 6 (May 1994): 1502–1546.

5. By "tracing legitimacy to popular authorization," I mean treating such authorization as a sufficient condition for the exercise of political power.

6. See John Hart Ely, *Democracy and Distrust* (Cambridge, Mass.: Harvard University Press, 1980); and Robert Dahl, *Democracy and Its Critics* (New Haven: Yale University Press, 1989).

7. See Dahl's concerns about judicial review in *Democracy and Its Critics,* 183.

8. It is of course open to a democratic pluralist to hold that such infringements are unjust and that the people ought not to reject them.

9. On the distinction between aggregative and deliberative views, and its bearing on the possibility of reconciling commitments to values of liberty and equality within a conception of democracy, see my review of Dahl's *Democracy and Its Critics,* in *Journal of Politics* 53 (1991): 221–225. For discussion of the related distinction between strategic and deliberative conceptions, see David Estlund, "Who's Afraid of Deliberative Democracy? On the Strategic/Deliberative Dichotomy in Recent Constitutional Jurisprudence," *Texas Law Review* 7, no. 7 (June 1993): 1437–1477. Estlund identifies

strategic theories with views that make use of the idea of utility-maximization. I think that the crucial issue is whether a conception of democracy emphasizes the idea of providing reasons acceptable to others.

10. In *Democracy and Its Critics*, chaps. 6–8, Robert Dahl derives conditions on democratic procedure from a principle of equal consideration and a presumption of personal autonomy.

11. When, for example, legislation relies on racial classifications—or at least on malign racial classification—we have reason to suspect that discriminatory preferences prompted the legislation. And if they did, then the procedural-democratic pedigree of the regulation is arguably corrupt. See Ely, *Democracy and Distrust*, chap. 6; and Ronald Dworkin, *Law's Empire* (Cambridge, Mass.: Harvard University Press, 1986), chap. 10. For a less social-psychological view of unacceptable procedural pedigree, see Bruce Ackerman, "Beyond Carolene Products," *Harvard Law Review* 98 (1985): 713–746. Unfortunately, the Supreme Court has recently endorsed the view that "malign racial classification" is a pleonasm, and "benign racial classification" a contradiction in terms. See *Richmond v. Croson*, 488 U.S. 469 (1989); *Shaw v. Reno*, 113 S. Ct. 2816 (1993); and *Miller v. Johnson*, slip op. (1995). For an alternative view, see *Metro Broadcasting v. FCC*, 497 U.S. 547 (1990).

12. The distinction between rights required to prevent discrimination and rights required to protect fundamental interests plays a central role in equal protection doctrine. See Laurence Tribe, *American Constitutional Law* (Mineola, N.Y.: Foundation Press, 1988), chap. 16. On the importance of paying attention to the content of views in an account of free exercise, see Ronald Dworkin, *Life's Dominion* (New York: Knopf, 1993), 162–166.

13. On the role of the idea of democracy as more than a political idea, see Gordon Wood, *The Radicalism of the American Revolution* (New York: Knopf, 1992), esp. 232.

14. See Cohen, "Deliberation and Democratic Legitimacy," 24.

15. On the idea of an epistemic conception, see Jules Coleman and John Ferejohn, "Democracy and Social Choice," *Ethics* 97 (October 1986): 6–25; and Joshua Cohen, "An Epistemic Conception of Democracy," *Ethics* 97 (October 1986): 26–38.

16. T. M. Scanlon, "Contractualism and Utilitarianism," in Amartya Sen and Bernard Williams, eds., *Utilitarianism and Beyond* (Cambridge: Cambridge University Press, 1982). The point of contrast in the text is prompted by Scanlon's discussion of the role of maximin reasoning in moral contractualism in "What Do We Owe Each Other?" (unpublished typescript, July 1994), chap. 5, 47–54.

17. On this last point the key to the case for religious liberty is that the content of a view assigns stringent obligations to a person who holds it. But specifically religious content is not essential.

18. This account of religious liberty may seem to rest on the idea of a natural right to religious liberty—to say, in effect, that reasons will count as acceptable in a deliberative process only if they accept this right. If the idea of a natural right to religious liberty simply comes to the claim that there is a right that can be abridged only on pain of illegitimacy, then the deliberative view includes natural rights. But natural rights views have claimed more than this: they offer an explanation of the

basis of fundamental rights in human nature, or natural law, or a prepolitical normative order to which political society must conform. The idea of democratic legitimacy does not depend on that explanation—though it asserts nothing inconsistent with it. It suffices that religious liberties have an explanation tied to the idea of democratic legitimacy. For the purposes of political argument, nothing more needs to be said, positively or negatively.

19. Roberto Unger argues that a system of immunity rights is one component of a democratic order, because "freedom as participation presupposes freedom as immunity." Rejecting the view of "critics of traditional democratic theory" who hold that "participatory opportunities [are] a more than satisfactory substitute for immunity guarantees," Unger sees immunity rights as necessary if a citizen is to have the "safety that encourages him to participate actively and independently in collective decision making." In *False Necessity* (Cambridge: Cambridge University Press, 1987), 525. I agree with Unger's observations, but I think that a conception of democracy can make a less instrumental place for certain liberties, even when those liberties are not procedural.

20. This discussion draws on my "Freedom of Expression," *Philosophy and Public Affairs* 22 (Summer 1993): 207–263.

21. See Alexander Meiklejohn, *Free Speech and Its Relation to Self-Government* (New York: Harper & Row, 1948); and Cass R. Sunstein, *Democracy and the Problem of Free Speech* (New York: Free Press, 1993). See also Robert Bork, "Neutral Principles and Some First Amendment Problems," *Indiana Law Journal* 47, no. 1 (Fall 1971): 1–35; Ely, *Democracy and Distrust;* and Owen Fiss, "Why the State?" *Harvard Law Review* 100 (1987): 781–794.

22. This is Sunstein's account of political speech in *Democracy and the Problem of Free Speech*, 130.

23. I do not mean to suggest that stringent protection ought to be confined to expression animated by such compelling reasons. The conventional democratic defense of rights of expression also provides a basis for stringent protection. My aim is to supplement that rationale.

24. *Democracy and Its Critics*, 283.

25. Ibid., 306–308.

26. The vices of a sales tax, for example, depend on the nature and level of exemptions, the presence (or not) of tax credits, and the nature of the policies that the revenue pays for.

27. See John Rawls, *Theory of Justice* (Cambridge, Mass.: Harvard University Press, 1971), 513. For discussion of the connections between the difference principle and an ideal of democracy, see Joshua Cohen, "Democratic Equality," *Ethics* 99 (July 1989): 736–743. Another view that might be used to illustrate the points in the text is Dworkin's equality of resources. See Ronald Dworkin, "What is Equality? Part 2: Equality of Resources," *Philosophy and Public Affairs* 10 (1981): 283–345.

28. See Rawls, *Theory of Justice*, 36–37.

29. On the requirement of opportunities for effective influence, see Rawls, *Political Liberalism*, 327–330. For a discussion of the constitutional dimension of the problem, see *Davis v. Bandemer* 478 U.S. 109, 132 (1986). The Court here acknowledges equal protection troubles when the "electoral system is arranged in a manner that will consistently degrade a voter's or group of voters' influence on political process as a whole." Low-Beer distinguishes a requirement of equally weighted votes, at stake in apportionment issues, from equally meaningful votes, at stake in gerrymandering cases. The value threatened by gerrymandering is better understood, I believe, as political influence more generally, not simply voting strength. See John Low-Beer, "The Constitutional Imperative of Proportional Representation," *Yale Law Journal* 94 (1984): 163–188.

30. Among the concerns that fall under this requirement are vote dilution due to racial and political gerrymandering, and unequal influence due to campaign finance arrangements, restrictive rules on ballot access, and regulations of political parties.

31. Historically, the deliberative conception of politics was associated with highly exclusivist forms of parliamentarism; moreover, according to one influential line of thought, mass democracy destroyed the possibility of deliberative political decision making. According to Carl Schmitt, "The belief in parliamentarism, in government by discussion, belongs to the intellectual world of liberalism. It does not belong to democracy." Moreover, "the development of modern mass democracy has made argumentative public discussion an empty formality." See *The Crisis of Parliamentary Democracy*, trans. Ellen Kennedy (Cambridge, Mass.: MIT Press, 1985), 6, 8.

32. Thus Beitz's account of political equality connects the interests in recognition and equitable treatment with assurances of equally weighted votes and fair access. What he calls the "deliberative interest," by contrast, simply requires well-conducted political debate. See Charles R. Beitz, *Political Equality* (Princeton: Princeton University Press, 1989).

33. See the discussion of the interest in equitable treatment in Beitz, *Political Equality*, 110–114. This interest plays an important role in the apportionment cases decided by the Supreme Court in the early 1960s. "No right is more precious in a free country than that of having a voice in the election of those who make the laws under which, as good citizens, we must live. Other rights, even the most basic, are illusory if the right to vote is undermined." *Gray v. Sanders*, cited in *Reynolds v. Sims* 377 U.S. 533, at 558 (1964). Or again: "Especially since the right to exercise the franchise in a free and unimpaired manner is *preservative of other basic civil and political rights*, any alleged infringement of the right of citizens to vote must be carefully and meticulously scrutinized." *Reynolds v. Sims*, at 562.

34. This may seem puzzling. Making the safe assumption that incumbents have advantages in raising funds, it might seem clear that challengers would fare better under a system of spending restrictions. But, according to one influential line of argument, background incumbency advantages make challengers *more dependent* on money. Thus a challenger is better off running with $300,000 against an incumbent with $500,000 than running with $250,000 against an incumbent with $250,000. See Gary Jacobson, "Enough Is Too Much: Money and Competition in House Elections," in *Elections in America*, ed. Kay Lehman Schlozman (Boston: Allen and Unwin, 1987), 173–195. For criticisms of Jacobson's view, see Donald Philip Green and Jonathan S. Krasno, "Salvation for the Spendthrift Incumbent: Reestimating the Effects of

Campaign Spending in House Elections," *American Journal of Political Science* 32, no. 4 (November 1988): 884–907.

35. I say a "regime" of unrestricted expenditures because the choice among systems of financing is a choice among alternative schemes of permissions and restrictions, not a choice between regulation and nonregulation.

36. 424 U.S. 1 (1976), 48–49.

37. *Buckley*, at 26–27.

38. See *Gray v. Sanders*, 372 U.S. 368 (1963); *Wesberry v. Sanders*, 376 U.S. 1 (1964); and *Reynolds v. Sims*, 377 U.S. 533 (1964). The tension between the apportionment decisions and *Buckley* is noted in Rawls, *Political Liberalism*, 361; and David A. Strauss, "Corruption, Equality, and Campaign Finance Reform," *Columbia Law Review* 94, no. 4 (May 1994): 1382–1383. The Court itself has retreated from the *Buckley* position, acknowledging possibilities of corruption involving unfair influence without quid pro quo, and the permissibility of regulating expenditures—at least in the case of for-profit corporations—in order to avoid such corruption. See *Austin v. Michigan Chamber of Commerce*, 494 U.S. 652, 660 (1990).

39. A problem with relying principally on spending restrictions is the capacity of contributors and candidates to maneuver around restrictions. See Frank Sorauf, *Inside Campaign Finance: Myths and Realities* (New Haven: Yale University Press, 1992). Increase the level of public subsidy, and you reduce the incentives to such maneuvering.

40. The United States is one of four OECD countries with contribution limits. All the other political systems rely more substantially than the United States on public financing; the Scandinavian countries have no contribution or expenditure limits and rely entirely on public funding. See Ellen S. Miller and Joel Rogers, *The World of Campaign Finance* (Madison and Washington, D.C.: Center for a New Democracy and Center for Responsive Politics, 1992).

41. For a description of a scheme of public financing animated by concerns about equality and deliberation, see Jamin Raskin and John Bonifaz, "The Constitutional Imperative and Practical Superiority of Democratically Financed Elections," *Columbia Law Review* 94, no. 4 (May 1994): 1160–1203.

42. For an interesting public financing proposal, built around support for parties that would be distributed by congressional leadership, see Daniel Hays Lowenstein, "The Root of All Evil Is Deeply Rooted," *Hofstra Law Review* 18, no. 2 (Fall 1989): 351–355.

43. On voucher systems, see Bruce Ackerman, "Crediting the Voters: A New Beginning for Campaign Finance," *American Prospect* (Spring 1993); and Edward Foley, "Equal Dollars per Voter: A Constitutional Principle of Campaign Finance," *Columbia Law Review* 94, no. 4 (May 1994): 1204–1257.

44. A broadly parallel concern arises in connection with the role of race-conscious measures in drawing lines around electoral districts. Given a background of racial bloc voting, the principle of participation may suggest a need for race-conscious districting to ensure opportunities for effective influence. But race-conscious district-

ing arguably works against deliberative politics. According to Lani Guinier, cumulative voting would address this tension. Like other forms of proportional representation, cumulative voting combines increased chances of effective minority influence with voluntary constituencies that may encourage deliberation. See her "Second Proms and Second Primaries: The Limits of Majority Rule," *Boston Review* 17, no. 5 (September–October 1992): 32–34; and *The Tyranny of the Majority* (New York: Basic Books, 1994).

45. This section of the paper draws on Joshua Cohen and Joel Rogers, "Solidarity, Democracy, Association," in Wolfgang Streeck, ed., *Staat und Verbände*, special issue of *Politischen Vierteljahresschrift* (Wiesbaden: Westdeutscher Verlag, 1994), 136–159.

46. This concern emerges naturally from criticisms of modern pluralism. See, for example, Theodore Lowi, *The End of Liberalism: The Second Republic of the United States,* 2d ed. (New York: Norton, 1979). For discussion of associative democracy as a response to the problem of faction, see Joshua Cohen and Joel Rogers, "Secondary Associations in Democratic Governance," *Politics and Society* 20 (December 1992): 393–472.

47. Or it can set them only in very abstract terms, for example, as requirements of "reasonableness" or "due care."

48. For discussion of the problem of shifting standards as it applies to the more general problem of measures of business performance, see Charles Sabel, "A Measure of Federalism: Assessing Manufacturing Technology Centers," *Research Policy* 5 (1996): 281–307.

49. Though to the extent that they receive public support, they are to be subject to constitutional constraints, in particular guarantees of equal protection.

50. This claim depends, of course, on the background assumption of a democratic state protecting basic liberties and ensuring equal protection.

# Contributors

**James Bohman** is Professor of Philosophy at Saint Louis University. His books include *Public Deliberation: Pluralism, Complexity, and Democracy* (MIT Press, 1996) and *New Philosophy of Social Science: Problems of Indeterminacy* (MIT Press, 1991); with Matthias Lutz-Bachmann he has edited *Perpetual Peace: Essays on Kant's Cosmopolitan Ideal* (MIT Press, 1997).

**Thomas Christiano** is Associate Professor of Philosophy at the University of Arizona. He is author of *The Rule of the Many: Fundamental Issues in Democratic Theory* (Westview, 1996); recent articles include "Voting and Democracy" (1995) and "Democratic Equality and the Problem of Persistent Minorities" (1994).

**Joshua Cohen** is Professor of Philosophy and Political Science at Massachusetts Institute of Technology. His books include *Association and Democracy in the Modern World* (Verso, 1995) and (with Joel Rogers) *On Democracy: Toward a Transformation of American Society* (Penguin, 1983).

**Jon Elster** is Professor of Political Science at Columbia University. He has authored and edited many books in political theory, including *Local Justice* (Russell Sage, 1992) and *The Cement of Society: A Study of Social Order* (Cambridge University Press, 1989).

**David Estlund** is Associate Professor of Philosophy at Brown University. He is editor (with Martha Nussbaum) of *Sex, Preference, and Family: Essays on Law and Nature* (Oxford University Press, 1996); his articles include "Who's Afraid of Deliberative Democracy?: On the Strategic/Deliberative Dichotomy in Recent Jurisprudence" (1993) and "Democracy without Preference" (1990).

**Gerald Gaus** is Professor of Philosophy at the University of Queensland, Australia. His books include *Justificatory Liberalism: An Essay on Epistemology* *and Political Theory* (Oxford University Press, 1996) and *Value and Justification: The Foundations of Liberal Theory* (Cambridge University Press, 1990).

**Jürgen Habermas** is Professor Emeritus of Philosophy at the University of Frankfurt, Germany. Some of his most influential works are *Legitimation Crisis* (Beacon Press, 1975) and the two volume *The Theory of Communicative Action,* (Beacon Press, 1984, 1987). His most recent work on democracy and the law is *Between Facts and Norms: Contributions to a Discourse Theory* of *Law and Democracy* (MIT Press, 1996).

**James Johnson** is Assistant Professor of Political Science at the University of Rochester. He is author of a number of articles including (with Jack Knight) "The Political Consequences of Pragmatism" (1996) and "Public Choice and the Rule of Law: Rational Choice Theories of Statutory Interpretation" (1994).

**Jack Knight** is Associate Professor of Political Science at Washington University. He is editor (with Itai Sened) of *Explaining Social Institutions* (University of Michigan Press, 1996) and author of *Institutions and Social Conflict* (Cambridge University Press, 1992).

**Frank Michelman** is Professor of Law at Harvard University. Some recent publications include "Bringing the Law to Life: A Plea for Disenchantment" (1989) and "Law's Republic" (1988).

**John Rawls** is Professor Emeritus of Philosophy at Harvard University. He is well known for his *Theory of Justice* (Harvard University Press, 1971) and *Political Liberalism* (Columbia University Press, 1993).

**William Rehg** is Assistant Professor of Philosophy at Saint Louis University. He is author of *Insight and Solidarity: A Study of the Discourse Ethics of Jürgen Habermas* (University of California Press, 1994) and (with James Bohman) "Deliberation and Discourse."

**Henry Richardson** is Associate Professor of Philosophy at Georgetown University. He is author of *Practical Reasoning about Final Ends* (Cambridge University Press, 1994) and editor (with B. Douglass and G. Mara) of *Liberalism and the Good* (Routledge, 1990).

**Iris Marion Young** is Professor of Philosophy at the University of Pittsburgh. She is author of *Justice and the Politics of Difference* (Princeton University Press, 1990) and *Throwing Like a Girl and Other Essays in Feminist Philosophy and Social Theory* (Indiana University Press, 1990).

# Index